Writing Effective Business Rules

Writing Effective Business Rules
A Practical Method

Graham Witt

AMSTERDAM • BOSTON • HEIDELBERG • LONDON
NEW YORK • OXFORD • PARIS • SAN DIEGO
SAN FRANCISCO • SINGAPORE • SYDNEY • TOKYO
Morgan Kaufmann is an imprint of Elsevier

Acquiring Editor: Rachel Roumeliotis
Development Editor: Robyn Day
Project Manager: André Cuello
Designer: Alisa Andreola

Morgan Kaufmann is an imprint of Elsevier
225 Wyman Street, Waltham, MA 02451, USA

Library of Congress Cataloging-in-Publication Data
Application submitted

British Library Cataloguing-in-Publication Data
A catalogue record for this book is available from the British Library.

ISBN: 978-0-12-385051-5

Printed in the United States of America
12   13   14   15   16   10   9   8   7   6   5   4   3   2   1

For information on all MK publications visit our website at www.mkp.com

"To Isabel, who shares my love of language"

Contents

Acknowledgments xiii

Introduction xv

CHAPTER 1   The world of rules 1

   1.1 What is a business rule? 1

      1.1.1 Laws of physics.. 2

      1.1.2 Legislation, regulations, external standards, and best practices 2

      1.1.3 Rule or business rule? 3

      1.1.4 System rule or business rule? 3

   1.2 Why rules are important 4

   1.3 Best practice rule management.. 5

   1.4 The nature of the problem 6

   1.5 The solutions 8

      1.5.1 Constrained natural language...................................... 8

      1.5.2 The benefits of a rule repository 10

      1.5.3 The benefits of rule metadata 10

   1.6 Summary.. 11

CHAPTER 2   How rules work 13

   2.1 Operative rules 13

   2.2 Definitional (structural) rules.. 14

   2.3 Normative, prescriptive, and descriptive rules................. 15

   2.4 Business processes 15

      2.4.1 Characteristics of a business process.......................... 16

      2.4.2 How rules govern business processes.......................... 17

   2.5 Rules in user interfaces 19

   2.6 Rules governing electronic messages 20

   2.7 Rules ensuring database integrity 20

   2.8 Human activities other than business processes 21

   2.9 Summary.. 22

CHAPTER 3   A brief history of rules 25

   3.1 Implementing rules.. 25

      3.1.1 Rules in program code 25

      3.1.2 Decision tables.. 27

      3.1.3 Rule sets in data 28

      3.1.4 Database constraints 30

      3.1.5 Graphical user interface building tools 31

      3.1.6 Constraints in XML schemas..................................... 31

      3.1.7 Rules engines.. 33

3.2 Documenting rules 33
    3.2.1 Rules in data models.. 34
    3.2.2 Rules in business process models... 40
3.3 Recent developments... 41
    3.3.1 Ross's rule taxonomy and diagramming notation....................................... 41
    3.3.2 Expressing rules in natural language.. 42
    3.3.3 The Business Rules Approach 53
    3.3.4 The Business Rules Manifesto.. 53
    3.3.5 The SBVR... 56
    3.3.6 Rules and rule statements 56
    3.3.7 Rule statements and advice statements 57
    3.3.8 Types of rule statements 57
    3.3.9 Types of advice statements... 61
3.4 Summary.. 62

CHAPTER 4   Types of rules **65**
4.1 Rules governing the physical world 65
    4.1.1 Mandatory and optional attributes and relationships 65
    4.1.2 Single-valued and multi-valued attributes and relationships....................... 66
    4.1.3 Variant and invariant attributes and relationships...................................... 66
    4.1.4 Constraints between attributes 66
    4.1.5 The impact of the physical world on an organization's rule book 66
4.2 Legislation and regulations 67
4.3 Organizational constructs... 68
4.4 Rules governing the collection and recording of data.. 69
    4.4.1 Data cardinality rules 70
    4.4.2 Data content rules.. 70
    4.4.3 Dynamic data constraints 71
4.5 Taking account of the physical world in data rules 72
    4.5.1 Distinguishing the physical world and data about it 72
    4.5.2 Ensuring that data does not describe an impossible situation...................... 75
    4.5.3 Do we even need definitional rules? 78
    4.5.4 Do we need so many operative rules? 79
    4.5.5 Data specifying an illegal or unsafe situation... 79
    4.5.6 The impact of the physical world on rule expression 80
4.6 Rules governing other business processes.. 81
4.7 Rules governing which parties can perform business processes.............................. 82
4.8 Rules governing human activities other than business processes 84
4.9 A complete taxonomy of rules 84
    4.9.1 Definitional rules 85
    4.9.2 Data rules... 88

4.9.3 Activity rules 96
4.9.4 Party rules 98
4.10 Summary 99

CHAPTER 5 **The building blocks of natural language rule statements** **101**
    5.1 Nouns 102
        5.1.1 Countable and non-countable nouns 102
        5.1.2 Simple and compound nouns 103
        5.1.3 Use of nouns in rule statements and fact types 104
    5.2 Proper names 104
    5.3 Verbs 105
        5.3.1 Transitive, intransitive, and intensive verbs 106
        5.3.2 Forms of verbs 106
        5.3.3 Compound verbs 109
        5.3.4 Auxiliary verbs 111
        5.3.5 Verbs involving 'that', 'if', or 'whether' 111
    5.4 Determiners 112
        5.4.1 Articles 112
        5.4.2 Specific determiners 113
        5.4.3 General determiners 114
        5.4.4 Determiners before countable and non-countable nouns 114
    5.5 Adjectives 115
    5.6 Prepositions 115
    5.7 Conjunctions 116
    5.8 Pronouns 117
    5.9 Literals 118
    5.10 The three uses of 'that' 120
    5.11 Summary 120

CHAPTER 6 **Fact models** **121**
    6.1 Fact models: An overview 121
        6.1.1 Typographical conventions 121
        6.1.2 Why build a fact model? 122
        6.1.3 Other models of the organization 124
        6.1.4 What is a fact model? 125
        6.1.5 What does a fact model consist of? 126
        6.1.6 Concepts 126
        6.1.7 Terms and definitions 127
        6.1.8 Facts and fact types 128
        6.1.9 Identification 128
        6.1.10 Attribute fact types 129

      6.1.11 Categorization schemes and categories 130

      6.1.12 Higher-order facts.. 132

  6.2 Terms and names 132

      6.2.1 Choice of words in a term 133

      6.2.2 Definitions 136

      6.2.3 The taxonomy of terms and proper names.. 138

  6.3 Fact types... 143

      6.3.1 Associative fact types.. 144

      6.3.2 Taxonomic fact types 151

      6.3.3 Derived fact types 153

      6.3.4 Object/identifier equivalence 153

  6.4 Building a fact model 154

      6.4.1 Bottom up.. 154

      6.4.2 Top down.. 155

      6.4.3 Concept and term discovery workshops.. 155

      6.4.4 Taxonomy publication.. 156

      6.4.5 Discovering fact types.. 156

      6.4.6 Deriving a fact model from a data model.. 156

  6.5 Using a fact model for other aspects of system specification............................ 157

      6.5.1 Building a data model from a fact model.. 157

      6.5.2 Building a process model.. 158

  6.6 Summary... 158

CHAPTER 7 **How to write quality natural language rule statements** **159**

  7.1 Typography and punctuation conventions in rule statements 159

  7.2 Rule statement anatomy.. 161

      7.2.1 Operative rule statements.. 161

      7.2.2 Definitional rule statements 164

      7.2.3 The subject of a rule statement 164

      7.2.4 Predicates in operative rule statements 172

      7.2.5 Conditional conjunctions.. 182

      7.2.6 Conditional clauses.. 183

      7.2.7 Qualifying clauses 185

      7.2.8 Qualifying clause or conditional clause?.. 187

  7.3 Why templates? 188

  7.4 Rule statement quality.. 189

      7.4.1 Fact type support for rule statements 190

      7.4.2 Ambiguity 194

      7.4.3 Self-contradiction.. 196

      7.4.4 Redundant qualifying and conditional clauses.................................... 199

      7.4.5 Duplicate rule statements 200

7.4.6 Overlapping rule statements..201
7.4.7 Contradictory rule statements 203
7.4.8 Using multiple complementary rule statements to state a single rule 203
7.5 Summary...204

CHAPTER 8 **An end-to-end rule management methodology** **205**
8.1 Rule discovery...205
8.1.1 Sources of rules 205
8.1.2 Collecting rules from those sources 206
8.2 Analyzing rules..207
8.2.1 The "data analysis" approach 207
8.2.2 The "raw rules" approach 214
8.3 Developing the rule statement vocabulary...227
8.3.1 Term and name metadata 227
8.3.2 Fact type metadata 228
8.4 Documenting rules 229
8.4.1 Rule metadata 229
8.5 Rule book quality assurance 230
8.6 Rule publication 230
8.7 Rule book and fact model maintenance 230
8.7.1 Adding a rule...231
8.7.2 Changing an existing rule 231
8.7.3 Retiring an existing rule...232
8.7.4 Adding an implemented data component...232
8.7.5 Modifying an existing implemented data component...............................233
8.7.6 Adding a software component 233
8.7.7 Modifying an existing software component..234
8.7.8 Changing the vocabulary..234
8.8 Summary..236

CHAPTER 9 **Rule statement templates and subtemplates**.. **237**
9.1 Using the templates to write rule statements...237
9.1.1 Rule statement templates 237
9.1.2 Subtemplates..239
9.2 Definitional rules..245
9.2.1 Formal term definitions..246
9.2.2 Categorization scheme enumerations..249
9.2.3 Category transition constraints...250
9.2.4 Complex concept structure rules...251
9.2.5 Valid value definitions 254
9.2.6 Data calculation rules..254
9.2.7 Standard format definitions..256

9.3 Data rules.. 257
    9.3.1 Data cardinality rules 258
    9.3.2 Data content rules.. 270
    9.3.3 Data update rules... 288
9.4 Activity rules... 290
    9.4.1 Activity restriction rules.. 291
    9.4.2 Process decision rules 297
9.5 Party rules... 298
    9.5.1 Party restriction rules 298
    9.5.2 Role separation and binding rules 299
    9.5.3 Information access rules... 300
    9.5.4 Responsibility rules 301
9.6 Summary.. 302

Bibliography **303**
Glossary **305**
Index.. **323**

Acknowledgments

I could not have written this book without the steadfast support and encouragement of my wife Isabel who was there for me, even when I was too distracted to be there for her. Writing a technical book in one's spare time while holding down a consulting career makes one a difficult person to live with. I also owe a debt of gratitude to Geoff Howard and Karen Richards of Ajilon, who have allowed me to work part-time so as to be able to put the time into this book that it required.

During my career I have had the good fortune to meet and have my imagination stimulated by a variety of thinkers. Foremost among these is Graeme Simsion, who not only launched my consulting career by inviting me to join Simsion Bowles and Associates, but also trusted me to co-author the second and third editions of his seminal book *Data Modeling Essentials*. Others from whom I have learnt many of the insights that have made their way into this book include Geoff Bowles, Chris Date, Harry Ellis, Terry Halpin, David Hay, Ron Ross, Hu Schroor, Alec Sharp, and Michael Stonebraker. More recently, the opportunity to work in a rules-rich environment alongside Colin Campbell of New South Wales Land & Property Information, and my Ajilon colleagues Greg Bowen, Emma Craig, and Pia Nicod, has enabled me to put many of the ideas in this book to the test.

Although this book is aimed at system design professionals, it is as much as anything a book about language. My love of language was initially stimulated by my late grandfather Jack Cade, who gave me copies of Frederick Bodmer's *Loom of Language* and *Roget's Thesaurus* during my teens. I have also been privileged to have had some wonderful language teachers over the years: Cornelius O'Neill, who taught me a year's worth of Latin over the course of my first Australian summer so that I could join the university stream at High School; Zorana Popović and Liljana Tasevska, who introduced me to the beauty of Serbian and Macedonian respectively.

This book would never have seen the light of day without the opportunity to trial the ideas therein in a series of articles in the online *Business Rules Journal*. Keri Anderson Healy has provided me with a forum to share my ideas, has edited those articles with care and intelligence, and has given me much useful advice in dealing with some of the pitfalls of crafting natural language business rules. I am also grateful to Don Baisley for sharing a number of useful insights.

My thanks are also due to all who responded so positively to Elsevier when approached with the initial proposal for this book: Glen Bell, Vanessa Cogan, Dagna Gaythorpe, David Hay (again), Keri Anderson Healy (again), and Michael Scofield. My thanks also go to Silvie Spreeuwenberg and my sister Gillian Essex, both of whom took considerable time out from their own busy careers to review the first draft: any remaining errors are, of course, my responsibility alone.

Finally, a big thank you to the team at Elsevier who have been a pleasure to work with in making this book a reality: Rick Adams, André Cuello, Robyn Day, Andrea Dierna, Steve Elliot, Jenifer Niles, and Rachel Roumeliotis.

Introduction

I was awoken by a pounding on the door of my room—long before was I sufficiently awake to answer the door, those outside had made clear they were policemen. But I wasn't in Australia, where I grew up, or Britain, where I was born. I was an overseas student in Eastern Europe, where nocturnal visits from the police were something to be feared.

By the time I let them into my room, I was completely awake, so, when they demanded to see my passport, I knew precisely where to find it. As it had been stamped at the border when I entered the country and I had met with the appropriate government authorities before commencing my course of study, I was confident that they would find nothing untoward. It transpired however that, as my course of study was longer than the 6 week limit imposed on tourist visas (such as the stamp that was in my passport), I should have obtained a longer term student visa.

In this situation, the officials charged with administering the rules for various kinds of visas knew those rules. However, I hadn't been informed as to what the rules were, although I was supposed to comply with them. If some information had been provided, even in one of the languages of my host country rather than English, I could have organized a translation, but with no information at all I was "in the dark."

This, of course, was not a matter of life and death: once I had the correct papers, all was well.

Failure to adhere to rules can be fatal however. Following an incident in 1972 in which a cargo hold door had blown off a McDonnell Douglas DC10, the aircraft manufacturer implemented a corrective measure to enable baggage handlers to establish that cargo hold doors were securely closed before takeoff. This measure involved the addition of a small window that allowed baggage handlers to see whether the door locking pins were in the correct position, and a placard beside the window advising them to do so.

A Turkish Airlines DC10 which crashed in 1974 killing all on board had had this modification implemented. However, investigation revealed that the baggage handler who closed the door before the aircraft's last takeoff (from Paris, France) had not been advised as to what the window was for. Furthermore, even though he could read and write three languages fluently, the instructions on the placard were in English, which he did not understand.

IS THIS BOOK FOR YOU?

Every community operates according to rules, be it a sovereign state, with laws governing the behavior of residents and visitors; a business wishing to minimize risk, reduce costs, and protect revenue; a not-for-profit organization; or any other type of community. Whatever the type of community, if a member of that community fails to comply with a rule, the outcome may range from financial loss to serious injury or death. Compliance is more likely if all community members are able to ascertain what rules apply in their circumstances.

This is best achieved if each rule is documented in a clear, unambiguous, and accessible statement in one or more of the natural languages[1] used by the community (e.g., English in the United

---

[1]As distinct from a programming language.

Kingdom, United States, Australia and New Zealand; English and French in Canada) using terminology that all community members (not only systems developers) understand. This has the added advantage that stakeholders can more easily review rules for relevance and correctness, approve them, change them as required, and so on.

In my 20 or so years of experience in consulting to organizations of all types (following many years as a systems analyst and developer), I have found that few organizations document their business rules in an ideal manner. Rules may be documented in different ways and in different places, indeed some may only exist as program code, in a database definition using DDL (data definition language), or as rules engine instructions. And while at least some may be documented in program specifications (and therefore in natural language), they are likely to be scattered across multiple specifications and embedded in other information, rather than collected into a separate dedicated resource.

Natural language rules, if properly written, are intelligible to business stakeholders. However, natural language has two disadvantages. The first is it can be ambiguous: some natural language statements can be interpreted in more than one way. The second disadvantage is that a given rule can be expressed in many different ways using natural language. As a result, similar rules can end up being expressed using quite different rule statements, which makes rule quality assurance more difficult.

There are of course many other indicators of good rule management practice (and I shall discuss these too), but I have found that organizations tend to do better on those other indicators if all rules have been properly documented in the first place, using natural language rule statements that are accessible to all stakeholders.

If you are fortunate enough to be working for, or consulting to, an organization that has managed to achieve an ideal rule documentation environment, this book may not be for you. If however you believe your employer or client(s) would benefit from improvement in the way their rules are documented, this book will provide you with a clearly described practical approach to assisting them to do so.

If you are serious about rules, you may well have encountered (Object Management Group, 2008), the Group's *Semantics of Business Vocabulary and Business Rules* (SBVR) (see Section 3.3.5 in Chapter 3). If you have been motivated to express rules in a manner that complies with the SBVR, but have been daunted by the sheer volume of theoretical detail set out in that ground-breaking document, this book may help you to not only better understand the matters raised in the SBVR but also produce quality SBVR-compliant rules.

I also believe that many of the techniques described in this book can improve the way we describe an organization's data and processes. If your remit includes data specification or process specification, you will also find value in this book.

WHAT THIS BOOK IS ABOUT

All organizations need to minimize exposure to risk, reduce costs, protect revenue, maintain market share, etc. Business rules, properly documented, managed, and implemented, enable organizations to do all those things. Many organizations specify their business rules in a manner that allows their developers to implement the required rules correctly. Program specifications, program code, DDL (data definition language), and rules engine instructions can all do that. These documentation methods, however, do not easily provide for business stakeholders to play an informed role in formulating rules, or allow those governed by the organization's rules to know what rules apply.

Properly constructed natural language rule statements provide all parties with the necessary information, to decide what rules are required, to implement them, or to comply with them. There is of course a significant problem with natural language statements. Unless carefully crafted, they may be ambiguous or unclear. This book is designed to help you specify an organization's business rules using natural language in a clear, succinct, unambiguous, and consistent manner.

While it is relatively easy to write a small suite of rules, maintaining consistency becomes more and more difficult as the number of rules increases. The techniques explained in this book will make it easier for you to author and manage a large set of quality business rules. These techniques comply with the requirements set out in the SBVR.

This book will not tell you how to implement rules in any programming language; for that you need the appropriate language guide. Nor will it tell you how to enter rules into a rules engine; again for that you need the user guide for the rules engine in question. Nor do I compare the user interfaces of various rules engines, which would admittedly be an interesting exercise. The focus of this book is the specification of rules clearly and unambiguously by human beings for other human beings.

HOW THIS BOOK IS ORGANIZED

Chapter 1
- defines some important technical terms to be used throughout this book;
- establishes why rules are important;
- describes the problems that face most organizations in managing rules; and
- describes the benefits of the approach described in this book to solving those problems.

Chapter 2
- distinguishes two fundamental types of rules: *operative rules* and *definitional rules* (or *structural rules*);
- describes how rules govern the business processes performed by organizations, their employees, customers, suppliers, and partners;
- describes how rules govern user interfaces and electronic messages and ensure database integrity; and
- describes how rules govern human behavior other than business processes.

Chapter 3
- describes how rule implementation and documentation has evolved over time; and
- includes some discussion of different types of rule statements—as categorized in recent business rules literature (including the SBVR)—and of how to express each type of rule statement in natural language.

Chapter 4 describes the various types of rules that may govern an organization, then collects those types into a complete *taxonomy*.

Chapter 5 discusses the various types of words we can use in the rule statements governing an organization.

Chapter 6 describes
- why a *fact model* should be built to support rule statement writing and other aspects of system specification;
- what a fact model consists of, and how it differs from other models and forms of documentation;
- how *nouns*, possibly qualified by *adjectives*, or (occasionally) other words, can be can be selected as *business terms*, defined, and given an appropriate place in the *taxonomy* of business terms;
- how *fact types* can be used to relate business terms (along with *verbs* and possibly *prepositions*); and
- useful techniques in developing a fact model.

Chapter 7 discusses the writing of quality natural language rule statements, in terms of
- the major components of a rule statement—such as the *subject*, the *predicate*, *conditional clauses*, and *qualifying clauses*—and the various forms these can take in rule statements of different types;
- the use of *templates* to generate quality rule statements of each type;
- quality criteria for rule statements, including the use of the fact model as a source of terms, verb phrases and prepositions in a rule statement.

Chapter 8 describes a complete end-to-end rule writing, documentation, and management methodology, with examples drawn from some typical business scenarios.

Chapter 9 lists the templates and subtemplates appropriate for each type of rule in the taxonomy set out in Chapter 4, together with, for each template or subtemplate
- examples of rule statements that can be generated from that template;
- a discussion of the meaning of each option in that template or subtemplate, and when it is appropriate or inappropriate to use that option;
- advice as to what terms, verbs, prepositions, and other words can be substituted in place of *placeholders* in that template; and
- advice as to what fact types are required when including terms, verbs, and prepositions in rule statements generated from that template.

HOW TO USE THIS BOOK

If you are as yet unfamiliar with business rules, I advise you to read each chapter in turn. If however you are an experienced business rule practitioner using this book for the first time as a reference for actually writing rule statements, you might want to head straight for Chapter 4 and read on from there. Once you've done that, further rule writing sessions can be undertaken using mainly Chapter 7 with occasional detours into Chapter 4 to check what type(s) of rule you're dealing with, Chapter 9 to answer any detailed rule statement syntax questions, and Chapter 8 to refresh your memory as to the appropriate procedures to follow.

SOME TYPOGRAPHICAL CONVENTIONS

By now you may have realized that each technical term used in this book is, at least on the first occasion, denoted by the use of a bold italic serif font, as in the case of ***rule statement*** in the following paragraph. Each of these terms is defined when first encountered and/or in the appropriate chapter of this book. In addition, each of these terms is defined in the Glossary at the end of this book.

Each ***rule statement***[2] in this book is

- given a unique identifier starting with the letter 'R'
- depicted using a sans serif font

as in the following example:

R1. Each sentence must *start with* an upper case letter.

Any rule statement that is marked with an initial dagger, as in the following example, is, for one or more reasons, not recommended; where such an example appears, the preferred alternative (in this case R1) will generally also be shown.

R2. †An upper case letter must *start* each sentence.

Two other markings are used before examples of inappropriate statements:

1. An asterisk is used before a syntactically incorrect sentence or phrase, as in "*how much customers is there."

2. A double dagger (‡) is used before a syntactically correct but meaningless sentence or phrase, as in "‡Each capital city *must be a category of* city."

Note that the ***nouns***[3] (the ***simple noun*** 'sentence' and the ***compound noun*** 'upper case letter')[4] in the example rule statements are underlined. We shall use the term ***business term*** (often abbreviated to ***term***[5]) to refer to any simple or compound noun that is used by an organization to refer to a concept of interest. Most terms in rule statements (and in various other contexts) are treated in this way throughout this book, but there are some exceptions, which are discussed in Section 7.1 in Chapter 7.

Note also that the ***verbs***[6] (i.e., the ***simple verb*** '*start*' and the ***prepositional verb*** '*start with*') in these rule statements are in italics. Most verbs and ***prepositions***[7] in rule statements are treated in this way throughout this book, but again there are some exceptions, notably the ***auxiliary verb***[8] '*must*'. These exceptions are also discussed in Section 7.1.

Proper names[9] (e.g., Los Angeles International) and ***literals***[10] (references to numeric values, textual values, categories within a categorization scheme, dates, times, or other time points) in rule statements are double underlined, as in '30 kg', 'LAX', 'approved', 'December 25', '9 am', 'Friday'.

---

[2]See Section 3.3.6 in Chapter 3 for a definition of the term ***rule statement***.
[3]See Section 5.1 in Chapter 5 for a definition of the term ***noun***.
[4]See Section 5.1.2 in Chapter 5 for definitions of the terms ***simple noun*** and ***compound noun***.
[5]See Section 6.2 in Chapter 6 for a definition of the term ***business term***.
[6]See Sections 5.3, 5.3.3, and 5.3.3.1 in Chapter 5 for definitions of the terms ***verb***, ***simple verb***, and ***prepositional verb***.
[7]See Section 5.6 in Chapter 5 for a definition of the term ***preposition***.
[8]See Section 5.3.4 in Chapter 5 for a definition of the term ***auxiliary verb***.
[9]See Section 5.2 in Chapter 5 for definitions of the terms ***common noun*** and ***proper name***.
[10]See Section 5.9 in Chapter 5 for a definition of the term ***literal***.

Finally, note that 'each' and 'an' are in a sans serif font but neither underlined nor in italics, as these are neither nouns nor verbs[11].

These conventions (underlining and italicization) are based on those used in the SBVR[12], which additionally distinguishes word types by color: 'teal' for ***common nouns***[9], blue for verbs and prepositions, green for proper names and literals, and orange for all other words in a rule statement.

---

[11]They are in fact, ***determiners***, defined in Section 5.4 in Chapter 5.
[12](Object Management Group, 2008).

The world of rules

This chapter
- defines some important technical terms used throughout this book;
- establishes why rules are important;
- describes the problems that face most organizations in managing rules;
- describes the benefits of the approach described in this book to solving those problems;
- discusses the various ways in which rules govern an organization and its employees, customers, suppliers, and partners;
- discusses how rule management has evolved over time.

1.1 WHAT IS A BUSINESS RULE?

Over time various authors have produced different definitions of the term **business rule**. Unfortunately some of these definitions have conflicted with others.

According to the Business Rules Group,[1] the first authoritative definition of the term 'business rule' appeared in the seminal 1995 report of the GUIDE Business Rules Project, entitled "Defining Business Rules—What Are They Really?" This definition reads: "*A business rule is a statement that defines or constrains some aspect of the business. It is intended to assert business structure or to control or influence the behavior of the business.*" The same definition appeared in the Business Rules Group's Final Report of July 2000.[2]

In 2001, von Halle[3] defined a business rule as "*a condition that govern[s] ... business event[s] so that [they] occur in such a way that is acceptable to the business.*" So far, so good.

By contrast, Ross[4] had in 1998 defined a business rule as "*a rule that is under business juris-diction.*" In 2008, the authors of the SBVR[5] chose to elaborate on this definition rather than the more general one and defined a business rule as "*a rule that is under business jurisdiction ... the semantic community can opt to change or discard the rule. Laws of physics may be relevant to a company (or other semantic community); legislation and regulations may be imposed on it; external standards and best practices may be adopted. These things are not business rules from the company's perspective.*" This narrower definition, in explicitly excluding "*laws of physics, ... legislation, ... regulations, ...*"

---

[1] www.BusinessRulesGroup.org.
[2] (Business Rules Group, 2000).
[3] (von Halle, 2001).
[4] (Ross, Business Rule Concepts—Getting to the Point of Knowledge, 1998).
[5] (Object Management Group, 2008).

external standards and best practices," places a significant proportion of the constraints on an organization, or the conditions that govern it, outside the set of business rules.

The business rules community has quite rightly, in the Business Rules Approach (discussed in Section 3.3.3 in Chapter 3) and the Business Rules Manifesto[6] (discussed in Section 3.3.4, also in Chapter 3), established guidelines for analysis, expression, and management of business rules, which should be applied to *all* rules that govern an organization, so let us look at the types of rules that fall outside the SBVR definition.

1.1.1 Laws of physics

All organizations are subject to the laws of physics. Therefore, since these cannot be violated, it might seem that an organization does not need to document such rules or include code in its application systems to ensure that such rules are not violated. However, many laws of physics need to be taken into account when establishing the rules governing the capture of information about the real world.

Consider a school timetabling system in which school days are divided into periods of, say, 45 min each and in which groups of students are assigned to a particular classroom for each of those periods, to be taught a particular subject by a particular teacher. At least two laws of physics need to be taken into account in such a system.

First, a person, or for that matter any concrete object, cannot be in more than one location at the one time.[7] Our school timetabling system should therefore (for example) prevent any teacher being timetabled to be in more than one classroom during the same timetable period.

Second, time is unidirectional (for all practical non-relativistic purposes). Nothing can therefore finish before it starts. Our school timetabling system should therefore also prevent (for example) a timetable period being defined with an end time earlier than its start time, or a part-time staff member's availability on a particular day starting after it finishes.

The school can, of course, "*opt to change or discard*" the rules that ensure that information representing such impossible situations cannot be entered into the timetabling system; these rules would then qualify as 'business rules' according to the SBVR definition. If it were to change or discard any such rules, however, the risk of producing an impractical timetable is increased, so it would make no sense to allow the school to do so.

1.1.2 Legislation, regulations, external standards, and best practices

Why should these be excluded from being analyzed, expressed, and managed in accordance with best practice, namely, the Business Rules Approach and the Business Rules Manifesto?

Failure to comply with legislation or regulation, for example, exposes the organization to the risk of litigation, leading to financial penalty and possibly loss of business through adverse publicity. Compliance with external standards typically yields efficiencies in dealing with other organizations, while compliance with best practice typically minimizes risk and/or ensures efficiency without "reinventing the wheel."

Any organization should therefore constrain its activities and (at the very least) those of its employees so as to comply with all relevant legislation and regulations, and stands to benefit from

---

[6](Business Rules Group, 2003).
[7]Apparently, some subatomic particles may be exempt from this limitation.

similarly constraining those activities so as to comply with relevant external standards and best practices.

Again, an organization can opt to change or discard the rules that ensure compliance with legislation and regulations so that these rules qualify as 'business rules' according to the SBVR definition. If, however, an organization were to change or discard any such rules, the risks of financial penalty and possible loss of business arising from litigation are increased, so again it makes no sense to allow an organization to do so, unless it believes it can 'get away with it.'

As an aside, I cannot help wondering whether the SBVR[8] restriction of the term 'business rule' might have been a contributing factor to the global financial crisis. If the financial services industry focused only on those rules that they could "*opt to change or discard*," this might have led to paying insufficient attention to the governance requirements of Sarbanes–Oxley[9] or Basel II.[10] A similar focus by the oil industry may arguably have led to 2010's disastrous oil spill in the Gulf of Mexico.

1.1.3 Rule or business rule?

Admittedly, the SBVR includes the more general term *rule* (signifying a superset of the set signified by the term *business rule*) with the definition "*one of a set of explicit or understood regulations or principles governing conduct or procedure within a particular area of activity... a law or principle that operates within a particular sphere of knowledge, describing, or prescribing what is possible or allowable*." This appears to cover not only business rules but also the other types of constraints excluded from the definition of *business rule*. It is significant that the Business Rules Manifesto[11] refers to "*rules*" 44 times but "*business rules*" only nine times.

Any business, indeed any organization, is governed by a wide variety of rules. While many of these will have been established by the organization itself and will therefore be able to be modified by the organization, others will reflect legislation or regulation, external standards or best practice, or even, as we have seen, laws of physics. Therefore, despite its title, this book focuses on *all* rules that might govern an organization, whether or not they would be considered to be business rules according to the SBVR definition.

1.1.4 System rule or business rule?

The GUIDE Business Rules Project[12] sensibly decided to focus only on "*constraints on the creation, updating and removal of persistent data in an information system*" rather than the rules that govern business practice or human behavior within an organization.

That decision, while understandable, actually applied two selection criteria to arrive at a manageable subset of an organization's rules. Even if an organization were to have no information systems, it would

---

[8](Object Management Group, 2008).

[9]The US Sarbanes–Oxley Act of 2002, which among other things has mandated more comprehensive audit report standards and rules.

[10]The Revised International Capital Framework, published by the Basel Committee on Banking Supervision in June 2004, which among other things describes more comprehensive measures and rules to ensure that a bank's capital is more closely aligned to its risk profile.

[11](Business Rules Group, 2003).

[12](Business Rules Group, 2000).

still need to ensure that all activities performed by its staff, and all interactions with customers and suppliers, were in accordance with relevant legislation and regulation as well as good business practice.

Clearly the acquisition of technology (including information systems) involves the consideration and implementation of rules governing how that technology is used, and the rules that the technology itself should enforce. For example, the organization might have a business rule that allows only authorized personnel access to certain parts of its premises. Technology systems, such as keypads that require a correct combination to be keyed in, or 'swipe card' readers, must be programmed with appropriate rules to support the organization's business rules.

In an ideal world, an organization's technology systems impose only those restrictions on processes (in particular, those of data capture and maintenance) that support adherence to the legislation, regulation, and business practice governing the organization: that is, all system rules support the organization's business rules. Sometimes, however, a system imposes rules that do not support any business rule. These may be additional constraints that make system design easier, agreed to by the organization as a trade-off against cheaper or earlier system delivery, or accepted as a non-compliant feature of a purchased system that is otherwise fit for purpose.

Sometimes such constraints are less justifiable. I recall developing a purchasing application and, during analysis of the relevant business rules, was assured that any one purchase order could only cover goods required by one department. In other words, if two departments required goods from the same supplier at the same time, two purchase orders would have to be raised (despite a significant cost overhead per purchase order). When I questioned this, it turned out to be not a business rule but a limitation of the existing system that had become ingrained in the organization's practice. Such limitations have been referred to by Ross[13] as *system rules* to distinguish them from business rules.

Most rule analysis exercises do focus only on those rules to be implemented in a new or updated application system, and most of those will be "*constraints on the creation, updating and removal of persistent data*" (as discussed in the GUIDE Business Rules Project[14]), although it is important to also analyze constraints on the execution of a process, as discussed in Section 2.4.2 in Chapter 2 as well as Sections 4.6 and 4.9.3 in Chapter 4. It can be of value to establish and document the ***motivation*** for each rule, which may be any of the following:

1. an already articulated business rule, which currently governs organizational behavior and must be supported by the new system;
2. an organizational objective, such as those listed in Section 1.2; and
3. an additional constraint to be introduced as part of the system design in the interests of simplicity and hence cheaper or earlier system delivery.

1.2 WHY RULES ARE IMPORTANT

Organizations choose to operate in accordance with rules for a variety of reasons. These include minimization of exposure to risk, cost reduction, revenue protection, maintenance of market share, etc. For example, the rules typically applied by lending institutions to establish the ability of a borrower to repay

---

[13](Ross, Are Integrity Constraints Business Rules? Not!, 2009).
[14](Business Rules Group, 2000).

a loan are driven by the need to minimize risk exposure. Financial institutions also apply rules to manage their overall exposure to risk across the set of accounts held by corporate customers (or retail customers with large loans). Internally defined rules may cover such matters as minimum prices (or maximum discounts) to protect revenue, completeness of information to support decision making (to ensure in turn risk minimization, cost reduction, or revenue generation), guidelines for rewarding customer loyalty (to minimize 'churn' and thus maintain market share and reduce costs)—these are of course only a small sample.

Enlightened organizations also constrain their business activities to ensure that they do not have a deleterious impact on the natural environment or the safety of employees and customers. Safety matters are governed by Occupational Health and Safety regulations (for employees) and product safety regulations (for customers). A really enlightened organization may even take into account the financial well-being of customers: for example, my mother's bank recently advised her of ways of reducing the fees she pays for their services; of course, whether this was as a result of any business rule is an interesting question.

1.3 BEST PRACTICE RULE MANAGEMENT

Given their importance, it is important that an organization's rules be managed in such a way as to achieve the following state of affairs:

1. All who are governed by those rules, who have a stake in those rules being complied with, or who are tasked with implementing those rules, know what rules are in force and which rules apply to each situation they may encounter; this includes the organization's employees, customers, suppliers, business partners, etc.
2. All rules that may be legitimately updated by the organization can be updated in a timely and inexpensive manner.

To achieve this ideal, the organization's rules need to be managed along the following lines:

1. Each rule is documented in one or more of the natural languages[15] used by those governed by that rule: for example, various dialects of English in the United Kingdom, the United States, and Australia, and English and French in Canada.
2. Each rule is documented in a single natural language statement in each of those natural languages (although it may be implemented using more than one programming language statement or declaration).
3. Each natural language rule statement uses business terminology rather than database table or column names or program module names.
4. Each natural language rule statement is unambiguous.
5. Each natural language rule statement is succinct (uses no more words than necessary).
6. All natural language rule statements are consistent in terms of vocabulary (terms used) and syntax (sentence structure).

---

[15]As distinct from a programming language.

7. All natural language rule statements are easily accessible and understandable by all who are governed by the stated rules, who have a stake in those rules being complied with, or who are tasked with implementing those rules.
8. All rules that may be legitimately updated by the organization are implemented in a manner that allows them to be updated as required without excessive expenditure of time and money.
9. Those who might require a rule to be changed know what rules can be changed and the impact of changing each of those rules.
10. Those who might require a rule to be changed or who are authorized to change any rule know what steps are required to update the statement and implementation(s) of that rule.

As I indicated in my introduction to this book, I have encountered few organizations that manage to achieve this ideal. There are many ways of documenting a rule: rules expressed in program code, DDL (data definition language), or rules engine instructions are unambiguous but not easily accessible or understandable by anyone other than the organization's application developers. Application development may be performed by contractors or outsourced, in which case there may be no one in the organization who can access and understand these rules. Rules documented in program specifications may at least have the advantage of being expressed in natural language (although they may instead be expressed in *pseudo-code*, which only partly resembles natural language) but those program specifications may not be available to all employees.

This situation, however, hardly meets the requirements listed above. First, each rule is hidden away in a large body of text, so not truly accessible. Second, rules are unlikely to be expressed using consistent syntax and vocabulary, unless expressed in pseudo-code (and sometimes not even then).

Another aspect of rule management that I rarely see done well is documentation of the impact of changing a rule. This has a number of aspects:

1. The likelihood of the rule changing, ranging from 'never' (in the case of a law of physics, for example) through 'rarely' (in the case of legislation or regulations) to 'often' (in the case of those internally defined rules deployed to fine-tune revenue): Airlines, for example, constantly fine-tune the numbers of discounted tickets available on each flight so as to strike the right balance between maximum loading (by ensuring every seat is booked) and maximum revenue (by minimizing the number of discount tickets on a high-demand flight).
2. The effects of the change on the organization's operations: Does the change have the potential to increase risk exposure, increase costs, or reduce revenue?
3. The effort required to change the rule: Where is the rule implemented? What other rules may be affected? How many system components (user interfaces, application system modules, database triggers, stored procedures, etc.) need to be updated? What testing and roll-out activities have to be performed?

1.4 THE NATURE OF THE PROBLEM

Given the importance of business rules, any system developed or acquired by an organization is of more value if that system ensures that the data it manages and the processes it performs comply with all relevant rules to which the organization is subject. Many older systems do not enforce compliance with all relevant rules. Other older systems may do so through program code. More modern systems may be governed by rules implemented in the database or a rules engine.

The rules governing an organization and its systems need to be documented in such a manner as to enable stakeholders to review them for relevance and correctness, approve them, change them as required, and so on. This requires in turn that all rule statements be easily accessible by all stakeholders, be in a standard format, and use business terminology (rather than database object names).

Unfortunately, current technology does not well support this requirement. Of course, rules engines expose all rule statements in a standard format, but, even if business terminology (rather than database object names) can be used in a rules engine, its standard format is unlikely to be particularly business-friendly. Many rules engines require a diagrammatic notation in which the objects that the rule governs or refers to are denoted by various symbols. Many others use a spreadsheet-style user interface. In an organization using a rules engine, therefore, business stakeholders either have to learn the notation and possibly become familiar with the relevant database object names, or rely on the rules engine specialist to explain what is meant by his or her arcane symbols.

Rules implemented in a database may be documented in (or in association with) the logical or conceptual data model (assuming one exists). This is fine (from the point of view of business stakeholders), provided that the model is available to them and has been set out in a manner that genuinely supports communication with business stakeholders—unfortunately such models are, in my experience, a rarity. It is rare to encounter a data model accompanied by a guide to the symbols used, but all too common to find a data model using not the organization's business terminology but terminology made up by the modeler, apparently in isolation.

A more common situation is that any rules are only documented in system functional specifications or program specifications. A major problem with this approach is that the rules documented in this way are most likely scattered throughout a series of large documents; even if the business stakeholders have access to those documents, do they know where to look for the rule statements?

Rules are usually documented in system specifications in either pseudo-code or natural language statements. Pseudo-code, such as

```
"if number-of-traffic-violations > 3 then perform reject-application",
```

has the advantage of being unambiguous but is often unintelligible to business stakeholders.

Natural language, on the other hand, has the advantage, if properly used, of being intelligible to business stakeholders. However, natural language can be ambiguous. Further, as we shall see in Sections 1.5.1.2 and 1.5.1.3, there are many different ways of expressing a given rule using natural language. This makes it all too easy to end up with similar rules expressed using quite different rule statements, which, as we shall see, makes rule quality assurance more difficult.

Managing changes to rules is, as we have seen, a complex matter. The questions that need to be answered when changing a rule will not be answered easily by inspection of the program code, database or rules engine in which it is implemented, and the system specification in which it is documented will generally not answer those questions either.

To summarize, there are three rule management problems faced by most organizations:

1. Their rule statements are not in a standard format and/or not using business terminology.
2. Their rule statements are not easily accessible by all stakeholders.
3. Their process for changing rules is complex.

1.5 THE SOLUTIONS

There are solutions to each of the rule management problems discussed in the previous section. While this book's principal focus is on a solution to the first of these problems, an effective solution to the other two problems is also described and forms part of the methodology described in Chapter 8.

1.5.1 Constrained natural language

The solution to the first rule management problem I described in Section 1.4 (rule statements not in a standard format and/or not using business terminology) is a *constrained natural language* (also known as a *controlled natural language*), namely a language exhibiting the following characteristics:

1. the vocabulary is constrained, to minimize the number of alternative ways of expressing the same rule;
2. the syntax (sentence structure) is constrained, for two reasons:
   a. to further minimize the number of alternative ways of expressing the same rule, and
   b. to remove at least some of the sources of ambiguity.

1.5.1.1 The benefits of expressing rules in natural language

The process of developing any application system component, whether it be a set of database tables, a program module, a set of business rules, or a *reusable service*, requires the following steps, once the overall system requirements have been established and documented:

1. establish the requirements that the component is to meet;
2. document the design of the component in a manner that can be understood by business stakeholders;
3. allow those business stakeholders to review the design, leading to an agreed final design;
4. implement the component according to that final design;
5. unit test;
6. integrate;
7. system test;
8. allow users to test the component against the established requirements; and
9. deploy.

This not only allows developers to implement the required components correctly but also allows business stakeholders to play an informed role in determining the function of the components to be implemented.

A set of business rules will be far better understood by business stakeholders if each rule is documented using a natural language statement rather than a programming language or pseudo-code statement.

1.5.1.2 The benefits of standardized vocabulary

It goes without saying that business stakeholders will understand rule statements better if those statements use business terminology rather than (for example) database table or column names or program module names. For this reason, I recommend organizations only use business terminology in rule statements.

This is easier than it sounds, however. Many business terms turn out to have different meanings depending on who is using them. For example, when consulting to an Australian airline, I discovered that at least six different meanings for the term 'service' were in common use, as in the following statements:

1. There are now more flights than ever on the Sydney–Melbourne service.
2. Your service to Brisbane is now ready for departure.
3. There is a breakfast service on each flight of more than an hour's duration departing before 8 am.
4. All staff are trained in customer service.
5. While an aircraft is in service, its location is reported every 5 min.
6. While the aircraft is undergoing service, all seats are to be replaced.

Differences are sometimes more subtle. For example, in an Australian state government department to which I have been consulting, one organization unit uses the term 'instrument' to refer to all documents of a certain type, whereas another organization unit uses the same term to refer to all documents of that type except certain special documents.

As we shall see in Chapter 6, it is necessary to establish what terms have single agreed meanings across the organization (and document those meanings).

We are not out of the woods yet! Most business terms have synonyms. For example, a customer may be referred to as a 'client' (or, in the airline industry, a 'passenger' or even 'guest'). Some may use the term 'birth date', while others prefer 'date of birth'. Thus the same rule could be expressed using any of the following statements:

R3. Each <u>account application</u> must *specify* the <u>birth date</u> *of* the <u>client</u>.
R4. Each <u>account application</u> must *specify* the <u>birth date</u> *of* the <u>customer</u>.
R5. Each <u>account application</u> must *specify* the <u>date of birth</u> *of* the <u>client</u>.
R6. Each <u>account application</u> must *specify* the <u>date of birth</u> *of* the <u>customer</u>.

However, it is not only terms that have synonyms: there are also various alternatives that could have been used in place of the verb *specify*, such as *include*, *state*, and so on. Even if the organization has agreed to standardize on <u>customer</u> and <u>date of birth</u>, we could still end up the following statements:

R7. Each <u>account application</u> must *include* the <u>date of birth</u> *of* the <u>customer</u>.
R8. Each <u>account application</u> must *state* the <u>date of birth</u> *of* the <u>customer</u>.

R3–R8 are alternative statements of the same rule. Yet more than one of these rule statements might be independently added to the organization's **rule book** (the collection of rules governing that organization) in either of the following scenarios:

1. multiple rule authors are working within the organization and not checking each other's work
2. the one rule author is working over an extended period of time and not checking his or her prior work (despite human memory being less than perfect).

Detection of such duplication can only be automated by a text processor that can do the following:

1. recognize synonyms of terms and equivalent verbs, and
2. perform some parsing of rule statements.

In the absence of any such support, it must be done manually. Given that the number of rules governing most organizations is in the thousands, this is time consuming, tedious, and error-prone.

As we shall see in Section 8.5 in Chapter 8, the organization's rule book must be consistent, in that no two rule statements conflict with or overlap each other (examples of such conflicts and overlaps are also to be found in Section 8.5). If rule statement authors use different synonyms, the process of checking for conflict and overlap is that much more difficult. Remember, such verification effort increases as the square of the number of rule statements.

1.5.1.3 The benefits of standardized syntax

Even if a standard vocabulary is used, checking rule statements for duplication, conflict, and overlap is made even more difficult if different sentence structures are used for rule statements of the same type. Consider the following:

R9. Each <u>account application</u> must *specify* the <u>date of birth</u> of the <u>customer</u>.
R10. †Each <u>account application</u> must *specify* the <u>customer</u>'s <u>date of birth</u>.[16]
R11. †The <u>date of birth</u> of the <u>customer</u> must be *specified* in each <u>account application</u>.
R12. †The <u>customer</u>'s <u>date of birth</u> must be *specified* in each <u>account application</u>.
R13. †It is obligatory that each <u>account application</u> *specifies* the <u>date of birth</u> of the <u>customer</u>.
R14. †It is obligatory that each <u>account application</u> *specifies* the <u>customer</u>'s <u>date of birth</u>.

Each of these rule statements expresses the same rule. If more than one of them is in the organization's rule book, detection of such duplication can only be achieved by either tedious manual inspection or investing in software that can recognize sentences with different structures as having the same meaning.

There is another benefit to be gained from consistent rule statement syntax. Translation of natural language rule statements to program code or rules engine input is made rather easier for the programmer or rules engine driver if rules of the same type are expressed using the same statement syntax. And software that automatically performs that translation is going to be considerably less expensive to develop or purchase if it does not have to cater for multiple statement forms for the same type of rule.

1.5.2 The benefits of a rule repository

The solution to the second rule management problem I described in Section 1.4 (rule statements not easily accessible by all stakeholders) is a rule repository in which all rules governing the organization can be recorded in the form of natural language rule statements.

1.5.3 The benefits of rule metadata

The solution to the third rule management problem I described in Section 1.4 (complexity of the rule change process) is the recording of relevant **metadata** about each rule: a small investment in rule metadata can return considerable benefits in terms of more efficient processes for changing those rules that need to be changed. For that reason, I have chosen to include in the methodology in Chapter 8 not only how to author well-formed rule statements but also how to record appropriate rule metadata, such as the following:

---

[16]Each rule statement example that, for one or more reasons, is not recommended is marked with an initial dagger, as in R10–R14 inclusive.

1. metadata about each rule, including
   a. its status: for example, 'proposed', 'in force', 'superseded';
   b. historic and proposed versions (if any);
   c. the effective and expiry dates of the current version, and any historic and proposed versions; and
   d. the databases, program modules, user interfaces, message schemas, and other system components in which the rule has been implemented;
2. metadata about the *terms* used in each rule statement, including
   a. an unambiguous definition (see Section 6.2.2 in Chapter 6);
   b. any current *synonyms* of the term and the communities that use those synonyms;
   c. any non-current synonyms of the term and the dates on which those synonyms were phased out;
   d. any synonyms of the term that are not to be used in business discourse for whatever reason;
   e. the plural form of the term, in particular, if it is one for which the plural form is not formed simply by the addition of 's': for example, 'bus', 'category', 'terminus', 'criterion', 'date of birth', 'man', 'child'[17];
   f. the *fact types* employing the term;
   g. the entities and/or attributes, in any data model produced for the organization, that represent the concept to which the term refers;
   h. the object classes and/or attributes, in any UML object class model produced for the organization, that represent the concept to which the term refers; and
   i. the database tables and/or columns, on-screen labels, XML tags, reusable services, and other application system components that form part of the system representation of the term;
3. metadata about the *connectors* (*verbs* or *prepositions*) used in each rule statement, including
   a. the *fact types* employing the connector.

The acquisition and effective deployment of a rule repository is a crucial enabler of the methodology described in Chapter 8.

1.6 SUMMARY

Rules include not only those that an organization creates for itself but also laws of physics, legislation, regulations, external standards, and best practices. Rules are important to organizations for many reasons, including risk mitigation, cost reduction, revenue protection, and maintenance of market share. Because of this, it is important that they be managed in such a way that employees, customers, suppliers, and other stakeholders know what rules are in force in each interaction they may have with the organization.

These rule documentation requirements are not best served by current technology (including rules engines) but can be met by documenting each rule in a succinct, unambiguous natural language rule statement using consistent business terminology and sentence structure and making those rule statements easily accessible (along with appropriate metadata) in a suitable repository.

It is also important that the organization knows what rules can be changed, the impact of changing any such rule, and the steps required to do so.

---

[17]The plural forms of these words are of course 'buses', 'categories', 'termini', 'criteria', 'dates of birth', 'men', 'children' respectively.

How rules work

This chapter first distinguishes two fundamental types of rules: **operative rules** and **definitional rules** (or **structural rules**). It then describes the various ways in which rules govern an organization:

1. some rules govern the business processes performed by organizations, their employees, customers, suppliers, and partners;
2. other rules govern user interfaces and electronic messages;
3. other rules ensure database integrity;
4. still other rules govern human behavior other than business processes.

2.1 OPERATIVE RULES

Operative rules state what must or must not happen in particular circumstances, as in the following examples:

R15. Each flight booking request *for* a return journey must *specify* the return date.

R16. A flight booking request *for* a one-way journey must not *specify* a return date.

R17. The departure date *specified in* each flight booking request must *be no earlier than* the booking date.

Operative rules can be contravened: someone filling out a request, application, order, etc. may omit the required information or supply information that is irrelevant or inappropriate. If such a rule is contravened, the person or system enforcing the rule should advise the person (or system) supplying the information that the rule has been contravened and indicate what information is required instead.

Note that this type of rule is not confined to whether information is to be provided or not. An operative rule may state restrictions on processes or activities, as in the following:

R18. A passenger may *board* a flight only after that passenger *undergoes* security screening.

Alternatively, it may state who must or must not perform a certain process or activity:

R19. The cabin crew member who *checks* that an aircraft door *is disarmed*[1] must not *be* the same cabin crew member who *disarmed* that aircraft door.

I shall explore how operative rules govern the provision of information, and processes generally, in Section 2.4.2.

---

[1]'Arming' of aircraft doors after closure but before takeoff ensures that, if a door is opened after a crash or emergency landing, an escape slide automatically inflates. On landing, of course, all doors must be disarmed.

2.2 DEFINITIONAL (STRUCTURAL) RULES

By contrast, **definitional rules** constrain how we define various constructs created by the organization (or the industry within which it operates). These rules are referred to in the SBVR as structural rules, but I prefer the term **definitional rules**, since only some of these rules are truly structural. The constructs that can be defined using definitional rules include the following:

1. Formal definitions of particular terms, such as

R20. An <u>infant passenger</u> *is* by definition a <u>passenger</u> whose <u>age</u> *is less than* $\underline{\underline{2\ years}}$[2] *at* the <u>time of travel</u>.[3]

R21. An <u>employee</u> *of* an <u>organization</u> *is* by definition a <u>person</u> who *is employed by* that <u>organization</u>.

R22. A <u>sister</u> *of* a <u>person</u> *is* by definition a <u>female person</u> who *has* the same <u>parents</u> *as* the first <u>person</u>.

2. In particular, formal definitions of time periods and points in time, such as

R23. <u>Close of business</u> *is* by definition $\underline{\underline{5\ pm}}$.

R24. <u>Christmas Day</u> *is* by definition <u>$\underline{\underline{December\ 25}}$</u>.

3. Enumerations of mutually exclusive sets of categories or statuses, such as

R25. A <u>flight</u> *is* by definition either a <u>domestic flight</u> or an <u>international flight</u>.

R26. A <u>journey</u> *is* by definition one of the following: a <u>one-way journey</u>, a <u>return journey</u>, or a <u>multi-stop journey</u>.

4. The structure of complex concepts, such as

R27. A <u>flight</u> *has* by definition exactly one <u>origin port</u>.

5. Necessary relationships between components of complex concepts, such as

R28. The <u>origin city</u> *of* the first <u>return flight</u> *of* a <u>return journey</u> *is* by definition *the same as* the <u>destination city</u> *of* the last <u>outgoing flight</u> *of* that <u>return journey</u>.

6. Valid values of measurements and quantities, such as

R29. <u>pH</u> *is* by definition *at least* $\underline{\underline{0}}$ and *at most* $\underline{\underline{14}}$.

7. Algorithms for calculating values, such as

R30. The <u>extension</u> *for* an <u>order line</u> *is* by definition *calculated as* the product of
- the <u>order quantity</u> *for* that <u>order line</u>,
- the <u>unit price</u> *for* that <u>order line</u>, and
- $\underline{\underline{1}}$ minus the <u>discount rate</u> *for* that <u>order line</u>.

---

[2]The SBVR convention is to mark quantities, dates, and times using a double underline.

[3]Note that the SBVR proposes alternative formulations for structural (definitional) rule statements, as described in Section 3.3.8.4 in Chapter 3. However, I do not recommend those formulations for practical business use, for the reasons given in that section.

8. In particular, definitions of conversion factors, such as

R31. 1 in *is* by definition *approximately equal to* 2.54 cm.

9. Standard formats, such as

R32. A valid port code[4] *is* by definition *composed of* exactly three letters.

2.3 NORMATIVE, PRESCRIPTIVE, AND DESCRIPTIVE RULES

Some practitioners prefer to categorize rules as either ***normative*** or ***descriptive***. The term 'normative' (or 'prescriptive') is used to characterize assertions that define what must be or should be (but which may not be) whereas the term 'descriptive' is used to characterize assertions that define what is of necessity the case. 'Normative rule' and 'prescriptive rule' are therefore synonyms of 'operative rule' (as defined in Section 2.1) and 'descriptive rule' is a synonym of 'definitional rule' or 'structural rule' (as defined in Section 2.2).

2.4 BUSINESS PROCESSES

A ***business process*** is an activity (or set of activities) that is managed by an organization to produce some result of value to that organization, its customers, its suppliers, and/or its partners.

A business process may be performed by a system without human intervention (e.g., account house-keeping performed at the end of each financial period, or the automatic reordering of any stores item that falls below a reorder point). Alternatively, a business process may be performed by a human being without any automated system support (e.g., the delivery of goods by a driver from a supplier's warehouse to a customer's premises, a storeman's counting of stores items during stocktaking).

However, the vast majority of business processes involve a collaboration between one or more human beings and one or more automated devices or systems (e.g., withdrawal of money from your bank account using an Automated Teller Machine (ATM) or over the counter; paying a bill by credit card over the phone or using an Internet facility provided by your bank; booking a flight on the Internet, over the phone or over the counter).

The majority of these interactions require that one of the human beings involved uses a form displayed on a computer monitor (an ***on-screen form***) but this is not essential. For example, automated phone transactions can be performed by the customer using only the telephone keypad or his or her voice.

An example of an even simpler device is a security keypad that unlocks a normally locked door only if the correct combination is keyed in. If any other combination is keyed in, the door must remain locked. In this system, there is a process (which unlocks the door if appropriate), input data (the combination), and a 'go/no-go' rule that only admits two outcomes (the door either unlocks or it does not). The rule is fired whenever input data are received (a combination is keyed into the keypad).

Alternatively, access control may be managed using a 'swipe card' reader. Here, the input data are whatever is encoded in the magnetic card: this may well include restrictions on the doors by which access is allowed, and/or times and days of the week for which access is allowed. In this situation, there

---

[4]'Port code' is the term used in the airline industry for the three-letter abbreviations used to identify airports, such as LAX (Los Angeles), LHR (London Heathrow), and SYD (Sydney).

are typically two rules: one leading to 'no-go' if the card is not recognized, and one leading to 'go' only if all of the following are true:

1. the card is recognized;
2. the card is programmed to allow access through this door;
3. the card is programmed to allow access at this particular time on this particular day of the week.

This is an example of a rule that responds not only to input data but also to environmental knowledge ("what day and time it is now").

A device may need spatial as well as temporal environmental knowledge. For instance, another system governed by rules is to be found at train stations in Sydney (Australia). On entering or leaving a station, most passengers are required to insert a ticket into a slot beside a normally closed barrier. An entry barrier opens only if the ticket meets all of the following criteria:

1. it is valid for travel from that station;
2. it has not expired;
3. it has not already been used for the maximum number of journeys allowed.

By contrast, an exit barrier opens if the ticket is valid for travel to that station and does not check for expiry or overuse.

Each barrier needs not only to read the ticket (the input data) but also to know whether it is in the geographical area covered by the ticket or not and (in the case of an entry barrier) know the date and time.

This system does not only include this 'go/no-go' rule. Both types of barriers also make a decision based on whether it would be legitimate to make any further journeys on the ticket (a single ticket can be used for only one journey and a return ticket for two, whereas a weekly ticket can be used for unlimited journeys within a week). If no more journeys are possible, the ticket is retained within the barrier, but in all other cases it is returned to the passenger. This decision would appear to render unnecessary the third clause in the 'go/no-go' rule for an entry barrier (the ticket has not already been used for the maximum number of journeys allowed). However, there are stations without barriers, so it cannot be assumed that (for example) a single ticket still in a passenger's possession has not yet been used.

I have chosen the examples in this section on account of their concrete physical nature and relative simplicity. More commonly, the business processes for which you will need to establish the rules are those that involve an on-screen form into which information can be entered by a person so as to achieve some desired result: for example, using the Internet to pay a bill or book a flight, or the company's Intranet to enter your weekly timesheet or apply for leave.

One final note on the use of environmental knowledge by a device: the development of applications for mobile devices is a growing field. Such devices are location-aware, enabling them to filter data based on their current location. As yet the developers of such applications may see little need to document the rules governing those applications, but as they become more sophisticated it will be interesting to see how developers ensure that all necessary rules are applied.

2.4.1 Characteristics of a business process

The examples in the previous section provide us with further characteristics of business processes:

1. All business processes are *recurrent*, in that they may occur more than once and generally many times. Each occurrence of a business process should have a well-defined start point and a well-defined end point: that is, it is possible for the participants to determine when each occurrence

of a process has started and when it has finished. For example, each withdrawal of money from an ATM starts with the insertion of one's bank card into the ATM and ends with the removal of the card, the money, and the docket recording the process (if any).

2. A business process may contain subprocesses. For example the Book Flight Online process provided by an airline typically consists of the following steps:
    a. Search Available Seats: the facility lists those flights that have available seats;
    b. Select Flights and Fares: the person using the facility selects the flight or flights and where more than one fare class is available on a flight, the preferred fare class for each flight;
    c. Review: the facility lists the selected flights and fares for confirmation;
    d. Identify Passengers: the person using the facility lists the names and other information about each passenger flying;
    e. Select Payment Option: the person using the facility enters details of the credit card or other means of payment;
    f. Confirm: the person using the facility confirms the payment.
3. A business process may be performed in different ways. For example, an airline may provide various means of booking a flight, such as online (via the airline's website or a travel agent's website), over the phone (direct to the airline), or via a travel agent (over the counter or over the phone).
4. Each occurrence of a business process is triggered by a certain type of event. This may be
    a. the arrival of a particular type of information: for example, a user enters information on a screen or a message arrives from another process;
    b. a clock or calendar event, whereby a particular time of day and/or date eventuates: for example, close of business each day, the end of the financial month or year, or some deadline such as 48 h after making a booking.

2.4.2 How rules govern business processes

Rules govern business processes in various ways, as illustrated in Figure 1:

1. A given business process may be permitted to occur only if certain pre-conditions are met. These may be any or all of the following:
    a. the completion of some other process (e.g., a passenger is permitted to board an aircraft only after that passenger has undergone security screening) or another occurrence of the same process (e.g., the airline employee checking boarding passengers will not start checking the documentation of a passenger until he or she has completed checking the documentation of the previous passenger);
    b. the presence of all necessary information (e.g., a passenger is permitted to board an aircraft only if he or she presents a boarding pass and—in the case of an international flight—passport);
    c. the completeness and correctness of all information provided (e.g., the boarding pass presented by a passenger when boarding an aircraft must include the correct flight number and date, and the passport presented by that passenger must include a likeness of the passenger and an expiry date at least 6 months in the future, while, if both are presented, the names on both must be the same);
    d. environmental conditions, such as a particular time period or even, now that many devices are location-aware, a particular place or geographical area: for example, a Sydney (Australia) train station barrier needs to know:
        i. whether it is in the geographical area covered by the ticket, and
        ii. (in the case of an entry barrier) the date and time.

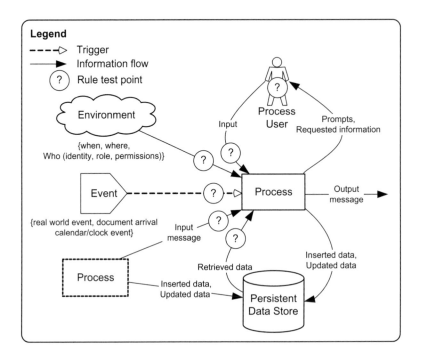

FIGURE 1

How rules govern business processes.

2. A business process may make decisions at certain points during the set of actions that take place (e.g., whether to retain a ticket presented at a train station barrier).
3. A business process may perform one or more calculations (e.g., the premium to be paid for comprehensive insurance on a motor vehicle, based on the value of the vehicle; the location where it is garaged; and the driving and claims history of the nominated driver).
4. There may be constraints on what individuals or roles are prohibited from performing a business process (or alternatively obliged to perform it). These constraints may
   a. be absolute, such as "only a user with administrative privileges may perform this process";
   b. ensure that two tasks are performed by the same person, such as a requirement that a shipping document must be signed by the person who packed the goods;
   c. (conversely) ensure that two tasks be performed by different persons, such as the requirement that the flight attendant who checks that an aircraft door is disarmed[5] must not be the same flight attendant who disarmed that door;
   d. avoid "vested interests", such as the common requirement that a document may be witnessed only by a person who is not related to the signatory.

---

[5]See the footnote to rule statement R19 in Section 2.1 for a definition of the airline industry term 'disarmed.'

2.5 **RULES IN USER INTERFACES**

An important class of rules governing business processes (as discussed in Section 2.4.2) consists of those that ensure the presence of all necessary information and the completeness and correctness of all information provided. The information input to each occurrence of a business process will in most cases be provided on a paper or electronic form or by way of an electronic message from another system. I shall consider in Section 2.6 the situation where input is by way of an electronic message and concentrate for now on information provided by way of a paper or electronic form.

Unless a process is completely manual, the information input to that process will inevitably be entered by way of an electronic user interface, even if the initial source of that information is a paper form.

Well-designed user interfaces govern what data can be entered so as to ensure data quality, prevent inappropriate outcomes, etc. Typically a user interface will do any or all of the following:

1. require that certain fields are filled in;
2. limit the possible contents of a field, by way of a 'combo box' providing a 'drop down list' or 'pick list';
3. limit the possible contents of a field to one of two values, representing 'yes' and 'no' respectively, by way of a check box;
4. allow only one of a group of yes/no items to be selected, by way of a group of 'radio buttons'; and/or
5. limit the possible contents of a field to a valid date, by way of a 'calendar gadget'.

Quite often, a user interface displays a representation of a row (record) of a database table, in which case the integrity constraints governing that table must all be supported in the user interface. For example, if a column that is mandatory in the database is represented in the user interface, the interface must be programmed to ensure that the field representing that column is filled in. This may of course be achieved by pre-loading the field with a **default value** each time it displays an otherwise blank electronic form.

After testing the entered data for compliance with the rules governing that data, the user interface must provide meaningful feedback to the user if any of the entered data are non-compliant. Some user interfaces produce rather cryptic messages that are perhaps meaningful only to a programmer. One great advantage of expressing rules in natural language is that the rule statement can also be used as an error message:

"The weekly course hours specified in each new student enrollment must not be greater than 40"

is more understandable than

"Range check error: wkly_crs_hrs !> 40".

It is important to provide the user with assistance to complete an on-screen form correctly before the data are entered and found to be non-compliant. A well-designed user interface should therefore include as much advice as is feasible before data entry as to what data fields must be filled in (even if only by way of an asterisk against each such field—which appears to have become a *de facto* standard). This advice may be on the on-screen form itself or a 'pop-up' that appears as each field is activated. Furthermore, where it is not feasible to constrain the content of a data field in advance by way of a combo box, 'calendar gadget', or other screen control, the user should be advised of any constraint on the data field content, such as a valid range, by means of a comment alongside the data field on the form.

Of course, rules can only be applied to ensure that information is complete, meaningful, and plausible, not that it is a correct representation of the operational environment. Consider the following scenario:

1. Projects #124 and #125, and my membership of the project teams for both of those projects, have been recorded in the timesheet system.
2. I worked for 8 h on Project #123 on a particular day.
3. I then recorded in a timesheet system that on that day I worked for 6 h on Project #124 and 2 h on Project #125.

In this scenario, the timesheet system is unlikely to detect an error, since all data entered are plausible:

1. my employee number, the project numbers, and the hours worked for each project have been entered;
2. my employee number and the project numbers are all valid;
3. both project numbers are valid in combination with my employee number; and
4. the hours recorded are valid durations adding up to 8 h.

In fact, any system relying on recording events after they have happened is subject to such errors, and rules are of no help in minimizing or eliminating such errors. By contrast, those systems that record intended activities before they occur and then constrain the activity are not subject to such errors. For example, if I book a flight to Los Angeles departing on May 1, I cannot fly to San Francisco on May 1 or Los Angeles on April 30 without changing that booking.

2.6 RULES GOVERNING ELECTRONIC MESSAGES

If the information input to a business process is by way of electronic messages from another system, it is still generally necessary to ensure the presence of all required information and the completeness and correctness of all information provided. If incoming messages are in XML format (rapidly becoming the dominant, if not the only, standard for messages), this may to some extent be achieved through constraints included in the XML schema for those messages (as described in Section 3.1.6 in Chapter 3) but all other rules governing message content must be implemented by the process itself.

2.7 RULES ENSURING DATABASE INTEGRITY

If the content of a persistent data store (such as a database) is to be meaningful, there are particular constraints on that content, mostly driven by the need for the database to be consistent rather than correct. As pointed out in (Date, Database in Depth—Relational Theory for Practitioners, 2005), these are not the same thing: a database can be consistent but not correct (in which case it represents a plausible alternative reality). However, if a database is not consistent, it cannot possibly be correct.

Various constraints can be imposed on a database to ensure its integrity: that is, consistency. These include the following:

1. ***Mandatory column constraints***: these require that a particular ***column*** in a ***table*** must have a value in every ***row*** (record) of that table: for example, each row in a table of purchase orders must include an order number and date raised as well as a customer number (a ***foreign key*** which implements a relationship to the table of customers);

2. ***Uniqueness constraints***: these include the requirement for each row to have a unique ***identifier*** (e.g., an order number in the case of a table of purchase orders), otherwise records cannot be distinguished (we cannot rely on a combination of customer number and date raised, since the same customer may raise more than one order on the same day). These constraints also include those that are necessary properties of the real-world situation represented by the data: for example, every seat allocation record for a particular flight on a particular day must have a different seat number, otherwise there will be two passengers allocated to the same seat, neither comfortable nor safe!

3. ***Referential integrity constraints***: these require that, in every row of a table, a particular column (or combination of columns) is either null (empty) or has a value or values that match the value(s) in a specific column or columns in either

   a. one of the rows of another table, or

   b. another row of the same table:

   for example, each customer number in a table of purchase orders must refer to an actual customer (there must be a corresponding record in the customer table);

4. ***Mandatory dependent row constraints***: these require that, where a row in one table can be associated with multiple rows in a second table, there must be at least one row in the second table for each row in the first table. For example, in a database holding information about orders (recorded in one table), each consisting of one or more order lines (recorded in another table), there must be at least one row in the Order Line table for each row in the Order table;

5. The often overlooked temporal equivalents of the last three of these constraints: for example, in a payroll system,

   a. there will generally be a requirement for the payroll records for an employee not to overlap in time: that is, no two payroll records for one employee can cover the same date: this is equivalent to a uniqueness constraint;

   b. there will generally be a requirement that no payroll record for an employee covers any date outside the employment period of that employee: this is equivalent to a referential integrity constraint;

   c. there may be a requirement for the payroll records for that employee to cover the entire employment period: that is, each date between the start date and the end date recorded in an employee record must be covered by a payroll record for that employee: this is equivalent to a mandatory dependent row constraint.

2.8 HUMAN ACTIVITIES OTHER THAN BUSINESS PROCESSES

In Section 2.4, I defined a ***business process*** as an activity (or set of activities) that is managed by an organization to produce some result of value to that organization, its customers, its suppliers, and/or its partners. However, there are many human beings within an organization's ecosystem: its employees; its personal customers; and in some cases, the employees of its corporate customers, suppliers, and partners. Furthermore, if the organization has premises that are open to the public (e.g., retail or passenger rail transport), it may attract other persons who are not customers. And it is an unfortunate fact that at least some of those human beings may engage in activities that not only do not add value but are detrimental to the organization or its stakeholders. Clearly these activities are not business processes.

An airline, for example, can characterize as business processes all of the following:

1. the activities of employees of the airline in scheduling, marketing, operations, maintenance, etc.;
2. customers' interactions with the airline via its website or over the phone (bookings, inquiries, and online check-in);
3. passengers' interactions with airline staff, automated check-in kiosks, or baggage handling equipment at an airport;
4. passengers' interactions with security or departure control staff between check-in and boarding;
5. travel agent's interactions with the airline online or over the phone.

However, there are other passenger activities that cannot be characterized as business processes but need to be restricted (e.g., using a laptop in flight) or completely prohibited (e.g., smoking in flight or during embarkation or disembarkation). Similarly, employees may be tempted to engage in activities that the business needs to restrict (e.g., employee use of company computers to access the Internet for personal reasons) or prohibit entirely (e.g., sexual harassment).

Such restrictions and prohibitions are not confined to customers and employees. A passenger rail transport company needs to restrict or prohibit various activities on trains or at train stations, not only by paying passengers but also by those who have not purchased a ticket.

For this reason, an organization may also need to identify and articulate rules restricting or prohibiting activities other than business processes.

2.9 SUMMARY

Operative rules (otherwise known as *normative rules* or *prescriptive rules*) state what must or must not happen in particular circumstances. Operative rules can be contravened: required information may be omitted, inappropriate information supplied, or an attempt may be made to perform a process that is prohibited. By contrast, *definitional rules* (otherwise known as *structural rules* or *descriptive rules*) constrain how we define various constructs created by the organization (or the industry within which it operates).

A *business process* is an activity (or set of activities) that produces some result. Rules can govern business processes in various ways:

1. A given business process may be permitted to occur only if certain pre-conditions are met, in particular the presence of all necessary information and the completeness and correctness of all information provided in a paper or electronic form or by way of an electronic message from another system.
2. A business process may make decisions at certain points during the set of actions that take place.
3. A business process may perform one or more calculations.

4. There may be constraints on which individuals or roles are prohibited from performing a business process.
5. There may be constraints on which individuals or roles are obliged to perform a business process.

Other rules ensure the integrity of a database; as well as *mandatory column constraints*, these include *uniqueness constraints*, *referential integrity constraints*, *mandatory dependent row constraints*, and the temporal equivalents of these.

An organization may also need rules to prohibit or restrict activities that may be detrimental to the organization or its stakeholders.

A brief history of rules

3

Rules have been with us long before there were computers, the Ten Commandments and the Code of Hammurabi[1] being but two examples. Both these sets of rules attempted to collect in one location natural language statements of a comprehensive set of rules by which the behavior of a particular community was to be governed. Since then, there has from time to time been conflict between, on the one hand, those who would make the law accessible only to a professional class specially trained in interpreting the law and, on the other hand, those who would make the law accessible to all. Recently, the latter school of thought has prevailed, with initiatives such as the 'Plain Language Law'[2].

3.1 IMPLEMENTING RULES

3.1.1 Rules in program code

Although some ***declarative programming languages*** have been developed—such as Prolog, SQL (Structured Query Language) and UML's OCL (Object Constraint Language)—by far the vast majority of business systems have been developed using ***procedural programming languages***—such as Cobol and PL/1 (from the 1960s onwards), Visual Basic and Java (in the 1990s), and .NET (in the 2000s). While a declarative programming language allows the programmer to specify desired outcomes or states, a procedural programming language only provides for sequences of commands to be performed, with some sets of commands being performed only if a certain logical condition is true. For example, if an undesirable condition arises, the program can display an error message and halt or return control to the user or operator. Alternatively, if a set of input data complies with all relevant rules, the program can proceed to update the database.

If rules are in program code, this presents us with a number of problems:

1. The complete set of rules spans multiple programs.
2. In each program there is non-rule code as well as rule code.
3. It is not always immediately obvious which is which.
4. Business stakeholders must learn the idiosyncrasies of the programming language to be able to understand each rule.

---

[1]This was a Babylonian law code enacted by the Babylonian king, Hammurabi, in about 1760 BCE, and consisting of 282 laws with defined punishments, some scaled according to the relative social status of offender and victim.
[2]*"Legislation that requires use of plain language in common agreements and contracts, such as those for consumer loans, home mortgages, insurance policies, and leasing and renting"*: (BusinessDictionary.com) (http://www.businessdictionary .com/definition/plain-language-law.html).

Cobol, PL/1, Visual Basic, .NET, and Java all use *if-statements* to specify conditional execution, which have much the same structure whatever the language: although there are minor lexical differences (such as the symbols used to separate statements and denote the end of the if-statement), each language has the following generic structure for an if-statement:

```
if <condition> then
   <action(s) to be taken if condition true>
else
   <action(s) to be taken if condition false>
```

For example, each of the following code fragments (in Cobol, PL/1, Visual Basic, .NET, and Java respectively) tests the value of a data item and produces an error message if that data item is out of range:

Cobol:

```
IF SHARE > 1
   DISPLAY ("Share must not be greater than 1")
ELSE
   IF SHARE = 0
      DISPLAY ("Share must not be zero")
   ELSE
      IF SHARE < 0
         DISPLAY ("Share must not be negative").
```

PL/1:

```
if share > 1 then
   put list ('Share must not be greater than 1');
else
   if share = 0 then
      put list ('Share must not be zero');
   else
      if share < 0 then
         put list ('Share must not be negative');
      endif;
   endif;
endif;
```

Visual Basic:

```
if Share > 1 then
   MsgBox ("Share must not be greater than 1")
elseif Share = 0 then
   MsgBox ("Share must not be zero")
elseif Share < 0 then
   MsgBox ("Share must not be negative")
end if
```

.NET:

```
if(Share > 1)
   Console.WriteLine("Share must not be greater than 1");
```

```
else
   if(Share = 0)
      Console.WriteLine("Share must not be zero");
   else
      if(Share < 0)
         Console.WriteLine("Share must not be negative");
```

Java:

```
if ( Share > 1 )
   System.out.println("Share must not be greater than 1");
else if ( Share = 0 ) {
   System.out.println("Share must not be zero");
} else if ( Share < 0 ) {
   System.out.println("Share must not be negative");
}
```

A key feature of procedural languages is that any condition that violates a rule must be tested after every statement that changes the data in question in any manner that might cause the data to violate that rule. For example, if a particular data item must never be negative, every statement that assigns a new value to that data item must be followed by an additional check that the data item is not negative (unless the assignment statement is adding a known positive value to that data item).

PL/1 is one of the languages that get around this problem by way of **on-statements**, which allow a condition and associated action to be specified at the beginning of a block of code. That condition will then be tested automatically each time there is a relevant change to any of the data item(s) covered by the condition, without that test having to be explicitly coded each time.

3.1.2 Decision tables

A **decision table** is a compact means of documenting the different decisions or actions to be taken in different sets of conditions: for example, what premium to charge for insurance depending on different risk factors, or indeed whether to issue a policy. There are two varieties of decision table:

1. a limited-entry decision table, as in Figure 1,
2. an extended-entry decision table, as in Figure 2.

The upper half of a limited-entry decision table lists the various conditions, one per row, on the left, and has a column on the right for each combination of conditions. The role of a condition in a combination of conditions is indicated by one of three symbols:

1. 'Y' indicates that that combination of conditions includes that condition;
2. 'N' indicates that that combination of conditions includes that condition negated;
3. a blank or (typically) a dash indicates that combination of conditions does not include that condition.

The lower half of a limited-entry decision table lists the various decisions or actions that may be taken, one per row, on the left, and indicates in each column on the right whether that decision or action is taken for that combination of conditions:

1. 'X' indicates that that decision or action is taken for that combination of conditions;
2. a dash indicates that that decision or action is not taken for that combination of conditions.

Daily?	Y	–	Y	–	Y	–
Weekly?	–	Y	–	Y	–	Y
Zone 1?	Y	Y	–	–	–	–
Zones 1 & 2?	–	–	Y	Y	–	–
Zone 2?	–	–	–	–	Y	Y
Fare = $5	X	–	–	–	–	–
Fare = $20	–	X	–	–	–	–
Fare = $8	–	–	X	–	–	–
Fare = $32	–	–	–	X	–	–
Fare = $4	–	–	–	–	X	–
Fare = $16	–	–	–	–	–	X

FIGURE 1

Example of a limited-entry decision table.

Duration	Daily	Weekly	Daily	Weekly	Daily	Weekly
Zone(s)?	1	1	1 & 2	1 & 2	2	2
Fare = ?	$5	$20	$8	$32	$4	$16

FIGURE 2

The same logic as an extended-entry decision table.

An extended-entry decision table differs by

1. including partial conditions on the left of the upper half and remainders of those conditions on the right, and/or
2. including partial decisions or actions on the left of the lower half and remainders of those decisions or actions on the right, as in Figure 2.

There are other forms of table that can represent such decision logic, as in Figure 3.

3.1.3 Rule sets in data

Implementing rules in program code gives rise to another problem: they cannot be modified without considerable effort. This is of course a good thing for rules that do not change in the real world. However, many rules do need to be changed from time to time.

For example, an airline might currently offer three classes of travel: first, business, and economy, but wish to increase market share by adding premium economy to the travel classes that it offers. If the program code used to process an online flight booking includes the following statement, that statement must be amended to allow for the additional travel class. This involves not only updating the program source code but compiling, testing, and releasing the new version of the program.

Zone(s) Duration	1	1 & 2	2
Daily	$5	$8	$4
Weekly	$20	$32	$16

FIGURE 3

An alternative representation of the same logic.

```
if not (Class = "First" and Class = "Business" and Class = "Economy") Then
   MsgBox ("Invalid Travel Class")
```

However, if the travel classes offered are held in a database table and the program compares the class entered into the booking form with the entries in that table, inclusion of an additional travel class requires only the insertion of an additional row into that table. The program code to perform the comparison is only marginally more complex:

```
if Lookup(ClassCode, "TravelClass", "ClassCode") = 0 Then
   MsgBox ("Invalid Travel Class")
```

This is arguably the most common use of data to manage a rule: holding the valid values of a data item in a column of a table. As well as enabling more agile changes to the rule, this technique is also useful where there are many valid values, such as there are for U.S. state codes. The first of the following two statements is certainly better than the second statement completed to show all fifty codes!

```
if Lookup (StateCode, "USState", "StateCode") = 0 Then
   MsgBox ("Invalid State Code")
if not (StateCode = "AL" and StateCode = "AK" and StateCode = ...) Then
   MsgBox ("Invalid State Code")
```

Database tables are also useful for holding sets of rules. For example, in a payroll system, it might be useful to record the following information in tables:

1. additional information about the categories in a categorization scheme: for example, which employee allowances are taxable and which are non-taxable;
2. minimum and maximum values: for example, the minimum and maximum annual salaries (or hourly rates) for employees of each grade;
3. valid combinations: for example, which allowance types may be paid to employees of each grade.

A cautionary tale is in order at this point: I recall a colleague who went to a great deal of trouble to include in a database design a number of tables that were intended to hold rule sets such as these. Unfortunately, due to a lack of communication between the data design and process design streams in the project (a far too common phenomenon in my experience), many of these rule sets were also hard-coded into the program logic! It was only when some of the rules needed to be changed that the resulting system deficiency was discovered: the appropriate manager updated the relevant values in the rule set tables, but found after doing so that the old values were still in force.

3.1.4 **Database constraints**

One feature of DBMSs (database management systems) is the ability to define data integrity rules. These include

1. the requirement for a column of a table to be **non-null**: that is, have a value in every row of that table;
2. the requirement for a column of a table to be **unique**: that is, have a different value in every row of that table;
3. the requirement for referential integrity between a **foreign key** and the corresponding **primary key**: that is, each row's value(s) in the column(s) making up the foreign key must match the value(s) in the primary key columns of one of the rows in a different table (or, in the case of a **recursive foreign key**, the same table);
4. constraints on the content of a column or columns in a row;
5. implicit constraints in numeric and date datatypes: for example, an integer column can only hold whole numbers, a date column can only hold valid dates.

For example, we can include the following data definition language (DDL) statements in a database specification:

```
CREATE TABLE Order_Line (
Order_No NUMBER(10) NOT NULL,
Line_No NUMBER(3) NOT NULL,
Product_Code VARCHAR2(10) NOT NULL,
Unit_Count NUMBER(4) NOT NULL
   CONSTRAINT CH_Unit_Count
      CHECK (Unit_Count > 0 AND Unit_Count < 9999),
Unit_Price NUMBER(7,2) NOT NULL
   CONSTRAINT CH_Unit_Price
      CHECK (Unit_Price > 0 AND Unit_Count < 99999.99),
Discount_Rate NUMBER(2,2)
   CONSTRAINT CH_Discount_Rate CHECK
      (Discount_Rate BETWEEN 0.05 AND 0.3),
CONSTRAINT PK_Order_Line PRIMARY KEY (Order_No, Line_No),
CONSTRAINT UK_Order_Line_01 UNIQUE (Order_No, Product_Code),
CONSTRAINT FK_Order_Order_Line_01 FOREIGN KEY (Order_No)
   REFERENCES Order(Order_No),
CONSTRAINT FK_Product_Order_Line_01 FOREIGN KEY (Product_Code)
   REFERENCES Product(Product_Code))
```

These statements specify, among other things, that

1. each Order Line must have an Order Number, Line Number, Product Code, Unit Count, and Unit Price (only the Discount Rate may be omitted);
2. each Order Number must be a numeral with no more than 10 digits;
3. each Line Number must be a numeral with no more than 3 digits;
4. each Product Code must have no more than 10 characters;
5. each Unit Count must be a positive integer (i.e., not zero, negative, or a fraction) no greater than 9999;

6. each Unit Price can have up to two decimal places, must be positive (i.e., not zero or negative), and cannot be greater than $99999.99;
7. the Discount Rate (if present) can have up to two decimal places and must be between 5% and 30%;
8. each Order Line must have a unique combination of Order Number and Line Number;
9. each Order Line must have a unique combination of Order Number and Product Code;
10. the Order Number in an Order Line must match an Order Number in the Order table; and
11. the Product Code in an Order Line must match a Product Code in the Product table.

3.1.5 Graphical user interface building tools

At the time online computing (as distinct from batch computing) first emerged, the appearance and behavior of the user interface was managed by way of programs written in conventional procedural programming languages, such as those described in Section 3.1.1.

A variety of graphical user interface building tools later evolved, providing facilities for programming the behavior of on-screen forms and their data fields. The relatively limited facilities provided by "dumb terminals" or "green screens" (typified by the IBM® 3270 screen) have given way to a range of facilities such as

1. checking the presence of data in a field when the user moves the cursor from that field;
2. checking the content of a field when data are entered into (or changed in) that field.

These facilities support rules such as those described in Section 2.5 in Chapter 2. These facilities tend to be much the same, whether the user interface is provided by a dedicated client application in a client-server environment or via a web interface running within a browser, such as Internet Explorer™ or Firefox™.

3.1.6 Constraints in XML schemas

XML (Extensible Markup Language) schemas can be coded to constrain the data in a message, in various ways such as the following:

1. implicit constraints on data content by way of the datatype, ranging from the use of a simple numeric or date datatype as in a DBMS to user-defined datatypes in which other restrictions on content can be specified: for example,
   ```
   <xs:simpleType name="PostalCodeType">
     <xs:restriction base="xs:string">
       <xs:minLength value="4"/>
       <xs:maxLength value="12"/>
       <xs:pattern value="([A-Z,0-9])*"/>
     </xs:restriction>
   </xs:simpleType>
   ```
   specifies that a Postal Code must contain at least 4 characters and at most 12 characters and each of those characters must be a letter or a digit;
2. restrictions on the minimum and maximum numbers of instances of a data item: for example,
   ```
   <xs:element name="AddresseeName" type="xs:string"
     minOccurs="1" maxOccurs="unbounded"/>
   ```

```
<xs:element name="StreetNumber" type="xs:string"
  minOccurs="0" maxOccurs="2"/>
<xs:element name="StreetName" type="xs:string"
  minOccurs="1" maxOccurs="2"/>
<xs:element name="LocalityName" type="xs:string"
  minOccurs="1" maxOccurs="1"/>
<xs:element name="PostalCode" type="xs:string"
  minOccurs="1" maxOccurs="1"/>
```

specifies that

a. there must be at least one Addressee Name but there is no upper limit to the number of Addressee Names that may be included,

b. there may be no Street Number or one or two Street Numbers,

c. there must be either one or two Street Names,

d. there must be one and only one Locality Name, and

e. there must be one and only one Postal Code;

3. the requirement that one of two or more alternatives must be included: for example,

```
<xs:choice>
  <xs:element name="clientReference" type="xs:string"/>
  <xs:element name="workspaceId" type="xs:string"/>
</xs:choice>
```

specifies that either a Client Reference or a Workspace ID must be present.

This type of structure can be used to implement more complex interdependencies, such as in the address structure above, in which a Street Number can in fact only be omitted (and must be omitted) if there are two Street Names, achieved by the following improvement on the schema fragment above:

```
<xs:element name="AddresseeName" type="xs:string"
  minOccurs="1" maxOccurs="unbounded"/>
<xs:choice>
  <xs:complexType name="OneStreetAddress"
    <xs:sequence>
      <xs:element name="StreetNumber" type="xs:string"
        minOccurs="1" maxOccurs="2"/>
      <xs:element name="StreetName" type="xs:string"
        minOccurs="1" maxOccurs="1"/>
    </xs:sequence>
  </xs:complexType>
  <xs:element name="StreetName" type="xs:string"
    minOccurs="2" maxOccurs="2"/>
</xs:choice>
<xs:element name="LocalityName" type="xs:string"
  minOccurs="1" maxOccurs="1"/>
<xs:element name="PostalCode" type="xs:string"
  minOccurs="1" maxOccurs="1"/>;
```

4. restrictions on the content of a data item to the values in an ***enumerated set***: for example,

```
<xs:simpleType name="DurationUnitType">
  <xs:restriction base="xs:string">
    <xs:enumeration value="year"/>
    <xs:enumeration value="month"/>
    <xs:enumeration value="week"/>
    <xs:enumeration value="day"/>
  </xs:restriction>
</xs:simpleType>
```

specifies that each Duration Unit must be one of the listed values.

3.1.7 **Rules engines**

Rules engines provide a means of not only collecting a number of rules into one accessible repository but implementing those rules. With the emphasis on implementation, however, comes a downside, in that the language used to express each rule is not one that business stakeholders will necessarily easily understand.

For a start, the visible representation of the rule may refer to database column names rather than the terms used by the business. Secondly, while many rules engine vendors claim that their tools have natural language interfaces, most if not all current rules engines use either a diagrammatic notation or a spreadsheet-style user interface. In either case, the commands or declarations to be entered require the use of a language that is more like a programming language than a natural business language. One exception was the Expert Rules product from Haley Systems, which has unfortunately been discontinued.

Furthermore, I have yet to see a rules engine deployed to manage all of an organization's rules. Typically an organization uses a rules engine to deal with a particular subset of the organization's rules, such as those determining whether an applicant for an insurance or financial product qualifies for that product and, if so, what premium, account opening fee, and/or interest rate that applicant should be charged.

3.2 **DOCUMENTING RULES**

So far we've been looking at the various methods available for the implementation of rules. Whether it be process, data, or rules, the IT industry has always tended to focus first on the implementation of those system components, and only later on how those components may be described in a manner that is understandable by business stakeholders. That is not to say that these rule implementation techniques are completely devoid of documentation: one can always read the program code, DDL, or XML, or open up the rules engine user interface! In each case, however, the business stakeholder untrained in the minutiae of the rule representation language or notation is unlikely to be able to comprehend accurately and with confidence the rules that have been implemented.

Of course, there have always been rule documents, such as legislation, rules and regulations, procedural manuals, and so on, for guiding human behavior either in front of or away from a computer. These, however, have varied widely in their use of language.

A serious approach to documenting rules so as to be understood consistently and confidently by all stakeholders is a relatively recent phenomenon.

3.2.1 **Rules in data models**

There are three principal methods of modeling data:

1. *Entity-Relationship Modeling* was initially described by Chen (1976), with variants subsequently developed by (among others) Charles Bachman, Richard Barker—described in (Barker, 1990)—and James Martin.
2. *ORM* (*Object-Role Modeling*) was developed initially by Gerardus Maria (Sjir) Nijssen in the 1970s and subsequently extended and formalized by him and Terry Halpin, leading to the publication of a number of ORM resources in 1989.[3] ORM is significantly different from the other methods in its approach to modeling data. In particular, it allows for the direct depiction of many more types of rules than either of the other methods.
3. *UML* (*Unified Modeling Language*) is a synthesis of three object-oriented modeling approaches:
   a. James Rumbaugh's Object Modeling Technique (OMT)
   b. Grady Booch's Booch Method
   c. Ivar Jacobson's Object-Oriented Software Engineering.
   Various versions of UML have been published by the OMG (Object Management Group) since 1997.[4] UML includes a variety of model types, including *object class models*, which are used in many organizations as an alternative to Entity-Relationship models.
   Each notation provides for modeling a different subset of the rules by which the integrity of a database can be maintained.

3.2.1.1 *Entity-relationship models*

Entity-Relationship Models (sometimes referred to as *ER Models*) focus on

1. *entities* (strictly speaking, *entity classes*): sets of similar things of interest to the business (e.g., 'Customer', 'Product', 'Order'), some of which may be *subtypes* of other entity classes; entity classes are represented in all Entity-Relationship Modeling variants by the use of rectangular boxes (with either square or rounded corners depending on the variant) although there are various ways of representing that one entity class is a subtype of another;
2. *attributes*: identifiers and properties of those entity classes (e.g., 'Customer Name', 'Product Code', 'Order Date', 'Order Quantity'), listed either within the relevant entity class box or separately from the diagram (depending on the variant);
3. *relationships*: sets of associations between instances of entity classes (e.g., 'Customer places Order', 'Order includes Order Line', 'Order Line is for Product'), represented in all Entity-Relationship Modeling variants by the use of lines between the relevant entity class boxes.

Some writers have claimed that Entity-Relationship models depict the business rules that govern the modeled data. This is true but only up to a point: in fact, only a few types of data constraints can be modeled graphically in all variants of Entity-Relationship modeling; these are as follows:

---

[3] In particular (Nijssen and Halpin, 1989).
[4] See (Object Management Group) (http://www.uml.org/) for a current specification and various other resources.

1. those that require that a relationship is mandatory: that is, that every instance of an entity class involved in a relationship must be associated with at least one instance of the other participating entity class: for example, every Order Line must be part of an Order;
2. those that require that each instance of an entity class participating in a relationship can only be associated with a single instance of the other participating entity class: for example, every Order Line must be part of just one Order;
3. those that require that an attribute is mandatory: that is, that every instance of an entity class has a value for that attribute: for example, every Order Line must have an Order Quantity;
4. those that require that one or more data items (attributes or relationships) has a unique value or set of values for each instance of the entity class: for example, every Order Line must have a combination of Order Number and Line Number that is different from that in all other Order Lines; in all variants, this can be achieved by marking those data items as the primary key of that entity class (some variants allow additional data items or sets of data items to be marked as having unique values);
5. those that define one entity class as a subtype of another entity class: for example, a Personal Customer is a particular type of Customer.

For example, the partial model depicted in Figure 4 specifies a number of constraints:

1. The following relationships are mandatory:
   a. each Order must refer to a Customer,
   b. each Order must include at least one Order Line,
   c. each Order Line must be part of an Order,
   d. each Order Line must specify a Product,
   e. each Corporate Customer must specify at least one Industry;

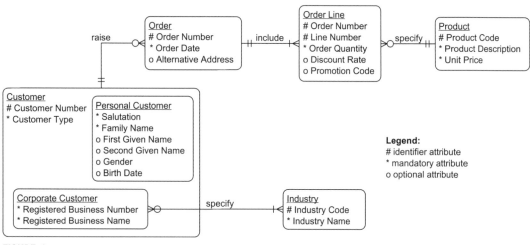

FIGURE 4

An Entity-Relationship Model.

by contrast,

   f. there may be Products that are not specified in any Order Line,

   g. there may be Customers that have not raised any current Order,

   h. there may be Industries that are not specified by any Corporate Customer.

2. The following relationships are mandatory and singular:

   a. each Order Line must be part of just one Order,

   b. each Order Line must specify just one Product;

by contrast,

   c. an Order can include more than one Order Line,

   d. a Product can be specified in more than one Order Line,

   e. a Customer can raise more than one Order.

3. The following attributes are mandatory:

   a. each Order must have an Order Number,

   b. each Order must specify an Order Date,

   c. each Order Line must have a Line Number,

   d. each Order Line must specify an Order Quantity,

   e. each Customer must have a Customer Number,

   f. each Customer must be recorded as being of a particular Customer Type,

   g. each Personal Customer must specify a Salutation,

   h. each Personal Customer must specify a Family Name,

   i. each Corporate Customer must have a Registered Business Number and Name,

   j. each Product must have a Unit Price,

   k. each Industry must have an Industry Code,

   l. each Industry must have an Industry Name;

by contrast,

   m. an Order does not have to specify an Alternative Address,

   n. an Order Line does not have to specify a Discount Rate or a Promotion Code,

   o. a Personal Customer does not have to specify a First Given Name, Second Given Name, Gender or Birth Date,

   p. a Personal Customer cannot have a Registered Business Number,

   q. a Corporate Customer cannot have a Gender or a Birth Date.

4. The following data items, for example, must have unique values:

   a. each Order must have a different Order Number,

   b. each Order Line must be for a different combination of Order Number and Line Number,

by contrast,

   c. two Orders may specify the same Order Date,

   d. two Order Lines may specify the same Order Quantity,

   e. two Order Lines may specify the same Promotion Code.

5. Each Customer is either a Personal Customer or a Corporate Customer but cannot be both.

6. Only a Corporate Customer can specify an Industry.

Of interest is an additional type of constraint that can be modeled in the Barker variant of Entity-Relationship Modeling, as implemented in the Oracle Designer ***CASE tool***. This variant allows a relationship to be marked as ***non-transferable***: for example, in the model above, the relationship between Orders and Order Lines is non-transferable, in that an Order Line cannot be transferred from one Order to another (nor can an Order be transferred from one Customer to another).

This is an example of a ***dynamic data constraint***. All other data constraints that can be modeled in an Entity-Relationship Model are ***static***, in that they define valid states of the database being modeled, rather than valid transitions. There are a number of dynamic constraints that should be considered when modeling persistent data: these are discussed in detail in Section 4.4.3 in Chapter 4.

3.2.1.2 Object-role modeling

Object-Role Modeling (commonly known as ***ORM***[5]) evolved from ***NIAM*** (originally "***Nijssen's Information Analysis Method***", later generalized to "***Natural Language Information Analysis Method***"), and for a time was sometimes referred to as ***Fact-Based Modeling***. ORM differs from Entity-Relationship modeling and UML in that it focuses on

1. ***object types***, used to model both entity classes and attributes, each represented using an ellipse (or a rectangle with rounded corners in ORM 3); an object type may be shown as a ***subtype*** of another (its ***supertype***) by way of a thick solid line between the relevant ellipses with an arrowhead at the supertype end;
2. ***fact types***, used to model sets of associations between instances of object types, each represented using a grid consisting of one or more boxes (see Figure 5);
3. ***roles***, used to model the part played by an object type in a fact type, each represented using a box in the relevant fact type grid connected by a solid line to the relevant object type ellipse (again see Figure 5).

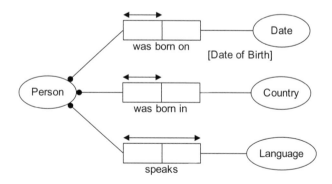

FIGURE 5

A simple ORM model.

---

[5](Halpin, Object Role Modeling).

ORM has a far richer set of data constraint notations than either Entity-Relationship Modeling or UML, some of which are illustrated in Figure 5. Data constraints that can be modeled graphically in ORM include the following:

1. A ***mandatory role constraint*** specifies the mandatory participation of each instance of a particular object type in at least one instance of a particular fact type: for example, an order must have at least one order line.

   A mandatory role constraint is indicated by a solid dot on the line connecting an object type ellipse to a fact type grid, at the end nearest the ellipse (as in Figure 5).

2. A ***uniqueness constraint*** specifies the restriction of each instance of a particular object type (or combination of instances of different object types) to participating in only one instance of a particular fact type: for example, an order line may be part of only one order.

   A uniqueness constraint is indicated by either

   a. (if there is only one role box, or more than one role box in the same fact type) a double-headed arrow[6] over the relevant role box(es) (as in Figure 5), or

   b. (if the role boxes are in different fact types) a circle containing the letter 'U', connected to each of the relevant role boxes by a dashed line.

3. A ***frequency constraint*** specifies further constraints (if any) on the number of instances of a particular fact type that an instance of a particular object type (or combination of instances of different object types) may participate in: for example, there is a limit of nine passengers in a standard flight booking.

   A frequency constraint is indicated by a numeral (e.g., '2'), range of numerals (e.g., '1..3') or inequality (e.g., '≤ 9') next to the relevant role box (or a line connecting two role boxes).

4. An ***inclusive-or constraint*** specifies that each instance of a particular object type must participate in at least one of a set of particular fact types: for example, a flight booking confirmation must specify a cellphone number, an e-mail address, or both.

   An inclusive-or constraint is indicated by a circle containing a solid dot, connected to each of the relevant role boxes by a dashed line.

5. An ***exclusion constraint*** specifies that no instance of a particular object type may participate in more than one of a set of particular fact types: for example, a loan application may be accepted, rejected, or (currently) neither but cannot be both accepted and rejected.

   An exclusion constraint is indicated by a circle containing the letter 'X', connected to each of the relevant role boxes by a dashed line.

6. An ***exclusive-or constraint*** specifies that each instance of a particular object type must participate in exactly one of two particular fact types: for example, a flight booking confirmation must specify either a credit card number or an electronic payment receipt but not both.

   An exclusive-or constraint is indicated by a circle containing the letter 'X' overlaid with a solid dot, connected to each of the relevant role boxes by a dashed line.

   An exclusive-or constraint may also be drawn between the arrows indicating ***subtypes*** of a ***supertype***.

---

[6]In ORM 3, a uniqueness constraint is indicated by a simple line without arrowheads over the role box(es).

7. A *value constraint* specifies the values that a particular object type may take: for example, the travel classes available when making a flight booking are 'first', 'business', 'premium economy', and 'economy' (coach).

   A value constraint is indicated by a list of values or value ranges within braces next to the object type ellipse.

8. A *subset constraint* specifies that all instances of a particular object type that participate in one particular fact type must participate in another particular fact type: for example, every customer issued with an invoice must have placed an order.

   A subset constraint is indicated in its simplest form by a dashed line between the relevant role boxes, adorned with

   a. a circle containing the symbol '$\subseteq$',

   b. an arrowhead at the end of the line nearest the second fact type.

9. A *set equality constraint* specifies that the set of instances of a particular object type that participate in one particular fact type must be identical to the set of instances of that object type that participate in another particular fact type: for example, every passenger booked to travel on the outgoing flight of a booked journey must be booked to travel on the corresponding return flight and vice versa.

   A set equality constraint is indicated in its simplest form by a dashed line between the relevant role boxes adorned with a circle containing the symbol '='.

10. In its simplest form, a *subtype constraint* specifies that each instance of a particular object type is an instance of another object type: for example, each Corporate Customer is a Customer.

    A subtype constraint is indicated by an arrow from the ellipse representing the subtype (in this case Corporate Customer) to the ellipse representing the supertype (in this case Customer).

11. A *derivation rule* is a rule by which values of a particular type can be derived or calculated: for example, the cost of an order line is the product unit cost multiplied by the order quantity, in turn multiplied by 100% minus the discount rate (if any).

    A derived fact type is indicated by an asterisk against the role box denoting the derivable value, and the appropriate formula (prefixed by an asterisk) written on the ORM diagram: for example, in this case,
    ```
    for each Order Line:
        cost = unit cost × order quantity × (1 - discount rate).
    ```

12. *Ring constraints* specify constraints on recursive relationships such as those described in Section 3.3.2.1.

3.2.1.3 UML
The *object class models* of *UML* (the *Unified Modeling Language*) focus on

1. *object classes*: more or less equivalent to *entity classes* (see Section 3.2.1.1), represented using rectangular boxes; an object class may be shown as a *subclass* (i.e., subtype) of another (its *superclass*) by way of a solid line between the relevant object class boxes with an open arrowhead at the superclass end;

2. *attributes*: equivalent to those in an Entity-Relationship Model, listed within the relevant object class box; and

3. *associations*: equivalent to *relationships* (see Section 3.2.1.1), represented using lines between the relevant object class boxes.

UML allows much the same data constraints to be modeled as Entity-Relationship Modeling. In addition,

1. like ORM but unlike Entity-Relationship Modeling, object class models provide for *frequency constraints* (see Section 3.2.1.2);
2. again, like ORM but unlike Entity-Relationship Modeling, *n-ary associations* can be specified, involving more than two object classes;
3. any constraints not formally provided by the notation can be stated in notes placed on the object class model diagram.

It also provides an Object Constraint Language (OCL). This, however, is a declarative programming language rather than a language in which to document rules for stakeholder consumption. For example,

1. To ensure that the number of passengers specified in a flight booking request is nine or less requires the following statement:
   ```
   context FlightBookingRequest inv:
      self.numberOfPassengers <= 9
   ```
   while to ensure that no more than 9 passenger names are listed in a flight booking confirmation requires the following statement:
   ```
   context FlightBookingConfirmation inv:
      self.passenger->size() <= 9.
   ```
2. To express the constraint that only a Personal Customer who has specified a first given name can specify a second given name requires the following statement:
   ```
   context FlightBookingRequest inv:
      {self.secondGivenName->isEmpty() or
       self.firstGivenName->notEmpty()}.
   ```

3.2.2 Rules in business process models

Various business process modeling notations have been used over the years, ranging from process flowcharts through data flow diagrams to current notations such as **BPMN**.[7]
   Among the situations that may be represented in *business process models* are

1. a *process sequence*, a set of processes in which each process other than the first must not start until the preceding process is completed: for example, a loan approval cannot occur until a credit check is completed and funds may not be disbursed until the loan approval is completed;
2. a *decision point* from which flow two or more sequences of processes depending on some logical condition, or, in BPMN terms, an *exclusive gateway* which allows only one of a set of following processes to proceed based on some condition established in the preceding process: for example, an airline passenger already in possession of a boarding pass proceeds either to a bag drop desk (if he or she has bags to be checked in) or directly to security screening (if he or she only has carry-on bags);
3. a *synchronizing gateway* which allows the following process to proceed only after all preceding processes are completed: for example, a pasta meal can be served only after both the pasta and the sauce have been cooked;

---

[7](Object Management Group) (www.bpmn.org), (Silver, 2009).

4. a *conditional start event* which causes the following process to be initiated when a particular condition becomes true: for example, a particular part is reordered when the quantity on hand drops below a pre-defined threshold (the 'reorder point');

5. a *timer event* which causes the following process to be initiated after a particular duration of time has elapsed: for example, if a cover note for vehicle insurance is not converted to a full policy within a particular period after the issue of the cover note (e.g., 7 days), the insurer must contact the party taking out the cover note;

6. an *interrupting event* which causes the process to which it is attached to be aborted: for example, if a case of real property transactions which has been lodged with a Land Registry is found to contain signed documents which have been changed since signature,[8] it is immediately returned to the party that submitted the case and no further processing occurs.

Note that, if a sequence is shown, one might infer that there is a true dependency, in that the second process must not start until the first process has finished. Often, however, the two processes share a resource (such as the person or role that performs those processes or the equipment required to perform those processes). Sometimes, it is not practical to perform both processes at the same time. And sometimes the sequence is merely one of convention, in that the two processes could equally correctly be performed in reverse sequence. For example, when getting ready for work

1. getting dressed definitely needs to occur after showering;
2. each person in the residence needs (most likely) to use the bathroom separately;
3. packing one's bag cannot practically be done while showering;
4. cleaning one's teeth can be done before or after (or even during) showering, but may always be done afterwards out of habit.

3.3 RECENT DEVELOPMENTS

3.3.1 Ross's rule taxonomy and diagramming notation

Various thought leaders have grappled with the need to expose rules to business stakeholders in a manner that would enable those stakeholders to review and approve those rules, change them as required, and so on.

Ross (1997) appears to have been the first to propose a comprehensive approach to documenting rules, which incorporated both a taxonomy of rules and a diagramming notation. The diagramming notation was rather complex, involving as it did a different symbol for each type of rule and a variety of linkages between symbols; this made it too complex to be truly understandable by the average business person. While there does not appear to have been much adoption of the Ross notation by practitioners, Ross's approach to rule classification provided a basis for further work in that field, including my own.

---

[8]This can be established by comparing the **hash key** built into the **digital signature** with the hash key generated from the current content of the signed document.

3.3.2 Expressing rules in natural language

Various authors have developed different approaches to expressing rules in natural language; each author has recognized that different types of rules require rule statements with different sentence patterns:

1. Halpin has produced a considerable body of work on natural language description of ORM models (including constraints) since the early 1990s, including (Halpin and Harding, Automated support for verbalization of conceptual schemas, 1993), (Halpin, Information Modeling and Relational Databases, 2001) and a series of articles on the Business Rules Community website[9];
2. At the 1999 Entity-Relationship conference in Paris, France, I delivered a paper[10] describing the technique by which business rules were modeled as natural language statements in a project to develop a school administration system.
3. Ross developed version 1.0 of the language RuleSpeak®[11] in 2001; this has been subsequently updated;
4. Morgan (2002) produced a set of syntactic templates for the construction of rule statements.
5. In (Simsion and Witt, Data Modeling Essentials, 2004), I described an approach to describing a data model and its associated rules using natural language *assertions*;
6. I have subsequently described, in a series of articles on the Business rules Community website,[12] a constrained natural language similar to that described in this book.

Note:

1. The references cited above are the earliest references to natural language rule expression by each author that I am aware of.
2. The extent to which any of the above authors has been influenced by preceding work in the field is not clear, and should not be inferred from the sequence of publication.

Each of these approaches is described in one of the following subsections.

3.3.2.1 Verbalization of ORM models

Halpin has defined appropriate "verbalizations" (sentence forms) for each type of rule that can be modeled in ORM. Unlike other authors, Halpin allows for alternative sentence forms for the same type of rule. The following are among the most useful:

1. A *mandatory role constraint* can be expressed using any of the following sentence forms:
    a. Each Order contains at least one Order Line.
    b. Each Order contains some Order Line.
    c. It is impossible that some Order contains no Order Line.
    d. No Order contains no Order Line.
    ORM also provides a sentence form for *statements of advice* indicating the absence of a mandatory constraint:
    e. It is possible that some Product is specified in no Order Line.[13]

---

[9]The first of these articles is (Halpin, Verbalizing Business Rules: Part 1, 2003).
[10](Witt, Modelling Business Rules for School Student Administration: a Case Study, 1999).
[11](Ross and Lam, 2001).
[12]The first of these articles is (Witt, A Practical Method of Developing Natural Language Rule Statements: Part 1, 2009).
[13]This reads somewhat unnaturally: a more natural form would be "It is possible that some Product is not referred to in any Order."

2. A *uniqueness constraint* can be expressed using either of the following sentence forms:

   a. Each Order Line is part of at most one Order.

   b. It is impossible that the same Order Line is part of more than one Order.

   Again ORM provides a sentence form for statements of advice indicating the absence of a uniqueness constraint:

   c. It is possible that the same Order includes more than one Order Line.

3. If a role is subject to both a mandatory constraint and a uniqueness constraint, these constraints can be combined in a single sentence form:

   a. Each Order Line is part of exactly one Order.

4. Both Entity-Relationship Modeling and UML allow for what are sometimes called *many-to-many relationships*. In the Customers and Orders model depicted in Section 3.2.1.1, the relationship between Corporate Customers and Industry Codes is such a relationship: a Corporate Customer may specify more than one Industry Code and an Industry Code may be specified by more than one Corporate Customer.[14] This relationship would be expressed using the following sentence form:

   a. It is possible that the same Corporate Customer specifies more than one Industry Code and that the same Industry Code is specified by more than one Corporate Customer.

   However, there is nothing in either Entity-Relationship Modeling or UML to prevent multiple records containing the same combination of Corporate Customer and Industry Code. ORM allows for the specification of a uniqueness constraint on such relationships to prevent this, expressed using the following sentence form:

   b. Each instance of Corporate Customer specifies Industry Code occurs only once.

5. ORM also allows for uniqueness constraints on *n-ary associations*. Diverging for a moment from the Customers and Orders example, consider a relationship in a school timetabling system between classrooms, time periods, and student groups: a uniqueness constraint applies which can be expressed using sentence forms such as the following:

   a. Given any Classroom and Time Period, that Classroom in that Time Period is timetabled for at most one Student Group.

   b. It is impossible that the same Classroom is timetabled for more than one Student Group in the same Time Period.

   Again ORM provides a sentence form for statements of advice indicating the absence of such a uniqueness constraint:

   c. It is possible that the same Classroom is timetabled for the same Student Group in more than one Time Period.

   Again ORM allows for the specification of a uniqueness constraint on such relationships to prevent multiple records containing the same combination of classroom, time period, and student group, expressed using the following sentence form:

   d. Each instance of Classroom timetabled for Student Group in Time Period occurs only once.

   Another sentence form available to express an ORM uniqueness constraint on an n-ary association is illustrated by the following example:

---

[14]While this relationship allows for more than one Industry Code per Customer, many will only specify one, and few (if any) would specify more than two. The word 'many' is therefore misleading. When I was a novice data modeler, I once asked a business stakeholder if a Customer could specify only one Industry Code or many: his reply was "no, not many, two at most." Halpin's verbalization resolves this issue.

    e. At most one Time Period has the same combination of Start Time Of Day and End Time Of Day.
N-ary associations can also be subject to mandatory constraints, as in the following example:
    f. Each Student Group has some Classroom timetabled for some Time Period.

6. A *frequency constraint* can be expressed using sentence forms such as the following:
    a. Each Corporate Customer specifies one or two instances of Industry Code.
    b. Each Corporate Customer specifies at most two instances of Industry Code.
    c. Given any Personal Customer and Promotion Code, there are at most three instances of Order Line where that Order Line is part of an Order by that Personal Customer and specifies that Promotion Code.

7. An *inclusive-or constraint* can be expressed using the following sentence form:
    a. Each Customer has a Salutation or a Registered Business Number.

8. An *exclusion constraint* can be expressed using sentence forms such as the following:
    a. No Customer that specifies a Gender also specifies a Registered Business Number.
    b. For each Customer at most one of the following is true:
        that Customer specifies a Gender;
        that Customer specifies a Registered Business Number.

9. An *exclusive-or constraint* can be expressed using sentence forms such as the following:
    a. Each Customer is a Personal Customer or a Corporate Customer but not both.
    b. For each Customer exactly one of the following is true:
        that Customer is a Personal Customer;
        that Customer is a Corporate Customer.
    c. Each Payment is an instance of exactly one of the following:
        a Cash Payment, a Credit Payment, an Electronic Funds Transfer.

10. A *value constraint* can be expressed using sentence forms such as the following:
    a. The possible values of Gender are 'Male', 'Female'.
    b. The possible values of Discount Rate are 0% to 25%.
    c. The possible values of Order Quantity are 1 or more.

11. A *subset constraint* can be expressed using sentence forms such as the following:
    a. Each Personal Customer who has specified a Second Given Name also has specified a First Given Name.
    b. If a Personal Customer has specified a Second Given Name then that Personal Customer has specified a First Given Name.

12. A *set equality constraint* can be expressed using sentence forms such as the following:
    a. Each Order Line that specifies a Discount Rate also specifies a Promotion Code and conversely.
    b. If an Order Line specifies a Discount Rate then that Order Line specifies a Promotion Code and conversely.

13. In its simplest form, a *subtype constraint* can be expressed using the following sentence form:
    a. Each Corporate Customer is a Customer.
More usefully, the subtypes of a supertype can be listed:
    b. Each Customer is a Corporate Customer or a Personal Customer.
The subtypes of a supertype are typically mutually exclusive, in that an instance of the supertype can only belong to one of the subtypes. While in some modeling environments this constraint can be assumed, it is safer to state the constraint explicitly:

    c. Each Customer is a Corporate Customer or a Personal Customer but not both.

    If a supertype has more than two subtypes, a different sentence form is required:

    d. Each Journey is exactly one of the following: Return Journey; One-Way Journey; Multi-stop Journey.

    If the different subtypes of a supertype are distinguishable by the values of a particular attribute, another sentence form is available:

    e. Each Corporate Customer is a Customer that is of Customer Type 'Corporate';

14. A *derivation rule* can be expressed using any appropriate formula: for example,

    a. For each Order Line:

        cost = unit cost × order quantity × (1 − discount rate).

15. *Ring constraints* (constraints on *recursive relationships*) can be expressed using sentence forms such as the following:

    a. No Country borders itself.

    b. If $Country_1$ borders $Country_2$, then $Country_2$ borders $Country_1$.

    c. If $Employee_1$ reports to $Employee_2$, then it is impossible[15] that $Employee_2$ reports to $Employee_1$.

    d. If an Employee reports to a Manager, then it is impossible that that Manager reports to that Employee.

    e. If $Person_1$ is a parent of $Person_2$ and $Person_2$ is a parent of $Person_3$, then it is forbidden that $Person_1$ is a parent of $Person_3$.

Halpin also provides some guidance as to the construction of quality rule statements.

3.3.2.2 *My 1999 paper*

(Witt, 1999) described a system acquisition project in which it was necessary to communicate business rules to a diverse audience:

1. the eventual users of the system;

2. those tendering to supply the system;

3. those customizing the acquired system;

4. those writing training and help materials for the customized system.

Although the project team had access to (Ross, 1997), it found that Ross's diagramming notation was too complex to be an effective communication tool in this context. As a result, I developed a consistent set of natural language rule statements with which to communicate with each stakeholder group.

    The recording of business rules for incorporation into specifications was organized along the following lines:

1. A significant class of rules was identified that determined the conduct of processes in various situations, either by the system or by the users of the system. These were documented within the process model against the process concerned.

---

[15]'Forbidden' may be substituted in place of 'impossible' in this example or the next to make them *deontic* constraints (obligations) rather than *alethic* constraints (necessities).

2. The remaining rules were divided into the following categories:

   a. those that constrain the creation of instances of an entity class;

   b. those that constrain the creation or modification of instances of a relationship between two entity classes;

   c. those that constrain the values that an attribute of an entity class may have on creation or modification;

   d. those that define the formula for calculating a derived quantity.

3. Those rules were documented as follows:

   a. Each rule in category a was documented in the project data dictionary as a note against the relevant entity class.

   b. Each rule in category b was documented in the project data dictionary as a note against the relevant relationship.

   c. Each rule in category c was documented in the project data dictionary as a note against the relevant attribute.

   d. Each derived quantity was also documented in the project data dictionary as a derived attribute of an entity class, and each rule in category 2.d was documented in the project data dictionary as a note against that attribute.

The rules were not presented as complete sentences, but rather as sentence stubs that could be appended to the entity class or relationship name (or attribute name qualified by the entity class name) to make complete sentences, a process which the project team discussed with each stakeholder group. For example, the following rule stubs were recorded against the End Date attribute in the Student Absence entity class:

```
if entered: must be valid date; must be >= Start Date;
   must be within reasonable range.16
```

These stubs, when appended to the attribute name ('End Date') qualified by the entity class name ('Student Absence'), were understood by all stakeholders to yield the following sentences:

```
If entered, the End Date of a Student Absence must be a valid date.
If entered, the End Date of a Student Absence must be >= Start Date.
If entered, the End Date of a Student Absence must be within reasonable range.
```

3.3.2.3 RuleSpeak

RuleSpeak includes a taxonomy of rules and sentence forms for each rule type. The taxonomy and sentence forms presented in version 1.0[17] have been simplified in version 2.2,[18] which consists of the following:

1. Business rule statements indicating that something is required:

   a. "… must …" indicates that something is mandatory;

   b. "… must be computed as …" indicates that a formula is to be used to compute some result;

---

[16]Note that the concept of "reasonable range" was separately defined for various types of data.

[17](Ross and Lam, 2001).

[18](Ross, RuleSpeak Sentence Forms – Specifying Natural-Language Business Rules in English, 2009).

    c. "...must be considered ...if ..." indicates that something is to be classified or derived a certain way if some condition(s) hold true;

    d. "...must be performed ...when ..." indicates that some process or procedure is to be performed when some condition(s) become true;

2. Business rule statements indicating that something is disallowed:

    a. "...must not ..." indicates that something is not allowed;

3. Business rule statements indicating that something is conditionally allowed:

    a. "...may ...only ..." indicates that something is allowed only in certain situations.

Ross's taxonomy also includes *statements of advice* indicating that something is either allowed or not required:

4. Statements of advice indicating that something is allowed:

    a. "...may ..." indicates that something is allowed;

5. Statements of advice indicating that something is not required:

    a. "...need not ..." indicates that something is not required.

Ross includes a statement "*The purpose of the Sentence Forms is to ensure that written Business Rules are more easily understood. They also help ensure that different practitioners working on a large set of Business Rules express the same ideas in the same way. Such consistency would not be possible if Business Rules were expressed in a completely 'free-form' manner.*" This is a reasonable statement with which most (if not all) business rule practitioners would agree. However, the sentence forms provided allow for considerable freedom, including the freedom to produce rule statements with significantly different syntax for rules of the same type. To be fair, the sentence forms are augmented by various principles governing the construction of quality rule statements.

3.3.2.4 Morgan's rule patterns

(Morgan, 2002) includes a small set of *rule patterns*,[19] which are much like the templates described in Chapter 9 of this book. The rule patterns include components which are each described informally, rather than being given formal syntactic definitions as in this book. Morgan's set of rule patterns is significantly less tied to a taxonomy of rules than either the templates in this book or Halpin's sentence forms. Like Ross and Halpin, Morgan sets out various principles governing the construction of quality rule statements.

    The following components that can be included in a rule pattern:

1. det: either nothing or one of the following *determiners*[20]: 'A', 'An', 'The', 'Each', 'Every';

2. subject: a *business term*,[21] optionally qualified by "other descriptive elements";

3. characteristic: "the business behavior that must take place or a relationship that must be enforced"[22];

---

[19]Actually rule statement patterns.

[20]See Section 5.4 in Chapter 5 for a definition of *determiner*.

[21]See Section 6.1.7 in Chapter 6 for a definition of *business term*.

[22]Note that this differs from the use of the term *characteristic* in the SBVR, in which it is synonymous with *unary fact type*, defined in Section 6.3.1.3.1 in Chapter 6.

4. fact: "a relationship between terms identifiable in the fact model, together with defined constraints ...";
5. fact list: a list of facts;
6. numeral: a "numeric parameter";
7. result: "any value, not necessarily numeric, that has some business meaning ...";
8. algorithm: a definition of the calculation or derivation of a result;
9. classification: a definition of a term;
10. enum-list: "a list of enumerated values .... ."

The notation used by Morgan for his rule patterns is similar to the one used in this book for templates, but subtly different. Therefore, to avoid confusion, I have presented Morgan's rule patterns using my own template notation (described in Section 9.1.1 of Chapter 9) rather than his. Morgan defines the following rule patterns:

1. a *basic constraint*: either:
   ```
   <det> <subject> {must|should} {not|} <characteristic>
       {{if|unless} <fact>|}.
   ```
   or:
   ```
   <det> <subject> may <characteristic> only if <fact>
   ```
   For example, "A next day order must not be accepted if the order value is less than $30."

2. a *list constraint*: either:
   ```
   <det> <subject> {must|should} {not|} <characteristic>
       {if|unless} at least <numeral>
       {and not more than <numeral>|} of the following is true:
       <fact list>.
   ```
   or:
   ```
   <det> <subject> may <characteristic> only if
       at least <numeral>
       {and not more than <numeral>|} of the following is true:
       <fact list>.
   ```
   For example, "A next day order must not be accepted if at least one of the following is true:
   – the order is received after 15:00
   – the order is received on a Friday or a Saturday
   – the order is received on the day before a public holiday."

3. a *classification*: either:
   ```
   <det> <subject> is {not|} defined as <classification>
       {{if|unless} <fact>|}.
   ```
   or:
   ```
   <det> <subject> must {not|} be considered as <classification>
       {{if|unless} <fact>|}.
   ```
   For example, "A Person is defined as Adult if the Age of that Person is more than 18 years."

4. a *computation*: either:
   ```
   <det> <result> is defined as <algorithm>.
   ```
   or:
   ```
   <det> <result> = <algorithm>.
   ```
   For example, "The cost of an Order Line is defined as unit cost × order quantity × (1 − discount rate)."

5. An *enumeration*:

```
<det> <result> must be chosen from the following {open|closed|} enumeration:
   <enum list>.
```

For example, "The Gender of a Person must be chosen from the following closed enumeration: 'Male', 'Female'."

3.3.2.5 Assertions

The assertions technique described in (Simsion and Witt, Data Modeling Essentials, 2004) is designed to provide a complete verbal description of a data model and associated constraints using the appropriate templates for each type of data model artifact or constraint being described. These templates use the notation described in Section 9.1.1 of Chapter 9. The types of assertions relevant to business rules include the following:

1. entity class assertions:

    a. entity class definitions, of the form

```
{A|An} <Entity Class Name> is <Entity Class Definition>.
```

    For example, "A Customer is a business or a person that has purchased at least one product."

    b. subtype definitions, of the form

```
{A|An} <Entity Class Name> is a type of <Superclass Name>,
   namely <Entity Class Definition>.
```

    For example, "A Corporate Customer is a type of Customer, namely a Customer that is a business rather than a person."

2. relationship assertions:

    a. non-recursive relationship assertions, of the form

```
Each <Entity Class 1 Name> {must|may}
   <Relationship Name>
   {just one <Entity Class 2 Name>|
   one or more <Entity Class 2 Plural Name>}
   that {may|must not} change over time.
```

    For example, "Each Order Line must specify just one Product that must not change over time.[23]"

    b. recursive relationship assertions, of the form

```
Each <Entity Class Name> {must|may}
   <Relationship Name>
   {just one other <Entity Class Name>|
   one or more other <Entity Class Plural Name>}
   that {may|must not} change over time.
```

    For example, "Each Employee may supervise one or more other Employees that may change over time."

    c. additional assertions for optional relationships:

        i. non-recursive:

```
Not every <Entity Class 1 Name> has to
   <Relationship Name>
   {{a|an} <Entity Class 2 Name>|
   <Entity Class 2 Plural Name>}.
```

---

[23]This constraint does not, of course, prevent cancellation of one Order Line and its replacement by another referring to a different Product.

    ii. recursive:

```
Not every <Entity Class 1 Name> has to
  <Relationship Name>
  {another <Entity Class 2 Name>|
  other <Entity Class 2 Plural Name>}.
```

For example, "Not every Product has to be specified in an Order Line."

  d. additional assertions for relationships, each instance of which may be optional initially but must ultimately be mandatory:

```
Each <Entity Class 1 Name> should ultimately
  <Relationship Name>
  {{a|an} <Entity Class 2 Name>|
  <Entity Class 2 Plural Name>}.
```

For example, "Each Product should ultimately be specified in an Order Line."

3. attribute assertions and assertion pairs:

  a. assertion pairs for single-valued attributes of entity classes:

    i.
```
Each <Entity Class Name> {must|may} have
  {a|an} <Attribute Name>
  which is <Attribute Definition>.
```

    ii. `No <Entity Class Name> may have more than one <Attribute Name>.`

For example, "Each Product must have a Unit Price, which is the standard price paid by a Customer for one unit of that Product. No Product may have more than one Unit Price."

  b. assertion pairs for multi-valued attributes of entity classes:

    i.
```
Each <Entity Class Name> {must|may} have
  <Attribute Plural Name>
  which are <Attribute Definition>.
```

    ii. `{A|An} <Entity Class Name> may have more than one <Attribute Name>.`

For example, "Each Flight must have Operating Days, which are the days of the week on which that Flight operates. A Flight may have more than one Operating Day."

  c. additional assertions for optional attributes of entity classes:

    i.
```
Not every <Entity class Name> has to have
  {a|an} <Attribute Name>.
```

For example, "Not every Order has to have an Alternative Address."

  d. assertion pairs for single-valued attributes of relationships:

    i.
```
Each combination of
  <Entity Class 1 Name> and <Entity Class 2 Name>
  {must|may} have
  {a|an} <Attribute Name>
  which is <Attribute Definition>.
```

    ii.
```
No combination of
  <Entity Class 1 Name> and <Entity Class 2 Name>
  may have more than one <Attribute Name>.
```

For example (where only one enrollment per student per course is allowed), "Each combination of Student and Course must have an Enrollment Date which is the date on which that Student's enrollment for that Course is received by the University's administrative office. No combination of Student and Course may have more than one Enrollment Date."

e. assertion pairs for multi-valued attributes of relationships:

    i. Each combination of
        <Entity Class 1 Name> and <Entity Class 2 Name>
        {must|may} have
        <Attribute Plural Name>
        which are <Attribute Definition>.

    ii. A combination of
        <Entity Class 1 Name> and <Entity Class 2 Name>
        may have more than one <Attribute Name>.

For example (where more than one enrollment per student per course is allowed), "Each combination of Student and Course must have Enrollment Dates which are the dates on which that Student's enrollment for that Course is received by the University's administrative office. A combination of Student and Course may have more than one Enrollment Date."

f. additional assertions for optional attributes of relationships:

    i. Not every combination of
        <Entity Class 1 Name> and <Entity Class 2 Name> has to have
        {a|an} <Attribute Name>.[24]

For example, "Not every combination of Student and Course has to have an Examination Date."

g. assertions for attributes assigned particular attribute types:

    i. The <Attribute Name> of {a|an} <Entity Class Name> is
        (and exhibits the properties of) {a|an} <Attribute Type Name>.

For example, "The Order Quantity of an Order Line is (and exhibits the properties of) an Integer."

4. assertions for *intersection entity classes*: these are alternatives to the assertions above for attributes of relationships:

    a. assertions for each intersection entity class which implements a binary relationship for which only one combination of each pair of instances is allowed: for example, an Enrollment entity class where each Student is prohibited from enrolling more than once in a Course; for each such entity class a set of three assertions is required:

        i. There can only be one <Data Item Name> for each combination of
            <Associated Entity Class 1 Name> and
            <Associated Entity Class 2 Name>.

        ii. For any particular <Associated Entity Class 1 Name>
            a different <Data Item Name> can occur for
            each <Associated Entity Class 2 Name>.

        iii. For any particular <Associated Entity Class 2 Name>
            a different <Data Item Name> can occur for
            each <Associated Entity Class 1 Name>.

---

[24]Note that this particular form was not included in (Simsion and Witt, Data Modeling Essentials, 2004).

In each case, <Data Item Name> is either an attribute name or the name of an entity class associated with the intersection entity class via a non-identifying relationship.

For example, "There can only be one Enrollment Date for each combination of Student and Course. For any particular Student a different Enrollment Date can occur for each Course. For any particular Course a different Enrollment Date can occur for each Student."

b. assertions for each intersection entity class which implements either an n-ary relationship or a binary relationship for which more than one combination of each pair of instances is allowed: for example, an Enrollment entity class where a Student is permitted to enroll more than once in a Course; each such entity class requires one assertion of form i., plus n assertions of form ii. (where n is the "arity" of the n-ary relationship: 2 for binary, 3 for ternary and so on):

i. There can only be one <Data Item Name> for each combination of <Identifier Component 1 Name>, <Identifier Component 2 Name>, ... and <Identifier Component n Name>.

ii. For any particular combination of <Identifier Component 1 Name>, ... and <Identifier Component n Name> a different <Data Item Name> can occur for each <Identifier Component m Name>.

For example, "There can only be one Achievement Score for each combination of Student, Course, and Enrollment Date. For any particular combination of Student and Course a different Achievement Score can occur for each Enrollment Date. For any particular combination of Student and Enrollment Date Course, a different Achievement Score can occur for each Course. For any particular combination of Course and Enrollment Date, a different Achievement Score can occur for each Student."

5. constraint assertions:

a. single data item uniqueness constraint assertions:

No two <Entity Class Plural Name> can have the same <Attribute Name>.

For example, "No two Orders can have the same Order Number."

b. multiple data item uniqueness constraint assertions:

No two <Entity Class Plural Name> can have the same combination of <Data Item 1 Name>, <Data Item 2 Name>, ... and <Data Item n Name>.

For example, "No two Order Lines can have the same combination of Order Number and Line Number."

c. general attribute constraint assertions:

The <Attribute Name> of {a|an} <Entity Class Name> <Attribute Constraint>.

For example, "The Order Quantity of an Order Line must be greater than 0."

d. general entity class constraint assertions:

{A|An} <Entity Class Name> <Entity Class Constraint>.

For example, "A Student Absence must not overlap in time with another Student Absence for the same Student."[25]

---

[25]Note that this particular example was worded less rigorously in (Simsion and Witt, 2004).

3.3.3 **The Business Rules Approach**

The Business Rules Approach took a broader perspective: it was developed as a system specification and implementation approach that treats rules as equal to, and independent of, data and process. A description of it can be found on the Business Rules Group website[26] and in (Ross, Principles of the Business Rule Approach, 2003).

3.3.4 **The Business Rules Manifesto**

The principles of the Business Rules Approach were subsequently distilled into the Business Rules Manifesto. Subtitled "The Principles of Rule Independence", version 2.0[27] of this document, edited by Ronald Ross, was published by the Business Rules Group in November 2003. It is reproduced here in full as allowed for by the copyright notice.[28]

Article 1. *"Primary Requirements, Not Secondary*
    1.1. *"Rules are a first-class citizen of the requirements world.*
    1.2. *"Rules are essential for, and a discrete part of, business models and technology models.*
Article 2. *"Separate From Processes, Not Contained In Them*
    2.1. *"Rules are explicit constraints on behavior and/or provide support to behavior.*
    2.2. *"Rules are not process and not procedure. They should not be embedded in either of these.*
    2.3. *"Rules apply* across *processes and procedures. There should be one cohesive body of rules, enforced consistently across all relevant areas of business activity.*
Article 3. *"Deliberate Knowledge, Not A By-Product*
    3.1. *"Rules build on facts, and facts build on concepts as expressed by terms.*
    3.2. *"Terms express business concepts: facts make assertions about these concepts: rules constrain and support these facts.*
    3.3. *"Rules must be explicit. No rule is ever assumed about any concept or fact.*
    3.4. *"Rules are basic to what the business knows about itself—that is, to basic business knowledge.*
    3.5. *"Rules need to be nurtured, protected, and managed.*
Article 4. *"Declarative, Not Procedural*
    4.1. *"Rules should be expressed declaratively in natural-language sentences for the business audience.*
    4.2. *"If something cannot be expressed, it is not a rule.*
    4.3. *"A set of statements is declarative only if the set has no implicit sequencing.*
    4.4. *"Any statements of rules that require constructs other than terms and facts imply assumptions about a system implementation.*
    4.5. *"A rule statement is distinct from any enforcement defined for it. A rule and its enforcement are separate concerns.*

---

[26](Business Rules Group) (www.businessrulesgroup.org/bra.shtml).
[27](Business Rules Group, 2003).
[28]"Copyright, 2003. Business Rules Group.
   Permission is granted for unlimited reproduction and distribution of this document under the following conditions: (a) The copyright and this permission notice are clearly included. (b) The work is clearly credited to the Business Rules Group. (c) No part of the document, including title, content, copyright, and permission notice, is altered, abridged or extended in any manner."

4.6. "*Rules should be defined independently of responsibility for the* who, where, when, *or* how *of their enforcement.*

4.7. "*Exceptions to rules are expressed by other rules.*

Article 5. "*Well-Formed Expression, Not Ad Hoc*

5.1. "*Business rules should be expressed in such a way that they can be validated for correctness by business people.*

5.2. "*Business rules should be expressed in such a way that they can be verified against each other for consistency.*

5.3. "*Formal logics, such as predicate logic, are fundamental to well-formed expression of rules in business terms, as well as to the technologies that implement business rules.*

Article 6. "*Rule-Based Architecture, Not Indirect Implementation*

6.1. "*A business rules application is intentionally built to accommodate continuous change in business rules. The platform on which the application runs should support such continuous change.*

6.2. "*Executing rules directly—for example in a rules engine—is a better implementation strategy than transcribing the rules into some procedural form.*

6.3. "*A business rule system must always be able to explain the reasoning by which it arrives at conclusions or takes action.*

6.4. "*Rules are based on truth values. How a rule's truth value is determined or maintained is hidden from users.*

6.5. "*The relationship between events and rules is generally many-to-many.*

Article 7. "*Rule-Guided Processes, Not Exception-Based Programming*

7.1. "*Rules define the boundary between acceptable and unacceptable business activity.*

7.2. "*Rules often require special or selective handling of detected violations. Such rule violation activity is activity like any other activity.*

7.3. "*To ensure maximum consistency and reusability, the handling of unacceptable business activity should be separable from the handling of acceptable business activity.*

Article 8. "*For the Sake of the Business, Not Technology*

8.1. "*Rules are about business practice and guidance; therefore, rules are motivated by business goals and objectives and are shaped by various influences.*

8.2. "*Rules always cost the business something.*

8.3. "*The cost of rule enforcement must be balanced against business risks, and against business opportunities that might otherwise be lost.*

8.4. "'*More rules' is not better. Usually fewer 'good rules' is better.*

8.5. "*An effective system can be based on a small number of rules. Additional, more discriminating rules can be subsequently added, so that over time the system becomes smarter.*

Article 9. "*Of, By, and For Business People, Not IT People*

9.1. "*Rules should arise from knowledgeable business people.*

9.2. "*Business people should have tools available to help them formulate, validate, and manage rules.*

9.3. "*Business people should have tools available to help them verify business rules against each other for consistency.*

Article 10. *"Managing Business Logic, Not Hardware/Software Platforms*
    10.1. *"Business rules are a vital business asset.*
    10.2. *"In the long run, rules are more important to the business than hardware/software platforms.*
    10.3. *"Business rules should be organized and stored in such a way that they can be readily redeployed to new hardware/software platforms.*
    10.4. *"Rules, and the ability to change them effectively, are fundamental to improving business adaptability."*

All points made in the manifesto are worthy of consideration, and should be followed by any organization that takes rules seriously. A number of points have significantly influenced the position I have taken in this book, in particular

1. *"rules . . . should not be embedded in"* process or procedure (Clause 2.2): the source of truth for a rule should never be a piece of program code, nor should rule statements (or allusions to rules) be scattered through a process specification;
2. *"there should be one cohesive body of rules"* (Clause 2.3): if all rules are expressed in natural language, as required by the *Semantics of Business Vocabulary and Business Rules* (SBVR) and as promoted by this book, the body of rules is cohesive in terms of comparability, consistency, and orderly development;
3. *"rules build on fact [types], and fact [types]build on concepts as expressed by terms"* (Clause 3.1): Chapter 6 describes how terms are selected to refer to concepts, and how fact types are built from terms, while Chapter 7 describes how fact types support rule statements and Chapters 8 and 9 provide specific examples of how fact types support rule statements;
4. *"rules must be explicit"* (Clause 3.3): every rule required must be expressed in a natural language rule statement; the methodology described in Chapter 8 describes steps that ensure that all required rules are captured;
5. *"rules should be expressed declaratively in natural-language sentences for the business audience"* (Clause 4.1): that is of course the chief focus of this book;
6. *"business people should have tools available to help them formulate, validate, and manage rules [and] verify business rules against each other for consistency"* (Clauses 9.2 and 9.3): the most powerful tool to meet this need is a set of natural language rule statements with a consistent vocabulary and syntax and stored in one accessible repository;
7. *"rules, and the ability to change them effectively, are fundamental to improving business adaptability"* (Clause 10.4): the solutions briefly discussed in Section 1.5 in Chapter 1 and the change management methodology described in Section 8.7 in Chapter 8 address this requirement.

I must confess, however, that I have an issue with the wording of a few of the clauses:

1. The use of the term 'fact' to refer to what are certainly not facts but what might be more reasonably called 'fact types' is inappropriate (see Section 6.3 in Chapter 6). This is why, in discussing Clause 3.1, I have amended it to refer to fact types rather than facts. For example, a fact might be "Employee #1234 is assigned to Project #567"; this is an instance of the fact type "Employee is assigned to Project". While there might be a case for referring to a specific employee or project in a rule statement, the more likely requirement is for rule statements that refer to the assignment

generally of employees to projects, as in "An Employee must not be assigned to more than one Project at the same time."

2. All rule statements require syntactic elements (such as 'each' and 'must') in addition to terms and verb phrases from fact types, so Clause 4.4 ("*Any statements of rules that require constructs other than terms and facts imply assumptions about a system implementation.*") is overly restrictive.
3. The inclusion of data modeling jargon ("*many-to-many*") in Clause 6.5 is perhaps inappropriate, given the overall business focus of the manifesto.

3.3.5 The SBVR

In January 2008, the OMG (Object Management Group) released version 1.0 of the SBVR. This document is significant in that it represents a comprehensive analysis of the linguistic and logical concepts underlying natural language discourse about an enterprise and its activities, in particular the rules that govern an enterprise. The complexity necessary for this analysis, however, means that it is not an easy read for even seasoned practitioners, particularly if they are not well versed in the theories of language and logic.

Unfortunately, this version of the SBVR takes positions with which I cannot entirely agree:

1. I have already indicated that I believe the use of the term 'business rule' to refer only to those rules that are "*under business jurisdiction*" inappropriately narrows the scope of the Business Rules Approach.
2. The SBVR definition of 'rule statement' ("*a guidance statement that expresses an operative business rule or a structural rule*") excludes operative rules that are not under business jurisdiction, for no obviously good reason.
3. In recognizing that an organization is not necessarily interested in recording all information about the real world, it proposes that there be two models of the world: a 'reality model' (of the real world) and an 'in-practice model' (of the organization's view of the real world), each with different constraints on the same real-world objects. I deal with this in some detail (and propose an alternative approach) in Section 4.5.1 in Chapter 4.

3.3.6 Rules and rule statements

It is important to make a distinction between a *rule* and the various *rule statements* that can be used to express it. Each rule statement may be clear or unclear, ambiguous or unambiguous, and may use natural business language, technical language, or programming code. This book focuses on rule statements that use natural business language, the vast majority of which are both clear and unambiguous, but I will occasionally provide examples of unclear or ambiguous rule statements by way of illustration.

The SBVR does make this distinction (between rules and rule statements). Unfortunately, the SBVR definition of 'rule statement' ("*a guidance statement that expresses an operative business rule or a structural rule*") excludes those operative rules that are not business rules, for no obviously good reason. (Remember that, according to the SBVR, not all rules are business rules.) In this book, I shall use the term *rule statement* with the following meaning: "a guidance statement that expresses an operative or definitional[29] rule."

Interestingly, the year before he defined the term *business rule* as "*a rule that is under business jurisdiction,*" Ross (The Business Rule Book—Classifying, Defining, and Modeling Rules, 1997)

---

[29]Note that I use the term *definitional rule* instead of *structural rule* to refer to the same concept.

had defined the same term as "*a … requirement … expressed in non-procedural and non-technical form … [which] represents a statement about business behavior.*" While this definition did not exclude "*laws of physics, … legislation, … regulations, … external standards and best practices,*" it restricted business rules to those that are properly expressed. I agree that it is important to ensure that all rules governing an enterprise are expressed declaratively and in natural language, but these are quality criteria governing rule statements rather than restrictions on what makes a business rule.

3.3.7 Rule statements and advice statements

Although it is important to clearly state prohibited or obligatory behavior (using **rule statements**), it may be just as important to clearly state what is allowed or not obligatory. This can be done using **advice statements**, such as "*an employment application may omit the applicant's date of birth.*"

Why are these important? To quote the SBVR:

> "*There are many possible reasons, but probably foremost among them are to re-assure workers or others that some degree of freedom does exist; to use as a basis for admonishing workers about applying some rule that actually does not exist; or to 'remember' the resolutions to some rule-related issue where the outcome was in favor of 'no rule.'*"

The importance of advice statements became very clear during a demonstration of an electronic public transport ticketing system for which I prepared the business rules. In this system, a server maintained, among other things, the decision tables that governed the behavior of the ticket vending machines, train station barriers, etc.

Each ticket vending machine was designed to shut down each night for data upload and system maintenance after the arrival of the last train at that station and then reopen the following morning before the departure of the first train. Passengers could therefore either purchase tickets the night before on arrival at their home stations or in the morning before getting on the train. Thus, as well as the rules about ticket pricing and validity, there were rules that determined the optimum times for each machine to shut down and reopen.

Since the last train was after midnight at most stations, I deliberately excluded a rule statement requiring the shutdown time to be later in the day than the reopening time. However, I neglected to include the advice "*the shutdown time may be earlier in the day than the reopening time.*" The programmer developing the user interface by which operators could adjust system rules (including machine operating hours) decided to include a rule that rejected any attempt to program a machine to shut down earlier in the day than the reopening time.

Of course, during the demonstration, when we tried to enter some typical real-world data (shut down at 1:30 am, reopen at 4:30 am), it was rejected, to our embarrassment.

Advice statements are described in Section 3.3.9.

3.3.8 Types of rule statements

Before we move on to discuss different types of rules (in Chapter 4), I wish to consider the various ways in which we can categorize the rule statements that can be used to express those rules.

3.3.8.1 Procedural and declarative rule statements

Procedural rule statements state what is to be done if a certain condition or set of conditions occurs. The fragments of program code in Section 3.1.1 are all procedural.

Declarative rule statements, on the other hand, merely state the condition or set of conditions that some information, process, person, or thing is to comply with, and leaves unstated the action to be taken if that condition or set of conditions is not complied with.

In this book, except where indicated, we shall confine ourselves to declarative rule statements.

3.3.8.2 Structural assertions, action assertions, and derivations

The Business Rules Group's Final Report of July 2000[30] ("the Final Report") distinguishes the following types of rule statements:

1. *Structural assertions* include both definitions of terms and what the Final Report refers to as "*facts relating terms to each other*" (although I prefer the term *fact type* to *fact*, as I shall explain in Section 6.3 in Chapter 6).
2. *Action assertions* (or *constraints*) define allowable actions; given the Final Report's focus on "*constraints on the creation, updating and removal of persistent data in an information system,*" these define allowable changes to data.
3. *Derivations* "*define how knowledge in one form may be transformed into other knowledge, possibly in a different form.*"

While this book does cover fact types, and includes guidelines for correctly structuring fact types, it deals with them separately from rule statements (as does the SBVR). Definitions of terms may be informal, in which case they form part of the overall fact model (see Section 6.2.2 in Chapter 6) or formal, in which case they are expressed as definitional rules (see Section 2.2 in Chapter 2, Sections 4.3 and 4.9.1 in Chapter 4, and Section 9.2.1 in Chapter 9).

Action assertions, as defined in the Final Report, are statements of operative rules.

Derivations, as defined in the Final Report, are statements of how values are either calculated or inferred. In this book, these rules are treated as definitional rules.

3.3.8.3 Operative rule statements

Later in this chapter we shall see that there are many types of operative rules and a number of types of definitional rules. However, irrespective of type, every operative rule can be expressed using one of the following:

1. An *obligation statement* expresses an obligation, typically one that obliges
   a. an item of information to be present or to have a valid value;
   b. a process to occur or to behave in a particular manner;
   c. a person to have a particular attribute, to perform a particular action, or to behave in a particular manner; or
   d. a thing to be present or to be in a particular state.

---

[30](Business Rules Group, 2000).

There are various approaches to the standard expression of obligation statements. In this book, as in RuleSpeak,[31] all obligation statements include the word 'must' without an immediately following 'not': for example,

R33. Each <u>flight booking request</u> *for* a <u>return journey</u> must *specify* the <u>departure date</u>.

2. A *prohibition statement* expresses a prohibition, typically one that prohibits
   a. the presence of, or an invalid value of, an item of information;
   b. the occurrence of, or a particular behavior by, a process;
   c. a particular attribute or action of, or a particular behavior by, a person; or
   d. the presence of, or a particular state of, a thing.
Again there are various approaches to the standard expression of prohibition statements. In this book, again as in RuleSpeak, all prohibition statements include the words 'must not': for example,

R34. A <u>flight booking request</u> *for* a <u>one-way journey</u> must not *specify* a <u>return date</u>.

3. A *restricted permission statement* allows a situation to exist only if a particular condition applies, typically
   a. an item of information may be present or absent, or may have particular values, only if a particular condition applies;
   b. a process may occur or fail to occur, or may behave in a particular manner, only if a particular condition applies;
   c. a person may have (or not have) a particular attribute, may perform a particular action, or may behave in a particular manner, only if a particular condition applies; or
   d. a thing may be present or absent, or may be in a particular state, only if a particular condition applies.
Again, there are various approaches to the standard expression of restricted permission statements. In this book, again as in RuleSpeak, all restricted permission statements include the word 'may' followed eventually by the word 'only' immediately before the clause expressing the condition: for example,

R35. Each <u>flight booking request</u> may *specify* a <u>return date</u> only if that <u>flight booking request</u> *is for* a <u>return journey</u>.

Comparison of rule statements R34 and R35 reveals that it is possible to express the same rule as either a prohibition statement or a restricted permission statement. The methodology to be described in this book will include indications as to which is the most appropriate form for each type of rule.

Although the SBVR allows for these formulations, it proposes alternative formulations for these three types of rule statements:

1. An obligation statement starts with the clause 'it is obligatory that': for example,

R36. †It is obligatory that each <u>flight booking request</u> *for* a <u>return journey</u> *specifies* the <u>departure date</u>.[32,33]

---

[31](Ross, RuleSpeak Sentence Forms - Specifying Natural-Language Business Rules in English, 2009).
[32]Each rule statement example that, for one or more reasons, is not recommended is marked with an initial dagger, as in R36–R44 inclusive.
[33]The majority of examples of rule statements of this type in the SBVR use the *third person singular present indicative* form of the verb (as in R36) although some examples use the *subjunctive* form of the verb (in this case '*specify*' rather than '*specifies*').

2. A prohibition statement starts with the clause 'it is prohibited that': for example,

R37. †It is prohibited that a <u>flight booking request</u> *for* a <u>one-way journey</u> *specifies* a <u>return date</u>.

3. A restricted permission statement starts with the clause 'it is permitted that' followed eventually by the word 'only' immediately before the clause expressing the condition: for example,

R38. †It is permitted that each <u>flight booking request</u> *specifies* a <u>return date</u> only if that <u>flight booking request</u> *is for* a <u>return journey</u>.

I believe these formulations are less successful in supporting our objective of clarity, for two reasons:

1. They each use more words to say the same thing, without the benefit of significantly more clarity or precision.[34]
2. Each of the rule statements R36, R37 and R38 is intended to test instances of <u>flight booking request</u>, yet, unlike R33, R34, and R35 (which are also intended to test instances of <u>flight booking request</u>), the subject of R36, R37, and R38 is in each case 'it'. This violates what I believe to be an important principle of rule statement formulation, namely that the subject of the rule statement be the term referring to the set of objects to be tested by the rule. This principle is discussed further in Section 7.2.3 in Chapter 7.

For these reasons, I do not recommend these formulations for practical business use. I have therefore not configured any templates to produce these formulations, and will not be citing further examples using these formulations.

3.3.8.4 Definitional (structural) rule statements
Both the SBVR and RuleSpeak (which is described in an Annex to the SBVR) also propose three corresponding types of definitional (structural) rule statements:

1. A *necessity statement* expresses a necessity: that is, something that is necessarily the case: for example, that a person have a birth date. The standard SBVR formulation starts with the clause 'it is necessary that', whereas in RuleSpeak each necessity statement includes the word 'always': for example,

R39. †It is necessary that each <u>person</u> *has* a <u>birth date</u>.
R40. †Each <u>person</u> always *has* a <u>birth date</u>.

2. An *impossibility statement* expresses an impossibility: that is, states that something is impossible: for example, that a person be born in more than one country. The standard SBVR formulation starts with the clause 'it is impossible that', whereas in RuleSpeak each impossibility statement includes the word 'never': for example,

R41. †It is impossible that the same <u>person</u> *be born in* more than one <u>country</u>.
R42. †The same <u>person</u> *is* never *born in* more than one <u>country</u>.

3. A *restricted possibility statement* expresses a situation that is possible only if a particular condition applies. The standard SBVR formulation starts with the clause 'it is possible that', whereas in

---

[34]One possible motivation for using formulations that do not include the word 'must' is that 'must' can be interpreted in three ways: (a) *alethic*: stating a logical conclusion, as in "he must be out" (since he is not home), (b) *epistemic* (asserting a belief, as in "surely he must be out"); (c) *deontic* (stating an obligation, as in "he must be out before the doors are locked"). However one can reasonably assume that 'must' in a rule statement has only a deontic interpretation.

RuleSpeak each restricted possibility statement includes 'can' followed eventually by the word 'only' immediately before the clause expressing the condition: for example,

R43. † It is possible that a <u>journey</u> *is* a <u>return journey</u> only if the <u>journey</u> *involves* a <u>return flight</u>.
R44. † A <u>journey</u> can *be* a <u>return journey</u> only if the <u>journey</u> *involves* a <u>return flight</u>.

I believe that none of these formulations supports our objective of clarity, for the following reasons:

1. While the difference between 'impossible' and 'prohibited' may be clear to the average employee or customer of an organization, the difference between 'necessary' and 'obligatory' is rather too subtle for common use. I have frequently encountered even well-educated business people use 'necessary' when they mean 'obligatory': for example, "it is necessary for applications for leave to be submitted on the appropriate form".
2. The use of 'always' or 'never' in a rule statement suggests that the rule stated is time-independent rather than time-dependent. For example, the existence of a rule statement of the form "each <u>person</u> always *has* a <u>birth date</u>" suggests that there may be attributes of a person that they have only for a certain period of time (as indeed there are: for example, marriage date, retirement date). Meanwhile, the inclusion of 'never' in the rule statement "The same <u>rental car</u> *is* never *owned by* more than one <u>branch</u>." suggests that the rule statement would be more precise if it were worded "The same <u>rental car</u> *is* never *owned by* more than one <u>branch</u> at the same time."
3. It is not clear how RuleSpeak would use 'always' to express the rule statement "It is necessary that each <u>person</u> *was born in* at most one <u>country</u>".

For these reasons, I do not recommend these formulations for practical business use. I have therefore not configured any templates to produce these formulations, and will not be citing further examples using these formulations (except as counter-examples). Examples of formulations I do recommend for definitional rules are to be found in Section 2.2 in Chapter 2: all use the phrase 'by definition'.

3.3.9 Types of advice statements

In the same way that a rule may be operative or definitional (structural), an advice statement may be

1. a *statement of advice of permission*, stating the absence of an operative rule; or
2. a *statement of advice of possibility*, stating the absence of a definitional (structural) rule.

3.3.9.1 Statements of advice of permission

Every statement of advice of permission can be expressed using one of the following:

1. A *permission statement*, for which the standard SBVR formulation starts with the clause 'It is permitted that': for example, "It is permitted that the <u>rental duration</u> *of* a <u>rental</u> *is more than* 90 <u>rental days</u>."

    In RuleSpeak, permission statements include the word 'may' without a following 'only': for example, "The <u>rental duration</u> *of* a <u>rental</u> may *be more than* 90 <u>rental days</u>."
2. A *non-obligation statement*, for which the standard SBVR formulation starts with the clause 'It is not obligatory that': for example, 'It is not obligatory that the <u>rental duration</u> *of* a <u>rental</u> *is less than* 91 <u>rental days</u>'.

    In RuleSpeak, non-obligation statements include the words 'need not': for example, "The <u>rental duration</u> *of* a <u>rental</u> need not *be less than* 91 <u>rental days</u>."

Again, I believe the standard SBVR formulations are less successful than the RuleSpeak formulations in supporting our objective of clarity for the same reasons that apply to operative rule statements:

1. They use more words to say the same thing.
2. The subject of the advice statement is in each case 'it', rather than the term referring to the set of objects that are governed by the advice.

3.3.9.2 Statements of advice of possibility

Every statement of advice of possibility can be expressed using one of the following:

1. A *possibility statement*, for which the standard SBVR formulation starts with the clause 'It is possible that': for example, "It is possible that a <u>journey</u> *does* not *include* a <u>return flight</u>."
   In RuleSpeak, possibility statements include the word 'sometimes': for example, "A <u>journey</u> sometimes *does not include* a <u>return flight</u>."
2. A *non-necessity statement*, for which the standard SBVR formulation starts with the clause 'It is not necessary that': for example, "It is not necessary that a <u>journey</u> *includes* a <u>return flight</u>."
   In RuleSpeak, non-necessity statements include the words 'not always' without a following 'only': for example, "A <u>journey</u> does not always *include* a <u>return flight</u>."

The standard SBVR formulations for these statements suffer from the same issues as those for the other statement types we have looked at. Moreover, the use of 'sometimes' or 'not always' in the RuleSpeak formulations suggests that the advice stated is time-independent rather than time-dependent. For these reasons, I do not recommend these formulations for practical business use. Examples of formulations I do recommend for definitional rules are to be found in Section 4.9.1 in Chapter 4.

3.4 SUMMARY

The Information Technology (IT) industry focused initially on the implementation (rather than documentation) of rules. Program code, mainly procedural, was for some time the only option, but over time alternative platforms for the implementation of rules emerged, such as databases (in terms of both rule sets in data and database constraints), graphical user interface building tools, XML schemas and, most recently, rules engines (although the last-named have not yet seriously replaced any of the other implementation platforms).

While, to some extent, some of these implementation methods can be self-documenting, none provides for the documentation of rules in a manner that is understandable by business stakeholders. The various data modeling disciplines (Entity-Relationship Modeling, Object-Role Modeling, and UML) provide for various subsets of the required data constraint types, and Business Process Models provide for some process constraints.

To meet the need for rules to be understood by all stakeholders, various authors have proposed broadly similar approaches to natural language expression of the rules governing an enterprise and its systems.

The Business Rules Approach (summarized in the Business Rules Manifesto) provides a system specification and implementation approach that treats rules as equal to, and independent of, data and process.

It is important to distinguish rules from the statements that are used to express those rules. The SBVR, published by the Object Management Group (OMG), provides a comprehensive analysis of the linguistic and logical concepts underlying business rules and rule statements: that is, their expression in natural language. Unfortunately, the complexity necessary for this analysis means that even seasoned practitioners may find it difficult to follow in places.

There are various ways of categorizing rule statements, one being the distinction between procedural and declarative statements: in line with the Business Rules Approach, the SBVR and this book both limit themselves to declarative statements. These in turn are categorized by the SBVR (and this book) as either operative or definitional (structural). Operative rule statements in turn are categorized as obligation statements, prohibition statements, or restricted permission statements, while definitional rule statements are categorized as necessity statements, impossibility statements, or restricted possibility statements.

Where a programmer or user may assume the existence of a rule that does not in fact exist, the absence of that rule can be stated by way of an advice statement.

Types of rules

A critical prerequisite for writing quality rule statements is a clear understanding of what type of rule you are dealing with on each occasion. This is somewhat complicated by the fact that the environment in which an organization operates consists of a number of facets that can each contribute to the rules governing that organization.

These facets include

1. the physical world in which the organization operates;
2. the legislative and regulatory environment in which the organization operates, either as
   a. an enforcer of that legislation or regulations (e.g., a government body requiring those with whom it deals to comply with such legislation or regulations), or
   b. an organization governed by that legislation or regulations (e.g., a bank required to obtain particular identification from new customers, or supply a regulatory body with certain information);
3. the concepts that the organization creates (or inherits from science, the industry within which it operates, or the relevant regulatory bodies) to describe aspects of its operations;
4. the information that the organization needs to collect, record, and provide to other parties;
5. the business processes that the organization performs;
6. the parties with which the organization interacts;
7. the activities (other than business processes) that those parties may engage in.

In this chapter, we look at each of these facets and review the various types of rules that occur within each facet. We will see that a rule within one facet may either give rise to one or more rules in another facet, or affect how we need to express one or more rules in another facet.

This chapter concludes (in Section 4.9) by collecting the various rule types we have encountered into a single taxonomy, with some guidelines as to how to correctly classify any rule that you might encounter.

4.1 RULES GOVERNING THE PHYSICAL WORLD

Objects in the physical world (people, places, and things) have certain attributes and participate in certain relationships.

4.1.1 Mandatory and optional attributes and relationships

Some attributes of physical world objects are mandatory, in that every instance of that type of object has that attribute. For example, each person, living or deceased, has a date of birth. By contrast, while each deceased person has a date of death, living persons do not yet have one.

This is also true of relationships: each person was born in a particular place, and that place was at that time in a particular country.[1]

4.1.2 Single-valued and multi-valued attributes and relationships

Some attributes of physical world objects are single-valued, in that no instance of that type of object has more than one value of that attribute at the same time. For example, each person has only one date of birth. By contrast, while some cars are of only one color, a car may be multi-colored.

Similarly with relationships: a person or thing cannot be in more than one place at the one time. In particular, a person can only be born in one country; in contrast, people may be simultaneously citizens of more than one country.[2]

4.1.3 Variant and invariant attributes and relationships

Some attributes of physical world objects are invariant, in that each instance of that type of object has a value for that attribute that does not change. For example, each person has only one date of birth, which does not change. By contrast, although each person has only one weight at any given time, that weight (unfortunately!) changes over time.

Similarly with relationships: a person's country of birth does not change[3] although his or her country of residence can change.

4.1.4 Constraints between attributes

Some attributes of a physical world object may be constrained by other attributes, in the sense that a change in one is necessarily reflected in a change in another. For example, the range of a vehicle (in miles) is the total fuel tank capacity (in gallons) multiplied by the fuel consumption rate (in miles per gallon). If either the total fuel tank capacity or the fuel consumption rate of a vehicle is changed, the range of that vehicle will necessarily also change.

Other sets of attributes may not be so tightly coupled, but may be still be constrained by each other. Typically, one attribute must necessarily be either greater than or less than another. This is often true of pairs of dates: a person's date of death cannot be earlier than his or her date of birth; and the effective date of a contract cannot be later than the expiry date of that contract. This type of constraint is discussed in some more detail in Section 4.5.2.4.

4.1.5 The impact of the physical world on an organization's rule book

No organization needs rules to ensure that (for example) each person it deals with has exactly one date of birth. Nor does an organization need rules to ensure that that date of birth does not change or fall after that person's date of death (if any).

---

[1] I use the phrase "at that time" since some places can end up as part of another country: for example, a place formerly in Yugoslavia, Czechoslovakia, or Sudan.

[2] While some countries require that a new citizen renounce any existing citizenships of other countries, this is not true of every country. For example, while I am now a citizen of Australia, I have not had to renounce my U.K. citizenship.

[3] Of course, the name of that country might change (e.g., Burma is now Myanmar), and/or (as explained in footnote 1) the person's birth place might end up as part of another country.

However, as we shall see, organizations often need rules about the capture and retention of data about the physical world. As we shall see in Section 4.5, such rules

1. need to ensure that the data captured do not describe an impossible physical world situation;
2. need to be worded so as to take account of the properties of the physical world;
3. should not be written as if they govern the physical world itself.

4.2 LEGISLATION AND REGULATIONS

Every organization operates in a legislative and regulatory environment that governs the operations of the organization and its employees, and which may also govern its customers, suppliers, and/or partners.

For example, banks operating in Australia are required by legislation[4] to obtain multiple forms of identification from applicants for new accounts. The intention of this regulation is to reduce the likelihood that a new account is used for money-laundering or financing terrorism. Since some forms of identification are harder to forge than others, the legislation

1. lists for each type of identification a point score (e.g., 70 points for a birth certificate or current passport, 40 points for an Australian driving license, 25 points for a credit card); and
2. stipulates that the identification provided by each applicant must carry a total score of at least 100.

Each bank operating in Australia is governed by that regulation, and has no choice in the matter. Thus, according to the definition of "business rule" in the Semantics of Business Vocabulary and Rules (SBVR), these rules are not business rules from the perspective of a bank, since that bank cannot "opt to discard or change the rule." Yet these are operative rules: a party applying for a new account may fail to provide enough correct information. However, according to the SBVR, there is no such thing as an operative rule that is not a business rule.

Another Australian example comes from the field of real property transactions. Each Australian state government has enacted legislation as to the conduct of such transactions, and in particular the information to be provided by parties to those transactions. There is a Land Registry in each state, responsible for accepting and registering the legal instruments documenting these transactions. The Land Registry in each state is governed by the information requirements stated in the legislation in force in that state. A Land Registry has no choice in the matter: each information requirement specified in the legislation is to be adhered to without modification.

Again, according to the SBVR definition of 'business rule', each such rule is not a business rule from the perspective of that Land Registry since that registry cannot "opt to discard or change the rule." At the same time, each such rule is an operative rule rather than structural rule since it can be violated by a negligent conveyancer or by a member of the public who has opted for self-conveyance but has not read or understood the legislation.

It has been put to me by authors of the SBVR that in this situation there are two separate sets of items:

1. the legislation (which does not consist of rules but of motivations for rules) written in legal language, difficult to understand, and
2. the rules governing the Land Registry, which is written in language more easily understood by employees and the public.

---

[4]*The Financial Transaction Reports Act, 1988.*

My view is that the legislation does indeed include rules, and, even if the department has developed alternative wordings of each rule stated in the legislation, these are merely alternative rule statements for the same rules rather than separate rules.[5] This position appears to have put me at odds with the business rules community, since I am talking about operative rules that (according to the community) are not business rules, which (again according to the community) do not exist.

Finally, an international example: the airline industry worldwide is bound by numerous items of legislation governing identification of passengers, inspection of bags, passenger and aircrew behavior, etc. Again, the legislation contains rules (indeed clauses of the relevant legislation are often displayed verbatim on airline websites and on placards at airports and on aircraft). Again, the rules are operative. Again, an airline is not in a position to "opt to discard or change" these rules. Again, we have operative rules that (according to the community) are not business rules.

All of this is not to say that there are not many situations in which organizations create additional rules, governing their employees, customers, and/or suppliers, which derive from (and are distinct from) the legislation or regulations that govern the organization. For example, governments in many countries and states have laws prohibiting the supply of alcoholic drinks to persons below a certain age, 18 years or 21 years as the case may be. While such a law is certainly one of the rules governing a bar in that country or state (and is an operative rule that the bar cannot "opt to discard or change" without risking a penalty), the bar will generally create additional rules governing activities by their bar staff, such as "each patron who looks younger than 25 years must present a photo ID before being served".

As these examples illustrate, legislation and regulations often govern the collection and recording of information, but may also govern other processes, or govern which roles may perform particular processes. Rules governing the collection and recording of information are discussed further in Section 4.4; rules governing other business processes are discussed further in Section 4.6; rules governing which roles may perform particular processes are discussed further in Section 4.7; and rules governing human activities other than business processes are discussed further in Section 4.8.

4.3 ORGANIZATIONAL CONSTRUCTS

Organizations not only operate within the physical world and an environment of legislation and regulation but create various constructs by which to describe aspects of their business (or inherit those constructs from science, industry, or regulatory bodies). These constructs include

1. terms chosen to describe specific concepts of interest (such as 'loan application', 'probationary employee', 'high value customer', 'close of business', or 'financial year'), each with a definition;
2. categorization schemes, based on physical properties (such as 'gender') or derived properties (such as 'credit rating' or 'marital status'), each with a set of categories and (in some cases) rules governing the allowed transitions between categories or statuses (e.g., a person's marital status cannot transition from 'divorced' to 'never married');

---

[5]See Section 3.3.6 for a discussion of the difference between rules and rule statements.

3. concepts with internal structure, of which the following are two examples from the airline industry:
   a. when an airline defines a 'flight', it is defined with one origin port, one destination port, one departure time, and one arrival time;
   b. similarly, the concept of a 'return journey' is defined as one or more passengers traveling on a pair of flights (the same passengers on each flight) in which
      i. the origin port of the second (return) flight is the same as the destination port of the first (outgoing) flight, and
      ii. the origin port of the outgoing flight is the same as the destination port of the return flight;
4. measurement units to be used with quantities of particular types: for example, miles (or kilometers) for distance, pH for acidity or alkalinity, along with
   a. conversion factors between different units (e.g., 1 mile is approximately 1.6 kilometers),
   b. valid values of measurements (e.g., the pH measure of acidity or alkalinity ranges from 0 to 14 inclusive);
5. standard calculations: for example, the standard means of calculating a business's 'total year-to-date sales' may be the total value (net of all included taxes and delivery charges) of all orders raised since January 1 in the current year;
6. standard formats for representing information: for example, whether, say, Christmas day 2010 is to be represented as '25/12/2010' (as in the United Kingdom or Australia), '12/25/2010' (as in the United States) or '25 December 2010' (to avoid any confusion);
7. the properties of relationships between objects of the same type, such as reporting relationships in an organization, borders between countries, and so on.

Before we move on, let me address a question that some of you may be prompted to ask at this point, as to why I have included at least one physical phenomenon among my examples of organizational constructs. While acidity/alkalinity is indeed a physical phenomenon, the use of pH to measure it is a human invention, as is the use of miles and kilometers to measure distances between objects in the physical world. The fact that miles are used in the United States and kilometers are used in most other nations should make clear that these are human inventions used to describe physical phenomena rather than the phenomena themselves.

A detailed taxonomy of rules governing organizational constructs is provided in Section 4.9.1.

4.4 RULES GOVERNING THE COLLECTION AND RECORDING OF DATA

Each organization needs to collect and retain data about the environment in which it operates, in particular the physical world objects of interest and the organizational constructs it uses. The data collected are subsequently used by the organization, either operationally (e.g., handling bookings) or in decision making (e.g., making discounted seats available, allocating aircraft to flights, or purchasing more aircraft). To support these processes, those data need to correctly represent the physical world objects and organizational constructs of interest.

As noted in Section 2.5 in Chapter 2, rules cannot ensure that data recorded by an organization correctly represent that organization's operational environment unless they are collected "before the event". However, rules can ensure that the data are complete, meaningful, and plausible.

As also discussed in Chapter 2, rules governing the collection and recording of data operate in three distinct environments:

1. the user interfaces whereby human operators enter data into systems;
2. electronic messages whereby one system transfers data to another;
3. persistent data stores, typically databases, where data is recorded for future use.

In each of these environments, much the same types of rules operate: in particular, each environment requires

1. rules ensuring that particular data items are present: for example, an online shopping user interface requires data identifying the purchaser, the product being purchased, and the payment mechanism, as does the database in which orders are recorded;
2. rules ensuring that data items contain values that are valid in the circumstances: for example, a leave application entered into an employee self-service system must specify only an allowed leave type, must specify valid dates, and must specify an end date that is no earlier than the start date.

4.4.1 Data cardinality rules

Rules that ensure that particular data items are present are commonly referred to as **mandatory data rules**, but these constitute a specific subset of a broader set of rules (**data cardinality rules**), including

1. those that prohibit data in certain situations: for example, in a flight booking system a request for a one-way journey should not specify a return date as well as a departure date;
2. those that allow only one instance of a particular data item in a single transaction: for example, in an employee self-service system a single leave request can only specify one leave type, one start date, and one end date;
3. those that require more than one instance of a particular data item in each transaction of a particular type: for example, typically an application to rent an apartment must furnish the names of three persons who can provide references.

A detailed taxonomy of data cardinality rules is provided in Section 4.9.2.1.

4.4.2 Data content rules

Rules that ensure that data items contain valid values (referred to in this book as **data content rules**) include

1. those that require that the content of a data item be one of a particular set of values: for example, in an online shopping system, each order line must specify one of the product codes in the product catalog and must specify one of the acceptable methods of payment;
2. those that require that a value contained in a data item be within a particular range: for example, in an online shopping system, each basket item must specify an order quantity of at least 1;
3. those that require that the values contained in two or more data items be different from each other: for example, in a flight booking request, the origin and destination cities must be different;
4. those that require that a value contained in a data item be different from every other value either
   a. already recorded for that data item (e.g., in a human resources system, a new employee record must specify an employee ID that is different from all existing employee IDs), or

     b. in other instances of that data item in the form being entered (e.g., again in a human resources system, a new allowance for an existing employee must be of a type that is not only different from all other existing allowances for that employee but different from all other new allowances being added at the same time);

5. those that require that multiple data items are consistent with each other: these rules include
       a. those that require that the values contained in two data items in a transaction or record have a particular relationship to each other: for example, the end date of a period of leave must be no earlier than the start date of that period of leave;
       b. those that require that the values contained in two or more data items form a valid combination: for example, in a postal address, the place name, state, and postal code[6] must be a valid combination;
       c. those that require that one set of data items be identical to another set: for example, the set of vendors specified in some real estate transactions must be identical to the current set of registered proprietors;
       d. those that impose a constraint on a *set function* over the values contained in a set of data items: for example, the sum of the shares held by the proprietors of a parcel of real property must equal 1;

6. *temporal data constraints*: those that require that a data item representing a particular date or time fall within a certain temporal range, and those that prescribe or prohibit relationships between data items representing time periods: for example,
       a. the time periods specified in an employee's leave records must not overlap,
       b. the time periods specified in an employee's pay records must be contiguous,
       c. the time periods specified in an employee's leave and pay records must not fall outside that employee's employment period;

7. *spatial data constraints*: those that prescribe or prohibit relationships between data items representing spatial properties (points, line segments, or polygons): for example, in a record of a real estate subdivision, the data items representing the polygons constituting the individual parcels in that subdivision must not imply any overlap and must (together with those representing the polygons constituting roads and common land) jointly cover the entire subdivision;

8. those that require that a data item have a particular format.

A detailed taxonomy of data content rules is provided in Section 4.9.2.2.

4.4.3 Dynamic data constraints

An important (and often overlooked) class of rules is those that govern changes to information already recorded. These are *dynamic* data constraints in that they are concerned with allowed relationships between old and new values of a data item. By contrast, the data rules so far discussed are *static* data constraints, concerned only with the presence or absence of a value or what that value is.

    The simplest dynamic data constraints are those that prohibit changes to data after it is recorded. Accounting systems typically require that, once a transaction is recorded, it cannot be changed: if it

---

[6]"Zip code" in the US.

turns out to have been entered incorrectly, a reversal transaction must be entered that reverses the effect of the original transaction, and then the correct transaction must be entered. Other dynamic data constraints include

1. those that limit the changes in a data item to a set of valid transitions: for example, if a system allows a person's marital status to be recorded as 'never married', 'married', '*de facto* (common law)', 'widowed', 'separated', or 'divorced', any person's transition from any status to a status of 'never married' is impossible[7];
2. those that require that a numeric value can only increase or decrease: for example, some employment arrangements prohibit a reduction in a person's hourly pay rate.

Thus a dynamic data constraint is concerned with

1. whether update of a data item is permitted, or
2. if so, what restrictions there are on the new value of that data item in terms of the existing value.

For this reason, they are more commonly known as ***data update rules***. A detailed taxonomy of data update rules is provided in Section 4.9.2.3.

4.5 TAKING ACCOUNT OF THE PHYSICAL WORLD IN DATA RULES

We have seen in Section 4.1.5 that rules are not required to ensure that objects in the physical world have particular attributes and relationships, or that those attributes and relationships behave in a particular way. However, an organization does need rule statements with which to ensure that data captured do not describe an impossible physical world situation, such as

1. a physical property or construct having an impossible value, as discussed in Section 4.5.2.1;
2. an impossible transition in some physical property or construct, as discussed in Section 4.5.2.2;
3. a person or thing being in more than one place at the same time, as discussed in Section 4.5.2.3;
4. an event, arrangement, or lifecycle stage ending before it starts (e.g., a person's date of death preceding his or her date of birth), as discussed in Section 4.5.2.4.

Furthermore, each rule statement referring to data about the physical world needs to be worded so as to take account of the properties of the physical world: this is discussed in Section 4.5.6.

Finally, it is important that rules governing data about the physical world are not written as if they govern the physical world itself: this is discussed in Section 4.5.1.

4.5.1 Distinguishing the physical world and data about it

A famous work[8] by the Belgian surrealist artist René Magritte depicts a smoker's pipe above the words "ceci n'est pas une pipe" ("this is not a pipe"). And a character in one of the episodes of the British radio comedy series The Goon Show tried to placate a creditor with the line "Here, take this picture of a five pound note". The humor in both cases is based on the fact that a representation of a thing in the physical world is not the same as the thing represented.

---

[7]See also Section 4.5.2.2 on the subject of impossible transitions.
[8]*The Treachery of Images*, 1929.

Every person has a date of birth. While some organizations may decide that they need to record the date of birth of every employee, others may decide otherwise. An organization that does decide to record every employee's date of birth does not need a rule to state that every employee of that organization has a date of birth (that is a given), but it does need a rule to state that the date of birth must be recorded for every employee. By contrast, an organization that decides otherwise needs neither rule. Importantly, the physical world in which each of those organizations operates is the same: one in which every person has a date of birth. The only difference lies in the presence or absence of a rule as to whether the date of birth must be recorded for every employee.

By contrast, version 1.0 of the SBVR proposes two different models: a "reality model" and an "in-practice model":

> *"Suppose the following two fact types are of interest: Employee was born on Date; Employee has Phone Number. In the real world, each employee is born, and may have more than one phone number. Hence the reality model includes the constraint 'Each Employee was born on at least one Date' (sic) and allows that 'It is possible that the same Employee has more than one Phone Number.' [If] the business decides to make it optional whether it knows an employee's date of birth, [and] is interested in knowing at most one phone number for any given employee, . . . the in-practice model excludes the reality constraint 'Each Employee was born on at least one Date', but it includes the following constraint that does not apply in the reality model: 'Each Employee has at most one Phone Number'."*

This seems to me to be an unnecessarily complex way of modeling the information requirements of an organization. In my opinion, there should only be one model (rather than two), in which the rules governing information requirements are written in terms of information requirements rather than some alternative reality.

Let's consider just dates of birth for the moment. The assertion "*each Employee was born on at least one Date*" (which might be better worded as "*each Employee was born on exactly one Date*", "*each Employee has exactly one Date of Birth*", or perhaps "*Each Employee has a Date of Birth*") is a statement about the real world. If the organization needs to record the date of birth of every employee, it needs an additional rule of the form "*each Employee Record must specify that Employee's Date of Birth*". If the organization does not need to record the date of birth of every employee, it omits that rule; if necessary, it can instead include an advice of the form "*an Employee Record need not specify that Employee's Date of Birth*".

Similarly, the assertion "*an Employee may have more than one Phone Number*" is a statement about the real world. If the organization does not need to record more than one phone number for any employee, it needs a rule statement expressing that information requirement (of the form "*an Employee Record must not specify more than one Phone Number*") rather than a false statement about reality (of the form proposed in the SBVR: "*each Employee has at most one Phone Number*").

A requirement to record information may depend on circumstances. For example, an insurance business may decide that it must collect the date of birth of each customer purchasing personal life insurance, so as to be able to calculate appropriate premiums. If, however, a customer is only purchasing home insurance, the business does not need to collect his or her date of birth. The business therefore needs a rule that requires that each customer provide his or her date of birth if purchasing personal life insurance.

One can only assume that the SBVR approach would require an "in-practice model" in which "*each Person purchasing Personal Life Insurance was born on at least one Date*". What is actually required is a rule statement expressing the information requirement, of the form "*each Application for a Personal Life Insurance Policy must specify the Date of Birth of the Person whose Life is to be covered by that Policy*". An advice of the form "*an Application for a Home Insurance Policy need not specify the Date of Birth of the Person covered by that Policy*" may also be included.

The 'date of birth' examples cited so far cover the situation in which something that is universal (persons' dates of birth) does not always need to be recorded. The reverse situation may also arise. Not every person has a union membership expiry date but, if an organization employs only union members, every employee has a union membership expiry date. Two rules characterize this situation: "*a Person may be employed by the Company only if that Person is a Union Member*" and "*each Employee Record must specify that Employee's Union Membership Expiry Date*".

4.5.1.1 Missing data

We have seen (with dates of birth) that a set of physical world objects can each possess a property that is only recorded by an organization for some of those objects. What does it mean when we encounter a data item that, while present in the records for some objects, is missing from the records for others?

Consider again dates of birth. If the organization has recorded the dates of birth of some customers but not of others, this may be due (as discussed in the previous section) to the purchase of different products by those customers combined with a different data collection policy with respect to those products. It may of course reflect something quite different: a change of policy over time with respect to data collection. Alternatively, it may be that the organization has made it optional whether customers supply their dates of birth, in which case the absence of a customer's date of birth means 'date of birth not supplied'.

Given that a significant proportion of Australian residents were born outside Australia, some Australian organizations record the date of arrival in Australia of persons born outside Australia. Interestingly, as many such persons arrived in Australia as small children many years ago, not every Australian immigrant knows their date of arrival in Australia. In this case, absence of a value in the 'date of arrival in Australia' data item can mean any of the following:

1. 'not applicable' (for those born in Australia)
2. 'not known'
3. 'known but not supplied'.

These reasons for absence (or at least some of them) can equally apply to categories such as gender (which may be unknown if a person is recording information about another person; or known but not supplied if a person opts not to supply his or her gender; or even not applicable if we are discussing parties in general—including organizations—rather than just persons).

Given that absence of data can be for different reasons, it is often important to record the reason for the absence of data rather than merely omit it. (Date, 2005) (and many of Date's earlier works) supply many sound arguments why omitting data can lead to all manner of anomalies. However, this often leads to additional 'reasons for absence' categories being added to categorization schemes: for example, while gender in the physical world includes only categories such as 'male' and 'female', information about gender may include additional categories such as 'not known' and 'known but not supplied'. I discuss this dichotomy further in Section 4.5.2.1.

4.5.2 Ensuring that data does not describe an impossible situation

An important class of rule statements ensures that data captured does not describe an impossible physical world situation. Such situations include

1. data specifying impossible values of physical properties: for example, pH less than 0 or more than 14;
2. data specifying impossible transitions between values of a property of a person or thing: for example, a person's transition from 'married' to 'never married';
3. data specifying impossible placement of persons or things: for example, a person in more than one place at the one time, or a vehicle required to exceed a practical speed limit;
4. data specifying impossible sequences of events: for example, a person's death occurring before his or her birth;
5. data specifying complex concepts with impossible structures: for example, a flight booking with different sets of passengers flying on different stages of the proposed journey.

Let's now look at each of these requirements in turn.

4.5.2.1 Data specifying impossible values

We have seen in Section 2.2 in Chapter 2 that a definitional rule can be used to limit the values of a particular measurement. One of the rule statements in Section 2.2 is reproduced again here:

R45. pH *is* by definition *at least* 0 and *at most* 14.

However, while that rule, being a definitional rule, cannot be violated, it is still necessary to prevent a user entering data about the physical and chemical properties of water samples from entering a pH value that is outside that range. To do so, an operative rule (a data content rule) is also required:

R46. The pH *specified in* each water sample record must *be at least* 0 and *at most* 14.

Some physical properties have value ranges that are less clear cut. For example, while the temperature of liquid water at normal sea level atmospheric pressure must be between 32°F (0°C) and 212°F (100°C), the temperature of water samples taken from a river will exhibit a much smaller range in practice. In this type of situation, "sanity check" rules can be useful: for example,

R47. A water sample record may *specify* a water temperature *less than* 32°F or *more than* 60°F only if the sample tester who *tested* the sample *specified in* that water sample record *has* confirmed that water temperature.

Similarly, there may be a definitional rule restricting the values of a category, such as R48 below. While this rule cannot be violated, it is still necessary to prevent a user entering an invalid category. To do so, an operative rule (a data content rule) is also required, such as R49.

R48. The travel class of each leg of a journey is by definition first class, business class, premium economy class, or economy class.

R49. The travel class specified in each flight booking request must be 'first class', 'business class', 'premium economy class', or 'economy class'.[9]

I discussed in Section 4.5.1.1 the inclusion of additional pseudo-categories such as 'not known' and 'known but not supplied' in categorization schemes. This may lead a rule author to create an operative rule that differs from the corresponding definitional rule by the inclusion of such pseudo-categories, but this is not appropriate. In the information world, a valid physical world category is either specified or not specified: thus R52 is the correct formulation rather than R51 if a person is permitted not to specify his or her gender.

R50. The gender of a person is by definition either male or female.

R51. †The gender specified in each enrollment application must be 'male', 'female', or 'known but not supplied'.[10]

R52. The gender (if any) specified in each enrollment application must be 'male' or 'female'.

4.5.2.2 Data specifying impossible transitions

Definitional rules can be used to specify allowed or disallowed transitions between categories or statuses: for example,

R53. A transition of the marital status of a person from married, widowed, separated, or divorced to never married is by definition impossible.

R54. A transition of the marital status of a person from widowed to divorced is by definition impossible.

Again, corresponding operative rules may be required to prevent the specification of invalid transitions in recorded data: for example, R55 (operative) corresponds to R53 (definitional). However, while R54 is a true statement about the physical world, R56 (which appears to correspond to R54) is not true of the world of information, since a widowed person may be married then divorced between consecutive occasions on which that person's marital status is recorded.

R55. The marital status of an employee may be updated to never married only if the marital status that is currently recorded for that employee is unknown.

R56. †The marital status of an employee must not be updated to divorced if the marital status that is currently recorded for that employee is widowed.

4.5.2.3 Data specifying impossible placement

It is a law of physics that no person or thing can be in more than one place at the one time. We do not need a rule to ensure that. However, it is important that data representing an impossible situation are not recorded. Allowing a timetabling system to show a teacher assigned to two classrooms at the same time is clearly unacceptable. A data content rule is required to constrain teacher assignments to classrooms:

---

[9]Note that in R49, but not in R48, each category value is enclosed in quote marks. This is because R49 defines the textual literals that can be legitimately included in a flight booking request form, whereas R48 defines the possible values of an organizational construct.

[10]Each rule statement example that, for one or more reasons, is not recommended is marked with an initial dagger, as in R51.

R57. An <u>assignment</u> *of* a <u>teacher</u> *to* a <u>classroom</u> must not *be for* the same <u>timetable period</u> *as* any other <u>assignment</u> *of* that <u>teacher</u> *to* a <u>classroom</u>.

Not only are people and things prevented from being in more than one place at the one time, they also require time to move from one place to another. Failure to appreciate this has on two occasions impacted my working life:

1. Some years ago I taught in a large suburban high school that was spread over a campus that took at least 5 min to cross. Despite this, each timetable period after the first started at the same time as the previous period finished, even though staff were often timetabled for duties at opposite ends of the campus in consecutive periods. After being cautioned more than once for arriving late for a lesson, I took to leaving some lessons 5 min early. This unfortunately led to a new problem: a class of teenagers soon finds creative ways of spending unsupervised time.
2. Recently, I worked for some months for a major Australian business with offices in various locations in the Sydney central business district. In this situation, it could take up to 10 min to get from one office to another; however, while MS Outlook™ alerted meeting organizers if I already had another meeting at the same time, it did not provide them with an alert if I already had a meeting in another location immediately preceding or following the planned meeting. Needless to say, people often arrived late for meetings or had to leave meetings early.

However, many systems do take account of the time required to move from one place to another. For example,

1. Transport timetabling systems are typically programmed to prevent vehicles being timetabled between different locations in such a way as to require speeds that are impractical.[11]
2. London's Heathrow airport has prominent signs advising passengers of the time required to reach the furthest departure gates.
3. European rail journey planning systems prevent connections that do not allow adequate time for transferring from one platform to another at the connecting station.
4. Online flight booking systems similarly require minimum transit times at connecting airports, as in the data content rule expressed by the following rule statement:

R58. The <u>arrival time</u> *of* each <u>outgoing flight</u> (other than the last)
    specified in each <u>flight booking confirmation</u>
    that *specifies* more than one <u>outgoing flight</u>
  must *precede* the <u>departure time</u> *of* the next <u>outgoing flight</u>
    specified in that <u>flight booking confirmation</u>
    by at least the <u>minimum international transit time</u>
    for the <u>port</u> *at* which those <u>flights</u> *connect*
  if any <u>outgoing flight</u>
    specified in that <u>flight booking confirmation</u>
    is international.

---

[11]They are also typically programmed to prevent vehicles being timetabled between different locations in such a way as to require speeds that are illegal or unsafe, but that is a slightly different matter, dealt with in Section 4.5.5.

4.5.2.4 Data specifying impossible sequences

A person's death cannot occur before his or her birth. Similarly a student's graduation cannot occur before his or her enrollment in the faculty from which he or she graduates. We do not need a rule to prevent either of these impossible situations. However, if data about persons are being recorded, it is important that the data recorded do not represent an impossible situation. Allowing a student's record to show a graduation date earlier than his or her enrollment date compromises data quality and possibly process logic. A data content rule is required, not to constrain the actual dates but the specifications of those dates, in either a form (as in R59) or a database record (as in R60):

R59. The combination of enrollment date and graduation date *specified in* each student graduation form must *be* such that the graduation date *is later than* the enrollment date.

R60. The combination of enrollment date and graduation date *specified in* each student record must *be* such that the graduation date *is later than* the enrollment date.

4.5.2.5 Data specifying impossible structures for complex concepts

We have seen in Section 2.2 of Chapter 2 that a definitional rule can be used to define the structure of organizational constructs. One of the rule statements in Section 2.2 is reproduced again here:

R61. The origin city *of* the return flight *of* a return journey *is* by definition *the same as* the destination city *of* the outgoing flight *of* that return journey.

However, while that rule, being a definitional rule, cannot be violated, it is still necessary to prevent a user entering data about a journey that conflicts with that definitional rule. To do so, an operative rule is also required:

R62. The origin city *specified for* the return flight *of* a return journey must *be the same as* the destination city *specified for* the outgoing flight *of* that return journey.

4.5.3 Do we even need definitional rules?

We have now seen a number of situations where it is necessary to create an operative rule that "mirrors" a definitional rule. This might prompt the question, "do we even need definitional rules?" If your only concern is reducing errors in entered data, there is a case for specifying only the relevant operative rules. However, definitional rules have value inasmuch as they describe the physical world and concepts with which the organization deals.

One way in which definitional rules can be quite useful is to reduce verbosity in operative rule statements. At a Land Registry in one of the Australian states, there are numerous rules governing real property transactions. Many of these govern some rather than all transaction types, leading to rule statements like R63. There were many such rule statements, each with the same list of transaction types. The rule author decided to create a definitional rule with rule statement R64, allowing R63 to be rewritten as R65.

R63. Each <u>real property transaction</u> *for* which the <u>transaction type</u> *is*

<u>'Transfer With Monetary Consideration'</u>,

<u>'Transfer Without Monetary Consideration'</u>,

<u>'Transfer Under Power Of Sale'</u>,

<u>'Mortgage'</u>,

<u>'Discharge Of Mortgage'</u>, or

<u>'Withdrawal Of Caveat'</u>

must *specify* the <u>full name</u> *of* each <u>party relinquishing</u>.

R64. A <u>real property relinquishing transaction</u> *is* by definition a <u>real property transaction</u> *for* which the <u>transaction type</u> *is*

<u>'Transfer With Monetary Consideration'</u>,

<u>'Transfer Without Monetary Consideration'</u>,

<u>'Transfer Under Power Of Sale'</u>,

<u>'Mortgage'</u>,

<u>'Discharge Of Mortgage'</u>, or

<u>'Withdrawal Of Caveat'</u>.

R65. Each <u>real property relinquishing transaction</u> must *specify* the <u>full name</u> *of* each <u>party relinquishing</u>.

4.5.4 Do we need so many operative rules?

Given that many modern user interfaces incorporate quite comprehensive data validation, I have found that some rule authors are tempted to omit those rules that can be enforced by the user interface, such as mandatory data items or data items that are limited to a specific set of values by way of a 'combo box'/'drop down list'/'pick list'. This is inappropriate. All rules governing the use of an application system, including those that are to be enforced by the user interface, must be documented as part of the application system design, and must be published to users and other stakeholders.

4.5.5 Data specifying an illegal or unsafe situation

Should a system be prevented from recording data that specifies an illegal or unsafe situation? That depends on whether the data specify situations that are yet to occur or situations that have already occurred. For example, transport timetabling systems are typically programmed to prevent vehicles being timetabled between different locations in such a way as to require speeds that are illegal or unsafe. This is because the data in timetabling systems specify situations that are yet to occur, and, since most organizations have an interest in preventing illegal or unsafe situations, the timetabling system can play a part in such prevention.

By contrast, a system that records actual vehicle locations at various times should be allowed to record pairs of times and locations that indicate unsafe or illegal speeds. This is generally the case with systems that record data after the event, as these provide a means of monitoring and correcting unsafe or illegal behavior. For example, a system that records details of the construction and usage of buildings in each area of a city must allow for the entry of data describing any building that is in violation of the zoning regulations for the area in which it is located.

As a further example, consider a case management system for a medical practice. Such a system should prevent a doctor prescribing two medications for the same patient that are unsafe in combination, and can do so by way of a rule that prevents the entry of the second of those prescriptions. The same system, however, should allow for the recording of all existing medications being taken by a new patient, including any unsafe combinations.

4.5.6 The impact of the physical world on rule expression

As stated in Section 4.1.5, each rule statement referring to information about the physical world needs to be worded differently depending on the properties of the physical world object(s) it refers to.

4.5.6.1 Mandatory and optional attributes and relationships

The fact that some attributes and relationships of physical world objects are mandatory, while some are optional, affects the way in which rule statements referring to those attributes or relationships must be expressed.

For example, since not every person has a date of entry into Australia (many were born there!), any rule statement referring to that date must be worded to allow for the possibility that a person may not have such a date, as in R66 or R67:

R66. Each application for employment must *specify* the date of entry into Australia *of* the applicant if that applicant *was* not *born in* Australia[12].

R67. Each application for employment must *specify* the date of entry into Australia (if any) *of* the applicant.

Contrast these rule statements with R68.

R68. Each application for employment must *specify* the date of birth *of* the applicant.

4.5.6.2 Single-valued and multi-valued attributes and relationships

Any rule statement that refers to an attribute or relationship of a physical world object should be formulated to take account of whether that attribute or relationship is necessarily single-valued or may be multi-valued. For example, a rule statement referring to an applicant's date of birth can use the noun phrase 'the date of birth *of* the applicant'. By contrast, a rule statement referring to an applicant's medical condition(s) must use either 'the medical conditions *of* the applicant' or 'one of the medical conditions *of* the applicant' rather than 'the medical condition *of* the applicant'.

---

[12]The SBVR convention is to mark proper names (as well as literals such as references to textual values, quantities, dates, and times) using a double underline.

4.5.6.3 Variant and invariant attributes and relationships

Any rule statement that refers to a variant attribute or relationship may need to be worded to take that into account: for example,

R69. Each <u>application for life insurance</u>
    must *specify* the <u>weight</u> *of* the <u>applicant</u> *at* the <u>time of application</u>.

The phrase '*at* the <u>time of application</u>' is clearly not necessary in a rule statement referring to an invariant attribute such as the applicant's date of birth.

4.6 RULES GOVERNING OTHER BUSINESS PROCESSES

Of course, an organization performs many other business processes in addition to collecting data about its operational environment. These processes are also governed by rules, which can be categorized as follows:

1. those prohibiting a process from occurring in certain circumstances;
2. those placing an obligation on a process to occur in specific situations;
3. those determining what action a process is to take in specific situations.

Rules that restrict the circumstances in which a process can occur (referred to in this book as ***activity restriction rules***[13]) include the following:

1. those that limit a process to a particular time period: for example, online check-in for a flight can only take place in the time period from 24 h before the scheduled departure time of that flight until 30 min before departure of a domestic flight or 90 min before departure of an international flight;
2. those that prohibit a process during a particular time period: for example, the cabin crew must not serve meals or refreshments
    a. after pushback from the gate until the seatbelt signs have been switched off,
    b. during descent and landing, or
    c. during turbulence;
3. those that prohibit a process from occurring unless some event or other process has previously occurred or some prerequisite condition exists: for example, a passenger may board a flight only if the aircraft is ready for boarding and that passenger
    a. has checked in for that flight,
    b. has undergone security screening, and
    c. presents a boarding pass that specifies the number and departure date of that flight:
    in addition, a passenger may board an international flight only if that passenger
    d. has undergone departure control, and
    e. presents a passport that specifies that passenger's name, bears a likeness of that passenger, and expires at least 6 months after the departure date of that flight.

---

[13]They are referred to as activity restriction rules rather than process restriction rules since they can govern activities other than business processes, as we shall see in Section 4.8.

Rules that place an obligation on a business process to occur in specific situations (referred to in this book as **_activity obligation rules_**[14]) ideally require that process to occur within a maximum time after a particular event (such as the completion of some other process): for example,

1. A service level agreement may dictate that certain events must be responded to within a particular time period: for example, each incoming paper form must be processed within 1 business day of receipt of that form.
2. A reorder process must be performed before midnight on any day that the stock level of a spare part or consumable drops below the reorder point for that item.
3. Weekly or monthly processing must be performed during the business day following the completion of the relevant week or month respectively, whereas quarterly or end of financial year processing must be performed during the 5 business days following the completion of the relevant quarter or financial year respectively.
4. A customer may be required to respond to an offer before a certain date to qualify for a particular product or discount.

Less satisfactory are those that merely require a business process to occur as soon as practical after a particular event: the possibility of such rules cannot be entirely ruled out.

Rules that determine what action a business process is to take in specific situations are referred to in this book as **_process decision rules_**[15]: for example,

1. A ticket validation process occurring as a passenger exits a station may be programmed to capture a ticket on which no more journeys can be made but return any other ticket.
2. A motor vehicle insurance policy application process may increase the premium (or reject the application) if provided with information about the vehicle, driver, or garaging location that increases the risk of a claim.

A detailed taxonomy of rules governing business processes is provided in Section 4.9.3.

4.7 RULES GOVERNING WHICH PARTIES CAN PERFORM BUSINESS PROCESSES

Some rules govern the parties (individuals or organizations) or roles that are allowed to perform a business process or use information. These rules are rarely in terms of specific individuals, being more often in terms of roles that may be played by parties (e.g., The Captain, The First Officer, The Chief Flight Attendant). Other rules, however, may refer to organizations: either specific departments within the business (e.g., The Purchasing Department) or specific external organizations (businesses or specific government departments).

Consider the rules encountered so far in this chapter: none of these rules requires knowledge of who is supplying the data or performing the process to determine whether the rule has been violated. For

---

[14]Since these rules may be relevant to activities other than business processes, they are referred to as activity obligation rules rather than process obligation rules.
[15]These rules are not relevant to activities other than business processes, so are referred to as process decision rules rather than activity decision rules.

example, anyone can fill in a flight booking request and confirmation online provided they have a credit card or can make an electronic payment; any person can pass through an entry barrier at a train station if that person presents a current ticket valid for travel from that station, on that day, and at that time.

There are, however, restrictions on who can perform some processes or activities or play some roles. These may be based on age, as in the following:

1. A person who is less than 2 years of age is prohibited from traveling alone by air.
2. A person who is 70 years of age or older is prohibited from obtaining travel insurance with some (if not all) insurance companies.

Alternatively, a restriction may be based on some other physical characteristic or capability, as in the following:

1. A cabin crew member[16] must be at least 160 cm (5′3″) tall.
2. A passenger who is unable to open an aircraft door in an emergency is prohibited from being allocated to a seat in an exit row.

For an activity requiring particular skills and/or involving physical or financial risks, a person may only perform that activity if that person has been certified as having been appropriately trained, tested, and certified in the appropriate skills, as in the following:

1. A person who does not hold a current commercial pilot license is prohibited from being rostered on a flight crew.
2. A person is prohibited from being rostered on a flight crew if that person does not hold type endorsements appropriate to all aircraft types to be flown by that flight crew.
3. A person who does not hold a current command endorsement is prohibited from being rostered as pilot in command on a flight crew.

It should be clear that compliance or non-compliance with each of these rules depends on who is being proposed for the process or activity. For example, I can obtain travel insurance since I am less than 70 years of age, and be allocated to an exit row seat in compliance since I can open an aircraft door in an emergency, while my mother can do neither. And neither of us can be rostered on a flight crew, whereas there are plenty of people who are qualified to be so rostered.

Some situations require separation of responsibilities, in that the same person (or organization) is prohibited from performing two activities. For example, the activities of disarming an aircraft door and checking that that door is disarmed are prohibited from being performed by the same cabin crew member.[17]

Still other situations require that the person (or organization) performing the second of two activities must be the same as the person (or organization) who performed the first of those activities. For example, the flight crew member who signs the pre-flight check report must be the same flight crew member who performed the pre-flight check documented in that pre-flight check report.

Finally, there are rules that define the responsibility of particular parties or roles for performing certain processes or paying certain fees, duties, or taxes.

---

[16]'Cabin crew member' is now the preferred term in some parts of the airline industry for persons previously known as 'flight attendants'.

[17]'Arming' of aircraft doors after closure but before takeoff ensures that, if a door is opened after a crash or emergency landing, an escape slide automatically inflates. On landing, of course, all doors must be disarmed.

A detailed taxonomy of rules governing which parties can perform business processes is provided in Section 4.9.4.

4.8 RULES GOVERNING HUMAN ACTIVITIES OTHER THAN BUSINESS PROCESSES

An organization may require rules governing activities by customers (or others) that cannot be characterized as business processes. These rules can be categorized as follows:

1. those restricting when and where an activity may occur (e.g., an airline passenger must not operate any electronic device
   a. after pushback from the gate until the seatbelt signs have been switched off, nor
   b. during descent and landing);
2. those completely prohibiting an activity (e.g., an airline passenger must not smoke at any time during a flight or during embarkation or disembarkation).

These are often overlooked by business rules projects, since they are rarely amenable to automation. If the purpose of a business rules project is to catalog rules to be automated, such omission is justified, but, if the project purpose is to catalog all rules that govern an organization or some functional area thereof, these rules should either be included or explicitly stated as being out of scope.

A detailed taxonomy of rules governing all activities is provided in Section 4.9.3.

4.9 A COMPLETE TAXONOMY OF RULES

It turns out that there are really only four fundamental categories of rule, each with fewer than a dozen subcategories. This taxonomy is set out in full in this section; each rule category and subcategory is referenced in Chapter 9, which sets out which template(s) should be used for each subcategory.

The fundamental rule types are

1. *definitional rules*: each of these rules constrains how we define a construct created or used by the organization or the industry within which it operates;
2. *data rules*: each of these rules (all of which are operative rules) constrains the data included in a transaction (a form or message) or a persistent dataset (e.g., a database record);
3. *activity rules*: each of these rules (all of which are operative rules) constrains the operation of one or more business processes or other activities;
4. *party rules*: each of these rules (all of which are operative rules) restricts the parties who can perform a process or activity or play a role.

A critical step in writing a set of quality rule statements is correctly classifying the rule that you are trying to write. So, how do we know if we have a definitional rule, a data rule, an activity rule, or a party rule? The best way to establish this is by a process of elimination:

1. If the rule cannot be violated, it is a *definitional rule*.
2. If the outcome of testing the rule depends on who is involved (i.e., if one person performs the action, the rule is complied with, but if another person performs the action, the rule is contravened), the rule is a *party rule*.

3. If the rule is concerned only with the presence or absence of one or more data items, how many instances of a data item there are, or the content of one or more data items, the rule is a ***data rule***.
4. If none of the above, the rule is an ***activity rule***.

4.9.1 Definitional rules

Definitional rules can in turn be categorized as

1. ***formal term definitions***, which define business terms formally:
   a. ***formal intensional definitions*** (described in Section 4.9.1.1.1)
   b. ***formal extensional definitions*** (described in Section 4.9.1.1.2)
   c. ***symbolic literal definitions*** (described in Section 4.9.1.1.3);
2. ***categorization scheme enumerations***, which define members of ***categorization schemes*** (described in Section 4.9.1.2);
3. ***category transition constraints***, which define constraints on the transitions between categories in a categorization scheme (described in Section 4.9.1.3);
4. ***complex concept structure rules***, which define constraints on the components of complex concepts:
   a. ***complex concept cardinality rules*** (described in Section 4.9.1.4.1)
   b. ***complex concept equivalence rules*** (described in Section 4.9.1.4.2)
   c. ***complex concept set constraints*** (described in Section 4.9.1.4.3);
5. ***valid value definitions***, which define the valid values of measures (described in Section 4.9.1.5);
6. ***data calculation rules***, which define algorithms or formulae for named quantities or conversion factors between units:
   a. ***data calculation algorithms*** (described in Section 4.9.1.6.1)
   b. ***conversion factor definitions*** (described in Section 4.9.1.6.2);
7. ***standard format definitions***, which define standard formats for data items (described in Section 4.9.1.7).

4.9.1.1 Formal term definitions

A ***formal term definition*** defines a particular business term in a formal manner.

4.9.1.1.1 Formal intensional definitions

A ***formal intensional definition*** defines the subject business term using an ***intensional definition***: one that cites both a ***hypernym*** (a term that refers to a superset of the set referred to by the original term) and the characteristics that distinguish members of the set referred to by the original term: for example,

R70. A senior passenger
  is by definition
  a passenger whose age *is at least* 70 years *at* the time of travel.[18]

R71. An employer *of* a person
  is by definition
  an organization that *employs* that person.

---

[18]Note that the SBVR proposes alternative formulations for structural (definitional) rule statements, as described in Section 3.3.8.4 in Chapter 3. However, I do not recommend those formulations for practical business use, for the reasons given in that section.

4.9.1.1.2 Formal extensional definitions

A *formal extensional definition* defines the subject business term by using an *extensional definition*: one that lists a complete set of *hyponyms* (terms that refer to subsets of the set referred to by the original term): for example,

R72. An immediate family member *of* a person
is by definition
a parent, sibling, spouse, or child *of* that person.

4.9.1.1.3 Symbolic literal definitions

A *symbolic literal definition* defines the subject business term using one or more *literals*: for example,

R73. End of financial year
is by definition
June 30.[19]

R74. A calendar year
is by definition
365 days or 366 days *from* a January 1 *to* the following December 31.

4.9.1.2 Categorization scheme enumerations

A *categorization scheme enumeration* defines the members of a *categorization scheme* that is both *mutually exclusive* (i.e., no individual object can be a member of more than one category in the categorization scheme) and *jointly exhaustive* (i.e., each member of the class with which the categorization scheme is associated belongs to a category in the categorization scheme).

One way of expressing this type of rule is in terms of subsets of the categorized term, by way of a formal extensional definition (already discussed in Section 4.9.1.1.2): for example,

R75. A person
is by definition
either an adult or a minor.

R76. A payment
is by definition
one of the following: a cash payment, a credit card payment, or an
electronic funds transfer payment.

Another way of expressing this type of rule is in terms of allowed values of a category attribute: for example,

R77. The gender *of* a person
is by definition
either male or female.

R78. The status *of* an employee
is by definition
one of the following: probational, permanent, or temporary.

---

[19]This is the case in Australia; other dates apply in other countries.

4.9.1.3 Category transition constraints

A *category transition constraint* specifies allowed or disallowed transitions between categories or statuses: for example,

R79. A transition *of* the status *of* a customer *from* current *to* prospect
is by definition
impossible.

4.9.1.4 Complex concept structure rules

A *complex concept structure rule* defines a particular constraint on one or more components of a complex concept.

4.9.1.4.1 Complex concept cardinality rules

A *complex concept cardinality rule* defines the number of (or minimum and/or maximum number of) components of a particular type within a particular concept: for example,

R80. A flight
has by definition
exactly one destination port.

4.9.1.4.2 Complex concept equivalence rules

A *complex concept equivalence rule* defines a pair of components within a particular concept that are of necessity the same: for example,

R81. The destination city *of* the last or only return flight *of* a return journey
is by definition
the same as the origin city of the first or only outgoing flight *of* that return journey.

4.9.1.4.3 Complex concept set constraints

A *complex concept set constraint* defines two sets of components within a particular concept that must be identical: for example,

R82. The set of passengers
booked on each flight
specified in a flight booking confirmation
is by definition
the same as the set of passengers
booked on each other flight
specified in that flight booking confirmation.

4.9.1.5 Valid value definitions

A *valid value definition* defines the valid values of a particular measure as a range or (occasionally) as a list of discrete values: for example,

R83. Water temperature
is by definition
at least 0°C and *at most* 100°C.

4.9.1.6 Data calculation rules

A *data calculation rule* defines the algorithm or formula for a particular quantity or a conversion factor between two units.

4.9.1.6.1 Data calculation algorithms

A *data calculation algorithm* defines how a particular quantity or amount (whether for operational purposes, such as a fee, or for business intelligence purposes, such as a performance measure) is calculated: for example,

R84. The year-to-date sales total *for* a product *on* a date
    is by definition *calculated as*
    the sum of the extension *for* each order line *for* that product that
    • *has* an order date *within* the same calendar year *as* that date and
    • *was* not *cancelled within* the same calendar year *as* that date.

4.9.1.6.2 Conversion factor definitions

A *conversion factor definition* defines a conversion factor between two units of measurement: for example,

R85. 1 ft
    is by definition *equal to*
    12 in.

4.9.1.7 Standard format definitions

A *standard format definition* defines the standard format for data items of a particular type in terms of individual characters (as in R86) and/or component data items (as in R87): for example,

R86. A valid product code
    is by definition *composed of*
    exactly 2 letters followed by 6 digits.
R87. A valid flight number
    is by definition *composed of*
    a valid airline code followed by up to 4 digits.

4.9.2 Data rules

Data rules can in turn be categorized as

1. *data cardinality rules*, which place restrictions on the maximum or minimum number of occurrences of data items:
   a. *mandatory data rules* (described in Section 4.9.2.1.1), of the following subcategories:
      i. *mandatory data item rules*
      ii. *mandatory option selection rules*
      iii. *mandatory group rules*
   b. *prohibited data rules* (described in Section 4.9.2.1.2)
   c. *maximum cardinality rules* (described in Section 4.9.2.1.3)
   d. *multiple data rules* (described in Section 4.9.2.1.4)
   e. *dependent cardinality rules* (described in Section 4.9.2.1.5);

2. *data content rules*, which place restrictions on the values contained in data items:
   a. *value set rules* (described in Section 4.9.2.2.1)
   b. *range rules* (described in Section 4.9.2.2.2)
   c. *equality rules* (described in Section 4.9.2.2.3)
   d. *uniqueness constraints* (described in Section 4.9.2.2.4)
   e. *data consistency rules* (described in Section 4.9.2.2.5)
   f. *temporal data constraints* (described in Section 4.9.2.2.6), of the following subcategories:
      i. *simple temporal data constraints*
      ii. *temporal data non-overlap constraints*
      iii. *temporal data completeness constraints*
      iv. *temporal data inclusion constraints*
      v. *temporal single record constraints*
   g. *spatial data constraints* (described in Section 4.9.2.2.7)
   h. *data item format rules* (described in Section 4.9.2.2.8);
3. *data update rules*, which either prohibit update of a data item or place restrictions on the new value of a data item in terms of the existing value:
   a. *data update prohibition rules* (described in Section 4.9.2.3.1)
   b. *state transition constraints* (described in Section 4.9.2.3.2)
   c. *monotonic transition constraints* (described in Section 4.9.2.3.3).

4.9.2.1 Data cardinality rules

A *data cardinality rule* requires the presence or absence of a data item and/or places a restriction on the maximum or minimum number of occurrences of a data item.

4.9.2.1.1 Mandatory data rules

A *mandatory data rule* mandates the presence of data: that is, requires that a data item be entered in a transaction form or present in a message, or that a persistent data record include a value for a data item. There are three subcategories of mandatory data rule:

1. a *mandatory data item rule* requires that a particular data item be present: for example,

R88. Each flight booking request
must *specify* exactly one departure date.

R89. Each flight booking confirmation
must *specify* at least one passenger name.

R90. Each flight booking confirmation *for* a return journey
must *specify* exactly two flights.

R91. Each flight booking confirmation
must *specify* exactly one travel class *for* each flight.

R92. Each flight booking confirmation
must *specify* exactly one set of passport details *for* each passenger
if any flight *specified in* that flight booking confirmation *is international*.

R93. Each combination of departure date, flight number, and departure city
must *be allocated* exactly one departure time.

2. a ***mandatory option selection rule*** requires that one of a set of pre-defined options be specified: for example,

R94. Each flight booking request
must *specify* whether it *is for* a return journey, a one-way journey, or a multi-stop journey.

R95. Each flight booking request
must *specify* whether or not the travel dates *specified in* that flight booking request *are* moveable.

3. a ***mandatory group rule*** requires that at least one of a group of data items be present: for example,

R96. Each flight booking confirmation
must *specify* a mobile phone number, an e-mail address, or both.

R97. Each flight booking confirmation
must *specify* a credit card or an electronic funds transfer payment receipt but not both.

R98. Each flight booking confirmation
must *specify* exactly one of the following:
a postal address, an e-mail address, or a fax number.

4.9.2.1.2 Prohibited data rules

A ***prohibited data rule*** mandates the absence of some data item in a particular situation: for example,

R99. A flight booking request *for* a one-way journey
must not *specify* a return date.

4.9.2.1.3 Maximum cardinality rules

A ***maximum cardinality rule*** places an upper limit (usually but not necessarily one) on how many instances of a particular data item there may be: for example,

R100. A flight booking confirmation
must not *specify* more than one insurance option.

R101. A flight booking confirmation
must not *specify* more than one frequent flier membership
for any one passenger.

R102. A combination of departure date, flight number, and departure city
must not *be allocated* more than one passenger
for any one seat number.

4.9.2.1.4 Multiple data rules

A ***multiple data rule*** mandates the presence of two or more instances of a particular data item in a particular situation: for example,

R103. Each flight booking confirmation *for* a return journey
must *specify* at least two flights.

4.9.2.1.5 Dependent cardinality rules

A *dependent cardinality rule* mandates how many of a particular data item must be present based on the value of another data item: for example,

R104. The number of <u>passenger names</u>
  specified in each <u>flight booking confirmation</u>
must *be equal to*
the <u>number of passengers</u>
  specified in the <u>flight booking request</u>
  that *gives rise to* that <u>flight booking confirmation</u>.

4.9.2.2 Data content rules

A *data content rule* places a restriction on the values contained in a data item or set of data items (rather than whether they must be present and how many there may or must be).

4.9.2.2.1 Value set rules

A *value set rule* requires either

1. that the content of a data item be (or not be) one of a particular set of values (either a fixed set, as in R105, or a set that may change over time, as in R106), or
2. that the content of a combination of data items match or not match a corresponding combination in a set of records, as in R107.

R105. The <u>travel class</u> *specified in* each <u>flight booking request</u>
  must be 'first class', 'business class', 'premium economy class', or 'economy class'.
R106. The <u>origin city</u> specified in each <u>flight booking request</u>
  must *be* one of the <u>cities</u> served by the <u>airline</u>.

R107 illustrates how a value set rule can be used to ensure that the values contained in two or more data items form a valid combination.

R107. The combination of <u>place name</u> and <u>postal code</u>
  included in the <u>postal address</u> (if any)
  specified in each <u>insurance application</u>
must *be* one of the combinations of <u>place name</u> and <u>postal code</u>
  allocated by the <u>postal authority</u>
  of the <u>country</u>
  in which that <u>postal address</u> *is located*.

4.9.2.2.2 Range rules

A *range rule* requires that the content of a data item be a value within a particular inclusive or exclusive single-bounded (as in R108) or double-bounded (as in R109) range: for example,

R108. The <u>number of passengers</u> *specified in* each <u>flight booking request</u>
  must *be at least* 1.
R109. The <u>number of passengers</u> *specified in* each <u>flight booking request</u>
  must *be at least* 1 and *at most* 9.
R110. The <u>departure date</u> *specified in* each <u>flight booking request</u>
  must *be no earlier than* <u>today</u>.

4.9.2.2.3 Equality rules

An *equality rule* requires that the content of a data item be the same as or not the same as that of some other data item: for example,

R111. The <u>origin city</u>
    of the <u>outgoing flight</u>
    specified in each <u>flight booking confirmation</u>
  must *be the same as* the <u>origin city</u>
    specified in the <u>flight booking request</u>
    that *gives rise to* that <u>flight booking confirmation</u>.

R112. The <u>destination city</u> *specified in* each <u>flight booking request</u>
  must *be different from* the <u>origin city</u> *specified in* that <u>flight booking request</u>.

4.9.2.2.4 Uniqueness constraints

A *uniqueness constraint* requires that the content of a data item (or combination or set[20] of data items) be different from that of the corresponding data item(s) in the same or other records or transactions: for example,

R113. The <u>record locator</u>
    allocated to each <u>flight booking confirmation</u>
  must *be different from* the <u>record locator</u>
    allocated to any other <u>flight booking confirmation</u>.

R114. The combination of
    <u>departure date</u>, <u>flight number</u>, <u>departure city</u>, and <u>seat number</u>
    specified in each <u>seat allocation</u>
  must *be different from*
  the combination of
    <u>departure date</u>, <u>flight number</u>, <u>departure city</u>, and <u>seat number</u>
    specified in any other <u>seat allocation</u>.

4.9.2.2.5 Data consistency rules

A *data consistency rule* requires the content of multiple data items to be consistent with each other, other than as provided for by a value set rule, range rule, or equality rule: for example,

R115. The combination of <u>start date</u> and <u>end date</u>
    specified in each <u>leave application</u>
  must *be* such that the <u>end date</u> *is no earlier than* the <u>start date</u>.

R116. The sum of the <u>shares</u> *held by* the <u>proprietors</u> *of* each <u>real property parcel</u> must *be equal to* 1.

4.9.2.2.6 Temporal data constraints

A *temporal data constraint* constrains one or more *temporal data* items (data items that represent time points or time periods). There are various subcategories of temporal constraint.

A *simple temporal data constraint* requires that a particular date or time fall within a certain temporal range: for example,

---

[20]The difference between a combination and a set of data items is discussed in Section 7.2.3.2.2 in Chapter 7.

R117. The return date (if any) *specified in* each flight booking request
must *be no earlier than*
the departure date *specified in* that flight booking request.

Other temporal constraints prescribe or prohibit relationships between time periods. The following rule statements illustrate the most common of these constraints:

1. In many situations there is a ***temporal data non-overlap constraint***—a requirement that the time periods specified in a set of records (e.g., an employee's leave records) do not overlap each other: for example,

R118. The time period *specified in* each employee leave record
must not *overlap*
the time period *specified in* any other employee leave record
for the same employee.

2. There is often also a ***temporal data completeness constraint***—a requirement that the time periods specified in a set of records (e.g., an employee's pay records) be contiguous and between them completely span some other time period (in this case that employee's employment period): for example,

R119. Each day *within* the employment period
specified in each employee record
must *be within*
the time period *specified in* exactly one employee pay record
for the same employee.

Note that the 'exactly one' determiner implies the corresponding temporal data non-overlap constraint. If the non-overlap constraint does not apply but the completeness constraint applies, the determiner 'at least one' should be used instead.

3. There is often also a ***temporal data inclusion constraint***—a requirement that the time periods specified in a set of records (e.g., an employee's leave and pay records) do not fall outside some other time period (in this case that employee's employment period): for example,

R120. Each day *within* the time period
specified in each employee leave record
must *be within*
the time period *specified in* the employment record
for the same employee.

4. A less obvious requirement—raised in (Date, Darwen, & Lorentzos, Temporal Data and the Relational Model, 2003)—arises from the fact that it is theoretically possible to create two records with two contiguous time periods and all other content identical. For example, if Employee #123 was regraded on 1 January 2010 and 5 April 2011, there should be a single employee grade record for Employee #123 that covers the period 1 January 2010 to 4 April 2011. There is of course nothing to stop us recording this situation using two otherwise identical employee grade records covering the periods 1 January 2010 to 4 April 2010 and 5 April 2010 to 4 April 2011. However, to do so causes a variety of problems: for example, a query as to which employees changed grade in April 2010 would erroneously include Employee #123. Creation of such multiple records can be prevented by requiring (in this case) that a new grade record be created only for a change of grade, as in R121. Date, Darwen, & Lorentzos (2003) refer to such multiple records as "circumlocution"; given

the fact that these constraints require a temporal state of affairs to be recorded using a single record rather than multiple records, I refer to them as ***temporal single record constraints***.

R121. Each <u>grade</u> *specified in* an <u>employee grade record</u>
must *be different from*
the <u>grade</u> *specified in* the latest of the earlier <u>employee grade records</u>
for the same <u>employee</u>.

5. Finally, there may be a requirement to restrict a date to a working day (typically but not necessarily any day other than a Saturday, Sunday, or public holiday). An example of such a ***day type constraint*** is

R122. The <u>payment due date</u> *specified in* each <u>invoice</u>
must *be* a <u>working day</u>.

This, of course, requires a ***formal term definition*** to define '<u>working day</u>'.

4.9.2.2.7 Spatial data constraints

A ***spatial data constraint*** prescribes or prohibits relationships between data items representing spatial properties (points, line segments or polygons): for example,

R123. The <u>polygon</u>
that *constitutes* each <u>individual parcel</u>
in a <u>real estate subdivision</u>
must not *overlap*
the <u>polygon</u>
that *constitutes* any other <u>individual parcel</u>
in any <u>real estate subdivision</u>.

R123 is an example of a non-overlap constraint (analogous to a ***temporal data non-overlap constraint***) in that it requires that the polygons specified in a dataset do not overlap each other. Other types of spatial data constraints governing polygon data are

1. completeness constraints, which require that the polygons specified in a dataset are contiguous and between them completely span some other polygon;
2. inclusion constraints, which require that a polygon specified in a dataset does not fall outside some other polygon.

Spatial data constraints can also govern line segment data. For example, a line segment specified in a dataset may be

1. obliged to be entirely (or at least partly) within a polygon
2. obliged to be entirely (or at least partly) outside a polygon
3. obliged to intersect (or at least meet) another line segment
4. prohibited from intersecting or meeting another line segment.

Spatial data constraints can also govern point data. For example, a point specified in a dataset may be

1. obliged to be within a polygon
2. obliged to be outside a polygon
3. obliged to be on a line segment
4. prohibited from being on a line segment.

4.9.2.2.8 Data item format rules

A *data item format rule* specifies the required format of a data item: for example,

R124. The <u>mobile phone number</u> (if any)
　　　specified in each <u>flight booking confirmation</u>
　　must *be* a valid <u>phone number</u>.

A data item format rule generally requires a corresponding **standard format definition** to define the actual format of the data item: for example, R124 requires R125[21]:

R125. A valid <u>phone number</u>
　　is by definition
　　composed of from 9 to 12 <u>digits</u>.

4.9.2.3 Data update rules

A *data update rule* either prohibits update of a data item or places restrictions on the new value of a data item in terms of its existing value.

4.9.2.3.1 Data update prohibition rules

A *data update prohibition rule* prohibits update of a particular data item or set of data items: for example,

R126. A <u>data item</u> *in* a <u>financial transaction</u>
　　must not *be updated*.

In particular, a data update prohibition rule can be used to specify that a recorded relationship is **non-transferable**: for example,

R127. An <u>order</u>
　　must not *be transferred from* one <u>customer</u> *to* another <u>customer</u>.

4.9.2.3.2 State transition constraints

A *state transition constraint* limits the changes in a data item to a set of valid transitions: for example,

R128. The <u>marital status</u> *of* an <u>employee</u>
　　may *be updated to* <u>never married</u>
　　only if the <u>marital status</u>
　　　that *is currently recorded for* that <u>employee</u>
　　　is <u>unknown</u>.

4.9.2.3.3 Monotonic transition constraints

A *monotonic transition constraint* requires that a numeric value either only increase or only decrease: for example, some employment arrangements prohibit a reduction in a person's hourly pay rate:

R129. The <u>hourly pay rate</u> *of* an <u>employee</u>
　　must not *be decreased*.

---

[21]An exception may be made (i.e., the standard format definition may be omitted) for axiomatic terms such as <u>unsigned integer</u>.

4.9.3 Activity rules

Activity rules can in turn be categorized as

1. *activity restriction rules*, which restrict a business process or other activity in some way:
    a. *activity time limit rules* (described in Section 4.9.3.1.1)
    b. *activity exclusion period rules* (described in Section 4.9.3.1.2)
    c. *activity pre-condition rules* (described in Section 4.9.3.1.3)
    d. *activity prohibition rules* (described in Section 4.9.3.1.4)
    e. *activity conflict rules* (described in Section 4.9.3.1.5)
    f. *information retention rules* (described in Section 4.9.3.1.6);
2. *activity obligation rules* (described in Section 4.9.3.2);
3. *process decision rules* (described in Section 4.9.3.3).

4.9.3.1 Activity restriction rules

An *activity restriction rule* restricts a business process or other activity in some way.

4.9.3.1.1 Activity time limit rules

An *activity time limit rule* restricts a business process or other activity to within a particular time period: for example,

R130. Online check-in *for* a flight
    may *occur*
        only *during* the 24 h *before* the departure time *of* that flight.
R131. Acknowledgment *of* an order
    must *occur*
        during the 24 h *after* the receipt *of* that order.

4.9.3.1.2 Activity exclusion period rules

An *activity exclusion period rule* prohibits a business process or other activity during a particular time period: for example,

R132. Online check-in *for* a flight
    must not *occur*
        earlier than 24 h *before* the departure time *of* that flight.[22]
R133. An electronic device
    must not *be operated on* an aircraft
    at any time *after* pushback[23] *of* that aircraft
    until a cabin crew member *advises* that
        electronic devices *may be operated safely.*

4.9.3.1.3 Activity pre-condition rules

An *activity pre-condition rule* prohibits a business process or other activity unless some other activity or event has previously occurred or some prerequisite condition exists: for example,

---

[22]Note that this rule statement is an alternative way of expressing the same rule as R130.
[23]'Pushback' is the reversal of an aircraft from the gate before taxying and takeoff.

R134. A passenger
may *board* a flight
only after that passenger *checks in for* that flight.

4.9.3.1.4 Activity prohibition rules

An *activity prohibition rule* prohibits a business process or other activity if some event or other process has previously occurred or some dangerous or illegal condition exists: for example,

R135. A driver
must not *operate* any vehicle
if that driver *is intoxicated.*

4.9.3.1.5 Activity conflict rules

An *activity conflict rule* restricts the simultaneous occurrence of multiple processes or other activities: for example,

R136. A folder
must not *be renamed*
while any file *within* that folder *is open for editing.*

4.9.3.1.6 Information retention rules

An *information retention rule* defines the minimum period for which a particular type of information is retained[24]: for example,

R137. Information
that *is relevant to* Australian income tax payment *in* a financial year
must not *be deleted*
during the 7 years *after* the end *of* that financial year.

4.9.3.2 Activity obligation rules

An *activity obligation rule* requires a business process or other activity to occur either within a maximum time after a particular event (such as the completion of some other process) or when particular conditions apply: for example,

R138. Each electronic device that *is being used on* an aircraft
must *be switched off*
no later than 1 min *after* the start *of* the descent *of* that aircraft.

4.9.3.3 Process decision rules

A *process decision rule* determines what action a business process or device is to take in specific situations: for example,

R139. Each ticket barrier
must *retain* each ticket that *is* not *valid for* any more journeys.

---

[24]It may not be obvious that this is an activity restriction rule, but it is a prohibition of the deletion or destruction of information.

4.9.4 Party rules

Party rules can in turn be categorized as

1. *party restriction rules* (described in Section 4.9.4.1);
2. *role separation rules* (described in Section 4.9.4.2);
3. *role binding rules* (described in Section 4.9.4.3);
4. *information access rules* (described in Section 4.9.4.4);
5. *responsibility rules* (described in Section 4.9.4.5).

4.9.4.1 Party restriction rules

A *party restriction rule* places restrictions on who can perform some processes or activities or play some roles, based on age, some other physical characteristic or capability, or training, testing, and certification in the appropriate skills: for example,

R140. A person
may *travel alone*
only if the age *of* that person *is at least* 2 years.

R141. A person
may *be employed as* a cabin crew member
only if the height *of* that person *is* at least 160 cm.

R142. A passenger
may *be allocated to* a seat *in* an exit row
only if that passenger *is able to open an aircraft door.*

R143. A person
may *be rostered on* a flight crew
only if that person *holds* an airline transport pilot license
that *is current*
and a type endorsement
that *is current for* each aircraft type *to be flown by* that flight crew.

4.9.4.2 Role separation rules

A *role separation rule* prohibits the same party from performing two activities: for example,

R144. The cabin crew member
who *checks* that an aircraft door *is disarmed*
must not *be* the same cabin crew member
who *disarmed* that aircraft door.

4.9.4.3 Role binding rules

A *role binding rule* requires that the party performing the second of two activities be the same as the party who performed the first of those activities: for example,

R145. The flight crew member
who *signs* the pre-flight check report
must *be* the same flight crew member
who *performed* the pre-flight check
documented in that pre-flight check report.

4.9.4.4 Information access rules

An *information access rule* defines who can view, create, or update particular information: for example,

R146. The <u>leave records</u> *of* an <u>employee</u>
may *be viewed by* only
    that <u>employee</u>,
    the <u>supervisor</u> *of* that <u>employee</u>,
    or a <u>human resources officer</u>.

4.9.4.5 Responsibility rules

A *responsibility rule* defines who is responsible for performing a particular process or liable for a particular fee, duty, or tax: for example,

R147. <u>Stamp duty</u>[25] *on* a <u>real property transfer</u>
must *be paid by* the <u>parties receiving</u>.

4.10 SUMMARY

While organizations do not need to state rules about the physical world in which they operate, they often need rules about the capture and retention of data about the physical world. These rules

1. need to ensure that data captured does not describe an impossible physical world situation;
2. need to be worded so as to take account of the properties of the physical world;
3. should not be written as if they govern the physical world itself.

Constructs created by the organization or the industry within which it operates are defined using definitional rules. As well as these definitional rules, an organization requires operative rules to govern not only the capture and retention of data but business processes and human activities other than business processes. Some of these rules are specific as to which parties or roles can perform particular processes.

The legislative and regulatory environment in which an organization operates governs the operations of that organization and its employees, and may also govern its customers, suppliers, and/or partners. This environment should not be overlooked as a source of operative rules.

Each major class of rules (definitional rules, data rules, activity rules, and party rules) includes a number of subclasses that define constructs or govern data or activities in particular ways. This taxonomy, set out in full in Section 4.9, is referenced in Chapter 9, which sets out which template(s) should be used for each subcategory of rule.

---

[25]A tax levied by Australian states on parties undertaking real property (real estate) transactions.

The building blocks of natural language rule statements

The phrase 'natural language rule statement' is rather cumbersome; so, from this point on in this book, any reference to 'rule statement' should be taken to mean 'natural language rule statement'.

Each rule statement is a sentence in a natural language (English in the case of all the examples in the book). It therefore consists of words of various types (or *word classes*): *nouns*, *verbs*, etc. Depending on when and where you went to school, you may be well-versed in English grammar, in which case you may want to skip this section and move straight to Chapter 6, or you may need an introduction to (or refresh of) how these word classes can be used.

Linguists agree that it is difficult to define word classes. To quote David Crystal in (Crystal, 2006): "*Modern linguists are reluctant to use the notional definitions found in traditional grammar—such as a noun being the 'name of something'. The vagueness of these definitions has often been criticized: is* beauty *a 'thing'? Is not the adjective* red *also a 'name' of a color? To supplement definitions based on meaning, there is now a focus on the structural features that signal the way in which groups of words behave in a language*". As a result, although this book does attempt to define each relevant word class in terms of the types of real-world concepts that words in that class can *signify* (refer to), it also defines each word class in terms of its behavior: that is, the usage of words in that class by competent speakers or writers of English. In addition, each class is illustrated with examples of words in that class.

Of course, just to make matters even more confusing, many words belong to more than one word class. For example, 'right' may be a *noun* (as in "you have the right to remain silent"), an *adjective* ("you were right to say that"), an *adverb* ("you have done that right"), or a *verb* ("we tried to right the fallen signpost"). Matters are not helped by our tendency to reuse words in one class as if they were in another: 'mentor' was originally only a noun (as in "I am your mentor") but is now also used by some as a verb ("I want you to mentor him"). Verbs can also be reused as nouns: 'upgrade' was used as a verb (as in "I can upgrade you to business class") but is now also a noun ("bronze frequent flier members receive one complimentary upgrade each year").

Two techniques can be used to characterize word classes:

1. the word classes of other words that members of the word class may precede or follow: for example, the *articles* 'a', 'an', and 'the' can precede *nouns* but not *verbs*;
2. the *inflections* that members of the word class exhibit: that is, the changes that occur to those words in certain contexts.

Clearly, we cannot use the first technique alone, since to do so would involve circular definitions, each word class being defined in terms of other word classes. Fortunately, two of the word classes we need (*nouns* and *verbs*) exhibit unique inflections in English. This is indeed fortunate, since English nouns and verbs are far less inflected than those in most other Indo-European languages, in particular German and the Slavic languages (Bulgarian, Croatian, Polish, Russian, Serbian, etc.).

Of course, if the word class contains only a few words, it is possible to list those words. This is the case with *articles*: 'a', 'an', and 'the'.

Before we move on to examine each word class, remember that this book proposes a *constrained natural language*. This means that not all English words of any class are available for use in rule statements in the language proposed in this book. Words of a particular class may be excluded on account of some property (e.g., there are limitations on the use of nouns that are not *countable*, as described in Section 5.1.1). Alternatively, only a few words of a particular class may be employed (as with *determiners* and *pronouns*, described in Sections 5.4 and 5.8 respectively).

5.1 NOUNS

What is a *noun*? We could start by saying that it is a word (or words) that we can use to refer to one or more instances of a concept: that is, a person, organization, place, or concrete or abstract thing (such as an event, arrangement, quality, etc.): for example, 'author', 'government department', 'country', 'wide-body aircraft', 'payment', 'contract', 'weight'. As Crystal points out, this definition might lead some to exclude abstract nouns like 'beauty' or include adjectives like 'red'.

Fortunately, every English noun exhibits a behavioral characteristic that is exhibited only by nouns, namely we can refer to a quality, characteristic, property, circumstance, or asset of an object signified by a noun by way of a *suffix* indicating possession. For singular or plural nouns not ending in 's', this suffix is "'s" ("apostrophe s"), as in "author's" or "children's".[1] For singular or plural nouns ending in 's', the suffix is either "'s" (as in "Thomas's bags") or the apostrophe without the following 's' (as in "passengers' bags"). This inflection is referred to as the *genitive case* in studies of some languages (e.g., Latin, Greek, German, or the Slavic languages).

Unfortunately, some nouns only rarely take this form. However, there are alternative distinguishing behavioral characteristics of the various subclasses of English nouns that are discussed in the following sections.

5.1.1 Countable and non-countable nouns

A *countable noun* (or *count noun*) is a noun that can be meaningfully used after the word 'each'. For example, it makes sense to say "each customer ...", "each order ...", or "each business day", whereas it does not make sense to say "*each information ..." or "*each governance ..."[2]: 'customer', 'order', and 'business day' are therefore countable nouns, whereas 'information' and 'governance' are *non-countable nouns* (or *mass nouns*).

As described in (Finch, 2005), the following additional characteristics distinguish countable from non-countable nouns:

1. Each countable noun has both *singular* or *plural* forms (e.g., 'author', 'authors'), whereas a non-countable noun has only the one form: usually singular, as in the examples above, but occasionally plural: for example, 'goods'.[3]

---

[1]This is not to be confused with the "apostrophe s" that is a shortened form of 'is' as in "it's", "how's", "who's", "when's", or "where's", or a shortened form of 'us' as in "let's".
[2]Syntactically incorrect constructions are conventionally indicated by way of an initial asterisk.
[3]A *proper name* (as we shall see in Section 5.2) also has only the one form: again usually singular (e.g., 'Australia'), but occasionally plural (e.g., 'The United States').

2. A singular countable noun requires a preceding ***determiner*** (see Section 5.4) such as an ***article*** ('a', 'an', or 'the'), when used in a sentence. Thus "*author signs book" is an invalid statement[4], whereas "each author signs his book" is valid. By contrast, non-countable nouns need no preceding determiner when used in a sentence: in fact many determiners (in particular 'a' or 'an') are invalid before a non-countable noun. Thus "information is useful" is a valid statement, whereas "*an information is useful" is invalid.

3. Countable nouns (but not non-countable nouns) can be used after an ***indefinite article*** ('a' or 'an'). Thus "*an information" and "*a governance" are both invalid.

An additional distinction is that "how many ... are there" is only valid around a countable noun, whereas "how much ... is there" is only valid around a non-countable noun. Thus "how many customers are there" and "how much information is there" are valid, whereas "*how much customers is there" and "*how many information are there" are invalid.

Some nouns can be used in both countable and non-countable senses. For example, as pointed out in (Finch, 2005), in a restaurant we can order "a coffee", "two coffees", etc. so that the waiter brings the correct number ('coffee' here is countable), whereas in a supermarket we buy "coffee", not "*a coffee" or "*coffees" ('coffee' here is non-countable). Similarly, many nouns (in particular those signifying abstract concepts such as 'religion') may be used in both a non-countable sense (as in "religion plays a significant role in politics") and a countable sense (as in "representatives of each of the monotheistic religions attended").

5.1.2 Simple and compound nouns

Most of the example nouns listed so far in this chapter consist of only one word. For convenience we can refer to these as ***simple nouns***. A ***compound noun***, by contrast, consists of more than one word. There are various forms of compound noun, including

1. a simple noun preceded by one or more ***pre-modifiers***, each of which may be
   a. an ***adjectival*** (an ***adjective***[5] or a simple noun acting as an adjective): for example, 'business unit', 'domestic flight', 'group purchasing contract', 'electronic transfer payment receipt', or
   b. (occasionally) a ***cardinal number*** (e.g., 'one-way flight') or ***ordinal number***[6] (e.g., 'first-time buyer');
   the last or only noun in each such construction is known as the ***head noun***; in the examples above, the head nouns are 'unit', 'flight', 'contract', 'receipt', 'flight', and 'buyer' respectively;

2. a simple noun followed by a ***post-modifier***:
   a. an adjective: for example, 'Attorney General', 'court-martial',
   b. a ***preposition***[7] and another simple noun (e.g., 'date of birth', 'mother-in-law');
   in these constructions the first or only noun is the head noun; in the examples above, the head nouns are 'Attorney', 'court', 'date', and 'mother' respectively;

---

[4]This form (i.e., without determiners) is however valid as a ***fact type*** (see Section 6.3 in Chapter 6).
[5]See Section 5.5 for a definition of ***adjective***.
[6]See Sections 5.4.3.1 and 5.4.2.1 for definitions of ***cardinal number*** and ***ordinal number*** respectively.
[7]See Section 5.6 for a definition of ***preposition***.

3. (occasionally) two simple nouns joined by a ***conjunction***[8] (e.g., 'parent or guardian', 'terms and conditions'); in these constructions, each of the nouns is a head noun.

Occasionally, other word classes may be employed to act as nouns, as in 'management buy-out', in which 'buy out'—normally a ***phrasal verb***[9]—is being used as a noun.

Note that the words in a compound noun may be separated by spaces or hyphens. There are also compound nouns in which the constituent words are written without intervening spaces or hyphens: for example, 'lawsuit', 'checkup', 'checkout'.

5.1.3 Use of nouns in rule statements and fact types

Both simple and compound nouns may be used in rule statements. While countable nouns can be used almost anywhere in a rule statement, non-countable nouns may only be used

1. in a ***compound noun***, but not as the ***head noun***
2. in a ***compound verb***.[10]

As we shall see in Chapter 6, we can manage the quality and consistency of our rule statements by way of a ***fact model*** (a set of ***fact types***). By convention, only the singular forms of simple nouns (and head nouns of compound nouns) are used in fact types,[11] as in the following example:

F1 airline *serves* city[12]

While most nouns in rule statements are singular, plural nouns may also be used in rule statements, as in the following example:

R148. Each city *specified in* each flight booking request
must *be* one of the cities *served by* the airline.

If we need to use a noun in a fact type that makes sense only in the plural form, a useful technique is to prefix that noun with 'set of'. Thus, instead of the plural 'terms and conditions', we can use 'set of terms and conditions', the head noun of which ('set') is singular.

5.2 PROPER NAMES

Most of the nouns used as examples so far in this discussion are ***common nouns***. A common noun can be used to refer to either a set of similar persons, organizations, places, or things, or any member of that set. For example, 'city' can be used to refer to a set of places, as in "most cities have historic buildings", or to assert that an individual place belongs to that set, as in "Sydney is a city".

---

[8]See Section 5.7 for a definition of ***conjunction***.
[9]See Section 5.3.3.1 for a definition of ***phrasal verb***.
[10]See Section 5.3.3 for a definition of ***compound verb***.
[11]An apparent exception to this convention is that some fact types may include proper names in the plural form, as described in Section 5.2.
[12]Each fact type in this book is given a unique identifier starting with the letter 'F' and depicted using a sans serif font.

Unlike a common noun, each *proper name* is the name of a single entity instance, such as

1. a person: for example, 'Albert Einstein';
2. a business or other organization: for example, 'Qantas', 'The World Health Organization', 'Médecins sans Frontiers';
3. a place (continent, country, region, city or town, ocean, river, lake, mountain, building, etc.): for example, 'Asia', 'Australia', 'The Midwest', 'Sydney', 'The Atlantic Ocean', 'The River Nile', 'Lake Ontario', 'Mont Blanc', 'The Empire State Building';
4. a time period (day or month): for example, 'Friday', 'July', 'Christmas Day', 'Hanukkah', 'Ramadan';
5. a musical or other artistic work: for example, 'Jailhouse Rock', 'Mona Lisa';
6. a brand or product name: for example, 'Macintosh', 'Prius'.

Note that a proper name may start with 'the', as in 'The World Health Organization'; this is part of the name, as distinct from 'the' which can appear before a common noun, as in 'the capital city'.

Historically, proper names were considered to be nouns and are still referred to in some literature as *proper nouns*. In the Semantics of Business Vocabulary and Rules (SBVR), they are referred to simply as *names*.

Note that a proper name may be in plural form but refer to a single composite entity instance: for example, 'The United States of America', 'The United Nations'.

Proper names appear only in one category of fact type, namely, *assortment fact types*, as in the following example:

F2 The United States *is a* country.

Proper names may also be used in rule statements, as in the following example:

R149. Each city *specified in* each domestic flight booking request
          must *be* a city *in* The United States.

5.3 VERBS

When I studied English grammar at school, a *verb* was defined as a "doing word": that is, one that refers to an action performed by a person or thing (e.g., 'create', 'specify', 'prevent'). Various linguists have identified that verbs are rather more versatile than that. In particular, Halliday (1985)[13] proposed a *functional grammar* (now more often referred to as a *systemic functional grammar*), in which he identified the various types of processes that verbs may refer to, namely,

1. material processes: actions performed in the physical world, such as 'open', as in 'open the bag', or 'open the door';
2. mental processes, such as 'like', 'know', 'think', 'understand';
3. behavioral processes: physiological or psychological behaviors, such as 'laugh', 'sneeze', 'walk', 'sleep';
4. verbal processes, such as 'say', 'tell', 'inform', 'explain', 'specify', 'ask';

---

[13]A third edition has been published as (Halliday & Matthiessen, 2004).

5. relational processes, such as those expressed using 'be' or 'have'[14];

6. existential processes, also using the verb 'be' after 'there', as in "there is a place".

A behavioral definition of the concept 'verb' is also available. Every English verb other than a ***modal auxiliary***[15] exhibits the following two behavioral characteristics, which are only exhibited by verbs:

1. It inflects, in that the form after 'he', 'she', 'it', or a singular noun (e.g., 'is' and 'specifies') is different from the form after 'they' or a plural noun ('are' and 'specify' respectively).

2. It has a form (the ***infinitive***) that can follow the ***modal auxiliaries*** (including 'must' and 'may'). Except for 'is'/'are' (for which the infinitive form is 'be'), the infinitive form of all verbs is the same as the form after 'they' or a plural noun.

5.3.1 Transitive, intransitive, and intensive verbs

Traditionally, English verbs have been classified as either

1. ***transitive***, requiring not only a subject but at least one object: for example, 'create', 'specify', 'prevent' (a person or thing cannot just create, specify, or prevent; he, she or it must create, specify, or prevent something), or

2. ***intransitive***, requiring only a subject: for example, 'exist', 'occur' (a person or thing can just exist or occur but cannot "*exist something" or "*occur something"[16]).

Some verbs may be used transitively or intransitively: for example, 'close' as in "the door closes" and "the attendant closes the door".

Halliday's analysis of different processes signified by verbs (listed at the start of Section 5.3) suggests that the verb 'be' is rather different from other verbs. This verb is now often referred to as being ***intensive*** or ***circumstantial*** rather than ***transitive***, as the words following the verb are not an ***object*** distinct from the ***subject*** (as with other verbs) but a reference to another facet of the subject or to one of its qualities, characteristics, attributes (i.e., a ***complement***), or its circumstance.

5.3.2 Forms of verbs

A verb has different forms which are used in different contexts. The principal ways in which a verb varies are

1. ***tense***, expressing whether an action, relationship, or state of being is in the past, present, or future;

2. ***aspect***, expressing whether an activity is continuous and/or at an indeterminate time;

---

[14]Halliday defined six subclasses of relational processes:
 1. intensive attributive, as in "Mary is nice";
 2. intensive identifying, as in "Isabel is my wife";
 3. circumstantial attributive, as in "the meeting is tomorrow";
 4. circumstantial identifying, as in "tomorrow is Friday";
 5. possessive attributive, as in "John has a car";
 6. possessive identifying, as in "the car is Bill's".
[15]The modal auxiliaries in English are 'may'/'might', 'must', 'can'/'could', 'shall'/'should', 'will'/'would'.
[16]Syntactically incorrect constructions are conventionally indicated by way of an initial asterisk.

3. **mood**, expressing whether an action, relationship, or state of being is actual, hypothetical, anticipated, or commanded;
4. **first**, **second**, or **third person** and **singular** or **plural number**, expressing who performs the action,
participates in the relationship, or exhibits the state of being;
5. **infinitive** form for use after verbs like 'must' and 'may';
6. **active** or **passive voice**, expressing whether the subject of the verb is the person or thing performing
the action or the person or thing on which the action is performed;
7. **positive** or **negated** form, expressing whether or not the action, relationship, or state of being exists
(or is to exist).

Each of these dimensions of verb variation is discussed in one of the following sections.

5.3.2.1 Tense

When a verb is used to express an action, relationship, or state of being which is current, the **present
tense** is used (e.g., 'specify', 'am specifying'), whereas if the action, relationship, or state of being is to
occur in the future, a **future tense** is used (e.g., 'will specify', 'will have specified'), and if the action or
relationship has occurred in the past, one of a number of different **past tenses** is used (e.g., 'specified',
'have specified', 'were specifying', 'used to specify', 'had specified').

Only present tense forms of verbs are used in fact types. Rule statements use mainly present tense
forms; however, rule statements that refer to a previous activity or process may use past tense verbs: for
example,

R150. Each <u>passenger</u>
must *board* the <u>flight</u> *for* which that <u>passenger</u> *has checked in*
no later than <u>15 min</u> *before* the <u>departure time</u> *of* that <u>flight</u>.

5.3.2.2 Aspect

When a verb is used to express continuous activity, the **progressive aspect** is used (e.g., 'am specifying', 'was specifying', 'will be specifying') rather than the **simple form** of the verb (e.g., 'specify',
'specified', 'will specify').

When a verb is used to indicate that the time of the activity is indeterminate, the **perfect aspect** is
used (e.g. 'have specified', 'had specified', 'will have specified').[17]

A verb can simultaneously exhibit both progressive and perfect aspects: for example, 'have been
specifying', 'had been specifying', 'will have been specifying').

Only simple forms are used in fact types. Rule statements use mainly simple forms and rarely (if
ever) use the progressive aspect. However, rule statements (such as R150 in the previous section) that
refer to a previous activity or process may use the perfect aspect.

5.3.2.3 Mood

Where a verb is used to express an actual action, relationship, or state of being, the **indicative mood** is
used. This can take either of two forms: the **declarative mood**, as in "the form specifies the departure
date", or the **interrogative mood**, as in "does the form specify the departure date?"

---

[17]Note that this not to be confused with the **perfective aspect**, used in some languages to indicate a completed activity.

However, if the action or relationship is hypothetical or anticipated, the ***subjunctive mood*** is used, as in "if the form were to specify the departure date, . . .".

Finally, one can command someone (or something) to do (or not do) something, using the ***imperative mood***, as in "fasten your seatbelts" or "do not pass this point".

Only the declarative form of the indicative mood is used in fact types or rule statements. Note that, although organizations frequently use commands in the imperative mood to express rules that their customers or employees are required to obey, the business rule community has standardized on rule statements containing 'must' or 'must not' rather than using the imperative mood.

5.3.2.4 Person and number

A verb in the present tense after 'he', 'she', or 'it' (the ***third person singular personal pronouns***) or a singular noun (e.g., "it specifies", "the application specifies") has a different form from that used after 'they' (the ***third person plural personal pronoun***) or a plural noun (e.g., "they specify", "the applications specify").

As the first of these forms ('specifies' in this example)

1. is not used after 'I', 'we' (***first person pronouns***), or 'you' (the ***second person pronoun***),
2. is not used after 'they' (the ***third person plural personal pronoun***),
3. appears only in the present tense,
4. should not be used in the ***subjunctive*** or ***imperative mood***,[18]

this is the ***third person singular present indicative*** form ("3PSPI" for short).

Only the 3PSPI form is used in fact types. Rule statements only use third person forms (except after 'must' or 'may': see the next section): the singular form after a singular noun, or the plural form after a plural noun: for example, "the application specifies a payment method", "the applications specify different payment methods".

5.3.2.5 The infinitive

After a ***modal auxiliary***, such as 'must' or 'may', the ***infinitive*** form is required: for example, 'specify' in the case of 'specifies'. As discussed previously, this just happens to be the same as the form used after 'they' or a plural noun (for all verbs except 'be').

The infinitive form is not used in fact types but is used in rule statements after 'must' or 'may': for example, "each application must specify a payment method".

5.3.2.6 Voice

If the subject of a verb is also the person or thing performing the action (the ***actor*** or ***agent***), the ***active voice*** is used (e.g., 'presents' as in "the passenger presents a boarding pass"), whereas if the subject of

---

[18]Nowadays, however, the 3PSPI form is often used in clauses that ought to be in the subjunctive mood. For example (Object Management Group, 2008), uses both indicative and subjunctive forms in examples following modal operators such as "It is obligatory that . . .", "It is permitted that . . .", and "It is prohibited that . . .". The indicative form ('is') is used in "It is obligatory that each rental specifies a car group.", "It is permitted that the drop-off branch of a rental is not the return branch of the rental.", and "It is prohibited that a rental be open if a driver of the rental is a barred driver.", but the subjunctive form ('be') is used in "It is permitted that a rental be open only if no driver of the rental is a barred driver." and "It is not obligatory that the drop-off branch of a rental be the return branch of the rental".

the verb is the person or thing on which the action is performed (the *patient* or *target*), the *passive voice* is used (e.g., 'is presented by' as in "a boarding pass is presented by the passenger").

A similar distinction may be used for some verbs expressing relationships rather than actions: for example, "the folder contains two files" and "two files are contained in the folder".

The passive form of a verb uses the verb 'be' (usually in the form 'is' or 'are') and the preposition 'by' enclosing the *past participle* of the verb: for example, 'presented' in the example earlier in this section. For *regular verbs* (like 'present' and 'specify'), the past participle is the same as the *simple past tense*; for *irregular verbs* (like 'give' and 'take'), the past participle ('given', 'taken') is different from the simple past tense ('gave', 'took').

As we shall see, both active and passive forms are used in fact types and rule statements. For example, "each flight booking request must specify a destination city", "the destination city that is specified in a flight booking request must be one of the cities served by the airline".

5.3.2.7 Negation

If we wish to refer to the absence of an action or relationship, we can negate the appropriate verb.

For all verb forms starting with an *auxiliary verb* ('is'/'are', 'has'/'have', 'must', 'may', 'might', 'can', 'could', 'shall', 'should', 'will', 'would') this involves the inclusion of 'not' after the auxiliary verb. For example, "is performed by" becomes "is not performed by", "has run" becomes "has not run".

For most other verb forms, negation involves replacing the verb by 'does not'/'do not' followed by the infinitive form of the verb. For example, "runs" becomes "does not run".

As we shall see in Section 5.3.3.2, two verbs may be joined by 'to', as in "try to stay awake", "need to be". Depending on the first verb in the construction, it may be able to be negated by replacing 'to' by 'not', thus "need not be" is an alternative to "does not need to be". However, be careful of negated forms that include 'not to': "try not to fall asleep" does not have the same meaning as "do not try to fall asleep".

Negated verbs are not used in fact types but can be used in rule statements. For example, "a flight booking request for a one-way journey must not specify a return date".

5.3.3 Compound verbs

Apart from the passive form of a verb, there are other multi-word formulations involving the verb 'be', the past participle of another verb, and a preposition. These are known as *compound verbs* whereas the verbs we have encountered so far in this chapter are *simple verbs*.

1. Whereas 'be married by' is the passive of 'marry' ("the priest marries the couple"/"the couple are married by the priest") the form 'be married to' can be used to express the relationship between a person and his or her spouse, as in "John is married to Maria". The *past participle* 'married' behaves just like an adjective: both attributive, as in "a married man" and predicative, as in "Ahmed is married". Other prepositions can also be used after the verb 'be' and a past participle, as in 'be associated with', 'be labeled with', 'be allocated to', 'be assigned to', 'be linked to', 'be specified in', 'be filed in', 'be recorded on', 'be registered on'.

2. Adjectives other than past participles can be used between the verb 'be' and a preposition, to form a phrase that behaves like a transitive verb, as in 'be responsible for', 'be similar to', or an intensive verb, as in 'be identical to', 'be equal to'.

3. Adjectives or past participles can be used after the verb 'be', to form a phrase that behaves like an intransitive verb, as in 'be present', 'be available', 'be excluded'.
4. Nouns, with or without a preceding article (see Section 5.4.1) can also be used with the verb 'be' and a preposition, to form a phrase that behaves like a transitive verb, as in 'be part of', 'be a category of', 'take the place of', 'be a match for'.
5. Nouns can also be used after the verb 'be' and a preposition, to form a phrase that behaves like an intransitive verb, as in 'be on duty', 'be in service'.

The verb 'have' can also be used with a noun and a preposition to form a phrase that behaves like a transitive verb, as in 'have responsibility for'.

5.3.3.1 Prepositional and phrasal verbs

Verbs (including 'be', but not 'have') can be used with prepositions to form ***prepositional verbs*** that behave like transitive verbs, as in 'apply for', 'buy into', 'act as'. Similar to prepositional verbs are ***phrasal verbs***, such as 'check out', 'look up'. The principal difference between prepositional and phrasal verbs is that, in a phrasal verb, the preposition can either precede or follow the object of the verb. One can check out something or check something out, look up something or look something up. 'Check out' and 'look up' are thus phrasal verbs. In fact, the prepositions in phrasal verbs ('out' and 'up' in these examples) act as ***adverbs*** (words that qualify the meaning of a verb, such as 'well' or 'completely').

However, while one can apply for something, buy into something, or act as someone, "*apply something for", "*buy something into", and "*act something as" are invalid constructions.[19] 'Apply for', 'buy into', and 'act as' are therefore prepositional rather than phrasal verbs.

Prepositional and phrasal verbs frequently have multiple meanings: for example, 'go off' has at least six. The same combination of verb and preposition can behave as either a prepositional verb or a phrasal verb depending on the meaning. For example, 'turn on' is a prepositional verb in the phrase "turn on a dime"[20] but a phrasal verb in "turn on the light". While one can say "turn the light on", one cannot say "*turn a dime on".

Some phrasal verbs can be used intransitively, such as 'give up': one can give up one's passport or simply give up.

Combined phrasal/prepositional verbs also exist, involving two prepositions, of which the first is acting as an adverb: for example, 'check up on'.

Phrasal verbs can be used as nouns: for example, 'check up', 'fit out'. When a phrasal verb is used as a noun, the constituent words may be joined by a hyphen (as in 'check-up', 'fit-out'), or written without intervening spaces or hyphens (as in 'checkup').

5.3.3.2 Verbs involving 'to'

Another type of compound verb involves a simple verb followed by 'to' and the infinitive form of another verb: for example, 'try to behave', 'need to know', 'wish to advise'.

---

[19]Syntactically incorrect constructions are conventionally indicated by way of an initial asterisk.
[20]"Turn on a sixpence" in the UK or Australia.

5.3.4 **Auxiliary verbs**

There are three classes of *auxiliary verb*:

1. As well as being able to stand alone as simple verbs, 'is'/'are', 'has'/'have', and 'does'/'do' can be used in front of a simple verb to generate different forms of that verb, as we have seen above: these are not used in this way in fact types but may be used in this way in rule statements.
2. The auxiliary verb 'will' cannot stand alone as a simple verb, but can be used in front of a simple verb to generate the future tense of that verb, as we have seen above: again, 'will' is not used in this way in fact types but may be used in this way in rule statements.[21]
3. There are also the *modal auxiliaries*: 'must', 'may', 'might', 'can', 'could', 'shall', 'should' and 'would'. Of these, none is used in fact types but every rule statement in both RuleSpeak and the constrained natural language used in this book must use either 'must' or 'may'.

Modal auxiliaries exhibit various *modalities*: for example:

1. The auxiliary 'must' can exhibit any of the following modalities:
   a. *alethic modality*, in which 'must' is interpreted as stating a logical conclusion, as in "he must be out" (since he is not home);
   b. *deontic modality*, in which 'must' is interpreted as stating an obligation, as in "he must be out before the doors are locked": in this modality, 'must' can be replaced by "is/are obliged to";
   c. *epistemic modality*, in which 'must' is interpreted as asserting a belief, as in "surely he must be out".
   In a rule statement, 'must' is always to be interpreted as expressing the deontic modality.

2. Similarly 'may' can exhibit either of the following modalities:
   a. *alethic modality*, in which 'may' is interpreted as stating a possibility: for example, "he may come home" can mean "it is possible that he will come home";
   b. *deontic modality*, in which 'may' is interpreted as stating a permission: for example, "he may come home" can mean "he is allowed to come home".
   In a rule statement, 'may' is always to be interpreted as expressing the deontic modality.

5.3.5 **Verbs involving 'that', 'if', or 'whether'**

Another interesting class of verbs consists of those that either state or question the truth of a proposition, such as 'state', 'ask', 'question', or 'check', as in "the witness stated that he had not seen the assailant clearly", "I asked if this were true", "She questioned whether he could have done it", or "The flight attendant checked that all passengers' seat belts were fastened". In each of these, the verb is separated from the following proposition by a conjunction ('that', 'if', or 'whether'). Note that

1. 'that' may be omitted after such verbs: for example, "The flight attendant checked all passengers' seat belts were fastened";

---

[21]Note that, in sentences like "I will", the following verb (e.g., 'take', as in "take this woman to be my lawful wedded wife") has been omitted. 'Will' is also used in a non-auxiliary fashion, as in "He willed the traffic light to stay green".

2. after some verbs, including 'check', 'that' may be replaced by 'whether' or 'whether or not'; the last example above would then read "The flight attendant checked whether all passengers' seat belts were fastened" or "The flight attendant checked whether or not all passengers' seat belts were fastened".

5.4 DETERMINERS

One or more ***determiners*** can be used before a noun to provide some information as to which (or how many) instances of the noun's concept are being referred to. As we shall see in Section 5.5, adjectives also do this. While there are various differences between determiners and adjectives, none of them applies to all determiners or all adjectives, so I will not cover them in this book. Indeed, there is no one definitive list of determiners agreed on by all linguists.

Fortunately, only a few of the many determiners available in the English language are used in rule statements (none is used in fact types) so we can list them all.

Without doubt, the most commonly used determiners are ***articles***.

5.4.1 Articles

There are two types of articles:

1. the ***indefinite articles***: 'a' and 'an';
2. the ***definite article***: 'the'.

An indefinite article is used before a singular noun when referring to an unspecified single instance: for example, 'a customer', 'an address', 'a product', 'an order'.

The definite article 'the' can be used before a singular or plural noun. I find that it is frequently misused: it can only be used legitimately before a singular noun when referring to

1. the only instance of that concept that exists, as in "the Earth";
2. the only instance of that concept that exists in the context already established, as in "the defendant" (in a court case);
3. (where an instance of the concept has already been referred to) the instance already referred to (by inclusion of 'same' after 'the'), as in "the same day";
4. (where two instances of the concept exist—or exist in the context already established—and one has already been referred to) the other instance (by inclusion of 'other' after 'the'), as in "the other party";
5. the only instance of that concept that meets the criterion or criteria specified:
  a. by one or more attributive adjectives or nouns between 'the' and the noun, as in "the eldest son", "the hardware shop",
  b. in a qualifying clause (see Section 7.2.7 in Chapter 7) after the noun, as in "the person named in the application",
  c. in both a qualifying clause and one or more attributive adjectives or nouns between 'the' and the noun, as in "the destination city specified in the flight booking request".

Similarly 'the' can only be used legitimately before a plural noun when referring to

1. all instances of a concept, as in "the Australian states";
2. all instances of a concept that exist in the context already established, as in "the people" (in a constitution);

3. (where particular instances of the concept have already been referred to) the instances already referred to (by inclusion of 'same' after 'the'), as in "the same products";
4. (where particular instances of the concept have already been referred to) all other instances (by inclusion of 'other' after 'the'), as in "the other rooms";
5. the only instances of that concept that meet the criterion or criteria specified:
   a. by one or more attributive adjectives or nouns between 'the' and the noun, as in "the updated records", "the Sydney offices",
   b. in a qualifying clause (see Section 7.2.7 in Chapter 7) after the noun, as in "the passengers specified in the booking",
   c. in both a qualifying clause and one or more attributive adjectives or nouns between 'the' and the noun, as in "the urgent orders placed by the customer".

5.4.2 Specific determiners

Specific determiners are used to limit the noun to referring only to a specific instance or instances. The definite article 'the' is a specific determiner, as are also

1. the *demonstrative determiners*: 'that' and 'those'[22];
2. the *ordinal numbers* ('first', 'second', 'third', etc.) and various other words defining position in a sequence, discussed in Section 5.4.2.1;
3. 'the same', 'the other', 'the only'.

Note that the possessive adjectives ('my', 'your', 'his', 'her', 'its', 'our', and 'their') are also specific determiners but are not used in rule statements.

5.4.2.1 Ordinal numbers

There is an infinite set of *ordinal numbers*: 'first', 'second', 'third', etc. Any of these may be used between 'the' and a noun to indicate which member of some sequence is referred to, as in "the first stop". There are other words or phrases that may be used in a similar way:

1. 'the last', where the number of members in the sequence is not known or can vary;
2. 'the first or only', when the statement refers to a sole instance or the first of a number of instances;
3. 'the last or only', when the statement refers to a sole instance or the last of a number of instances;
4. 'the second or any subsequent', when the statement refers to any instance except the first;
5. 'the previous' or 'the next', when the statement refers to the member before or after some other member previously referred to;
6. 'every second', 'every third', etc., as in "the carry-on bags of every fifth passenger must be checked for explosives".

Ordinal numbers may also be used in compound nouns. An ordinal number may be used before a pair of nouns to indicate which member of some sequence (signified by the first noun) is involved in a particular instance of some concept (signified by the second noun). Thus we can say 'first-person narrative', 'second-class citizen', 'third-world country', etc.

---

[22]'This' and 'these' are also demonstratives but are not used in the rule statements in this book.

5.4.3 General determiners

General determiners limit the number of instances referred to by a noun without being specific as to which instance or instances are referenced. The indefinite articles ('a' and 'an') are general determiners, as are also

1. the *cardinal numbers* ('one', 'two', 'ten', etc.) and various other words defining how many instances are involved (discussed in Section 5.4.3.1);
2. the *quantifiers* 'all', 'both', 'every', 'each', 'any', 'no', etc.;
3. 'another', 'other' (but not 'the other', which is a specific determiner);
4. 'either', 'neither'.

5.4.3.1 Cardinal numbers

There is an infinite set of *cardinal numbers*: 'one', 'two', 'three', etc. Any of these may be preceded by one of the following:

1. 'exactly' to express a more rigorous statement as to how many instances are involved, as in "each flight booking request must specify exactly one departure date";
2. 'at least' or 'from', to express the minimum number of instances involved, as in "each flight booking confirmation must specify at least one passenger name";
3. 'at most' (or 'up to'), to similarly express the maximum number of instances involved.

A cardinal number may be followed by 'of the', as in "the origin city specified in each flight booking request must be one of the cities served by the airline".

Cardinal numbers may also be used in compound nouns. A cardinal number may be used before two or more nouns to indicate how many of some part (signified by the first noun) are involved in an assembly of some kind (signified by the last noun). Thus we can say 'one-way flight', 'two-way radio', 'three-way intersection', 'four-wheel drive vehicle',[23] 'six-speed gearbox', 'hundred-point check',[24] etc.

5.4.4 Determiners before countable and non-countable nouns

Note that the following determiners can only precede *countable nouns*[25]:

1. cardinal and ordinal numbers;
2. 'the last', 'the first or only', 'the last or only', 'the second or any subsequent', 'the previous', 'the next', 'every second', 'every third', etc.;
3. 'those', 'the other', 'another', 'either', 'neither', 'both', 'every', 'each'.

For example, we cannot say "*one information . . .", "*the first governance . . .", "*either training", etc., as "information", "governance", and "training" are *non-countable nouns*.

---

[23]Note to North American readers: this is the term used in Australia for an SUV.
[24]An Australian government identity check system that assigns points to each type of identity document (e.g., 70 points for a birth certificate or passport, 25 points for a credit card) and requires a party opening a financial account to supply identity documents with a total of 100 points or more.
[25]See Section 5.1.1 for definitions of *countable noun* and *non-countable noun*.

5.5 ADJECTIVES

An *adjective* is a word that can be used as either

1. a *pre-modifier* of a noun (an *attributive adjective*), as in "checked bag", or
2. part of a *predicate* following a noun and the verb 'is' (in which case it is a *predicative adjective*), as in "this bag is checked".

For example, 'international' can precede 'flight' (as in "the international flight") or follow "flight is" (as in "this flight is international") and is therefore an adjective.

Note that not all adjectives can be used in both ways. For example, 'former' can only be used as an attributive adjective, as in "former employee" (we do not say "*the employee is former"[26]). By contrast, 'well', when used as an adjective, can only be used predicatively: we can say "the patient is well" but not "*the well patient".

The adjective 'valid' has a special use in a *standard format definition* rules (see Section 4.9.1.7 in Chapter 4). Other adjectives may appear only in *compound nouns* (see Section 5.1.2) or *compound verbs* (see Section 5.3.3) in a fact type or rule statement.

5.6 PREPOSITIONS

A *preposition* is one or more words that can be used in either or both of the following ways:

1. after the verb 'be' and before a noun to express a relationship between the object referenced by the noun before 'be' and the object referenced by the noun after the preposition, as with 'on' in "the message is on the screen";
2. after the verb 'go' and before a noun to express movement by the object referenced by the noun before the verb with respect to the object referenced by the noun after the preposition, as with 'into' in "the flight crew goes into the aircraft".[27]

Most of the relationships that can be thus expressed fall into one of the following categories:

1. locational: for example, 'on' and 'in' in "the cat is on the mat" and "your dinner is in the fridge" respectively; prepositions of this nature express the location of the object referenced by the first noun with respect to that of the object referenced by the second noun; other common locational prepositions include 'above', 'below', 'in front of', 'behind', 'beside', 'within', 'between', 'to' (as in "to London"), 'into', and 'onto';
2. temporal: for example, 'before', 'after', 'during'; prepositions of this nature express the date and/or time of the object referenced by the first noun with respect to that of the object referenced by the second noun;
3. causative: for example, 'due to', 'because of', 'as a result of'; prepositions of this nature express that the object referenced by the second noun is at least part of the cause of the object referenced by the first noun;

---

[26]Syntactically incorrect constructions are conventionally indicated by way of an initial asterisk.

[27]Note that these are not the only situations in which a preposition can occur; other situations include:
1. after other verbs, e.g. "enter into an agreement", "read through the document";
2. after nouns, e.g., "the fields on this form".

4. beneficiary: for example, 'for', 'to' (as in "to Pedro"); prepositions of this nature express that the object referenced by the second noun benefits in some way from the object referenced by the first noun;
5. possessive: for example, 'of'; prepositions of this nature express that the object referenced by the first noun belongs to the object referenced by the second noun;
6. perspective: for example, 'as'; prepositions of this nature express that the object referenced by the first noun can be considered from some perspective expressed by the second noun;
7. comparative: for example, 'the same as', 'different from', 'more than', 'less than', 'fewer than', 'equal to', 'later than', 'earlier than', 'the same time as'; prepositions of this nature express a comparison between the objects referenced by each noun.

Prepositions are used quite often in rule statements; the most common are 'of', 'by', and 'in'.

Prepositions may also be used in compound nouns (as described in Section 5.1.2) or compound verbs (as described in Section 5.3.3).

The most common preposition used in a compound noun is 'of' (as in 'date of birth'). Note that most compound nouns using the preposition 'of' can be alternatively expressed by removing 'of' and swapping the simple nouns: for example, a synonym of 'date of birth' is 'birth date'.

5.7 CONJUNCTIONS

Conjunctions have various uses. However, their only use in a fact model is to join two nouns in a few compound nouns. The conjunction most commonly used for this purpose is 'and' (as in "terms and conditions"), although a case might be made for the use of 'or' (as in 'parent or guardian').

In a rule statement, a ***conjunction*** can be used to join two nouns, clauses, or (less commonly) verbs, determiners, or prepositions. The conjunctions most commonly used in rule statements are

1. 'and' and 'or', used in rule statements to join
   a. nouns in a list, as in "cash, check, or credit", or
   b. subclauses in a ***qualifying clause*** or ***conditional clause***,[28] as in "that specifies that flight and specifies the departure date of that flight",
   c. values at each end of a range, as in "between 0 and 14 inclusive";
2. 'if' and 'unless', used in rule statements to introduce conditional clauses, as in "if that passenger presents a boarding pass".

The following conjunctions are also used for particular purposes:

1. 'but' is used in the phrase 'but not both' after a pair of nouns separated by 'or' to indicate that only one of the options signified by those nouns applies, as in "a credit card or an electronic transfer payment receipt but not both";
2. 'after' (which may be used as a conjunction as well as a ***preposition***) may be used to refer to a preceding process, as in "after that passenger undergoes check-in";

---

[28]See Sections 7.2.7 and 7.2.6 in Chapter 7 for definitions of ***qualifying clause*** and ***conditional clause*** respectively.

3. 'that', 'if', and 'whether' can be used after a verb that states or questions the truth of a proposition, such as 'state', 'ask', 'question', or 'check', as described in Section 5.3.5;
4. 'other than' may be used to introduce a qualifying clause, "a payment other than a cash payment".

Conjunctions may also be used in compound nouns, as described in Section 5.1.2.

5.8 PRONOUNS

Pronouns are words that may stand in place of nouns (or other pronouns) previously referred to: for example, 'him' as in "when Paul arrived, we recognized him". The following classes of pronouns are relevant to rule statements:

1. the *personal pronouns*: these include 'he', 'him', 'she', 'her', 'it', 'they', and 'them', but only 'it' is generally used in rule statements;
2. the *relative pronouns* (including 'that', 'who', 'which', 'whom', and 'whose'), which act as the subject or object of the first or only verb in a *relative clause* (see Section 7.2.7 in Chapter 7), as in the following examples:
   a. in "the house that Jack built", 'that' referring to 'house', is the object of 'built' in the relative clause "that Jack built",
   b. in "the girl who stole my heart", 'who', referring to 'girl', is the subject of 'stole' in the relative clause "who stole my heart",
   c. in "the port at which those flights connect", 'which', referring to 'port', is the object of the *prepositional verb* 'connect at' in the relative clause "at which those flights connect",
   d. in "those for whom the bell tolls", 'whom', referring to 'those', is the object of the prepositional verb 'toll for' in the relative clause "for whom the bell tolls",
   e. in "the person whose life is covered by the policy", 'whose', referring to 'person', identifies the life that is the subject of 'is covered by';
3. 'both', which can be used after a pair of nouns to refer equally to each noun in that pair, as in "a credit card or an electronic transfer payment receipt but not both".

Note that the use of pronouns in a sentence can render it ambiguous. For example, in R151, it is not immediately clear what 'it' refers to: the origin city (unlikely), the outgoing flight (possible but still unlikely), the flight booking confirmation (the most likely). R152 creates no such ambiguity.

R151. †The <u>origin city</u> *of* the <u>outgoing flight</u>
   specified in a <u>flight booking confirmation</u>
   must *be the same as* the <u>origin city</u>
   specified in the <u>flight booking request</u> that *gives rise to* it.[29]

R152. The <u>origin city</u> *of* the <u>outgoing flight</u>
   specified in a <u>flight booking confirmation</u>
   must *be the same as* the <u>origin city</u>
   specified in the <u>flight booking request</u>
   that *gives rise to* that <u>flight booking confirmation</u>.

---

[29]The dagger at the start of a rule statement indicates that it is in some way invalid as it stands.

For this reason, pronouns should only be used in rule statements in the following ways:

1. 'it' can be used if there is only one previous noun, as in R153;

R153. Each <u>flight booking request</u>
    must *specify* whether it *is for*
        a <u>return journey</u>, a <u>one-way journey</u>, or a <u>multi-stop journey</u>.

2. 'both' can be used immediately after a pair of nouns:
    a. separated by a comma and followed by 'or', as in R154, or
    b. separated by 'or' and followed by 'but not', as in R155;

R154. Each <u>flight booking confirmation</u>
    must *specify* a <u>mobile phone number</u>, an <u>e-mail address</u>, or both.
R155. Each <u>flight booking confirmation</u>
    must *specify*
        a <u>credit card</u> or an <u>electronic funds transfer payment receipt</u>
        but not both.

3. 'that' or 'who' can be used immediately after a noun to introduce a ***qualifying clause***, as in "a bag that weighs more than 20 kg", "a passenger who has checked in online";

4. 'which' or 'whom' can be used immediately after a ***preposition*** to introduce a qualifying clause, as in "the day on which that flight departs", "the passenger for whom the special meal has been prepared".

Another use of 'it' is as an ***impersonal pronoun***, referring not to a previous noun but to the world in general, as in "it is raining". Each of the standard SBVR rule statement formulations uses 'it' in this way:

1. "It is obligatory that …";
2. "It is prohibited that …";
3. "It is permitted that …";
4. "It is necessary that …";
5. "It is impossible that …";
6. "It is possible that …".

5.9 LITERALS

A *literal* is a reference to a numeric value, textual value, category in a categorization scheme, date, time, or other time point, which may be used in a rule statement to either

1. constrain the value of a data item, or an attribute of a real-world object, event, or process, in terms of that value, category, or time point (e.g., 1 and 9 in R156, 3 h in R158, high in R159, and 9 am in R160), or
2. limit the scope of that rule statement to situations in which a data item, or an attribute of a real-world object, event, or process, has a particular value or values, or is of a particular category (e.g., 30 kg in R157 and 'LAX' in R158).

R156. The <u>number of passengers</u> *specified in* each <u>flight booking request</u>
must *be* at least <u>1</u> and at most <u>9</u>.

R157. Each <u>bag</u> that *weighs more than* <u>30 kg</u>
must *be checked in at* the <u>oversize bag counter</u>.

R158. Each <u>transit time</u> *specified in* each <u>flight booking confirmation</u>
that *specifies* more than one <u>flight</u>
must *be at least* <u>3 h</u>
if the <u>port code</u> *of* the <u>connecting port</u>
for which that <u>transit time</u> *is specified*
is '<u>LAX</u>'.[30]

R159. The <u>importance</u> *of* an <u>e-mail</u>
is by definition
<u>high</u>, <u>normal</u>, or <u>low</u>.

R160. <u>Start of business</u>
is by definition
<u>9 am</u>.

As can be seen from these examples,

1. a numeric literal is simply a numeral (represented using digits rather than textually as in the ***cardinal numbers*** discussed in Section 5.4.3.1) optionally followed by a symbol defining the units (e.g., 'kg', 'h');
2. a textual literal is enclosed in single quotation marks;
3. a time point literal may be
   a. a date, in any format acceptable to the organization, with or without the year specified,
   b. a time of day, in any format acceptable to the organization, with or without the date specified.

Alternative time point literals include:

1. a month alone: for example, 'June',
2. a day of the week: for example, 'Friday'.

Time point literals may be included (singly or in combination) in phrases to express particular requirements: for example

1. a recurrent month, day of the month, or day of the week: for example, "July of each year", "the 3rd day of each month", "Wednesday of each week";
2. a particular month (or month and day) in a year related to the current year or year under discussion: for example, "June of the previous year", "30th April of the following year";
3. a particular day in a month related to the current month or month under discussion: for example, "the 15th day of that month", "the last day of the previous month", "the 7th day of the following month";
4. a day of the week in a week related to the current week or week under discussion: for example, "Thursday of the previous week";

---

[30]Note that an alternative way of expressing this rule statement would be to replace "if the <u>port code</u> *of* the <u>connecting port</u> is '<u>LAX</u>'" with "if the <u>connecting port</u> is <u>Los Angeles International</u>".

5. a time of day on a day of the week: for example, "5 pm on Friday of each week"[31];
6. a time of day on a particular day in a week related to the current week or week under discussion: for example, "midday on Tuesday of the following week".

5.10 THE THREE USES OF 'THAT'

As we have now seen, 'that' can be used in three distinct ways:

1. as a *conjunction* between a verb stating or questioning the truth of a proposition and that proposition, as in "the form specified that all passengers were adults" (in Section 5.3.5);
2. as a *determiner*, as in "I have the tickets for that flight" (in Section 5.4.2);
3. as a *relative pronoun* introducing a qualifying clause, as in "each bag that weighs more than 20 kg must be labeled with a 'heavy bag' label" (in Section 5.8).

5.11 SUMMARY

Natural language rule statements consist of words, each of which (each time it is used) belongs to a particular *word class*: *noun*, *verb*, etc. Some words belong to more than one class depending on their meaning and how they are used.

Each *noun* is either a *simple noun* or a *compound noun*, which, as well as at least one simple noun, may include *adjectives*, *prepositions*, and (occasionally) *numbers* or *conjunctions*.

Each *proper name* is the name of a single person, business (or other organization), place (continent, country, region, city, town, ocean, river, lake, mountain, building, etc.), time period (such as a day or month), musical or other artistic work, or brand or product name.

Each *verb* is either a *simple verb* or a *compound verb*. A compound verb includes a simple verb, plus an adjective, noun, one or more prepositions, and/or an *article*. Verbs can take many forms: while fact types use only the *third person singular present indicative* forms (in both the *active voice* and the *passive voice*), rule statements may use the other forms.

Determiners, adjectives, prepositions, conjunctions, and (occasionally) *pronouns* can be used in their own right (i.e., not as part of compound nouns or compound verbs) in rule statements; however, these words are never used in fact types except as parts of compound nouns or compound verbs.

Not all English words of any class are available for use in rule statements in the *constrained natural language* proposed in this book. For example, a *non-countable noun* may not be used alone but only in a compound noun (as a pre-modifier of a *countable noun*) or in a compound verb. Also only a few determiners and pronouns, out of the many available in English, are used in this constrained natural language.

Literals can also be used in rule statements: these express numeric or textual values, or time points, such as dates, times of day, or days of the week or month.

---

[31]Known in Australia as "beer o'clock".

Fact models

This chapter describes

- why a ***fact model*** should be built to support rule statement writing and other aspects of system specification;
- what a fact model consists of, and how it differs from other models and forms of documentation;
- how ***nouns***, possibly qualified by ***adjectives***, or (occasionally) other words, can be can be selected as ***business terms***, defined and given an appropriate place in the ***taxonomy*** of business terms; and
- how ***fact types*** can be used to relate business terms (along with ***verbs*** and possibly ***prepositions***).

6.1 FACT MODELS: AN OVERVIEW

In this section, we look at

1. why a fact model is useful,
2. how a fact model differs from other models and forms of documentation, and
3. what a fact model consists of.

In subsequent sections, we look at the following in detail:

1. business terms and proper names (Section 6.2)
2. fact types (Section 6.3)
3. building a fact model (Section 6.4)
4. using a fact model for other aspects of system specification (Section 6.5).

6.1.1 Typographical conventions

Each fact type in this book is given a unique identifier starting with the letter 'F' and depicted using a sans serif font. In this and subsequent chapters, all examples of fact model content are rendered as they would be in a fact type or rule statement: that is,

1. examples of ***terms*** are underlined;
2. examples of ***verbs***[1] and ***prepositions***[2] are in italics;

---

[1] See Section 5.3 in Chapter 5 for a definition of the term ***verb***.
[2] See Section 5.6 in Chapter 5 for a definition of the term ***preposition***.

3. examples of ***proper names***[3] and ***literals*** (references to numeric values, textual values, categories within a categorization scheme, dates, times, or other time points) are double underlined.

These conventions are based on those used in the Semantics of Business Vocabulary and Rules (SBVR)[4].

6.1.2 Why build a fact model?

6.1.2.1 Support for standardizing rule statement vocabulary

Section 1.5.1.2 in Chapter 1 makes the case for using a standardized vocabulary in an organization's rule statements. This is not simply a case of establishing a glossary of accepted **business terms**, but also involves agreeing on the **verbs** and/or **prepositions** to be used when associating particular terms in a rule statement.

For example, even if we agree on the business terms flight booking request and departure date, we still have to agree on the verb to be used in associating flight booking requests (and other transactions) with the data items that can be included in such transactions: is that *specify*, *include*, or *state*? Unless we establish a consensus as to the verbs to be used as well as the business terms, we risk ending up with multiple copies of essentially the same rule statement: for example, R161, R162, and R163:

R161. Each flight booking request
must *specify* exactly one departure date.
R162. Each flight booking request
must *include* exactly one departure date.
R163. Each flight booking request
must *state* exactly one departure date.

Whatever the consensus, it is best documented by way of a ***fact model***: a set of ***fact types*** that associate ***business terms*** using agreed ***verbs*** and/or ***prepositions***. A business term is a ***simple noun*** or a ***compound noun***; as we saw in Section 5.1.2 in Chapter 5, compound nouns are made up of ***simple nouns***, ***adjectives***, prepositions, and (occasionally) ***numbers***, ***conjunctions***, or even ***verbs***.

For example, if the organization decides that *specify* is the standard verb to be used to associate transactions with the data items that can be included in them, it can record the following fact type in the fact model:

F3. flight booking request *specifies* departure date

Of course, there are in any organization many transactions and many data items that can be included in transactions. Rather than have to create a fact type for each combination of transaction and data item (and run the risk of them using different verbs), a generalized fact type such as F4 can be created. Each transaction can then be included in a categorization fact type such as F5; similarly, each data item can be included in another categorization fact type such as F6. Each combination of

---

[3]See Section 5.2 in Chapter 5 for a definition of the term ***common noun***.
[4](Object Management Group, 2008).

transaction and data item then inherits the verb from F4. This concept of **inheritance** is discussed further in Section 6.3.3.

F4. transaction *specifies* data item
F5. flight booking request *is a category of* transaction
F6. departure date *is a category of* data item[5]

F3 (or the combination of F4, F5, and F6) can support a variety of other rule statements, such as

R164. The departure date *specified in* each flight booking request
must *be no earlier than* today.
R165. The return date (if any) *specified in* each flight booking request
must *be no earlier than* the departure date
specified in that flight booking request.

In turn, R165 requires one of the following additional fact types:

F7. flight booking request *specifies* return date
F8. return date *is a category of* data item

Of course, a particular pair of concepts may be associated in more than one way. I recall eating recently at a restaurant in which my order was taken on a hand-held electronic device, which was presumably to ensure that I got the meal I wanted and that my bill would be correct (neither of which was the case!). In such a system, the terms person and meal might be associated in each of the following fact types, each of which signifies a different relationship rather than different wording for the same relationship:

F9. person *orders* meal
F10. person *prepares* meal
F11. person *serves* meal
F12. person *pays for* meal[6]

6.1.2.2 Finding the right term
Having identified each concept of interest to the organization and the preferred term signifying each concept, we could simply list each term, with its definition, in alphabetical order. Such a collection, often referred to as a **business glossary** (or, if developed as a side effect of a data modeling exercise, a **data dictionary**), is reasonably useful if you already know the preferred term and only need to establish or confirm the definition assigned to that term.

Whatever preferred term is chosen for each concept, there are for most concepts many alternative terms, which new employees and customers may think are just as valid, and long-standing employees and customers may use out of habit. If these alternative wordings (or **synonyms**) are not included in the glossary, employees or customers will either have to try and imagine what the preferred term is (and no

---

[5]Note that that the SBVR uses a different form, namely <term 1> *is of the category* '<term 2>'. The form <term 1> *is a category of* <term 2> used in this book is after (Ross, 2003).
[6]Of course, one might alternatively use the specific person role names customer (or diner), kitchen staff member, and waitperson in F9, F10, and F11 respectively (and customer again in F12).

doubt come up with a few candidates) and then search for each candidate until one is found, or, worse, may assume that the concept is not included.

For example, you may know that the glossary includes a term to cover agreements made with customers: is one of these referred to as an <u>agreement</u>, a <u>contract</u>, or a <u>deal</u>? If the preferred term for this concept is <u>contract</u>, anyone who thinks in terms of <u>agreement</u> or <u>deal</u> will not find either and have to search the entire glossary unless they guess that it must be <u>contract</u>.

There are two ways of resolving this problem, both valuable, and neither replaces the other:

1. Record all possible synonyms in the glossary, marking each one except the preferred term with a cross-reference to the preferred term, thus:
   - <u>Agreement</u>: *see Contract*
   - <u>Contract</u>
   - <u>Deal</u>: *see Contract*
2. Organize terms into a **taxonomy**, in which each concept (except for a small set of top-level concepts) is recorded as being a specialized variety of some more general concept: for example, businesses, government bodies, and not-for-profit organizations are each particular types of organizations.

6.1.2.3 Other uses of a fact model

A fact model can also be used as a source of

1. business-friendly names of entity classes (or object classes), attributes, and relationships in conceptual or logical data models: (entity-relationship models, ORM (Object Role Modeling) models, or UML (Unified Modeling Language) object class models) (see Section 6.5.1);
2. meaningful tags in XML schemas (see Section 3.1.6 in Chapter 3 for some examples)[7];
3. names of processes in business process models (see Section 6.5.2);
4. terminology in system documentation: specifications, training manuals, help screens, etc.

6.1.3 Other models of the organization

There are various other means available to an organization to document the environment in which it operates, the processes it performs, the information it records, the systems it requires for those purposes, and the language it uses to describe its environment, processes, information, and system components:

1. A **business glossary** is generally a list of business terms with definitions, with little indication (except perhaps within those definitions) of the way in which the concepts signified by each term interact within the organization's environment. Since most (if not all) business glossaries are alphabetically sorted, they are not an ideal source of a big picture of the organization's environment, nor do they easily provide answers to questions of the form "what term is used for the concept . . ."[8], as discussed in Section 6.1.2.2.

---

[7]XML tags must not contain spaces, so "camel case" (e.g., 'dateOfBirth') is used for these. If they are also to be abbreviated, this should be done consistently: that is, using a single abbreviation for any given word or compound noun.
[8]That is, unless all possible synonyms are also included.

2. Various forms of ***business process model*** (e.g., Use Cases, BPMN—Business Process Modelling Notation—models) are available to document the processes an organization performs, and at least some of the rules governing those processes: in practice, these may or may not use business terminology to do so. Procedure manuals document human processes and human interactions with systems. System specifications document the processes performed by a system in detail.

3. Various forms of ***data model*** (entity-relationship models, ORM models, or UML object class models)— see Section 3.2.1 in Chapter 3—can be used to document the structures (and to some extent the content) of an organization's data resources (i.e., databases), and at least some of the rules governing those data. While these can also be used to document intersystem messages, some organizations do not do so, leaving such documentation to XML schemas (see Section 3.1.6 in Chapter 3). Again, in practice many of the entities (or object classes) and attributes in such models are not given meaningful business names, and rarely have adequate definitions. There have been various approaches to modeling the real world within which organizations operate: among them are Corporate Data Models (which have fallen out of fashion) and Information Architectures (which may or may not include data models as such).

4. A ***data dictionary*** can be used to specify the meaning of, and rules governing the content of, individual data items in an organization's data resources or intersystem messages. Again, in practice these data items are identified by the database column name or XML tag, which is often not a meaningful business name, although definitions are generally better than those in data models.

5. A ***rule book*** documents the rules governing an organization.

6.1.4 **What is a fact model?**

A ***fact model*** documents

1. the concepts that the staff within an organization need to understand and refer to in discourse within that organization, and that the customers, suppliers, and partners of that organization need to understand and refer to in discourse with that organization;

2. the preferred terminology to be used to refer to those concepts, as well as any other terminology in common use;

3. the attributes, properties, or characteristics exhibited by those concepts that are of interest to that organization;

4. the preferred terminology to be used to refer to those attributes, properties, or characteristics, as well as any other terminology in common use;

5. the relationships between those concepts that are of interest to that organization;

6. the preferred terminology to be used to refer to those relationships, as well as any other terminology in common use.

An alternative name for a fact model is ***structured business vocabulary***. As this name suggests, a fact model is more than merely a business glossary; it is structured, in that it documents the relationships between concepts referred to by business terms, in particular ***taxonomic relationships***, such as the following:

1. Both persons and organizations are parties with which arrangements can be entered into.

2. Minors and adults are both persons.

3. Organizations include businesses, government bodies, and registered not-for-profit organizations.

In the examples above

1. <u>party</u> is the ***hypernym***[9] of <u>person</u> and <u>organization</u>, while <u>person</u> and <u>organization</u> are ***hyponyms***[10] of party (the set of persons and the set of organizations are ***subsets*** of the set of parties);
2. <u>person</u> is a hypernym (as is <u>party</u>) of <u>minor</u> and <u>adult</u>, each of which is a hyponym of <u>person</u> (and <u>party</u>);
3. <u>organization</u> is a hypernym (as is <u>party</u>) of <u>business</u>, <u>government body</u>, and <u>registered not-for-profit organization</u>, each of which is a hyponym of <u>organization</u> (and <u>party</u>).

As we shall see, such taxonomic relationships provide a number of significant advantages, including the following:

1. A more useful means of organizing terms than alphabetically, allowing for both the big picture and detailed pictures of the organization's environment, and answering questions of the form "what term is used for the concept …?" (as discussed in Section 6.1.2.2);
2. The ability to define relationships and relationship terminology at a generalized organization-wide level, which are then inherited by the hyponyms of the terms in the generalized relationship (as in the example in Section 6.1.2.1);
3. The ability to develop the model in a more comprehensive and consistent manner through the emergence of patterns: for example, if it is understood that parties participate in arrangements, the model can be developed by considering which types of parties participate in which ways in which types of arrangements.

6.1.5 **What does a fact model consist of?**

A ***fact model*** consists of

1. ***business terms*** (or ***terms***), each being the preferred term for a concept to be used in discourse by the organization, each with
   a. a definition of the concept signified by that term,
   b. any ***synonyms*** (other terms in common use for that concept);
2. ***proper names*** (or ***names***) of individual instances of such concepts;
3. ***fact types***, each of which either
   a. relates two or more concepts, or
   b. documents a characteristic of a concept.

6.1.6 **Concepts**

Phenomena in the natural world exist whether or not any human beings have established any mental concepts of those phenomena: that is, perceived that those phenomena exist and that there are classes of phenomena to which more than one individual phenomenon belongs. For example, early in life we

---

[9]Alternatively, ***superclass name*** (if you are used to UML object class models), ***supertype name*** (if you are used to entity-relationship models), or ***superset term*** (if you are used to set theory).
[10]Alternatively, ***subclass name***, ***subtype name***, or ***subset term***.

establish that all human beings seem to share certain common characteristics. Other natural phenomena include other various types of animals (apart from human beings), plants, and landforms (mountains, valleys, etc.).

The physical world also includes concepts that exist only because human beings individually or as a group have created such concepts. These include anything manufactured or built, such as cities, buildings, and equipment.

Human beings have also created concepts that are at least partly abstract, such as families, organizations, market sectors, states, countries, contracts, accounts, and transactions.

Fortunately, unless we are working for a dictionary or thesaurus publisher, we only need to include in an organization's fact model those concepts that are

1. other organizations or persons with which the organization has dealings, and the roles played by those organizations or persons;
2. locations in which the organization or its customers or suppliers operate;
3. products and services that the organization provides to customers;
4. physical resources such as equipment items or consumables;
5. arrangements and agreements, including contracts;
6. financial accounts;
7. events that affect the organization, including customer and supplier activities, processes performed by the organization's staff, and all financial transactions;
8. organizational influences, such as legislation, regulations, policies, and business plans;
9. information resources;
10. relationships between any of the above;
11. attributes of any of the above.

6.1.7 Terms and definitions

For the members of an organization to be able to have a shared understanding of the concepts of interest, a consensus is necessary as to what *term*(s) are to be used when referring to particular concepts (*en masse* or individually). Thus some organizations refer to a human being as a person while others might, for various reasons, prefer the term human being, individual, or natural person. Having agreed on a preferred term—and also which *synonyms* (alternative terms) may be allowed in certain situations—it is also necessary to agree on which concepts are covered by that term. Does the term person cover someone who is *in utero* or now deceased? Does it cover fictional characters? While the answer to the second question is most likely to be 'no' in most organizations, different organizations might answer the first question differently.

Of course, it is not only the concepts themselves (the *entities* to a data modeler, or *object classes* to an object modeler) but their attributes, properties, or characteristics for which agreed terms (and definitions) are needed. Is the human characteristic that a train operating company takes into account when allocating shared sleeping accommodation to solo travelers to be called sex or gender? Having chosen the term, do we use it to mean particular biological characteristics (as the medical and insurance industries might choose) or merely how the person presents to the community?

Agreed terms and definitions for both entities (object classes) and attributes are fundamental components of a fact model. This is discussed in more detail in Section 6.2.

6.1.8 **Facts and fact types**

An organization's understanding of its environment is achieved through the assembly of various *facts* of interest. To an airline,

<u>Frequent Flier #123456</u> *resides in* <u>Sydney</u>,
<u>Frequent Flier #234567</u> *resides in* <u>Melbourne</u>, and
<u>Frequent Flier #345678</u> *resides in* <u>Brisbane</u>

are all facts that can be used, say, for marketing or tailoring the online experience of frequent flier program members. Similarly,

<u>Flight QF1</u> *operates from* <u>Sydney</u> *to* <u>London Heathrow</u>,
<u>Flight QF765</u> *operates from* <u>Sydney</u> *to* <u>Adelaide</u>, and
<u>Flight QF926</u> *operates from* <u>Sydney</u> *to* <u>Cairns</u>

are all facts that can be used both by the airline and its customers to identify services available between particular cities.

In each case, the organization has established multiple facts of the same type: in the first case each fact is of the form depicted in F13, while in the second case each fact is of the form depicted in F14.

F13. <u>frequent flier program member</u> *resides in* <u>city</u>
F14. <u>flight</u> *operates from* <u>port</u> *to* <u>port</u>

Since these forms are archetypes of similar facts, we can call them *fact types*. Specifically, they are both *associative fact types*, since they each provide a *pro forma* for one or more *associative facts*, namely facts that associate phenomena with each other: for example, people with the cities in which they reside, and flights with ports. Each fact type includes

1. *terms* (<u>frequent flier program member</u>, <u>city</u>, <u>flight</u>, <u>port</u>), which act as placeholders, in place of which can be substituted the name of any member of the set signified by the term;
2. a *fact symbol* ('*resides in*', '*operates from ... to*'), which consists of everything in the fact type other than the *terms*.

Each fact symbol consists of one or more *connectors*, each being a contiguous set of words, either a *verb phrase* or a *preposition*. Thus F13's fact symbol consists of the connector '*resides in*' while F14's consists of the two connectors '*operates from*' and '*to*'.

Fact types are discussed in more detail in Section 6.3.

6.1.9 **Identification**

To be able to express the facts in the previous section, an organization needs to have a means of identifying individual persons, cities, flights, and ports. Indeed, to express any fact of interest, one must be able to identify individual instances of each concept of interest. To be able to do this, the organization needs a *reference scheme* for each set of concepts of interest, namely one or more numbers, names, or codes that together uniquely identify each instance of the concept.

In the case of frequent flier program members, the membership number is sufficient since presumably no number has been allocated to more than one member. Of course, if the airline provides reciprocal services to members of allied airlines' frequent flier programs, the membership number alone is no longer sufficient but must be combined with either the name of the airline or a code which uniquely identifies the airline. Thus QF123456 (a Qantas frequent flier) and AA123456 (an American Airlines frequent flier) are highly unlikely to be the same person even though they have the same frequent flier program membership number.

Similarly, cities cannot be uniquely identified by name alone. To uniquely identify a city within Australia or the United States requires not only the name but the state code: for example, there are towns named Springfield in Illinois, Massachusetts, and Missouri, among others. If the set of cities of interest spans more than one country, the country name (or a code identifying the country) should be added, so as to distinguish, for example, London, UK, and London, Ontario, Canada[11].

A comparable problem exists with airports ('ports' in airline terminology). For this reason, ports are assigned unique three-letter codes by IATA (the International Air Transport Association), such as 'LAX', 'LHR', and 'SYD'.

Flights are of course identified by flight number, chosen by the airline to be unique. If flights by multiple airlines need to be considered, the addition of the airline identification code (e.g., 'QF' for Qantas, 'AA' for American Airlines) ensures unique identification.

A fact model should also identify the appropriate reference scheme(s) for each entity class or object class. This is discussed in more detail in Section 6.3.1.3.3.

6.1.10 Attribute fact types

Among the facts an organization may wish to record about employees, customers, or other persons of interest are the birth dates of at least some of those persons. These are not so much of interest *per se* but are useful as a means of calculating a person's age. This is because persons under a certain age may be restricted from certain activities (e.g., driving, marrying, signing a contract, traveling alone, purchasing certain products) and persons over a certain age may be restricted from certain activities or products (e.g., some types of insurance cover) or may obtain discounts or rebates on certain fees.

Thus we may have rules such as the following:

R166. A person
may *travel alone*
only if the age *of* that person *is at least* 2 years.

R167. A person
may *obtain* travel insurance
only if the age *of* that person *is less than* 70 years.

The attribute fact type that supports both these rule statements is

F15. age *is of* person

Note that not all attributes are appropriate to all entities (object classes). While height and weight may be recorded for at least some employees (such as flight and cabin crew), I am not aware of height or

---

[11]However, a problem with identifying cities in multiple countries is that not all countries are divided into states or the equivalent (e.g., states in the United States and Australia, counties in the United Kingdom, provinces in Canada, departments in France). For example, New Zealand has no such subdivisions. The reference scheme in this case therefore has to allow for the code identifying the state, county, province, department, etc., to be optional.

weight being recorded for any passengers by any airline (although it has been recommended on at least one occasion by the National Transportation Safety Board). And while height and various weights[12] are also appropriate attributes for aircraft, birth date is not (date of manufacture or date of entry into service are however likely to be required). Furthermore, none of these is an appropriate attribute for cities. Attribute fact types enable the organization to identify which attribute terms are appropriate to which entity class (or object class) terms. For example, the following fact types capture some of the above discussion:

F16. age *is of* person
F17. date of birth *is of* person
F18. height *is of* person
F19. weight *is of* person
F20. height *is of* aircraft model
F21. date of manufacture *is of* aircraft model
F22. date of entry into service *is of* aircraft model

Attribute fact types are discussed in detail in Section 6.3.1.3.

6.1.11 Categorization schemes and categories

All organizations classify in various ways the concepts that are of interest to them. For example, some organizations need to classify their employees or their customers by gender. Gender is a *categorization scheme* that applies in particular to persons. Outside the health and human services environment, this scheme usually includes two *categories*: male and female.

Note that the categories in a categorization scheme should be *mutually exclusive*: that is, no individual can be simultaneously be given more than one category within that scheme. The categories may or may not be *jointly exhaustive*: that is, there may be individuals that belong to no category within the scheme. For example, loan applications may be categorized as approved or rejected, but loan applications that have not yet been through the approval process are neither.

All of the categories discussed so far in this section are named using adjectives. Nouns can also be used for category names. For example, a bank may categorize its retail products as check account, savings account, credit card, personal loan, mortgage, etc. If preferred, categories named using adjectives can be given noun names by appending the term signifying the categorized concept. In this way, the categories above become male person, female person, approved loan application, and rejected loan application.

Sometimes, a categorization scheme is derived from a quantitative attribute (see Section 6.2.3.2.3), dividing the range of values that may be taken by that attribute into a series of bands. For example, airlines make a distinction between adults, children, and infants, since there are rules governing the respective numbers of adults, children, and infants allowed in a group of passengers traveling together. (Since each infant travels on an adult's lap rather than in a seat of their own, the number of infants must not exceed the number of adults; if there are children but no adults, special conditions apply.) While the names of the categories (adult, child, and infant) are obvious, there is no obvious name for the

---

[12]These include the unladen weight of an aircraft model and the calculated takeoff weight of an individual aircraft immediately before a particular flight.

categorization scheme. While <u>majority</u> is one possible name, it may not even be necessary in terms of user interface or system design to name the categorization scheme as well as the categories.

How do these categorization schemes and categories appear in rule statements? Let's look at some examples:

R168. A <u>sleeping berth booking request</u>
must *specify* the <u>gender</u> *of* the <u>passenger</u>.

R169. A <u>child passenger</u> who *is traveling alone*
must not *be seated next to* a <u>male passenger</u>.[13]

R170. <u>Disbursement</u> *of* a <u>loan application</u> that *is approved*
must *occur during* the <u>3 business days</u>
after the <u>approval</u> *of* that <u>loan application</u>.

R171. Each <u>application</u> *for* a <u>retail product</u> other than a <u>savings account</u>
must *be accompanied by* a <u>declaration of credit history</u>.

R172. The number of <u>infant passengers</u>
specified in a <u>flight booking confirmation</u>
must *be no more than* the number of <u>adult passengers</u>
specified in that <u>flight booking confirmation</u>.

R168 illustrates that a categorization scheme (<u>gender</u> in this case) can be referenced as if it were an attribute of the concept being categorized.

R169 illustrates one way of including an adjective in a rule statement, namely appending the term signifying the categorized concept to create a compound noun (as described in Section 5.1.2 in Chapter 5). Thus from <u>male</u> we get <u>male passenger</u>.

R170 illustrates the only other way of including an adjective in a rule statement, namely preceding the adjective with the verb '*is*', is to create a compound verb (as described in Section 5.3.3 in Chapter 5). Thus from <u>approved</u> we get '*is approved*'.

Unlike categories expressed using adjectives, categories expressed using nouns can be referred to in isolation. For example, we cannot use the word <u>approved</u> in a rule statement without naming the categorized concept (<u>loan application</u> in this case), but we can refer to a <u>savings account</u> in a rule statement without having to state that it is a type of retail product. However, R171 is an example of a rule statement that does include both a term (<u>retail product</u>) and the name of one of its categories (<u>savings account</u>).

R172 illustrates that, even with category names that are already nouns, it may be appropriate to append the term signifying the categorized concept to those category names in a rule statement. Rather than the category names <u>infant</u> and <u>adult</u>, the terms <u>infant passenger</u> and <u>adult passenger</u> are used.

What fact types do we need to document a categorization scheme and its categories along with the categorized concept? Let's consider first the categorization of passengers by gender: that is, as male or female. F23 names the categorization scheme and associates it with the categorized concept. F24 and F25 express the categories as compound verbs, while F26 and F27 express the categories as compound nouns.

---

[13]This rule is enforced by at least one airline to my knowledge, although it has caused considerable debate.

F23. gender *is of* passenger
F24. passenger *is male*
F25. passenger *is female*
F26. male passenger *is a category of* passenger
F27. female passenger *is a category of* passenger

However, there does not yet appear to be any way of associating a categorization scheme with its categories using fact types. This is not a problem for expression of business rules since a rule statement either refers to the categorization scheme (as in R168) or one or more of the categories (as in R169-R172).

6.1.12 Higher-order facts

We have now encountered fact types with one, two, and three terms. Facts (and thus fact types) involving four or more terms are also possible, such as

Employee #123 *passes* Order #9876 *to* Employee #345 *on* 5 May 2010, or
Customer #1234 *orders* 10 *of* Product #2345 *on* 6 June 2010.

The corresponding fact types are

F28. employee *passes* order *to* employee *on* date
F29. customer *orders* quantity *of* product *on* date

6.2 TERMS AND NAMES

A *business term* (referred to in the SBVR as a *term*) is a *simple noun* or *compound noun*[14] that an organization uses to refer to one or more instances of a concept: that is,

1. a party (a person or organization) or role played by a party: for example, customer, employee, supplier, organization unit;
2. a location: for example, country, state, city, suburb, street;
3. a concrete thing: for example, vehicle, physical asset, equipment item;
4. an abstract thing (such as an event, arrangement, quality, etc.): for example, transaction, account, duration.

Each term must also be a *countable noun*[15] and must be recorded in the *singular* form (i.e., not the *plural* form).

Some terms are used to signify relationships between other terms. For example, organizations employ persons. The term employment can be used to signify the relationship between an organization and a person employed by that organization; employment is therefore a *relationship term*. Furthermore, both the organization and the person in that relationship play specific roles: the organization plays

---

[14]See Section 5.1.2 in Chapter 5 for definitions of the terms *simple noun* and *compound noun*.
[15]See Section 5.1.1 in Chapter 5 for a definition of the term *countable noun*.

the role of employer, and the person plays the role of employee; <u>employer</u> and <u>employee</u> may therefore be referred to as *role terms*. Relationship terms correspond to *intersection entity classes* in entity-relationship models and *association classes* in UML object class models, while role terms correspond to roles in object class models and ORM models.

Some terms are used to signify attributes (properties or characteristics) of other terms. For example, each organization has a registered business name, and each person has a family name (or surname) and one or more given names. Each person also has a date of birth, a height, and a weight (which may or may not be of interest). Each employment has a start date. Each employee may have an employee number. <u>Registered business name</u>, <u>family name</u>, <u>given name</u>, <u>date of birth</u>, <u>height</u>, <u>weight</u>, <u>start date</u>, and <u>employee number</u> may all therefore be referred to as *attribute terms*. Attribute terms correspond to attributes in both entity-relationship models and UML object class models.

Terms that are not relationship terms, role terms or attribute terms may be referred to as *fundamental terms*. These correspond to entity classes (but not intersection entity classes) in entity-relationship models and to object classes (but not association classes) in UML object class models.

There are three important decisions to be made when creating a term in a fact model:

1. the choice of the word or words to be used in the term: for example, the use of <u>customer</u> or <u>client</u> as the preferred term (and whether the other is to be retained as a known synonym);
2. what that term actually signifies (which must be documented as a properly constructed definition): for example, the term <u>customer</u> is to be used only for another organization or a person that has purchased a product or service from us, or is in the process of doing so; the term includes those that have not made a purchase for some time, but excludes any <u>prospect</u>: that is, those that have been identified by marketing or sales staff but have not yet made a purchase;
3. its place in the taxonomy of terms: for example, a <u>customer</u> is a specific <u>party role</u>, alongside <u>employee</u> and <u>supplier</u>.

These three decisions interact, so we need first to discuss some of the implications of each aspect.

With proper names we have less choice as to the words to be used, and none with official names, such as place names or the names of organizations. Also, names only occasionally require definitions. However, each name should be correctly placed in the taxonomy: for example, <u>California</u> is a <u>US State</u>.

6.2.1 Choice of words in a term

Clearly, an important consideration when choosing the wording of a term is common usage within the organization. If only one term is ever used within the organization, the choice would seem to be simple. However, in this situation we need to ask whether the same term (or proper name) is used anywhere within the organization (or among customers or suppliers) to refer to a different concept: in other words, whether we have any *homonyms*.

6.2.1.1 Homonyms

These can arise in a variety of ways. For example, in one Australian Land Registry, the term <u>instrument</u> includes a particular document type in one section of the organization but excludes that same document type in another section. The solution in this case was not to change habits but to document the divergence in meaning.

In any Land Registry, the term <u>property</u> has a specific meaning to do with real estate. On acquiring a software tool that used the term <u>property</u> for something quite different, a new term was agreed on for the new concept, and the tool was customized to replace the term <u>property</u> with the new term on all screens.

As I previously observed in Section 1.5.1.2 in Chapter 1, <u>service</u> had at least six different meanings in one airline, so it was necessary to create one or more different terms for each meaning by (in most cases) prefixing <u>service</u> by a suitable noun or adjective: for example, <u>meal service</u>, <u>customer service</u>, <u>maintenance service</u>.

Another source of homonyms is the common practice in some organizations to use the same term for a type of event and the document raised to record events of that type: for example, <u>license application</u>. It may be appropriate to create a new term for the document, such as <u>license application document</u>, but this may not be acceptable.

Yet another rich source of homonyms is the names of countries and states, each of which can be used to refer either to an area of land or to a legal entity: for example, <u>Australia</u> is both a landmass and a country that can participate in international activities of various kinds. One way to distinguish the alternative meanings is to use the full name of the legal entity: for example, <u>Commonwealth of Australia</u>, <u>State of Victoria</u>, and the short name (<u>Australia</u>, <u>Victoria</u>) only for the area of land.

6.2.1.2 Synonyms

If more than one term (or proper name) is used for the same concept, we need to ask the following questions:

1. Are these different terms truly synonymous, or do they signify different sets of things? For example, in one organization where I consulted the terms <u>organization unit</u> and <u>branch</u> were treated by some as synonymous, yet I was later to discover that officially a branch was a particular type of organization unit: that is, not all organization units were branches. In another situation, I discovered that, while one term was used to refer to all documents of a particular type, an apparent synonym was used only to refer to such documents after they were registered.
2. Which term more correctly describes the concept? Alternatively, are any of the terms misleading to the untrained person?
3. Which term is most commonly used?

Sometimes, the term that is most commonly used is misleading; in this situation, there is a case for recommending adoption of the less commonly used but more accurate term as the preferred term.

6.2.1.3 Compound nouns as terms

Various problems can arise with compound nouns, the most common form of which is a head noun prefixed by one or more adjectives or other nouns. On one occasion, I encountered the term <u>external employee</u> which was used to signify the employees of customers, rather than employees of the organization itself. While this term was quite appropriate, the term <u>employee</u> was at the same time being used to refer only to employees of the organization. I argued that, where two terms differed only inasmuch as one term is the other term with a prefix (like <u>external employee</u> and <u>employee</u>), it is reasonable to assume that the term without the prefix covers all instances covered by the term with the prefix plus some others. In this case, it was reasonable to assume that the term <u>employee</u> covered all external employees (as well as others). It took some convincing but the organization eventually accepted that the term <u>internal employee</u> should be used for employees of the organization, and <u>employee</u> only used when referring to both employees of customers and employees of the organization itself. Shortly afterwards, I was vindicated when an online facility was provided that could be accessed by both sets of employees.

The rule of thumb here is that a term that is another term prefixed should be used only when the first term signifies a subset of the set signified by the second term: that is, the first term is a ***hyponym*** of the second. For example if <u>customer</u>, <u>retail customer</u>, and <u>wholesale customer</u> are all terms in use, the latter two are appropriate terms only if they signify types of <u>customer</u>.

Of course, there are other ways in which a compound noun can be constructed. One way is to append a noun to another term to create a term that signifies a concept in some way associated with the concept signified by the original term. For example,

1. as well as <u>order,</u> we can have <u>order line</u> signifying part of an order;
2. as well as <u>loan,</u> we can have <u>loan application</u> and <u>loan approval</u>, signifying events that occur in the lifecycle of a loan.

Another way (particularly when trying to name tables in a relational database) is to create a term signifying an association between two concepts by concatenating those concepts' terms: for example, if the organization records which suppliers supply which parts, a designer of a relational database in which this information is to be recorded will almost inevitably[16] create a table named 'Supplier_Product'. I find that business stakeholders rarely feel the need to name such relationships, and, if they do, generally prefer to append a third noun: for example, (in this case) 'availability', so as to yield <u>supplier product availability</u>.

It is important to note that such terms are rarely required to support rule statement writing. The fact model can document the relationship with a fact type rather than a term, as in F30, while a rule statement can have as its subject a reference to a combination of terms instead of a single term, as in R173.

F30. <u>supplier</u> *supplies* <u>product</u>
R173. Each record of a combination of <u>supplier</u> and <u>product</u>
        must *specify* the <u>latest supply date</u>.

Another potential problem with forming compound nouns is due to there being more than one method of forming a compound noun. The two most common methods are

1. prefixing an existing term with one or more adjectives or other nouns;
2. following an existing term with a preposition and another noun.

Thus we can use either the term <u>birth date</u> or <u>date of birth</u>. This in itself is not a problem. We can decide for each concept which form is to be the preferred term, and may even standardize, so that (for example) all terms referring to dates are of one form or the other. If we need to add a third noun, however, we cannot mix these methods. Note what happens if we do. At an Australian Land Registry recently, the terminology team was busy creating all the necessary terms to be used in rule statements. Having created the terms <u>interest in land</u> and <u>mortgage of estate</u>, they then required

---

[16]That is, unless they take advantage of object-relational capabilities in more recent versions of relational database management systems.

1. a term to signify the categorization scheme by which interests in land are categorized, and
2. a term to signify an instrument (official document) registering a mortgage of estate.

The team duly came up with <u>interest in land type</u> and <u>mortgage of estate instrument</u>, but these are not quite right. The term <u>interest in land type</u> appears to signify an interest in a type of land rather than a type of interest in land, and <u>mortgage of estate instrument</u> appears to signify the mortgage of an estate instrument (if there is such a thing) rather than an instrument registering a mortgage of estate. The correct terms are <u>type of interest in land</u> and <u>instrument for mortgage of estate</u>.

Note that, if the original terms are changed to <u>land interest</u> and <u>estate mortgage</u>, two options are now available for each of the new concepts:

1. either <u>land interest type</u> or <u>type of land interest</u>;
2. either <u>estate mortgage instrument</u> or <u>instrument for estate mortgage</u>.

Yet another problem can arise when a term is created by prefixing a noun with both an adjective and another noun. I was amused by a recent newspaper article about "Ancient DNA Experts": was 'ancient' a reference to the DNA or the experts? I also recall an HR system that included the screen legend "Short Employee Name" in which to enter an eight-character abbreviated form of each employee's name: I found myself wondering why short employees had a special data item of their own.

6.2.2 Definitions

Each term must have a definition which clearly and unambiguously defines which objects are and are not covered by the term.

The definition of a business term may be

1. *intensional*, in which the objects covered by the business term are defined as members of a more general class with one or more distinguishing characteristics: for example, <u>minor</u>: a <u>person</u> whose <u>age</u> is less than the <u>age of majority</u>;
2. *extensional*, in which the objects covered by the business term are listed: for example, <u>minor</u>: a <u>boy</u> or a <u>girl</u>.

Each definition should meet the following quality criteria:

1. Wherever possible, each definition should in the first instance be sourced from
   a. any existing business glossary,
   b. any procedural documentation produced by the organization,
   c. any relevant legislation,
   d. a specialized dictionary (if any) for the industry in which the organization operates,
   e. a general dictionary of the English language.
2. Each definition should be unambiguous.
3. No definition should be misleading, in the sense that any reader might infer either
   a. inclusion of inappropriate instances in the set signified by the term, or
   b. inappropriate exclusion of some instances from that set.
   Thus the definition should not be too general or too specific.

4. Each definition must use natural language syntax, so that "A <term> is a <definition>" forms a grammatical sentence. For example, "a party who lends money under the terms of a mortgage" is appropriate as a definition of mortgagee since "A mortgagee is a party who lends money under the terms of a mortgage" is a grammatical sentence.

5. Unless the term signifies a single instance—for example, State of Western Australia—there must be at least one *indefinite article* ('a' or 'an') in the definition. The *definite article* ('the') may be used in definitions as follows:

   a. if the term signifies a single instance, or

   b. if there is also at least one indefinite article elsewhere in the definition.

   Note that the initial article in a definition should only be 'the' if there is known to be only one instance of the object signified by the term in each instance of the described context. Thus "the six-character string identifying a flight booking" is appropriate as a definition of booking reference number since there is only one associated with each flight booking, but "the party who is lent money under the terms of a mortgage" is inappropriate as a definition of mortgagor since there may be more than one such party to a mortgage: the definition should read "a party who is lent money under the terms of a mortgage".

6. If any other business term is used in the definition (in the singular or plural form), it should ideally be marked in some way[17], if used with the meaning implied by the definition of that other term. However, if used with some other meaning (typically common usage), it should ideally be marked in some other way.

7. No term signifying a real-world object should be defined in terms of any data item or information object representing that real-world object. For example, the term customer should not be defined as "a party recorded in the customer database" but instead be defined in terms of the events and/or relationships that characterize a customer in the real world. The term customer database can then be defined as "the database in which details of customers are recorded".

Metadata associated with a definition (none of which should really appear in the definition itself) should include the source of the definition and example members of the set of objects signified by the term. For example, 'Federal Aviation Administration' and 'National Transportation Safety Board' might be recorded as examples of regulatory body by an airline.

If the term is likely to be misused, each of the excluded cases (concepts that might be considered to be included within the meaning of the term in question, but for which an alternative term is used) should be recorded, each with the alternative term. This is particularly important where it may not be clear whether the term signifies individual objects or classes of objects. For example, the term aircraft is used commonly to refer to either

1. individual aircraft, each with a separate tail number (registration number), as in "ten aircraft landed at Vancouver airport between 0900 and 1000 today", or

2. an aircraft model (e.g., 'Airbus 380'), as in "what aircraft is used on this flight?"

The term aircraft should therefore have, in addition to its definition, a statement that the term is not to be used to signify an aircraft model, for which the term aircraft model should instead be used.

---

[17]Ideally as an active hyperlink to the location of the other term in the fact model.

6.2.3 **The taxonomy of terms and proper names**

A *taxonomy* results from classifying the concepts to which an organization or community needs to refer, by recognition of either common or distinguishing properties, characteristics, behavior, or relationships.

For example, the organization can recognize that it deals in much the same way in terms of provision of products or services with both individual persons and organizations. It may be tempted to create the term customer to cover both persons and organizations, but not all persons and organizations are customers: persons may be employees and organizations may be suppliers, regulatory bodies, and so on. A more neutral term is party. Recognition of common features in the way persons and organizations are dealt with leads to the creation of the *hypernym* party embracing both person and organization.

At the same time, the organization may recognize that not all persons are dealt with in the same way, in particular that children are dealt with differently from adults. Recognition of this fact leads to the creation of the *hyponyms* adult and child referring to different types of person. Of course, there is more than one way to categorize persons: gender may also be relevant[18]. In this case, the subset terms male person and female person can be created.

Note that the terms adult and child are mutually exclusive (if properly defined): no person can be both an adult and a child. Similarly, the terms male person and female person are mutually exclusive: no person can be both a male person and a female person. However, the terms adult and male person are not mutually exclusive: a person can be both an adult and a male person. What we have done is to divide the class of persons into two mutually exclusive *categorization schemes*: one distinguishes adults and children, the other distinguishes male and female persons.

Note that, if any term is used to signify multiple concepts (e.g., the term table signifies either an artifact in a database or an item of furniture), it will appear in multiple positions in the taxonomy, with a specific definition in each position. I recommend that each occurrence of such a term be marked in some way to indicate that there are other occurrences of the same term. For example, in a taxonomy I produced for one Australian government body, each such term was rendered as a hyperlink which when clicked navigated the user to the next occurrence of the same term (clicking on the last occurrence of the term navigated the user to the first occurrence of the same term).

I discuss in more detail how to build the taxonomy of terms in Section 6.4.

6.2.3.1 *Examples of taxonomies*

Perhaps the best known example of a taxonomy is the Linnaean taxonomy of organisms. Another well-known taxonomic classification is to be found in Roget's Thesaurus, although this is not, strictly speaking, a taxonomy, since it includes within each grouping verbs, adjectives and adverbs as well as nouns. I still have the 3rd edition published in 1962, in which there are eight top-level classes, each containing a number of subclasses, each of which in turn contains a number of sections containing all words dealing with a specific concept. The top-level classes are

1. Abstract Relations
2. Space
3. Physics

---

[18]Despite the very reasonable requirement in most organizations that persons are dealt with in the same way irrespective of gender, there are various organizations (e.g., in the health sector) in which it is important to distinguish persons by gender.

4. Matter
5. Sensation
6. Intellect
7. Volition
8. Affections.

Similarly the IBM Financial Services Data Model has nine top-level "data concepts" within which all financial services concepts are grouped:

1. Arrangement
2. Business Direction Item
3. Condition
4. Classification
5. Event
6. Involved Party
7. Location
8. Product
9. Resource Item.

In developing business taxonomies for a variety of clients, I have found that the following set of top-level concepts is a very useful starting point:

1. party: a person or organization (not necessarily legally constituted) that may play one or more party roles;
2. party role: a role played by a party with respect to the organization (e.g., customer, employee, supplier, service provider, partner, regulator) or with respect to some arrangement or event (e.g., vendor, purchaser, applicant);
3. geospatial feature (or location): any place where the organization or its customers or suppliers operates, any physical address from or to which goods or communications may be sent, or any geopolitical or organizational division of the earth's surface (e.g., country, state, region, city, postal zone, building, room, port, terminal, gate, physical address);
4. product/service: any product or service that the organization provides to customers;
5. physical resource: any equipment item, furniture, building, or consumable used by the organization in its operations;
6. arrangement: any agreement, contract, or other ongoing arrangement, such as a financial account, fund, insurance policy, lease, program, or project in which the enterprise is involved or has an interest;
7. event: anything that happens that affects the organization, such as a customer or supplier activity, a process performed by the organization's staff, or a financial transaction;
8. organizational influence: anything which influences the actions of the organization, its employees and/or its customers, or how those actions are performed, such as items of legislation, regulations, policies, business plans, performance indicators, standard amounts and rates, maxima and minima, and external issues (political, industrial, social, economic, demographic, or environmental) that influence the operation or behavior of the enterprise;
9. information resource: any set or item of information held or used at any time by the organization, such as a record, file, database, intersystem message, or data item therein, including all representations of any other concept;

10. relationship: any association between any of the above concepts or representations thereof;
11. attribute: any simple or complex attribute, property, characteristic, or categorization scheme of any of the above;
12. category: any category within any categorization scheme.

Each organization will of course include different sets of terms under each of these top-level terms (reflecting its particular interests and scope of operations). Some organizations may indeed wish to add, delete, or rename one or more top-level terms. One area in which all organizations tend to end up with the same concepts (if not the same terms) is under attribute. For this reason, the next section sets out a taxonomy of attribute and data item terms that I have found to be almost universal.

6.2.3.2 Attributes and data items

Before considering the taxonomy of attribute and data item terms, it is important to be clear on a number of things:

1. Objects in the physical world have attributes: for example, at any given time, a person may have a family name, one or more given names, a date of birth, a height, a weight, and so on.
2. Information resources recording information about physical world objects include data items that represent the attributes of those physical world objects: for example, an employee database is likely to include columns holding data items representing each employee's family and given names, and, possibly, date of birth, height, and weight. These data items are not attributes of those information resources.
3. Those information resources and individual records, as well as data items therein, may however have attributes, such as date last updated, number of records, size, and so on.
4. The taxonomy set out below is a taxonomy of attributes of physical world objects. An analogous taxonomy of data items can be created, if required, with the same structure. To avoid confusion, each term in the taxonomy of data items is named by replacing 'attribute' with 'data item': for example, the data item term corresponding to category attribute is category data item.

Each attribute is one of the following:

1. identifier attribute: an *identifier attribute* exists purely to identify entity instances and does not imply any properties of those instances (e.g., order number, product code, line number)[19];
2. category attribute: a *category attribute* can only take one of a defined set of values, each representing a *category* in the relevant *categorization scheme* (e.g., product type, customer credit rating, payment method, delivery status);
3. quantitative attribute: a *quantitative attribute* (or *arithmetic attribute*) is one on which some arithmetic can be performed (e.g., addition, subtraction), and on which comparisons other than '=' and '≠'[20] can be performed (e.g., order quantity, order date, unit price, discount rate);
4. text attribute: a *text attribute* can hold any string of characters that the user may choose to enter (e.g., customer name, product name, product type description, delivery instructions text).

---

[19]Note that, while these attributes almost always arise in the first instance as data items in systems, they are often subsequently used by human beings to identify the physical world objects concerned: for example, account numbers, customer numbers, credit card numbers, postal codes (zip codes).

[20]Note that the comparisons '=' and '≠' can be performed on any type of attribute.

6.2.3.2.1 Identifier attributes

Each <u>identifier attribute</u> is one of the following:

1. <u>system-generated identifier</u>: an identifier generated automatically without user intervention whenever a new instance is created (e.g., <u>customer number</u>, <u>order number</u>), which
   a. may be generated in sequence although there is no particular requirement to do so,
   b. is not necessarily numeric: for example, the six-character booking reference 'number' assigned to an airline reservation,
   c. may or may not be visible to users;
2. <u>administrator-defined identifier</u>: an identifier suitable only for low-volume entities but ideal for these (e.g., <u>department code</u>, <u>product code</u>), which
   a. requires some means for new identifiers to be loaded into each relevant system as required,
   b. may be numeric or alphanumeric;
3. <u>externally defined identifier</u>: an identifier defined by a standards authority or other external party (e.g., <u>country code</u>, <u>currency code</u>, <u>state code</u>, <u>postal code</u>), which
   a. is ideally loaded into a database in bulk from a dataset provided by the defining authority,
   b. may be numeric or alphanumeric;
4. <u>tie-breaker attribute</u> (or <u>tie-breaker</u>): an attribute used in conjunction with other attributes for the sole purpose of providing a unique multi-attribute identifier (e.g., <u>line no</u> in an <u>order line</u> entity class), which is inevitably
   a. system-generated, and
   b. numeric to allow for a simple means of generating new unique values.

6.2.3.2.2 Category attributes

Category attributes are typically administrator-defined, but some may be externally defined. Externally (on screens and reports), each category is represented using a unique character string (e.g., 'Cash', 'Check', 'Credit Card', 'Charge Card', 'Debit Card') but may be represented internally using a shorter code or an integer value. The internal representations may even be used externally if users are familiar with them and their meanings.

A particular kind of category attribute is the ***Boolean attribute*** (***flag attribute*** or ***indicator attribute***): this can take a "Yes" or "No" answer to a suitably worded question about the entity instance, in which case the question should appear as a legend on screens and reports alongside the answer (usually represented externally as a check box or as a text field that can hold 'Y' or 'N' and internally as either 1/0, 'Y'/'N', or 'T'/'F').

6.2.3.2.3 Quantitative attributes

Each <u>quantitative attribute</u> is one of the following:

1. <u>simple arithmetic attribute</u>: an attribute for which the question "*Is this attribute greater than ...?*" makes sense
   a. <u>count attribute</u>: a dimensionless (unitless) attribute that answers a question of the form "*How many ...?*" (e.g., <u>vehicle count</u>, <u>employee count</u>);
   b. <u>ordinal attribute</u>: a dimensionless (unitless) attribute that answers a question of the form "*In what sequence ...?*" (e.g., <u>period number</u>, <u>task sequence number</u>);

   c. currency amount attribute: an attribute that answers a question of the form "*How much ...?*", specifies an amount of money, and requires a currency unit ($US, $A, GBP, etc.) (e.g., unit price, payment amount, outstanding balance);

   d. dimension attribute: an attribute that answers a question of the form "*How long ...?*"; "*How high ...?*"; "*How wide ...?*"; "*How heavy ...?*"; etc., and that can only be interpreted in conjunction with a unit (mm, g, etc.) (e.g., room width, unit weight);

   e. factor attribute: an attribute that is (conceptually) the result of dividing one quantitative attribute by another and that requires a unit ($/h, m/s, etc.) unless both quantitative attributes are of the same dimension, in which case it is a unitless ratio (or percentage) (e.g., interest rate, discount rate, hourly rate, blood alcohol concentration);

2. time point attribute: a dimensionless (unitless) attribute that answers a question of the form "*When ...?*"

   a. specific time point attribute: an attribute that answers a question of the form "*When ...?*" in relation to a single event:

     i. timestamp attribute (or datetime attribute), which specifies the date and time when something happened (e.g., transaction timestamp),

     ii. date attribute, which specifies the date on which something happened but not the time (e.g., order date),

     iii. month attribute, which specifies the month and year in which something happened (e.g., manufacture month),

     iv. year attribute, which specifies the year in which something happened, such as the year of arrival of an immigrant (e.g., arrival year);

   b. recurrent time point attribute: an attribute that answers a question of the form "*When ...?*" in relation to a recurrent event:

     i. time of day attribute, which specifies the time but not the date (e.g., departure time of day),

     ii. day of week attribute, which specifies only the day within a week (e.g., scheduled day of week),

     iii. day of month attribute, which specifies only the day within a month (e.g., mortgage repayment day of month),

     iv. day of year attribute, which specifies only the day within a year (e.g., annual renewal day of year),

     v. month of year attribute, which specifies only the month within a year (e.g., annual renewal month of year);

3. interval attribute (or duration attribute): an attribute that answers a question of the form "*For how long ...?*" and that requires a unit (e.g. s, min, h, days, weeks, months, years) (e.g., lesson duration, mortgage repayment period);

4. time period attribute: an attribute that answers a question of the form "*For what period of time ...?*" and consists of two dates, one marking the start of the period and the other the end (e.g., employment time period);

5. spatial attribute: an attribute that answers a question of the form "*Where ...?*" and that requires a datum and a coordinate unit, such as

   a. point attribute, which specifies a point in two- or three-dimensional space (e.g., lot centroid, start point),

  b. line segment attribute, which specifies a line segment in two- or three-dimensional space (e.g., road centerline),

  c. polygon attribute, which specifies a two-dimensional polygon in two- or three-dimensional space (e.g., postal code area).

6.3 FACT TYPES

Fact types are occasionally referred to in the literature (and in at least one rule repository tool) as "facts". Fortunately, the SBVR (Object Management Group, 2008) makes a clear distinction between *facts* and *fact types*. A fact is either

1. something which is the case or which has occurred, or
2. a true statement.

For example, "Canberra is the capital city of Australia" is a true statement (a fact), whereas "Sydney is the capital city of Australia" is a false statement.

  The artifact "city *is the capital city of* country" is not a statement as such but can be used as the *pro forma* for any number of statements, some of which will be true (i.e., facts) and some false, depending on which city and country names you include.

  Fact types are formed from ***business terms*** in any of the following ways:

1. associating a pair of terms using a ***verb phrase***, to form a ***binary fact type***: for example,

F31. customer *raises* order

2. associating sets of three or more terms with a verb phrase and one or more prepositions, to form a ***ternary fact type***, ***quaternary fact type***, or other ***higher-order fact type***: for example,

F32. person *plays* sport *for* country

3. associating a single term with an ***intransitive verb phrase***: for example,

F33. person *is deceased*

By convention all verb phrases in fact types are in the ***third person singular present indicative*** form (see Section 5.3.2.4 in Chapter 5)—for example, '*specifies*'—even though some alternative forms are required in rule statements. For example:

1. After 'must', 'must not', or 'may', the ***infinitive*** form is required: for example, '*specify*' in the case of '*specifies*'.
2. Some rule statements require the use of a verb phrase in the past tense: for example,

R174. Each passenger
  must *board* the flight *for* which that passenger *has checked in*
   no later than 15 min *before* the departure time *of* that flight.

Fact types can be categorized in two ways:

1. by the number of terms appearing in the fact type: a ***unary fact type*** includes only one term, a ***binary fact type*** includes two, a ***ternary fact type*** three, and so on;

2. by the relationship between those terms that is expressed in the fact type, which gives us the following categories:

    a. *associative fact types*, of the following subcategories:

        i. *named relationship fact types* (which can be binary, ternary, or higher order but not unary), described in Section 6.3.1.1;

        ii. *partitive fact types* (which can only be binary), described in Section 6.3.1.2;

        iii. *attribute fact types* (referred to in the SBVR as *is-property-of fact types*) (which also can only be binary), described (along with unary fact types) in Section 6.3.1.3;

    b. *taxonomic fact types*, of the following subcategories:

        i. *categorization fact types* (which also can only be binary), described in Section 6.3.2.1;

        ii. *assortment fact types* (which also can only be binary), described in Section 6.3.2.2.

6.3.1 Associative fact types

An associative fact type relates two or more *fundamental terms* (see Section 6.2) using a *verb phrase* and (if there are more than two terms) one or more *prepositions*. Two particular varieties of associative fact type are the *partitive fact type* and the *attribute fact type*, described in Sections 6.3.1.2 and 6.3.1.3 respectively. All other associative fact types are *named relationship fact types*.

6.3.1.1 Named relationship fact types

6.3.1.1.1 Binary named relationship fact types

The most common form of named relationship fact type is *binary*, in that it links two terms using a verb phrase: that is, it has the form

    <u>term 1</u> *<verb phrase>* <u>term 2</u>: for example,

F34. <u>flight booking request</u> *specifies* <u>departure date</u>
F35. <u>flight booking request</u> *specifies* <u>return date</u>

The purpose of such a fact type is to document the verb phrase to be used in any rule statements that need to refer to the relationship between instances of the two terms (in this case, a date in the context of a flight booking request). Thus rule statements can include such sequences as

    each <u>flight booking request</u> must *specify* a <u>departure date</u>,
    a <u>flight booking request</u> that *specifies* a <u>return date</u>, or
    if that <u>flight booking request</u> *specifies* a <u>return date</u>,

but not corresponding sequences with any other verb phrase (unless there are additional fact types signifying different relationships between flight booking requests and dates—see next paragraph).

The same two terms may legitimately appear in more than one binary named relationship fact type, but only if the two relationships signified are quite distinct. For example, F36 and F37 signify two quite distinct relationships, whereas F38 and F39 signify the same relationship, and therefore only one of these should appear in the same fact model.

F36. <u>employee</u> *reports to* <u>employee</u>
F37. <u>employee</u> *trains* <u>employee</u>
F38. <u>employee</u> *reports to* <u>employee</u>
F39. <u>employee</u> *is subordinate to* <u>employee</u>

Since we may need to include these terms in reverse order, each binary named relationship fact type also has a reverse form. The reverse form of F35 above is 'return date *is specified by* flight booking request'.

In this case, the reverse form is generated by swapping the two terms and replacing the **active verb phrase** by its form in the **passive voice**. There are occasions, however, when an alternative verb phrase is used, either because there is no convenient passive form or because it does not read well: for example, whereas one could derive '†employee *is reported to by* employee'[21] from 'employee *reports to* employee', it does not read well: 'employee *manages* employee' (or 'employee *is manager of* employee') reads better. Of course, the passive form of '*manages*' is '*is managed by*', in view of which you may wish to replace 'employee *reports to* employee' by 'employee *is managed by* employee' but, in Australia at least, the first form is more commonly used.

Whatever reverse form you select for each verb phrase used in a fact type, you should record each such verb phrase and its reverse form in your fact model in some way. If you are creating your fact model using a rule repository tool or fact modeling tool, it should

1. provide for the recording of standard verb phrases and their reverse forms: for example, record '*is specified by*' as the reverse form of '*specifies*', and

2. be able to display each fact type in both directions: for example, if you record 'flight booking request *specifies* return date' as a fact type, and '*is specified by*' has been recorded as the reverse form of '*specifies*', that fact type can be displayed in its original form or as 'return date *is specified by* flight booking request'.

If you are creating fact types manually, you should record the reverse form of each standard verb phrase to be used in fact types. You may wish to also record the reverse form explicitly at the same time as you create each fact type, and associate the original and reverse forms with each other in some way: for example, record 'flight booking request *specifies* return date' as associated with 'return date *is specified by* flight booking request'.

6.3.1.1.2 Higher order fact types

There are also **ternary fact types** (all of which are named relationship fact types) which link three terms, most often using a verb phrase and a preposition, in the form

<term 1> <verb phrase> <term 2> <preposition> <term 3>: for example,

F40. employee *passes* document *to* employee

You may occasionally encounter a **quaternary fact type** (with four terms), but, while there is no theoretical limit to the number of terms in a fact type, fact types with four or more terms are quite rare.

Ternary, quaternary, and higher order associative fact types may also have forms in which the terms are sequenced differently: for example, alternative forms of F40 are

document *is passed from* employee *to* employee,
employee *is passed* document *by* employee, or
employee *receives* document *from* employee.

---

[21]Syntactic constructions that are, for one reason or another, not recommended are indicated by an initial dagger.

A binary named relationship fact type corresponds to a relationship in an entity-relationship model or a binary association in a UML object class model. A ternary or higher order fact type has no direct means of representation in an entity-relationship model but can be represented as a ternary or higher order association in a UML object class model.

Note, however, that a binary named relationship fact type makes no assertion as to whether

1. each instance of <u>term 1</u> must be associated with an instance of <u>term 2</u> or there may be instances of <u>term 1</u> that are not associated with any instance of <u>term 2</u>;
2. each instance of <u>term 2</u> must be associated with an instance of <u>term 1</u> or there may be instances of <u>term 2</u> that are not associated with any instance of <u>term 1</u>;
3. each instance of <u>term 1</u> must be associated with no more than one instance of <u>term 2</u> or there may be instances of <u>term 1</u> that are associated with more than one instance of <u>term 2</u>;
4. each instance of <u>term 2</u> must be associated with no more than one instance of <u>term 1</u> or there may be instances of <u>term 2</u> that are associated with more than one instance of <u>term 1</u>.

Higher order fact types similarly make no such assertions about the terms used in those fact types.

A variety of ternary fact type that is particularly useful allows multiple instances of the same object to be associated with another object. For example, a flight booking request specifies an origin city and a destination city. Both the origin city and the destination city are cities and subject to rules about cities. However, the origin and destination cities in a flight booking request are not categories of city and so cannot inherit the properties and associations of a city as described in Section 6.3.3.

The origin and destination cities in a flight booking request are in fact roles played by cities. By using a ternary fact type, we can associate an object that plays a role, the role, and the context in which it plays that role:

F41. <u>flight booking request</u> *specifies* <u>city</u> *as* <u>origin city</u>
F42. <u>flight booking request</u> *specifies* <u>city</u> *as* <u>destination city</u>
F43. <u>flight booking request</u> *specifies* <u>date</u> *as* <u>departure date</u>
F44. <u>flight booking request</u> *specifies* <u>date</u> *as* <u>return date</u>

6.3.1.1.3 Using role terms in named relationship fact types
The fact that organizations employ persons can be signified by fact type F45.

F45. <u>organization</u> *employs* <u>person</u>

Since, as we saw in Section 6.2, an organization involved in such a relationship can be referred to as an <u>employer</u> and a person involved in such a relationship can be referred to as an <u>employee</u>, it may be tempting to reformulate this fact type as

<u>employer</u> *employs* <u>employee</u>.

However, I recommend that fact types use fundamental terms even if relevant role terms exist. Meanwhile, each role term should be defined using a ***formal term definition*** rule statement (as described in Section 4.9.1.1 in Chapter 4[22]):

---

[22]I am aware that the SBVR (Object Management Group, 2008) has defined "is role of" fact types but at the time of writing my understanding is that these are to be revamped in a subsequent version of the SBVR.

R175. An <u>employer</u> *of* a <u>person</u> *is* by definition
        an <u>organization</u> that *employs* that <u>person</u>.
R176. An <u>employee</u> *of* an <u>organization</u> *is* by definition
        a <u>person</u> who *is employed by* that <u>organization</u>.

6.3.1.2 Partitive fact types

A *partitive fact type* is a particular variety of binary associative fact type in which the nature of the relationship is that each object signified by one term is part of an object signified by the other term. A verb phrase commonly used for partitive fact types is '*is part of*', in which case these fact types have the form

    <u>term 1</u> *is part of* <u>term 2</u>: for example,

F46. <u>order line</u> *is part of* <u>order</u>

This category of fact type also has a reverse form: '<u>order</u> *includes* <u>order line</u>'.
    A related concept is that of **containment** for which the verb phrases '*is contained in*' and '*contains*' are more appropriate: for example,

F47. <u>file</u> *is contained in* <u>folder</u>

A partitive or containment fact type does make the assertion that each instance of <u>term 1</u> must be associated with no more than one instance of <u>term 2</u> but it makes none of the other assertions listed above for named relationship fact types.
    In addition, the reversed form of a partitive or containment fact type: that is,

    <u>term 2</u> *includes* <u>term 1</u> (or <u>term 2</u> *contains* <u>term 1</u>),

makes no assertion as to whether instances of <u>term 2</u> are precluded from including or containing any other objects: for example, F47 does not imply that a folder cannot contain other types of objects.
    A partitive or containment fact type corresponds to either an aggregation or a composition relationship in a UML object class model. Entity-relationship models, however, commonly make no distinction between aggregation or composition relationships and other relationships.

6.3.1.3 Fact types dealing with attributes

An entity class in an entity-relationship model or object class in a UML object class model generally has attributes. The association between an entity class (or object class) and any of its attributes is signified by

1. a *unary fact type* if the attribute is **Boolean**, or
2. an *attribute fact type* otherwise.

A particular variant of the attribute fact type is the **identification fact type**. Each of these is now described.

6.3.1.3.1 Unary fact types

A *unary fact type* signifies an association between a **Boolean** property or characteristic exhibited by instances of an entity class (or object class): that is, a characteristic that each instance either does or does not exhibit. Such a fact type has the form

<u>term 1</u> <verb phrase>,

in which <u>term 1</u> signifies the entity (class): for example,

F48. <u>person</u> smokes
F49. <u>person</u> is deceased

Such a fact type clearly has no reverse form. Note that the verb phrase must be **intransitive**, as distinct from a **transitive verb phrase** (one that requires an object as well as a subject, such as '*employs*' in '<u>organization</u> *employs* <u>person</u>'). Thus rule statements can include such sequences as

a <u>person</u> who *smokes*, or
if that <u>person</u> *smokes*.

6.3.1.3.2 Attribute fact types

An **attribute fact type** is used to signify any other (non-Boolean) property or characteristic of an entity class (or object class). Such a fact type has the form

<u>term 1</u> *has* <u>term 2</u>,

in which <u>term 1</u> signifies the entity class (or object class) and <u>term 2</u> signifies the property or characteristic, with the reverse form

<u>term 2</u> *is of* <u>term 1</u>: for example,

F50. <u>person</u> *has* <u>birth date</u>/
      <u>birth date</u> *is of* <u>person</u>

Thus rule statements can include such sequences as

a <u>person</u> who *has* a <u>birth date</u> that *is earlier than* <u>1/1/1950</u>,
a <u>person</u> whose <u>birth date</u> *is earlier than* <u>1/1/1950</u>, or
if the <u>birth date</u> *of* that <u>person</u> *is earlier than* <u>1/1/1950</u>.

6.3.1.3.3 Identification fact types

As we saw in Section 6.2.3.2.1, an **identifier attribute** is a particular type of attribute that exists purely to identify entity instances. An **identification fact type** is a particular variant of the attribute fact type that uses a more appropriate verb phrase to associate an entity class (or object class) with the relevant identifier attribute. Such a fact type has the form

<u>term 1</u> *is identified using* <u>term 2</u>,

in which <u>term 1</u> signifies the entity class (or object class) and <u>term 2</u> signifies the identifier, with the reverse form

<u>term 2</u> *identifies* <u>term 1</u>: for example,

F51. <u>person</u> *is identified using* <u>social security number</u>/
      <u>social security number</u> *identifies* <u>person</u>

But what if the entity class requires multiple attributes to identify each instance? For example, motor vehicle registration numbers in Australia are only unique within the state of registration: that is, two different vehicles registered in different states may have the same registration number. Thus to uniquely identify a registered motor vehicle in Australia, it is necessary to specify the state as well as the registration number. Using only identification fact types, the best we could do would be

F52. motor vehicle *is identified using* registration number/
registration number *identifies* motor vehicle
F53. motor vehicle *is identified using* state name/
state name *identifies* motor vehicle

However, neither of these fact types is appropriate, since neither registration number nor state name uniquely identifies a motor vehicle. If it is necessary to specify the **reference scheme** (means of identification) for each entity class or object class (and I believe it is), fact types like the following are required for each entity class or object class which has a multi-attribute reference scheme:

F54. motor vehicle *is identified using* motor vehicle identifier/
motor vehicle identifier *identifies* motor vehicle
F55. registration number *is part of* motor vehicle identifier/
motor vehicle identifier *includes* registration number
F56. state name *is part of* motor vehicle identifier/
motor vehicle identifier *includes* state name

6.3.1.3.4 Standard fact types for comparison of quantitative attributes

In Section 6.3.1.3.2, we encountered rule statement fragments in which a person's birth date was being compared with a specific date (as in "a person whose birth date *is earlier than* 1/1/1950"). Such comparisons are common in rule statements, and are based on a set of standard fact types that support comparison of quantitative attributes. The following fact types support date comparisons (F57 in particular supports the comparisons in Section 6.3.1.3.2):

F57. time point attribute *is earlier than* time point
F58. time point attribute *is later than* time point
F59. time point attribute *is no earlier than* time point
F60. time point attribute *is no later than* time point
F61. time point attribute *is on* time point

In each of these, time point refers to either a time point attribute or a time point literal. Alternative forms for the first four of these fact types support alternative wording in rule statements:

F62. time point attribute *is before* time point
F63. time point attribute *is after* time point
F64. time point attribute *is on or after* time point
F65. time point attribute *is on or before* time point

Corresponding fact types are available for simple arithmetic attributes:

F66. simple arithmetic attribute *is less than* quantity
F67. simple arithmetic attribute *is more than* quantity
F68. simple arithmetic attribute *is no less than* quantity
F69. simple arithmetic attribute *is no more than* quantity
F70. simple arithmetic attribute *is equal to* quantity

In each of these, quantity refers to either a simple arithmetic attribute or a quantity literal. There are also alternative forms for F66, F68, and F69:

F71. simple arithmetic attribute *is fewer than* quantity
F72. simple arithmetic attribute *is at least* quantity
F73. simple arithmetic attribute *is at most* quantity

Fact types are also available for comparing time periods with each other and time points with time periods:

F74. time period attribute *overlaps* time period
F75. time period attribute *is earlier than* time period
F76. time period attribute *is later than* time period
F77. time period attribute *is earlier than* time point
F78. time period attribute *is later than* time point
F79. time point attribute *is within* time period

In each of these, time point refers to either a time point attribute or a time point literal, while time period refers to either a time period attribute or a time period literal. Again, an alternative to each fact type using the connector '*is earlier than*' uses the connector '*is before*', while an alternative to each fact type using the connector '*is later than*' uses the connector '*is after*'.

Fact types are also available for comparing spatial data items, such as:

F80. point attribute *is on* line segment
F81. point attribute *is within* polygon
F82. line segment attribute *intersects* line segment
F83. line segment attribute *is within* polygon
F84. polygon attribute *is within* polygon
F85. polygon attribute *overlaps* polygon

In each of these, line segment refers to either a line segment attribute or a literal representing a line segment, while polygon refers to either a polygon attribute or a literal representing a polygon (such as the name of some region on the earth's surface).

6.3.1.3.5 Alternative forms of verb phrases involving attributes

You may be tempted to provide for alternative wordings when referring to attributes. For example, instead of

a person who *has* a birth date that *is earlier than* 1/1/1950, you may prefer

>   a <u>person</u> who *was born earlier than* <u>1/1/1950</u>.

While this is a common form of expression in everyday English, it poses a problem. Instead of a separate term for each attribute (e.g., <u>birth date</u>, <u>height</u>, <u>weight</u>) and a small set of fact types for comparing attributes (as in the previous section), we are using a verb phrase to represent the attribute. This would necessitate a separate fact type for each combination of attribute and comparison, and so is not recommended.

6.3.2 Taxonomic fact types

There are two special categories of fact type which we can use to define our taxonomy of terms:

1. *categorization fact types* (described in Section 6.3.2.1) that define a term's **hypernym** (the term signifying the superset of the set signified by the original term);
2. *assortment fact types* (described in Section 6.3.2.2) that define the set to which the individual concept signified by a **proper name** belongs.

6.3.2.1 Categorization fact types

Many of the terms we use are **hyponyms**, signifying particular types of the things signified by more general terms (**hypernyms**). For example, we may use the hyponyms <u>return journey</u> and <u>one-way journey</u> as well as the hypernym <u>journey</u>. Return journeys exhibit all the characteristics and associations of journeys but may have additional characteristics and associations exhibited only by return journeys (such as a return date). An association such as this is represented in an entity-relationship model as a supertype/subtype association or a UML object class model as a superclass/subclass association.

　　Categorization fact types are used to document this type of association and thus enable us to assemble the terms we use into a **taxonomy** (as described in Section 6.2.3). Such a fact type has the form

>   <u><term 1></u> *is categorized as* <u><term 2></u>[23],

in which '<u>term 1</u>' is the **hypernym** and '<u>term 2</u>' is the **hyponym**, with the reverse form

>   <u><term 2></u> *is a category of* <u><term 1></u>.

In the case of '<u>journey</u>', '<u>return journey</u>', and '<u>one-way journey</u>', the categorization fact types are

F86. <u>return journey</u> *is a category of* <u>journey</u>/
　　　　<u>journey</u> *is categorized as* <u>return journey</u>
F87. <u>one-way journey</u> *is a category of* <u>journey</u>/
　　　　<u>journey</u> *is categorized as* <u>one-way journey</u>

6.3.2.2 Assortment fact types

In Section 6.2, we saw that a **business term** is a term that refers to a set of similar things (e.g., <u>Country</u>) whereas a **proper name** is a term that refers to an individual concept (e.g., <u>Australia</u>). An **assortment**

---

[23]Note that the SBVR uses a different form, namely "<u><term 1></u> *is of the category* '<u><term 2></u>'". The form "<u><term 1></u> *is a category of* <u><term 2></u>" used in this book is after (Ross, Principles of the Business Rule Approach, 2003).

fact type is a means of recording for a proper name the set to which that individual concept belongs. For example,

F88. Australia *is a* country
F89. Sydney *is a* city

Strictly speaking, these are facts rather than fact types: each is a true statement rather than a *pro forma* for a number of statements.

6.3.2.3 Features of taxonomic fact types

Categorization and assortment fact types differ from the other categories of fact type in a number of ways. The most fundamental difference is what the terms in each fact type signify.

A fact type in any of the other categories signifies a set of relationships between instances of the two classes. Consider

F90. city *is the capital city of* country

This fact type embraces each of the following facts:

> Canberra *is the capital city of* Australia,
> Washington DC *is the capital city of* the United States of America,
> London *is the capital city of* the United Kingdom,
> and so on.

By contrast, a categorization fact type signifies a relationship between two sets: for example,

F91. capital city *is a category of* city

This fact type signifies a relationship between the set of cities and the set of capital cities: we cannot substitute the names of actual cities in place of either 'capital city' or 'city' in any meaningful way.

As a result, '*is categorized as*' and '*is a category of*' do not appear in rule statements. It clearly makes no sense to state

> ‡ Each capital city must *be a category of* city.[24]

This is because a rule statement governs individually each instance of its subject term (i.e., each capital city in the example above).

Similarly, it makes no sense to qualify references to capital cities, as in

> ‡ a capital city that *is a category of* city, or
> ‡ if that capital city *is a category of* city.

This is because these clauses each use a property of the set of capital cities as a selection criterion for members of that set, which is about as relevant as (for example) using whether or not a human being is a vertebrate as a selection criterion for members of that set when all human beings belong to a particular category of vertebrate.

Of course, one could legitimately write "a city that *is* a capital city", but this noun phrase can be replaced by "a capital city" in any rule statement without loss or alteration of meaning.

---

[24]The double dagger prefixing a rule statement fragment indicates that, although syntactically valid, it is a meaningless formulation.

However, there may be a case for including a categorization fact type in a rule statement, as in

if that <u>city</u> *is* a <u>capital city</u>.

A similar argument applies to assortment fact types: for example,

F92. <u>London</u> *is a* <u>city</u>

This fact type identifies a member of the set of cities: again, we cannot substitute the name of any actual city in place of <u>city</u> in any meaningful way (which is why a so-called assortment fact type is really a fact rather than a fact type).

Again, there may be a case for including an assortment fact type in a rule statement, as in

if that <u>city</u> *is* <u>London</u>.

6.3.3 Derived fact types

The most important role of categorization fact types is to support ***inheritance*** of other fact types down the taxonomy. For example, the categorization fact type F94 allows <u>return journey</u> to inherit fact type F93 from <u>journey</u> in the form of fact type F95.

F93. <u>flight booking request</u> *is for* <u>journey</u>
F94. <u>return journey</u> *is a category of* <u>journey</u>
F95. <u>flight booking request</u> *is for* <u>return journey</u>

Since F95 can be inferred from F93 and F94, F95 should not be explicitly recorded as well as F93.

Note that inheritance can operate across more than one level in a taxonomy. For example, F96 defines <u>multi-stop journey</u> as another ***hyponym*** of <u>journey</u> (along with <u>return journey</u>), and F97 defines <u>round-the-world journey</u> as a ***hyponym*** of <u>multi-stop journey</u>, and, as a result, as a ***hyponym*** of <u>journey</u>. Similarly, <u>journey</u> is a ***hypernym*** of <u>return journey</u>, <u>multi-stop journey</u>, and <u>round-the-world journey</u>.

F96. <u>multi-stop journey</u> *is a category of* <u>journey</u>
F97. <u>round-the-world journey</u> *is a category of* <u>multi-stop journey</u>

If you have two candidate fact types and the only difference between them is that a term in one is a hyponym of the corresponding term in the other fact type, the fact type with the hypernym should be recorded but not the fact type with the hyponym. Thus, for example, F98 and F99 should not be recorded since the terms <u>multi-stop journey</u> and <u>round-the-world journey</u> are hyponyms of <u>journey</u> in F93.

F98. <u>flight booking request</u> *is for* <u>multi-stop journey</u>
F99. <u>flight booking request</u> *is for* <u>round-the-world journey</u>

If there is an analogous fact type for more than one hyponym of a particular hypernym, they should be replaced by a single fact type using the hypernym. For example, if at least two of F95, F98, and F99 exist, they should be replaced by F93.

6.3.4 Object/identifier equivalence

If instances of a type of transaction include references to real-world objects, they often do so using the identifiers of those objects. For example, an order specifies one or more products, but does so using the product code of each product required. Thus fact types F100 and F101 are equivalent.

F100. order *specifies* product
F101. order *specifies* product code

Are both fact types required? No, either will do. It's a good idea, though, to decide which variety of fact type to use for each situation in which a transaction specifies a real-world object by way of its identifier, and make all such fact types consistent.

6.4 BUILDING A FACT MODEL

While the rule statement authoring methodology is covered in Chapter 8, many organizations opt to develop the fact model as an independent exercise, and only "top it up" as necessary to accommodate additional terminology encountered when writing rule statements. This section covers some of the issues you might encounter in fact model development, whether it be as an independent exercise or as part of the process of rule statement authoring.

There are two ways in which the terms to be included in an organization's fact model can be discovered:

1. "bottom up": identifying the terms in use in the organization, by
   a. examining any existing business glossary or procedural documentation produced by the organization, and/or
   b. conducting workshops or interviews with appropriate staff,
   then placing them appropriately within the taxonomy;
2. "top down": starting with one or more of the top-level concepts listed in Section 6.2.3.1 and brainstorming with appropriate staff what specific types of that top-level concept the organization deals with: for example, if the top-level concept 'party role' is chosen, one can workshop all the different party roles with which the organization deals.

Neither approach occurs in isolation: at any given moment, one may focus more on exploring concepts and naming them, or on trying to find homes for terms already identified, but for most of the time both these mental processes are occurring.

6.4.1 Bottom up

The "bottom up" approach yields terms easily but requires care in deciding where in the taxonomy each additional term fits. To again quote Crystal (2006): "*[Each] new [lexical] item has to find its place within the lexicon we have already acquired. And in joining the relevant set, it has to elbow its way in: we may have to change our mind about the sense of other items already there.*" For example, imagine we are assisting a bank to develop its product taxonomy, and we have already identified investment product, cash management product, and loan product as hyponyms of product. We now encounter mortgage product: is that a specific type of loan product or a completely different type of product that needs to placed alongside the existing three as a direct hyponym of product? We agree that a mortgage product is a specific type of loan product, so we make mortgage product a hyponym of loan product. This prompts the question: what other types of loan products are there? Someone mentions personal loans: a personal loan is another type of loan product, so we add personal loan product as another hyponym of <u>loan product</u>. Someone else points out that there are chattel mortgages as well as real estate mortgages. Do we add each of them as a hyponym of <u>mortgage product</u> or do we replace <u>mortgage product</u> by <u>real estate mortgage product</u> and <u>chattel mortgage product</u>? And so on.

6.4.2 Top down

The "top down" approach builds the taxonomy easily (provided you have a place to start) but requires care in the choice of terms. Some of the issues that need to be considered when choosing terms are discussed in Section 6.2.1. As for starting points from which to develop the taxonomy, I've found it useful to get stakeholders to consider the different lifecycles that objects exhibit. For example,

1. some objects would have needed to be mostly in place before the organization started business (with some occasional addition or modification once business got under way): for example,
   a. services and products,
   b. pre-existing parties, such as <u>organization unit</u>, <u>regulatory body</u>,
   c. categorization schemes, such as <u>customer type</u>, <u>transaction type</u>,
   d. other reference sets, such as <u>country</u>, <u>currency</u>, <u>state</u>, <u>language</u>;
2. some objects come into being as the organization does business, with instances that are generally long-lived: for example,
   a. other parties and party roles, such as <u>customer</u>, <u>supplier</u>, <u>employee</u>,
   b. long-term arrangements, such as <u>supply contract</u>, <u>employment contract</u>, <u>insurance policy</u>,
   c. assets, such as <u>equipment item</u>;
3. still other objects also come into being as the organization does business, but are generally transient (although information about them may be retained for some time): for example,
   a. transactions, such as <u>order</u>, <u>sale</u>, <u>purchase</u>, <u>payment</u>,
   b. other events and short-term arrangements, such as <u>project</u>, <u>equipment allocation</u>.

6.4.3 Concept and term discovery workshops

Each workshop should cover specific business functions or processes, with the appropriate stakeholders in attendance. Start by allowing stakeholders to take turns suggesting terms that are important in discussion of that business function or process. Record all terms in a manner visible to all participants (on a photocopying whiteboard or in a spreadsheet on a computer connected to a projector). Don't try to get an agreed definition of any term or its position in the taxonomy: just list them in the first instance, and then, after a reasonable number have been gathered, try and place terms under their most appropriate top-level concept.

Only then should definitions be attempted: deal with the terms within each top-level concept in turn. In this way, it is easier to ensure that definitions of different terms within a given top-level concept do not overlap. Of course, some terms will already be defined in existing documentation, such as policy manuals or legislation. For each of these, identify the appropriate source document if possible, or delegate someone to examine the documentation and supply the required definition. Other terms may lend themselves to an early consensus within the workshop group as a whole. If, however, discussion takes more than 5 or 10 min and no consensus is in sight, move on to the next term, and, at the end of the workshop, obtain agreement on, and enact, an appropriate process for obtaining acceptable definitions of the outstanding terms.

Given the highly intensive and iterative nature of this process, do not use a repository tool during workshops. A spreadsheet not only provides significantly faster data entry and modification facilities but also requires significantly less effort in tidying up outputs for presentation back to stakeholders. Once the taxonomy is reasonably stable, it can be imported into a repository.

6.4.4 Taxonomy publication

The best way to ensure acceptance of the taxonomy is to make it widely available to stakeholders, easy to access and easy to provide feedback. Wiki-style media are ideal for this. Feedback may include proposed changes to definitions (and possibly even terms), or reclassification of terms within the taxonomy, as stakeholders develop more understanding of the set of terms and their meanings.

6.4.5 Discovering fact types

In my experience, the most useful approach to discovering fact types is to consider in turn each pair of top-level concepts, such as party and location. What are the associations of interest between various types of parties and locations? For example:

F102. person *was born in* country
F103. person *is citizen of* country
F104. person *resides at* address
F105. organization *operates at* address
F106. employee *works at* branch

This should be repeated for each pair. Don't overlook associations between parties and other parties, or locations and other locations, such as

F107. organization *employs* person
F108. employee *reports to* employee
F109. organization *is part of* organization
F110. person *is married to* person
F111. person *is parent of* person
F112. address *is in* city
F113. city *is in* state
F114. state *is in* country

6.4.6 Deriving a fact model from a data model

If up-to-date data models are already in use, they may be able to be used as sources of terms and fact types by applying the correspondences documented in Section 6.5.1. This may, however, not be as easy as it sounds, since many data models use entity class and attribute names that are abbreviated and/or cryptic rather than reflecting business terminology. If that is the case, each business term created from examination of the data model should be mapped to the corresponding entity class name or attribute name (in reality, often a database table or column name). This mapping is best recorded against the term in the fact model repository rather than in the data model. This is for two reasons:

1. Given that fact model repositories have been around for significantly less time than data model repositories, there are more likely to be fewer fact model repositories (ideally only one) whereas there are likely to be numerous data models in different repositories.
2. Data model repositories are less likely to provide for such mappings.

6.5 USING A FACT MODEL FOR OTHER ASPECTS OF SYSTEM SPECIFICATION

6.5.1 Building a data model from a fact model

Earlier in this chapter, we observed correspondences between fact types of various kinds and various data model artifacts. To summarize:

1. A fundamental term corresponds to an entity in an entity-relationship model or an object class in a UML object class model.
2. An attribute term corresponds to an attribute in an entity-relationship model or UML object class model.
3. A unary fact type corresponds to the association between an entity (or object class) and one of its Boolean attributes.
4. A binary named relationship fact type corresponds to a relationship in an entity-relationship model or a binary association in a UML object class model.
5. A ternary or higher-order fact type corresponds to a ternary or higher order association in a UML object class model.
6. A partitive or containment fact type corresponds to either an aggregation or a composition relationship in a UML object class model.
7. An attribute fact type corresponds to the association between an entity or object class and one of its non-Boolean attributes.
8. A categorization fact type corresponds to a supertype/subtype association in an entity-relationship model or a superclass/subclass association in a UML object class model.

As a result of these correspondences, if a fact model has already been developed for an area of an organization's operations, it provides a ready source of artifacts with business-friendly names and definitions for inclusion in any data model required.

Of course, physical data models include the actual table and column names. These may be constrained by the target database management system to be no more than a certain length or not contain spaces. Neither of these constraints should be reflected in any data model shared with business stakeholders, which should use agreed business terminology for all names of entities (or object classes), attributes, and relationships. Table and column names should then, if necessary, be derived from the corresponding entity and attribute names by

1. either removal of spaces (to yield "camel case" names, e.g., 'dateOfBirth') or replacement of spaces by underscores (e.g., 'date_of_birth');
2. consistent replacement of particular words or compound nouns by standard abbreviations: that is, a single abbreviation for any given word or compound noun.

I am aware that there is a standard in the UML community for "camel case" names for object classes and attributes in particular. If this is absolutely necessary, those names should not also be abbreviated.

6.5.2 Building a process model

Processes in business process models should each be given a name of the form '<verb> <term>': for example, 'Enroll Student', 'Record Booking', 'Update Customer Address', 'Close Account'. Each term so used should be from the fact model and each combination of verb and term should appear in at least one fact type.

6.6 SUMMARY

To establish a consensus on the vocabulary to be used in an organization's rule statements, a *fact model* (a set of *fact types*) associates *nouns* and/or *proper names* using agreed *verbs* and/or *prepositions*.

A fact model can also be used as a source of business-friendly names of data and process model artifacts (entity classes, object classes, attributes, relationships, and business processes), meaningful tags in XML schemas, and terminology in system documentation.

A *fact model* (or *structured business vocabulary*) documents the concepts (including attributes and relationships) of interest to an organization and the terminology for those concepts (preferred and/or in common use) in the form of a *taxonomy* of *hyponyms* (terms signifying specific subsets of the sets signified by their more general *hypernyms*).

When adding terms to a fact model, care should be taken in the choice of words to be used in each term. Each term must have a definition that clearly and unambiguously defines which objects are and are not covered by the term, and a place in the taxonomy. Discovery of terms occurs through a combination of "top down" and "bottom up" approaches. One approach starts with top-level concepts and looks for and names specific types; the other approach tries to find a home in the taxonomy for terms identified by examining existing documentation or consulting appropriate staff.

As well as *unary fact types* (each involving a single term), *associative fact types* of various categories document relationships between instances of concepts. *Taxonomic fact types* by contrast document the taxonomy, supporting *inheritance* by *hyponyms* of fact types from their *hypernyms*.

Fact types can be discovered by considering pairs of top-level concepts in turn and documenting the associations of interest between various hyponyms of those concepts. Fact models can also be derived from data models.

How to write quality natural language rule statements

This chapter discusses the writing of quality natural language rule statements, in terms of
- the major components of a rule statement—such as the **subject**, the **predicate**, **conditional clauses**, and **qualifying clauses**—and the various forms these can take in rule statements of different types;
- the use of **templates** as the basis for quality rule statements of each type;
- quality criteria for rule statements, including the use of the fact model as a source of terms, verb phrases, and prepositions in a rule statement.

7.1 TYPOGRAPHY AND PUNCTUATION CONVENTIONS IN RULE STATEMENTS

To comply with the SBVR, rule statements in this book use the following typographical conventions:

1. Each **term** from the **fact model** is underlined with a continuous single underline: for example, <u>flight booking request</u>. Note that the special nouns listed in item 3.c below are not treated as terms.
2. Each **proper name** or **literal** value is underlined with a continuous double underline: for example, <u>Australia</u>, <u>30 kg</u>. Note that a cardinal number used to state how many of one object must be associated (or are associated) with another object (as in a data cardinality rule) is treated differently (see item 3.b.ii below).
3. Each of the following words and phrases is in upright text not underlined:
   a. the **modal auxiliaries** 'may' and 'must', and the verb modifier 'not';
   b. all **determiners**: for example,
      i. 'a', 'an', 'the' (except when part of a verb phrase such as '*is the same as*'),
      ii. any cardinal number when used to state how many of one object are associated with another object: for example, 'one', 'two', possibly preceded by 'at least', 'at most', 'more than', 'less than', or 'exactly',
      iii. any ordinal number: for example, 'first', 'second', also 'last', 'next',
      iv. 'all', 'another', 'any', 'both', 'each', 'either', 'every', 'no'[1], 'one', 'only', 'other', 'same', 'that', 'those', 'more';
   c. the special **nouns** 'definition', 'transition', 'combination', 'set', 'record', 'number', 'sum', 'total', 'maximum', 'minimum', 'average', 'mean', 'median', 'product', 'square', 'cube', 'root';

---

[1]Except when part of a verb phrase that expresses a comparison, such as '*be no earlier than*'.

   d. the preposition 'of' when following any of those special nouns, and also the preposition 'other than';

   e. any ***conjunction*** that does not form part of a term (such as <u>terms and conditions</u>): for example,

      i. 'and', 'or', 'but',

      ii. 'that', 'such that',

      iii. 'if', 'unless', 'whether',

      iv. 'after', 'before'[2], 'until', 'while';

   f. the phrases 'at least', 'at most', 'at any time' when qualifying the temporal conjunctions 'after', 'before', 'until', 'while';

   g. all ***pronouns***: for example, 'it', 'that', 'which', 'who', 'whose';

   h. any ***adjective*** that does not form part of a term or verb phrase: for example, 'earlier', 'earliest', 'later', 'latest', 'valid', 'impossible';

   i. the special phrase "the following";

   j. the arithmetic operators 'plus', 'minus', 'multiplied by', 'divided by'.

4. Each ***verb phrase*** from the fact model is in italics: for example, '*is specified by*'. Note that the verb phrases 'may' and 'must' are treated differently (see item 3.a above).

5. Each ***preposition*** is in italics: for example, '*of*', '*in*', except '*of*' after a special noun (as described above) and 'other than'.

Note that, as described in Section 5.10 in Chapter 5, 'that' may be a determiner, a conjunction, or a relative pronoun. Irrespective of its use, 'that' is always rendered in upright non-underlined text.

    It should also be noted that these typographic conventions have no semantic implication, but have been adopted only for clarity; they are not essential to presentation of a correctly formed rule statement. In other words, if your rule repository does not support italics or underlining, your rule statements can use the same font and style throughout and still be correctly formed.

    The following punctuation marks are the only ones used in rule statements in this book:

1. parentheses to enclose 'if any' (as in R177);

2. parentheses to enclose a conditional conjunction and conditional clause other than at the end of a rule statement (as in R178);

3. commas to separate items in a list (also as in R178).

These punctuation conventions are essential.

R177. The <u>postal address</u> (if any)
        specified in each <u>flight booking confirmation</u>
    must *include* exactly one <u>country name</u>.

R178. Each <u>online ticket purchase</u>
    must
    (if it *is* not *made by* an <u>account holder</u>)
    specify exactly one of the following:
        a <u>postal address</u>, an <u>e-mail address</u>, or a <u>fax number</u>.

---

[2]Note that 'after' and 'before' may also be used as prepositions, in which case they are rendered in italics.

A further convention I have adopted from Chapter 4 onward is to lay out each rule statement expressing an *operative rule*[3] in multiple lines as follows:

1. the subject of the statement on one line;
2. any qualifying clauses qualifying the subject, each on a separate indented line;
3. 'must', 'must not', or 'may', followed by the predicate, all on one line if possible, otherwise on multiple lines with the second and subsequent lines indented;
4. any qualifying clauses qualifying the predicate, each on a separate indented line;
5. if there is a conditional clause, 'if' or 'unless', followed by the conditional clause, all on one line if possible, otherwise on multiple lines with the second and subsequent lines indented.

Similarly, in Chapter 4 onward each rule statement expressing a *definitional rule*[4] is laid out in multiple lines as follows:

1. the subject of the statement on one line;
2. any qualifying clauses qualifying the subject, each on a separate indented line;
3. all or part of a verb phrase, followed by the phrase 'by definition', followed optionally by the remainder of the verb phrase;
4. the definition, all on one line if possible, otherwise on multiple lines with the second and subsequent lines indented.

7.2 RULE STATEMENT ANATOMY

This section discusses the major components of a rule statement—such as the **subject**, the **predicate**, **conditional clauses**, and **qualifying clauses**—and the various forms these can take in rule statements of different types.

7.2.1 Operative rule statements

An *operative rule statement* is a statement of an *operative rule*. Every operative rule statement in this book—and every operative rule statement you write if you follow the method outlined in this book—has one of the following general formulations:

T1. {Each|The} <operative rule statement subject>
   must <rule statement predicate>
   {{if|unless} <conditional clause>|}.[5]

T2. {A|An|The}[6] <operative rule statement subject>
   must not <rule statement predicate>
   {{if|unless} <conditional clause>|}.[7]

---

[3]See Section 2.1 in Chapter 2 for a definition of the term *operative rule*.
[4]See Section 2.2 in Chapter 2 for a definition of the term *definitional rule*.
[5]Rule statements conforming to this formulation are **obligation statements** as described in Section 3.3.8.3 in Chapter 3.
[6]'A', 'An', or 'The' is used rather than 'Each' in this type of rule statement since the use of 'Each' with 'must not' leads to awkward-sounding statements: for example, '†Each passenger must not *smoke*'.
[7]Rule statements conforming to this formulation are **prohibition statements** as described in Section 3.3.8.3 in Chapter 3.

T3. {Each|The} <operative rule statement subject>
may <rule statement predicate>
only <conditional conjunction> <conditional clause>.[8]

T4. {Each|The} <operative rule statement subject>
must
{({if|unless} <conditional clause>)|}
<rule statement predicate>.[9]

T5. {Each|The} <operative rule statement subject>
may <*verb phrase*>
only <qualified list>.[10]

Each formulation is expressed using a **template**, in which the various symbols have the following meanings:

1. Each item enclosed in "angle brackets" ('<' and '>') is a **placeholder**, in place of which any suitable text may be substituted. For example, any of the following may be substituted in place of <operative rule statement subject>:
   a. a term: for example, 'flight booking request',
   b. a term followed by a qualifying clause: for example, 'flight booking request *for* a one-way journey',
   c. a reference to a combination of items: for example, 'combination of enrollment date and graduation date', with or without a qualifying clause,
   d. a reference to a set of items: for example, 'set of passengers', with or without a qualifying clause.
2. Each pair of braces ('{' and '}') encloses a set of options (separated from each other by the bar symbol: '|'), one of which is included in the rule statement. For example,
   a. each rule statement conforming to formulation T1, T3, or T4 starts with either 'Each' or 'The';
   b. a conditional clause in a rule statement conforming to formulation T1, T2, or T4 is preceded by either 'if' or 'unless'.
3. If a pair of braces includes a bar symbol immediately before the closing brace, the **null option** is allowed: that is, you can, if necessary, include none of the options at that point in the rule statement. For example, each rule statement conforming to formulation T1, T2, or T4 may include or omit a conditional clause preceded by 'if' or 'unless'.
4. Sets of options may be nested. For example, in each of the templates above
   a. a conditional clause may be included or omitted,
   b. if included, the conditional clause should be preceded by either 'if' or 'unless'.
5. A further notation, introduced later in this section, uses square brackets to indicate that a syntactic element may be repeated indefinitely: this is described in more detail in Section 9.1.1.3 in Chapter 9.

---

[8]Rule statements conforming to this formulation are **restricted permission statements** as described in Section 3.3.8.3.
[9]This is a variant of T1, used whenever the rule predicate involves a list of items.
[10]This is a variant of T3, used to simplify **information access rules** (see Section 7.2.4.5).

6. Any text not enclosed in either "angle brackets" or braces (i.e., 'must', 'not', 'may', and 'only') is included in every rule statement conforming to the relevant template.

While there may be numerous options available as to what may be substituted in place of each place-holder, there are also restrictions:

1. If the designator in the placeholder is underlined with a single underline (e.g., <u>term</u>), any suit-able term from the fact model may be substituted. Chapter 9 discusses each rule type in turn and includes in that discussion an indication as to what terms are suitable in rule statements for that rule type.

2. If the placeholder is <*verb phrase*>, a verb phrase from a fact type in the fact model may be substituted, so long as the terms and any preposition in that fact type are also included in the rule statement.

3. Similarly, if the placeholder is <*preposition*>, a preposition from a fact type in the fact model may be substituted, so long as the verb phrase and terms in that fact type are also included in the rule statement.

4. If the placeholder is <<u>literal</u>>, any suitable literal may be substituted. Literals include numeric values, textual values, categories from categorization schemes, dates, times, and other time points.

5. If the placeholder is <positive integer>, any suitable cardinal number (e.g., 'one', 'two') may be substituted.

6. For every other placeholder, the available options are set out in a ***subtemplate***. For example, the subtemplate for <operative rule statement subject> is S1, which allows for one of the following, with or without a qualifying clause[11]:

   a. a term,
   b. 'combination of' followed by a list of terms, of which the last two are separated by 'and' (or a comma and 'and' if adhering to US punctuation standards) and each other pair of terms in the list is separated by a comma, or
   c. 'set of' followed by a term.

S1. <operative rule statement subject>::=
    {<<u>term</u>>|combination of [<<u>term</u>>, and]|set of <<u>term</u>>}
    {<qualifying clause>|}

What this subtemplate does not tell us, however, is the circumstances in which we can use each of these options, or, to put it another way, the rule statement subjects that are appropriate for each type of rule. This is discussed in Section 7.2.3. Rule statement predicates, conditional clauses, and conditional con-junctions are similarly discussed, in Sections 7.2.4, 7.2.5, and 7.2.6 respectively.

   Given the wide variety of rule types (as set out in Section 4.9 in Chapter 4), the five templates at the start of this section are too general for easy use in creating rule statements that correctly express each type of operative rule. Sections 9.3–9.5 in Chapter 9 list specific templates for each type of operative rule, along with more specific restrictions on suitable subject and predicate phras-ing. Chapter 9 also includes (in Section 9.1.2) a subtemplate for each distinct placeholder in the templates.

---

[11]Qualifying clauses are discussed in Section 7.2.7.

7.2.2 Definitional rule statements

A *definitional rule statement* is a statement of a *definitional rule*. Every definitional rule statement in this book—and every definitional rule statement you write if you follow the method outlined in this book—has the following general formulation:

T6. {A|An|The|} <definitional rule statement subject>
   {<qualifying clause>|}
   <*verb phrase*> by definition
   <definition>.

Again, this template is too general for easy use in creating rule statements that correctly express each type of definitional rule. Section 9.2 in Chapter 9 lists specific templates for each type of definitional rule, along with more specific restrictions on suitable phrasing of subjects and definitions.

7.2.3 The subject of a rule statement

With very few exceptions, every rule statement involves more than one term, of which only one can be the subject of that statement. For each type of rule statement, there are restrictions on which term can be the subject. For *definitional rule statements*, these restrictions vary depending on the type of rule, as described in Section 7.2.3.1. In any *operative rule statement*, the subject must be the term signifying the set of objects to be tested by the rule, as described in Sections 7.2.3.2–7.2.3.4. The discussion in Chapter 9 of the template(s) for each type of rule statement includes advice as to what the subject term (and any other terms) in the rule statement should be or not be.

Unfortunately, I often encounter operative rule statements that violate this principle, produced by practitioners new to business rules, and even sometimes by experienced practitioners.

For example a recent paper on business rules included the following rule statement:

R179. †A 'flammable' sticker
   must *be displayed on* a tank *containing* a combustible fuel.

Since the subject of that rule statement is 'flammable' sticker, the statement governs what is to be done with 'flammable' stickers (rather than tanks containing combustible fuel). Thus, if I have a 'flammable' sticker in my hand rather than on a tank, that sticker does not comply with the rule statement as written. If, however, I recast R179 as in R180, it is tanks rather than stickers which must be checked for compliance with the rule statement, and one can have a supply of spare stickers on hand.

R180. A tank that *contains* a combustible fuel
   must *be marked with* a 'flammable' sticker.

Other rules that are easy to express in a way that violates this principle are those governing activities that depend on preceding activities having been completed. If an activity is permitted to occur only after some other activity has been completed, the subject of the rule statement must be the term that signifies the later activity rather than the earlier.

Consider rule statements R181 and R182. The intention of each of these rule statements is to establish whether a passenger is permitted to board a flight. It is not a constraint on passengers checking in.

In fact, although a passenger is permitted only in extenuating circumstances (such as sudden serious ill-ness) to check in then not board the flight, it is permitted in those circumstances. R182 is therefore correct while R181 is incorrect.

R181. †Each passenger
must *check in for* a flight before that passenger *boards* that flight.

R182. A passenger
may *board* a flight
only after that passenger *checks in for* that flight.

Another variation on this kind of error arises with those rules that limit a data item to a particular set of values. The subject of a rule statement expressing this type of rule must always be the term signifying that data item, not the set of values.

For example, rule statement R183 reads as if the airline is obliged to serve each city specified in each flight booking request that it receives (which is clearly inappropriate). R184, by contrast, obliges those making flight booking requests to specify only cities served by the airline, which is appropriate.

R183. †The cities
served by the airline
must *include* the destination city
specified in each flight booking request.

R184. The destination city
specified in each flight booking request
must *be* one of the cities
served by the airline.

7.2.3.1 Subjects of definitional rule statements

For each type of definitional rule statement, there is only one term that can be the subject of that rule statement:

1. for a *formal term definition*, the term being defined;
2. for a *categorization scheme enumeration*, the term signifying a category attribute that is governed by that categorization scheme;
3. for a *category transition constraint*, the term 'transition';
4. for a *complex concept cardinality rule*, the term signifying that complex concept;
5. for a *complex concept equivalence rule*, the term signifying one of two components of that complex concept that must be the same;
6. for a *complex concept set constraint*, the phrase 'set of <term>' that signifies one of the two sets of components of that complex concept that must be identical;
7. for a *valid value definition*, the term signifying the measure for which the values are defined;
8. for a *data calculation algorithm*, the term signifying the quantity or amount to be calculated;
9. for a *conversion factor definition*, a literal consisting of the numeral '1' and one of the units for which the conversion is defined;
10. for a *standard format definition*, the phrase 'valid <term>' where <term> is the name used for attributes of that format.

7.2.3.2 Subjects of data rule statements

For each type of *data rule statement*, there are restrictions on what term can be the subject of that rule statement:

1. for a *data cardinality rule statement*, the term signifying the transaction (form or message) or persistent data record in which a data item is required or prohibited (see Section 7.2.3.2.1 for more details);
2. for a *data content rule statement*, the term signifying the data item, combination of data items, or set of data items for which the content is constrained (see Section 7.2.3.2.2 for more details);
3. for a *data update prohibition rule statement* that specifies a *non-transferable relationship*, the term signifying the record for which a relationship cannot be transferred;
4. for any other *data update rule statement*, either
   a. the term signifying the data item for which update is prohibited or restricted, or
   b. the term 'data item' if all data items for a particular transaction or record are prohibited from update.

7.2.3.2.1 Subjects of data cardinality rule statements

The subject of any *data cardinality rule statement* (except one for a *dependent cardinality rule*) must be the term signifying the transaction or persistent data record in which a data item is required or prohibited.

Each type of incoming form (paper or on-screen) should be assigned an agreed term (often one that signifies a particular transaction, such as 'leave application', 'order', or 'flight booking request') and that term should be used as the subject in any data cardinality rule statement governing data in that form.

Each type of incoming message (which should either be a request for a service or a response from a service) should also be assigned an agreed term. A good standard for terms signifying messages is to base them on the name of the service:

1. If the message is requesting a service, append the word 'request' to the service name: for example, 'digital signature validation request'.
2. If the message is a response from a service, append the word 'response' to the service name: for example, 'account details update response'.

Each type of persistent data record should also be assigned an agreed term. However, that term (e.g., a database table name) is often simply the term signifying the real-world objects about which information is held in that record type (e.g., 'employee'). While the real-world object has attributes, the record of that object contains data items which correspond to those attributes. If we use a term signifying a real-world object as the subject of a data cardinality rule statement, we get, for example, either R185 (which is an operative rule statement expressing a definitional rule) or R186 (which places an ambiguous obligation on employees: when must they specify their birth dates?). The correct formulation is R187, in which the word 'record' is added to the term signifying the real-world object about which information is held in that record type:

R185. † Each employee
     must *have* exactly one birth date.
R186. † Each employee
     must *specify* exactly one birth date.
R187. Each employee record
     must *specify* exactly one birth date.

Some persistent data records represent combinations of objects for which there is jointly no term (e.g., combinations of product and supplier for which minimum and maximum delivery lead times are recorded). While the database designer may have created a table with (in this case) a name like 'product supplier' (or 'supplier product'), such a name is misleading and (I hope) would not find favor as a business term. Rule statements about such combinations should use the construction 'record of a combination of . . .' as in R188. The phrase 'record of a' may be dropped if the verb phrase can be expressed in the ***passive voice***, as in R189.

R188. Each record of a combination of <u>product</u> and <u>supplier</u>
   must *specify* at most one <u>minimum delivery lead time</u>.
R189. Each combination of <u>flight number</u> and <u>departure city</u>
   must *be allocated* exactly one <u>departure time</u>.

The subject of a ***dependent cardinality rule statement*** must be formulated as follows:

1. 'number of'; followed by
2. the term signifying the data item for which the cardinality is being defined (e.g., '<u>passengers</u>' in R190, '<u>advance seat requests</u>' in R191); followed by
3. '*specified*'; followed by
4. if the data item for which the cardinality is being defined is part of a complex data item,[12] a prepositional phrase identifying that complex data item (e.g., '*for* each <u>flight</u>' in R191); followed by
5. '*in* each'; followed by
6. the term signifying the transaction or persistent data record in which the data item is required (e.g., '<u>flight booking confirmation</u>' in both R190 and R191).

R190. The number of <u>passenger names</u>
   specified in each <u>flight booking confirmation</u>
   must *be equal to* the <u>number of passengers</u>
   specified in the <u>flight booking request</u>
   that *gives rise to* that <u>flight booking confirmation</u>.
R191. The number of <u>advance seat requests</u>
   specified for each <u>flight</u>
   in each <u>flight booking confirmation</u>
   must *be no more than* the number of <u>passenger names</u>
   specified in that <u>flight booking confirmation</u>.

7.2.3.2.2 Subjects of data content rule statements
The subject of a ***data content rule statement*** must be one of the following:

1. If the rule constrains the value of a single data item (e.g., R192), the subject of the rule statement must be the term signifying that data item, followed by a suitable qualifying clause.[13]

R192. The <u>departure date</u>
   specified in each <u>flight booking request</u>
   must *be later than* the <u>date</u> *of* the <u>flight booking request</u>.

---

[12]Complex data items (and their handling in rule statements) are discussed in Section 7.2.3.2.2.
[13]Possible qualifying clauses are discussed later in this section.

2. A combination of data items is a collection of different data items that together provide information about an object: for example, the combination of flight number, date, and departure port that together distinguish the departures of aircraft from airports. If the rule constrains such a combination (e.g., R193), the subject of the rule statement must be formulated as follows:

   a. 'combination of'; followed by
   b. a list of the terms signifying the data items; followed by
   c. a suitable qualifying clause.

R193. The combination of <u>placename</u> and <u>postal code</u>
specified in each <u>order</u>
must *be* one of the combinations of <u>placename</u> and <u>postal code</u>
allocated by the <u>postal authority</u>.

3. A set of data items is a collection of data items, all signified by the same term, that each represent a member of some set of objects that are associated with some other object: for example, the set of passengers booked on each flight in a flight booking.

   a. If the rule constrains the values in such a set (e.g., R194), the subject of the rule statement must be formulated as follows:

   i. 'set of'; followed by
   ii. the term signifying the data item; followed by
   iii. a suitable qualifying clause.

R194. The set of <u>passengers</u>
specified for each <u>flight</u>
in each <u>flight booking confirmation</u>
must *be the same as* the set of <u>passengers</u>
specified for each other <u>flight</u>
in that <u>flight booking confirmation</u>.

   b. If the rule constrains a set function[14] of such a set (e.g., R195), the subject of the rule statement must be formulated as follows:

   i. the set function name; followed by
   ii. 'of', possibly followed by a suitable ***determiner*** (such as 'the' or 'all'); followed by
   iii. the term signifying the data item; followed by
   iv. a suitable qualifying clause.

R195. The sum of the <u>shares</u>
specified in a <u>nomination of beneficiaries</u>
must *be equal to* <u>1</u>.

The qualifying clause in the subject of a data content rule statement depends on the nature of the relationship of the governed data item to the form, message, transaction, or record in which it appears. In particular, the data item may be part of a ***complex data item*** or ***subform***, a feature commonly found in forms. These may be used in a number of ways:

---

[14]For example, 'number' (the number of items in the set), 'sum' (the sum of the values in the set), 'maximum' (the maximum value in the set).

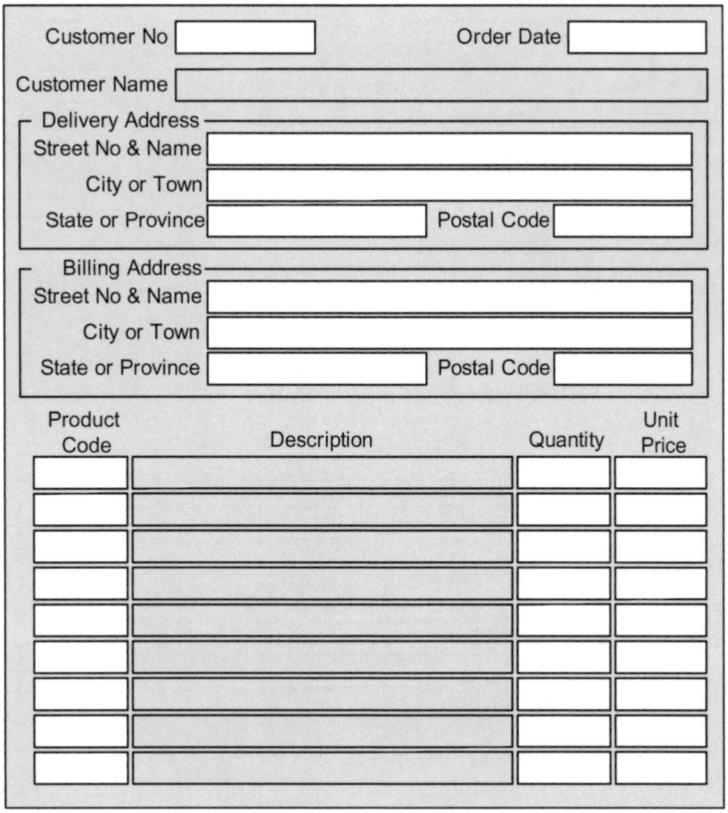

FIGURE 1

Order lines in an order form.

1. Multiple records, each containing similar sets of data, can be recorded in the one instance of the form: for example, the order lines (one for each product) in an order form, as in Figure 1;

2. A set of data, which may be optional as a whole, may consist of data items which are mandatory if the set is included: for example, a postal address may be optional in a form if other means of communication such as e-mail or telephone may be used, but, if the postal address is entered, there must be at least one street number and name, exactly one city or town, exactly one postal code, etc.

3. Sets of data may be grouped to make data entry easier: for example, delivery address and billing address, each of which consists of multiple data items, may both be included on the one form, again as in Figure 1.

This nested structure is also a feature of XML messages: an XML message is a complex data element consisting of both simple data elements (numbers, dates, text fields, etc.) and complex subelements, each consisting in turn of two or more simple or complex data elements. However, given the traditionally "flat" nature of database tables, there has until recently been no corresponding structure in persistent data, although object-relational DBMSs (database management systems)—such as Postgres, first described in (Stonebraker and Moore, 1996)—and recent versions of relational DBMSs provide analogous facilities such as *nested tables*.

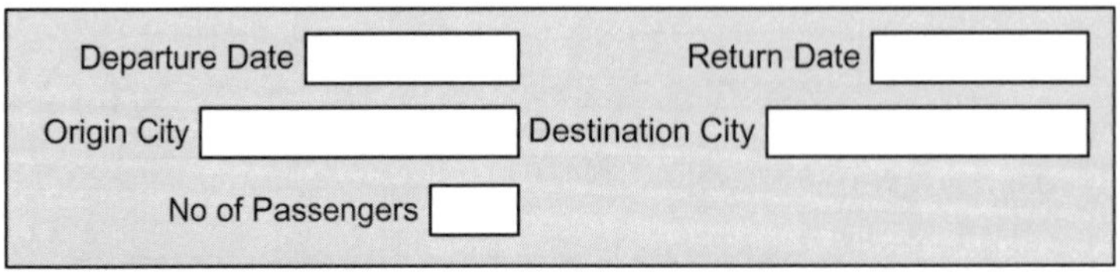

FIGURE 2

A flight booking request form.

Consider the flight booking request and confirmation forms depicted in Figures 2 and 3, with the following data items (among others):

1. a single mandatory departure date data item (not part of any other data item);
2. a single return date data item (not part of any other data item) that is prohibited if a one-way journey is being booked;

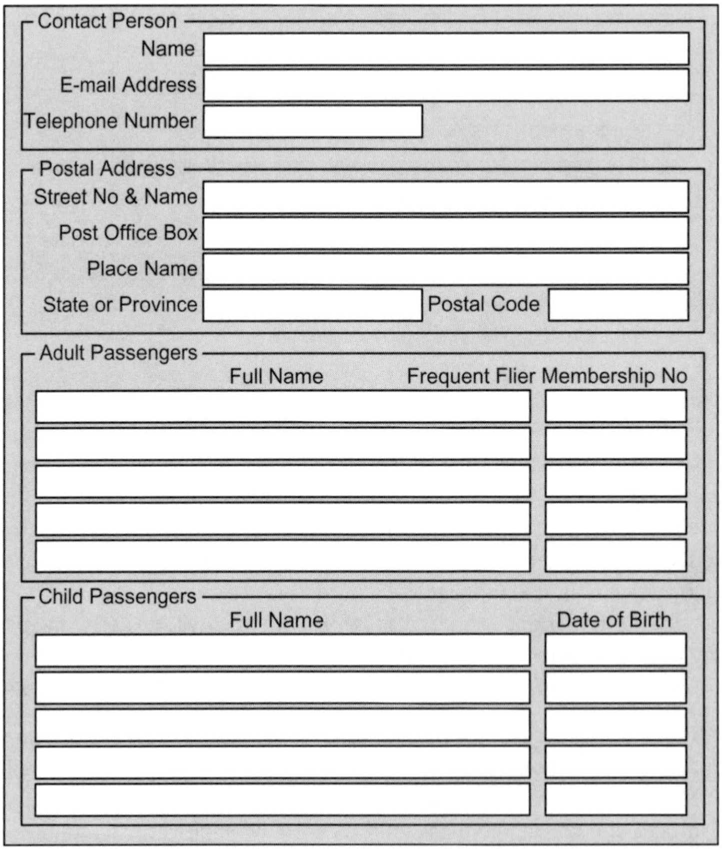

FIGURE 3

A flight booking confirmation form.

3. a single mandatory contact person data item, in which the name and telephone number are mandatory and the e-mail address is optional;
4. a single optional postal address data item, in which the place name and postal code are mandatory (the street number and name are optional as a box number may be provided instead);
5. a mandatory set of adult passenger data items (there must be at least one), for each of which
    a. the name is mandatory, and
    b. at most one frequent flier membership may be specified;
6. an optional set of child passenger data items (there may be none), in each of which the name and date of birth are mandatory.

As examples of **data content rule statements**, the following are some of the necessary **data item format rule statements** governing these data items:

R196. The departure date
      specified in each flight booking request
      must *be represented using* a valid date representation.
R197. The return date (if any)
      specified in each flight booking request
      must *be represented using* a valid date representation.
R198. The person name
      specified for the contact person
      in each flight booking confirmation
      must *be* a valid person name.
R199. The place name
      specified in the postal address (if any)
      in each flight booking confirmation
      must *be* a valid place name.
R200. The person name
      specified for each adult passenger
      in each flight booking confirmation
      must *be* a valid person name.
R201. The frequent flier membership number (if any)
      specified for each adult passenger
      in each flight booking confirmation
      must *be* a valid frequent flier membership number.
R202. The birth date
      specified for each child passenger (if any)
      in each flight booking confirmation
      must *be represented using* a valid date representation.

The differences are as follows:

1. In a data content rule statement governing a data item that is *not* part of a complex data item, the subject requires only a simple qualifying clause, which identifies the form, message, transaction, or record ('*specified in* each flight booking' in each of the above examples). By contrast, in a data content rule statement governing a data item that *is* part of a complex data item, the subject requires

a qualifying clause that includes an additional phrase (starting with '*for*' or '*in*') identifying the relevant complex data item (as in R198 to R202 inclusive).

2. In that additional phrase, '*for*' or '*in*' must be followed by
   a. 'the' if there can only be one of the complex data item;
   b. 'each' if there can be more than one of the complex data item.
3. '(if any)' should be added after
   a. the term signifying the subject data item, if that data item is optional;
   b. the term signifying the complex data item (if any) containing the subject data item, if that complex data item is optional.

7.2.3.3 Subjects of activity rule statements
The subject of an *activity rule statement* may be any of the following:

1. the term signifying the activity,
2. the term signifying the object of the activity, or
3. (occasionally) the term signifying the person or device that performs the activity.

7.2.3.4 Subjects of party rule statements
For each type of *party rule statement*, there is only one term that can be the subject of that rule statement:

1. for an *information access rule*, the term signifying the record or data item to which access is restricted;
2. for a *responsibility rule*, the term signifying the process, fee, duty, or tax for which a party is responsible or liable;
3. for any other *party rule*, the term signifying the type of party who may be restricted from performing a process or activity or playing a role.

7.2.4 Predicates in operative rule statements

Predicates in operative rule statements exhibit even more variation than subjects. As with subjects, each type of rule statement is restricted to one or two types of predicates, as specified in the template for each rule statement type in Chapter 9.

7.2.4.1 Predicates in data cardinality rule statements
The following are some of the necessary *data cardinality rule statements* governing the data items in the flight booking forms discussed in Section 7.2.3.2.2:

R203. Each flight booking request
　　　must *specify* exactly one departure date.
R204. A flight booking request
　　　　for a one-way journey
　　　must not *specify* a return date.
R205. Each flight booking confirmation
　　　must *specify* exactly one person name
　　　　for the contact person.

R206. Each <u>flight booking confirmation</u>
must *specify* exactly one <u>place name</u>
for the <u>postal address</u> (if any).
R207. Each <u>flight booking confirmation</u>
must *specify* exactly one <u>person name</u>
for each <u>adult passenger</u>.
R208. A <u>flight booking confirmation</u>
must not *specify* more than one <u>frequent flier membership number</u>
for any <u>adult passenger</u>.
R209. Each <u>flight booking confirmation</u>
must *specify* exactly one <u>birth date</u>
for each <u>child passenger</u> (if any).

The differences are as follows:

1. In a data cardinality rule statement governing a data item that is part of a complex data item, the predicate must include a qualifying clause (starting with '*for*' or '*in*') identifying the relevant complex data item (as in R205 to R209 inclusive). By contrast, in a data cardinality rule statement governing a data item that is not part of a complex data item, the predicate does not require such a clause.
2. In that qualifying clause, '*for*' or '*in*' must be followed by
   a. 'the' if there can only be one of the complex data item,
   b. 'each' or 'any' if there can be more than one of the complex data item:
      i. 'any' if the rule statement is a ***prohibition statement*** (containing 'must not'),
      ii. otherwise 'each'.
3. '(if any)' should be added after the term signifying the complex data item if that data item is optional.

Before we move on to consider some other types of data cardinality rule statements, I should point out that, if the predicate does include a qualifying clause identifying a complex data item, that qualifying clause can be extended to include other criteria. For example, R209 could alternatively be expressed as

R210. Each <u>flight booking</u>
must *specify* exactly one <u>birth date</u>
for each <u>passenger</u> whose <u>age</u> *is less than* <u>12 years</u>.

This is an example of a ***chained qualifying clause***. We shall meet more of these, in particular in Section 7.2.7.

There are other types of data cardinality rule statements, the syntax of which similarly varies depending on whether the subject data item is part of a complex data item. Consider first the following ***mandatory option selection rule statements***:

R211. Each <u>flight booking request</u>
must *specify*
whether it *is for*
a <u>return journey</u>, a <u>one-way journey</u>, or a <u>multi-stop journey</u>.

R212. Each <u>flight booking confirmation</u>
   must *specify*
      for each <u>passenger</u>
      whether that <u>passenger</u> *is*
      an <u>adult passenger</u>, a <u>child passenger</u>, or an <u>infant passenger</u>.

While R211 governs the form itself, R212 governs a complex data item within a form, and therefore requires the qualifying clause '*for* each <u>passenger</u>' identifying that complex data item. Note that this qualifying clause must appear immediately after the verb phrase ('*specify*') rather than after the object of the verb phrase as in the previous examples. This is also the case with **mandatory group rule statements**. Again, R213 governs the form itself, whereas R214, with a qualifying clause, governs a complex data item ('<u>contact person</u>').

R213. Each <u>flight booking confirmation</u>
   must *specify*
      a <u>credit card</u> or an <u>electronic funds transfer payment receipt</u> but not both.
R214. Each <u>flight booking confirmation</u>
   must *specify*
      for the <u>contact person</u>
      a <u>mobile phone number</u>, an <u>e-mail address</u>, or both.

7.2.4.2. *Predicates in data content rule statements*
The predicate of a **data content rule statement** constrains

1. the values or the format of a subject data item,
2. the values of a subject set of data items, or
3. the values of a subject combination of data items.[15]

7.2.4.2.1 Predicates constraining values of single data items
A constraint on the value of a single data item may limit that data item to

1. one of a set of discrete values (as in R215 and R216), in which case the rule is a **value set rule**;
2. a value within a range of values (as in R217, R218, and R219), in which case the rule is a **range rule**;
3. a particular value (as in R220), or any value other than a particular value (as in R221), in which case the rule is an **equality rule**;
4. a value different from the value in any other instance of the same data item (as in R222), in which case the rule is a **uniqueness constraint**.

Note that in each case, except that of a uniqueness constraint, the value(s) may be

  a. explicit values, as in R215 and R217,
  b. defined by a term, as in R216 and R218,
  c. an expression involving terms and/or explicit values, as in R219.

R215. The <u>payment method</u>
      specified in each <u>order form</u>
   must *be* '<u>credit card</u>' or '<u>direct debit</u>'.

---

[15] See Section 7.2.3.2.2 for a discussion of the difference between sets and combinations of data items.

R216. The <u>payment method</u>
    specified in each <u>order form</u>
  must *be* one of the <u>payment methods</u>
    accepted by the <u>vendor</u>.

R217. The <u>order quantity</u>
    specified in each <u>order line</u>
    in each <u>order form</u>
  must *be more than* <u>0</u>.

R218. The <u>return date</u> (if any)
    specified in each <u>flight booking request</u>
  must *be no earlier than* the <u>departure date</u>
    specified in that <u>flight booking request</u>.

R219. The <u>departure time</u>
    of the <u>return flight</u> (if any)
    specified in each <u>flight booking confirmation</u>
  must *be no earlier than* <u>1 h</u> *after* the <u>arrival time</u>
    of the <u>outgoing flight</u>
    specified in that <u>flight booking confirmation</u>.

R220. The <u>destination city</u>
    of the <u>outgoing flight</u>
    specified in a <u>flight booking confirmation</u>
  must *be the same as* the <u>destination city</u>
    specified in the <u>flight booking request</u>
    that *gives rise to* that <u>flight booking confirmation</u>.

R221. The <u>new full name</u>
    specified in each <u>change of name request</u>
  must *be different from* the <u>previous full name</u>
    specified in that <u>change of name request</u>.

R222. Each <u>city</u>
    specified in each <u>flight booking request</u>
    for a <u>round-the-world journey</u>
  must *be different from* any other <u>city</u>
    specified in that <u>flight booking request</u>.

There is an additional type of constraint on data items representing time periods: this type of constraint prohibits such a data item from representing a time period that overlaps another time period, as in R223.

R223. The <u>time period</u>
    specified in each <u>historic price record</u>
    for a <u>product variant</u>
  must not *overlap* the <u>time period</u>
    specified in any other <u>historic price record</u>
    for the same <u>product variant</u>.

There are analogous constraints on data items representing spatial properties (points, line segments, or polygons).

The forms that the predicates of such rule statements can take are as follows:

1. The predicate of a **value set rule** can take either of the following forms after the verb '*be*':
   a. a list of literals, being the values that the subject data item can take: for example,
      i. <u>0</u>, <u>1</u>, or <u>2</u>,
      ii. '<u>approved</u>' or '<u>rejected</u>'; or
   b. 'one of the', followed by a term and qualifying clause signifying the set of allowed values: for example,
      i. 'one of the <u>customer types</u> recognized by the <u>organization</u>',
      ii. 'one of the <u>products</u> available from that <u>supplier</u>'.
2. The predicate of a **range rule** must be formulated as follows:
   a. one of the following verb phrases expressing comparison:
      i. '*be less than*',
      ii. '*be more than*',
      iii. '*be no less than*' (or '*be at least*')
      iv. '*be no more than*' (or '*be at most*')
      v. '*be earlier than*' (or '*be before*')
      vi. '*be later than*' (or '*be after*')
      vii. '*be no earlier than*', or
      viii. '*be no later than*'; followed by
   b. one of the following, signifying the value with which the subject data item is being compared:
      i. an explicit value: for example,
         <u>1</u>,
      ii. a term with a preceding article (usually 'the') and a following qualifying clause: for example,
         'the <u>minimum value</u> of the <u>parameter</u>', or
      iii. an expression involving terms and/or explicit values: for example,
         '<u>4 h</u> before the <u>departure time</u> of the <u>flight</u>';
   c. optionally, the conjunction 'and' followed by another comparison verb phrase and value, term, or expression: this allows for such constructions as '*be at least* <u>1</u> and *at most* <u>9</u>'.[16]
3. The predicate of an **equality rule** must be formulated as follows:
   a. either '*be the same as*' or '*be different from*' ('*be equal to*' and '*be unequal to*' are alternatives); followed by
   b. any of the alternatives listed in item 2.b above: for example,
      'the <u>customer name</u> *specified in* the <u>order</u>'.
4. The predicate of a **uniqueness constraint** must be formulated as follows:
   a. the verb phrase '*be different from*'; followed by
   b. the determiner 'each other'; followed by
   c. a repetition of the subject term of the rule statement followed by a qualifying clause (see R222 above).

---

[16]Note that '*be*' is omitted from the second verb phrase, as in normal spoken and written English.

5. The predicate of a ***temporal data non-overlap constraint*** must be formulated as follows:
   a. the verb '*overlap*'; followed by
   b. a term with a preceding article (usually 'the') and a following qualifying clause (see R223 above).

7.2.4.2.2 Predicates constraining the format of data items

A constraint on the format of a data item (such as R224) requires that that data item be a valid instance of a standardized data item that has been defined using a definitional rule such as R227.[17]

R224. Each <u>flight</u>
   specified in each <u>flight booking confirmation</u>
   must *be represented using* a valid <u>flight number</u>.
R225. The <u>contact phone number</u>
   specified in each <u>order</u>
   must *be* a valid <u>phone number</u>.
R226. The <u>number of passengers</u>
   specified in each <u>flight booking request</u>
   must *be represented using* a valid <u>unsigned integer</u>.
R227. A valid <u>flight number</u>
   is by definition *composed of*
   2 or 3 <u>letters</u> followed by up to 4 <u>digits</u>.

The form that the predicates of such rule statements can take is as follows:

1. the verb phrase '*be*' or '*be represented using*'; followed by
2. the phrase 'a valid'; followed by
3. the term signifying the standardized data item.

7.2.4.2.3 Predicates constraining combinations of data items

A constraint on a combination of data items may

1. limit it to a set of allowed combinations: for example,

R228. The combination of <u>product category</u> and <u>discount rate</u>
   specified in each <u>order</u>
   must *be* one of the combinations of <u>product category</u> and <u>discount rate</u>
   allowed for in the <u>product catalog</u>.

2. require that it be different from any other instance of the same combination: for example,

R229. The combination of <u>employee ID</u> and <u>project code</u>
   specified in each <u>employee assignment</u>
   must *be different from* the combination of <u>employee ID</u> and <u>project code</u>
   specified in each other <u>employee assignment</u>.

3. impose an ordering on the values of the data items such that one is greater than (or later than) or not less than (or not earlier than) the other: for example,

---

[17]The definitional rule statement may be omitted for axiomatic terms such as <u>unsigned integer</u>.

R230. The combination of <u>minimum value</u> and <u>maximum value</u>
   specified for each <u>parameter</u>
   must *be* such that
      the <u>minimum value</u> *is no more than* the <u>maximum value</u>.

The forms that the predicates of such rule statements can take are as follows:

1. If the rule statement limits the combination of data items to a set of allowed combinations, the predicate must be formulated as follows (see R228 above for an example):
   a. '*be* one of the combinations of'; followed by
   b. a repetition of the list of terms making up the subject of the rule statement, followed by a qualifying clause.
2. If the rule statement requires that the combination of data items be different from any other instance of the same combination, the predicate must be formulated as follows (see R229 above for an example):
   a. the verb phrase '*be different from*'; followed by
   b. the phrase 'combination of'; followed by
   c. a repetition of the list of terms making up the subject of the rule statement; followed by a qualifying clause.
3. If the rule statement imposes an ordering on the values of the data items such that one is greater than (or later than) or not less than (or not earlier than) the other, the predicate must be formulated as follows (see R230 above for an example):
   a. the verb phrase '*be such that*'; followed by
   b. the term signifying one of the data items, with preceding article (usually 'the'); followed by
   c. one of the following verb phrases expressing comparison:
      i. '*is less than*'
      ii. '*is more than*'
      iii. '*is no less than*' (or '*is at least*')
      iv. '*is no more than*' (or '*is at most*')
      v. '*is earlier than*' (or '*is before*')
      vi. '*is later than*' (or '*is after*')
      vii. '*is no earlier than*' or
      viii. '*is no later than*'; followed by
   d. the term signifying the other data item, with preceding article (usually 'the').

7.2.4.2.4 Predicates constraining sets of data items
A predicate constraining a set of data items may limit that set to

1. being identical to another set;
2. being identical to the **union** of two or more sets (the set that contains all members that are in at least one of those sets);
3. being identical to the **intersection** of two or more sets (the set that contains all members that are in all of those sets);
4. being identical to the **difference** of two sets (the set that contains all members that are in one of those sets but not the other);

5. being a *subset* of another set (or union, intersection, or difference);
6. being a *superset* of another set (or union, intersection, or difference).

Subset constraints can be expressed as constraints on the members of the subject set:

1. If the subject set must be a subset of set *a*, each member of the subject set must be a member of set *a*.
2. If the subject set must be a subset of the union of sets *a* and *b*, each member of the subject set must be a member of set *a* or a member of set *b*.
3. If the subject set must be a subset of the intersection of sets *a* and *b*, each member of the subject set must be both a member of set *a* and a member of set *b*.
4. If the subject set must be a subset of the difference of sets *a* and *b*, each member of the subject set must be a member of set *a* and not a member of set *b*.

A requirement for two sets to be identical can be easily expressed, as in R231.

R231. The set of vendors
   specified in each vehicle transfer
   must *be the same as* the set of registered owners
   of the vehicle
   specified in that vehicle transfer.

This leaves those constraints that limit the subject set to

1. being identical to the union or intersection of other sets, or difference between two other sets; or
2. being a superset of another set, union, or intersection of sets, or difference between sets.

Expressing such rules using the set operators 'union', 'intersection', or 'difference' can yield clumsy statements that are not very clear, particularly when each set may require a complex phrase to define it. Consider R232:

R232. †The set of transacting parties
   specified in each real property transfer
   must *be the same as* the union of the set of registered proprietors
   of the property
   specified in that real property transfer
   and the set of registered mortgagees
   of the property
   specified in that real property transfer.

An alternative option is to create a term to represent the set expression, define that term using a definitional rule statement (e.g., R233), and then express the original rule as a requirement for two sets to be identical (e.g., R234).

R233. A party with interest
   with respect to a property
   is by definition
   a registered proprietor *of* that property
   or a registered mortgagee *of* that property.

R234. The set of <u>transacting parties</u>
    specified in each <u>real property transfer</u>
  must *be the same as* the set of <u>parties with interest</u>
    with respect to the <u>property</u>
    specified in that <u>real property transfer</u>.

If the subject set must be a superset of another set, union or intersection of sets, or difference between sets, the constraint is more clearly expressed by using the phrase '*include* all', as in the following:

R235. The set of <u>transacting parties</u>
    specified in each <u>real property transfer</u>
  must *include* all <u>registered proprietors</u>
    of the <u>property</u>
    specified in that <u>real property transfer</u>.

7.2.4.3 Predicates in data update rule statements

The predicate of a ***data update rule statement*** signifies the prohibited or restricted update action ('*be updated*', '*be transferred from* one <u>employee</u> *to* another <u>employee</u>', '*be updated to* <u>never married</u>', '*be decreased*' in the following examples).

R236. A <u>data item</u>
    in a <u>signed legal instrument</u>
  must not *be updated*.
R237. A <u>leave application</u>
  must not *be transferred from* one <u>employee</u> *to* another <u>employee</u>.
R238. The <u>marital status</u>
    of an <u>employee</u>
  may *be updated to* <u>never married</u>
  only if the <u>marital status</u>
    that *is currently recorded for* that <u>employee</u>
    is <u>unknown</u>.
R239. The <u>total actual work duration</u>
    specified in an <u>employee project assignment</u>
  must not *be decreased*.

7.2.4.4 Predicates in activity rule statements

Which predicates are allowed in an ***activity rule statement*** depends on what is signified by the subject of that statement:

1. If the subject of the rule statement is the term signifying the activity (as in R240 and R241), the predicate should be '*occur*', followed by any clause limiting the time of the activity (as in R241 but not R240, in which the clause limiting the time of the activity is part of the conditional clause following 'only').

R240. <u>Bag drop</u>
    for a <u>flight</u>
  may *occur*
  only *during* the <u>4 h</u> *before* the <u>departure time</u> *of* that <u>flight</u>.

R241. Acknowledgment
> *of* a service request
> > that *is made before* 2 pm
> must *occur before* 5 pm
> > *on* the day *of* that request.

2. If the subject is the term signifying the object of the activity (as in R242 and R243), the predicate should be the passive form of the verb phrase signifying that activity, followed if necessary by the term signifying the person or device that performs the activity (as in R243 but not R242).

R242. A daily ticket
> may *be used*
> only until 2 am
> > *on* the day
> > *after* the day
> > *on* which the ticket *is validated.*

R243. A multi-trip ticket
> must not *be used by* more than one passenger.

3. If the subject is the term signifying the person or device that performs the activity (as in R244, R245, and R246), the predicate should be the active form of the verb phrase signifying the activity, followed (if that verb phrase is *transitive*) by the term signifying the object or target of the activity (as in R244 and R246 but not R245).

R244. A passenger
> may *board* an international flight
> only after that passenger *undergoes* departure control.

R245. A passenger
> may *smoke*
> only after that passenger *has exited* the airport.

R246. A ticket barrier
> must *retain* each ticket
> > that *is expired.*

7.2.4.5 Predicates in party rule statements

Which predicates are allowed in a *party rule statement* depends on the particular type of party rule expressed by the rule statement:

1. For an *information access rule* (in which the subject is the term signifying the record or data item to which access is restricted), the predicate must be formulated as follows:
   a. a verb phrase signifying the data access activity:
      i. '*be viewed by*'
      ii. '*be created by*'
      iii. '*be updated by*', or
      iv. '*be deleted by*'; followed by
   b. the adverb 'only'; followed by
   c. a list of terms signifying the parties or roles allowed access, each followed by a qualifying clause as necessary.

R247. The <u>leave record</u>
  of an <u>employee</u>
  may *be viewed by* only that <u>employee</u>,
    the <u>supervisor</u> *of* that <u>employee</u>, or a <u>human resources officer</u>.

2. For a ***responsibility rule*** (in which the subject is the term signifying the process fee, duty, or tax for which a party is responsible or liable), the predicate must be formulated as follows:

   a. a verb phrase signifying performance of the process or payment of the fee, duty, or tax; followed by

   b. a term signifying the responsible party, followed a by qualifying clause as necessary.

R248. <u>Stamp duty</u>
    on a <u>real property transfer</u>
  must *be paid by* the <u>parties receiving</u>.

3. For a ***role separation rule*** or a ***role binding rule***, the predicate must be formulated as follows:

   a. the verb '*be*'; followed by

   b. the determiner 'the same' or 'one of the'; followed by

   c. a term signifying the restricted role, followed a by qualifying clause as necessary.

R249. The <u>representative</u>
      who *signs* a <u>real property transaction instrument</u>
      for the <u>vendor</u>
      specified in that <u>instrument</u>
    must not *be* the same <u>representative</u>
      who *signs* that <u>instrument</u>
      for the <u>purchaser</u>
      specified in that <u>instrument</u>.

4. For any other ***party rule*** (in which the subject is the term signifying the type of party who may be restricted from performing a process or activity or playing a role), the predicate must be formulated as follows:

   a. the verb phrase signifying the process, activity, or performance of the role; followed by

   b. the term signifying the object or target of the process or activity, or the role, if that verb phrase is transitive.

   For example, '*obtain* <u>travel insurance</u>' or '*be rostered as* a <u>driver</u>'.

7.2.5 Conditional conjunctions

A conditional conjunction is used in two ways in rule statements:

1. 'if' or 'unless' is used to precede a conditional clause;

2. various conjunctions may be used immediately after the word 'only' in a ***restricted permission statement***:

   a. 'if' is used if permission depends on a logical condition being true: for example,

R250. A <u>person</u>
    may *be rostered as* the <u>pilot in command</u>
        on a <u>flight crew</u>
    only if that <u>person</u> *holds* a <u>command endorsement</u>
        that *is current*.

b. 'after' is used if permission depends on a process being completed: for example,

R251. A <u>passenger</u>
    may *board* an <u>international flight</u>
    only after that <u>passenger</u> *undergoes* <u>departure control</u>.

c. 'during' or 'while' is used if permission depends on a process or state of affairs simultaneously occurring: for example,

R252. A <u>passenger</u>
    may *move about* the <u>cabin</u>
    only while the <u>seatbelt sign</u> *is extinguished*.

7.2.6 Conditional clauses

Conditional clauses can be used after conditional conjunctions to restrict the scope of a rule statement. Let's review some of the conditional clauses in rule statements we've encountered so far:

1. 'that <u>driver</u>
    is intoxicated';
2. 'that <u>applicant</u>
    was not *born in* <u>Australia</u>';
3. 'that <u>flight booking request</u>
    is for a <u>return journey</u>'.

In each of examples 1–3, there is a subject term (which is in each case a repetition of one of the terms in the subject of the rule statement) preceded by the determiner 'that' and followed by a predicate, consisting of a verb phrase, plus an object term or literal if the verb phrase is ***transitive***.

4. it
    is not *made by* an <u>account holder</u>'.

In example 4, there is a pronoun ('it') rather than a subject term (a pronoun is allowed here because there is only one term preceding it in the rule statement), again followed by a predicate.

5. 'the <u>port code</u>
    of the <u>connecting port</u>
        for which that <u>transit time</u> *is specified*
    is '<u>LAX</u>'';
6. 'the <u>age</u>
    of that <u>person</u>
    is at least <u>2 years</u>';

7. 'the <u>marital status</u>
   that *is currently recorded for* that <u>employee</u>
   is <u>unknown</u>';
8. 'any <u>flight</u>
   specified in that <u>flight booking confirmation</u>
   is international';
9. 'the <u>sample tester</u>
   who *tested* the <u>sample</u> *specified in* that <u>water sample record</u>
   has confirmed that <u>water temperature</u>'.

In each of the examples 5–9, the subject term is followed by a qualifying clause. We can also see that a wider variety of ***determiners***[18] is possible. Note, however, that in each case, although 'that' is not used before the subject of the conditional clause, it is used before one of the terms in the qualifying clause, namely the term that repeats one of the terms in the subject of the rule statement.

10. 'that <u>passenger</u>
    presents a <u>passport</u>
       that *specifies* the <u>name</u> *of* that <u>passenger</u>
       and *bears* a <u>likeness</u> *of* that <u>passenger</u>
       and *specifies* an <u>expiry date</u>
       that *is later than* <u>6 months</u> after the <u>date</u> *of* <u>departure control</u>'.

In example 10, the predicate includes a qualifying clause after the object term.

11. 'that <u>person</u>
    holds an <u>airline transport pilot license</u>
       that *is current*
    and *holds* a <u>type endorsement</u>
       that *is current for* each <u>aircraft type</u> *to be flown by* that <u>flight crew</u>'.

In example 11, there are two predicates separated by the conjunction 'and', each including an object term followed by a qualifying clause.

12. 'that <u>person</u>
    holds an <u>airline transport pilot license</u>
       that *is current*
    and a <u>type endorsement</u>
       that *is current for* each <u>aircraft type</u> *to be flown by* that <u>flight crew</u>'.

In example 12—which is an alternative rendering of example 11—the removal of the common verb *holds* means that there is now one predicate with two object terms (separated by the conjunction 'and'), each followed by a qualifying clause.

---

[18]See Section 7.1 for a list of determiners used in rule statements.

 A conditional clause may also specify conditions on multiple subjects: for example,

13. 'that <u>product</u>
   is out of stock
   and that <u>order</u>
   is urgent'.

There is, of course, no reason why a conditional clause cannot specify multiple conditions of which only one need apply, using 'or' rather than 'and': for example,

14. 'the <u>due date</u>
   is <u>Saturday</u>, <u>Sunday</u>, *or* a <u>public holiday</u>';
15. 'that <u>customer</u>
   has an <u>outstanding balance</u> *more than* <u>$1000</u>
   or *has made* more than one <u>payment</u> *after* the <u>due date</u> *for* that <u>payment</u>'.

7.2.7 Qualifying clauses

A *qualifying clause* (also known as a *restrictive relative clause*) can be used after a term in two ways:

1. Following the *subject term* of a rule statement, a qualifying clause restricts the scope of that rule statement to a subset of the set of objects signified by that term, rather than the set of all objects signified by that term. For example, R253 is a rule statement that applies only to those flight booking requests that are for a return journey, rather than all flight booking requests. If the qualifying clause '*for* a <u>return journey</u>' were removed, however, the rule statement would apply to all flight booking requests.

R253. Each <u>flight booking request</u>
     for a <u>return journey</u>
     must *specify* exactly one <u>return date</u>.

2. Following any other term in a rule statement, a qualifying clause makes any stated constraint more specific than if the qualifying clause were absent. For example, R254 is inadequate since a passenger can comply by presenting a passport with someone else's name or likeness or one that is about to expire. By contrast, the qualifying clause in R255 specifies all criteria with which the passport must comply.

R254. †A <u>passenger</u>
     may *pass through* <u>departure control</u>
     only if that <u>passenger</u> *presents* a <u>passport</u>.
R255. A <u>passenger</u>
     may *pass through* <u>departure control</u>
     only if that <u>passenger</u> *presents* a <u>passport</u>
       that *specifies* the <u>name</u> *of* that <u>passenger</u>
       and *bears* a <u>likeness</u> *of* that <u>passenger</u>
       and *specifies* an <u>expiry date</u>
       that *is later than* <u>6 months</u> *after* the <u>date</u> *of* <u>departure control</u>.

Qualifying clauses exhibit considerable variety. Let's review some of the qualifying clauses in rule statements we've encountered so far:

1. 'that *employs* that <u>person</u>';
2. 'who *is employed by* that <u>organization</u>';
3. 'that *specifies* more than one <u>outgoing flight</u>';
4. 'that *is* not *valid* for any more <u>journeys</u>';
5. 'that *weighs more than* <u>30 kg</u>'.

In each of examples 1–5, there is a **relative pronoun** ('that' or 'who'), a verb phrase (which may be negated, as in example 4), and either a **determiner** and a term or (as in example 5) a literal.

6. 'who *is traveling alone*'.

Example 6 differs in that the verb phrase, being **intransitive**, is not followed by a term or a literal.

7. 'who *checks* that an <u>aircraft door</u> *is disarmed*';

Example 7 differs again in that the verb phrase is one of those that states or questions the truth of a proposition. The verb phrase is therefore followed by 'that', 'if', or 'whether' and a clause consisting of a subject term and a predicate (just like a conditional clause).

8. '*specified in* each <u>flight booking request</u>';
9. '*served by* the <u>airline</u>'.

Examples 8 and 9 illustrate that, if a verb phrase starts with '*is*', '*is*' and the relative pronoun can be omitted. These examples are in fact short forms of:

10. 'who *is specified in* each <u>flight booking request</u>';
11. 'that *is served by* the <u>airline</u>'.

The following examples could be considered to be examples of the same principle, or simply illustrate the fact that a qualifying clause can consist of a preposition followed by either a determiner and a term or (as in example 15) a literal.

12. '*of* a <u>person</u>';
13. '*for* each <u>passenger</u>';
14. '*at* the <u>time of application</u>';
15. '*in* <u>The United States</u>'.

The next example is a qualifying clause that consists of a preposition followed by a **relative pronoun** ('which' or 'whom') and a clause consisting of a subject term and a predicate (again just like a conditional clause):

16. '*for* which that <u>passenger</u> *has checked in*'.

The next example is similar, but uses the relative pronoun 'whose' instead of '*of* whom':

17. 'whose <u>birth date</u> *is earlier than* <u>1/1/1950</u>'.

The next example illustrates another useful alternative form of a qualifying clause:

18. 'other than a <u>savings account</u>'.

This example is in fact a short form of

19. 'that *is* not a <u>savings account</u>'.

All of the above examples may be referred to as *simple qualifying clauses* (by contrast with the remaining examples). The next few examples illustrate that, if a qualifying clause ends in a term or a literal, that term or literal can itself be qualified by a qualifying clause, the whole being a *chained qualifying clause*. In particular, example 30 shows that chaining of qualifying clauses can in theory be continued as required.

20. 'that *constitutes* each individual parcel
in a real estate subdivision';

21. 'who *tested* the sample
specified in that water sample record';

22. '*of* the return flight
of a return journey';

23. '*for* the port
at which those flights *connect*';

24. 'whose age *is at least* 70 years
at the time of travel';

25. '*specified in* the flight booking request
that *gives rise to* that flight booking confirmation';

26. '*specified in* each flight booking confirmation
that *specifies* more than one flight';

27. '*booked on* each flight
specified in a flight booking confirmation';

28. '*included in* the postal address (if any)
specified in each insurance application';

29. '*specified in* another employee leave record
for the same employee';

30. '*allocated by* the postal authority
of the country
in which that postal address *is located*'.

The next example illustrates that a qualifying clause can be followed by one or more (in this case two) qualifying clauses, each preceded by 'and' (and without a preceding 'that'); the second added qualifying clause is in this case a chained qualifying clause made up of three simple qualifying clauses:

31. 'that *specifies* the name *of* that passenger
and *bears* a likeness *of* that passenger
and *specifies* an expiry date
that *is later than* 6 months
after the date *of* departure control'.

The next example illustrates a qualifying clause consisting of simple qualifying clauses separated by 'or':

32. '*less than* 32°F or *more than* 60°F.'

7.2.8 Qualifying clause or conditional clause?

Both qualifying clauses and conditional clauses restrict the scope of the rule statements in which they appear. Are they interchangeable? Let's recall one of the rule statements used as an example of one with a qualifying clause:

R256. Each <u>flight booking request</u>
   for a <u>return journey</u>
  must *specify* exactly one <u>return date</u>.

This rule statement can be alternatively expressed using a conditional clause:

R257. Each <u>flight booking request</u>
  must *specify* exactly one <u>return date</u>
  if that <u>flight booking request</u> *is for* a <u>return journey</u>.

Note, however, that

1. since a conditional clause needs to repeat the subject term, a rule statement with a conditional clause is more verbose than the equivalent rule statement with a qualifying clause;
2. as we have seen, qualifying clauses exhibit more variety.

However, this does not mean that conditional clauses do not have their place. In particular, if the condition is complex, involving a chain of criteria and/or a number of criteria joined by 'and' or 'or', the use of a long qualifying clause would separate the subject and predicate by an excessive number of words. These words are better placed in a conditional clause, which will either be at the end of the rule statement or enclosed in parentheses.

7.3 WHY TEMPLATES?

It has been suggested to me that templates do not assist the formulation of quality rule statements. Quite apart from the fact that this technique is being successfully employed by a large Australian government agency, I believe the following argument supports the use of templates.

 If we wish to state a particular rule, there are numerous rule statements that we might utter or write in an attempt to express that rule. Even if we limit ourselves only to statements that contain only meaningful correctly spelled words and that are syntactically correct, there are still many possibilities. We can go further and state that only terms from the organization's vocabulary are used and that the only sentence forms allowed are

  <subject phrase> must {not|} <predicate> {if <conditional clause>|} or
  <subject phrase> may only <predicate> if <conditional clause>.

This still allows for many possibilities:

1. rule statements that do not express the intended rule but some other rule, through the use of terms or verb phrases other than those required to express the intended rule;
2. rule statements that do not express the intended rule but some other rule, by misplacing the true subject of the intended rule: some examples of rule statements that violate this principle are discussed in Section 7.2.3;
3. rule statements that are ambiguous;
4. rule statements that express the intended rule in an unambiguous manner.

Clearly, only rule statements in the last of these four categories are appropriate. But there is likely to be more than one possible rule statement for any given rule even in the last category. For example, there is a requirement that each flight booking confirmation specify at least one passenger name. This require-ment can be expressed using numerous formulations, some invalid, others valid: for example,

1. †Each <u>flight booking request</u> must *specify* at least one <u>passenger name</u> (invalid: inappropriate term).
2. †Each <u>flight booking confirmation</u> must *contain* at least one <u>passenger name</u> (invalid: inappropriate verb phrase).
3. †There must *be* at least one <u>passenger name</u> *in* each <u>flight booking confirmation</u> (invalid: misplaced rule subject).
4. A <u>flight booking confirmation</u> must *specify* either one <u>passenger name</u> or more than one <u>passenger name</u> (valid: intended rule, unambiguous).
5. A <u>flight booking confirmation</u> must *specify* one or more <u>passenger names</u> (valid: intended rule, unambiguous).
6. A <u>flight booking confirmation</u> must *specify* at least one <u>passenger name</u> (valid: intended rule, unambiguous).
7. Each <u>flight booking confirmation</u> must *specify* at least one <u>passenger name</u> (valid: intended rule, unambiguous).

Within the organization there may be a preference for one of the valid formulations over the others, or one formulation may find less favor: for example, 4 may be seen as too verbose or 6 not as rigorous as 7. At the same time, there may be multiple formulations that seem equally appropriate: for example, 5 and 6. In just the same way as Australia has opted for driving on the left (despite there being nothing in-trinsically better about driving on the left instead of the right), it is better for everyone in an organi-zation to agree to use one formulation rather than the other, although the stakes are admittedly rather higher on the roads!

Templates provide a means of documenting the agreed rule statement formulation for each type of rule.

7.4 **RULE STATEMENT QUALITY**

The quality of a rule statement depends on it meeting a number of criteria:

1. Each word or phrase in the rule statement must be correctly spelt in the language used by the or-ganization: for example, US or Australian English.
2. Each term in the rule statement must be a term in the fact model used by the organization; in par-ticular, each term in the rule statement must be a preferred term rather than any synonym of a preferred term.
3. The rule statement must not include personal pronouns (such as 'you'[19]) or adverbs of time or place (such as 'here' or 'now').
4. The rule statement must include one of the following:
   a. 'by definition'
   b. 'must' or
   c. 'may' followed by 'only' at some point in the statement.

---

[19]The pronoun 'it' may be used in **mandatory option selection rule statements** (see Section 7.2.4.1), and may be used with care anywhere in a rule statement where only one term precedes the location where the pronoun is to be used.

5. The rule statement must form a syntactically correct sentence.
6. The rule statement should[20] conform to the rule statement template appropriate to the type of rule. This should ensure that criteria 3, 4, and 5 are met.
7. The rule statement must be based on fact types in the fact model (see Section 7.4.1). This should ensure that criterion 2 is met.
8. The subject of the rule statement must signify the object that is to be tested by the rule (see Section 7.2.3).
9. The rule statement must not be ambiguous (see Section 7.4.2).
10. The rule statement must not be self-contradictory (see Section 7.4.3).
11. The rule statement should not include any redundant qualifying or conditional clauses (see Section 7.4.4).
12. The rule statement must not duplicate any other rule statement (see Section 7.4.5).
13. The rule statement must not overlap (imply or be implied by) any other rule statement (see Section 7.4.6).
14. The rule statement must not contradict any other rule statement (see Section 7.4.7).
15. The rule statement should not be one of a set of complementary rule statements which between them express a single rule (see Section 7.4.8).

7.4.1 Fact type support for rule statements

Each rule statement must be based on fact types in the fact model (either explicitly stated, or derived as described in Section 6.3.3 in Chapter 6). What this means is that the verb phrases associated with each term in a rule statement must be associated with that term in a fact type. Let's look at a simple example to start with:

R258. Each flight booking request
must *specify* exactly one destination city.

The subject is 'flight booking request' and the predicate (after removal of the determiner) is '*specify* destination city'. If this rule statement is genuine, the following fact type should be present in the fact model:

F115. flight booking request *specifies* destination city

What if the rule statement includes a conditional clause? Again, the subject and the predicate (less any determiner) of the conditional clause should form one of the fact types in the fact model. Thus the conditional clause in R259 requires the fact type F116 (and the main clause requires F117).

R259. A person
may *be employed as* a driver
only if that person *holds* a current Australian driving license.
F116. person *holds* current Australian driving license
F117. person *is employed as* driver

---

[20]I have used 'should' rather than 'must' here as there are practitioners who disagree with the use of templates: disagreement on this one criterion should not cause rejection of this entire list.

If the predicate in the conditional clause involves a comparison between an attribute and a particular value, that conditional clause requires (at least) two fact types:

1. one, such as F119, connecting the attribute term (<u>age</u> in R260) to the relevant fundamental term ('<u>person</u>' in this case), and
2. one, such as F120, connecting the attribute term to the generic term covering values that the attribute may take ('<u>quantity</u>' in this case).

Again, the main clause requires a fact type that associates its subject and predicate (F118 in this case).

R260. A <u>person</u>
   may *obtain* <u>travel insurance</u>
   only if the <u>age</u> *of* that <u>person</u> *is less than* <u>70 years</u>.
F118. <u>person</u> *obtains* <u>travel insurance</u>
F119. <u>person</u> *has* <u>age</u>/
   <u>age</u> *is of* <u>person</u>
F120. <u>simple arithmetic attribute</u> *is less than* <u>quantity</u>

What if the rule statement includes a qualifying clause? Any qualifying clause requires a fact type which links the qualified term (the term immediately before the qualifying clause: '<u>number of passengers</u>' in R261) with the verb phrase introducing the qualifying clause and the term (if any) that follows that verb phrase. F121 (in its reverse form) fulfils that role for the qualifying clause in R261. A fact type is still required to associate the qualified term with the predicate: F122 in this case.

R261. The <u>number of passengers</u>
      specified in each <u>flight booking request</u>
   must *be no less than* <u>1</u>.
F121. <u>flight booking request</u> *specifies* <u>number of passengers</u>/
   <u>number of passengers</u> *is specified in* <u>flight booking request</u>
F122. <u>simple arithmetic attribute</u> *is no less than* <u>quantity</u>

Of course, a qualifying clause can be used to qualify the predicate rather than the subject: the same principles apply. Thus R262 requires the following fact types:

1. F123 (in its reverse form), to support the qualifying clause qualifying the subject;
2. F124 (in its reverse form), to support the qualifying clause qualifying the predicate.

R262. The <u>destination city</u>
      specified in each <u>flight booking request</u>
   must *be* one of the <u>cities</u>
      served by the <u>airline</u>.
F123. <u>flight booking request</u> *specifies* <u>destination city</u>/
   <u>destination city</u> *is specified in* <u>flight booking request</u>
F124. <u>airline</u> *serves* <u>city</u>/
   <u>city</u> *is served by* <u>airline</u>

The next example has both a qualifying clause and a conditional clause, and also includes a special kind of predicate in the conditional clause. This predicate, referring as it does to an ability or desire rather than an actual action or relationship, can be supported by a unary fact type.[21] To put it another way, we are not interested here in passengers actually opening doors (if so, we would require the fact type 'passenger *opens* aircraft door'). Thus R263 requires the following fact types:

1. F125, to support the main clause;
2. F126, to support the qualifying clause;
3. F127, to support the conditional clause.

R263. A passenger
      may *be allocated to* a seat
         in an exit row
      only if that passenger *is able to open an aircraft door.*

F125. passenger *is allocated to* seat

F126. seat *is in* exit row

F127. passenger *is able to open an aircraft door*

The next example illustrates a further point and reinforces a point made previously:

1. A ***ternary fact type*** (such as F128) may be more appropriate to associate three terms if the second and third terms are separated in the rule statement by a ***preposition*** ('*for*' here) rather than a verb.
2. Any term qualified by a qualifying clause (such as '<u>flight</u>' in R264) requires not only a fact type to associate it with the verb phrase and term in the qualifying clause (F130 in its reverse form in this case) but a fact type to associate it with its own predicate (F131).

As well as these, F129 (in its reverse form) is needed to support the qualifying clause qualifying 'passenger'.

R264. Each flight booking confirmation
      must *specify* exactly one set of passport details
         for each passenger
         specified in that flight booking confirmation
      if any flight
         specified in that flight booking confirmation
      is international.

F128. flight booking confirmation *specifies* set of passport details *for* passenger

F129. flight booking confirmation *specifies* passenger/
passenger *is specified in* flight booking confirmation

F130. flight booking confirmation *specifies* flight/
flight *is specified in* flight booking confirmation

F131. flight *is international*

Finally, you may recall that, in Section 5.3.5 in Chapter 5, I briefly discussed those verbs that state or question the truth of a proposition: these verbs are followed by 'that', 'whether' (optionally followed in turn by 'or not'), or 'if'. Examples of such verbs are '*specify*' (as in R265) and '*check*' (as in R266). Such verbs require a fact type in which the term after the verb is 'proposition'.

---

[21]This type of verb may occur anywhere in a rule statement: main clause, qualifying clause or conditional clause.

R265 therefore requires

1. F132, to support the subject of the main clause ('<u>flight booking request</u>'), the verb '*specify*', and the proposition specified;
2. F133, to support the qualifying clause after '<u>travel dates</u>';
3. F134, to support the proposition, namely whether the travel dates are movable.

Similarly, R266 requires

1. F135, to support the subject of the main clause ('<u>cabin crew member</u>'), the verb '*check*', and the proposition specified;
2. F136, to support the proposition, namely whether the door is disarmed;
3. F137, to support the predicate of the main clause ('*be* the same <u>cabin crew member</u>', which is a short form of '*be the same as* the <u>cabin crew member</u>');
4. F138, to support the second occurrence of '<u>cabin crew member</u>'.

R265. Each <u>flight booking request</u>
must *specify* whether or not the <u>travel dates</u>
specified in the <u>flight booking request</u>
are moveable.
F132. <u>flight booking request</u> *specifies* <u>proposition</u>
F133. <u>flight booking request</u> *specifies* <u>travel date</u>/
<u>travel date</u> *is specified in* <u>flight booking request</u>
F134. <u>travel date</u> *is moveable*
R266. The <u>cabin crew member</u>
who *checks* that an <u>aircraft door</u> *is disarmed*
must not *be* the same <u>cabin crew member</u>
who *disarmed* that <u>aircraft door.</u>
F135. <u>cabin crew member</u> *checks* <u>proposition</u>
F136. <u>aircraft door</u> *is disarmed*
F137. <u>person</u> *is the same as* <u>person</u>
F138. <u>cabin crew member</u> *disarms* <u>aircraft door</u>

Before we move on, note that R265 refers to '<u>travel dates</u>', whereas other rule statements relating to flight booking requests have referred to '<u>departure date</u>' and '<u>return date</u>'. This variation can be accommodated if we identify, by way of the following fact types, that the term '<u>travel date</u>' covers both departure date and return date.

F139. <u>departure date</u> *is a category of* <u>travel date</u>
F140. <u>return date</u> *is a category of* <u>travel date</u>

Generalized terms such as this can be used in another way. Consider the following rule statements:

R267. Each <u>flight booking request</u>
for a <u>return journey</u>
must *specify* the <u>return date.</u>
R268. A <u>flight booking request</u>
for a <u>one-way journey</u>
must not *specify* a <u>return date.</u>

The qualifying clauses in these rule statements could be supported by the following fact types:

F141. †flight booking request *is for* return journey[22]
F142. †flight booking request *is for* one-way journey

Alternatively, if it is recognized that each flight booking request is for a single journey that is a return journey or a one-way journey, the following fact types more accurately portray the relationship between flight booking requests and journeys:

F143. flight booking request *is for* journey
F144. return journey *is a category of* journey
F145. one-way journey *is a category of* journey

You may of course now be tempted to use F146 to model the fact that flight booking requests may specify two travel dates, a departure date, and (optionally) a return date, but since a single flight booking request may specify both those dates, F147 and F148 more accurately portray the relationship between flight booking requests and travel dates:

F146. †flight booking request *specifies* travel date
F147. flight booking request *specifies* departure date
F148. flight booking request *specifies* return date

7.4.2 Ambiguity

There are various ways in which a rule statement may be ambiguous. The following guidelines and examples cover just a few of the possible sources of ambiguity:

1. A rule statement should not include any ***personal pronouns*** (e.g., 'it', 'her') unless there is only one term before the pronoun, and the pronoun is to refer to that term. If more than one term precedes the pronoun, it is not always clear which term the pronoun refers to. For example, in R269, 'it' could refer to either the origin city or the destination city.

R269. †Each flight booking request
             that *specifies* an origin city
             that *is outside* Australia
             and a destination city
             that *is within* Australia
         must *specify* whether it *is* the city of residence *of* each passenger.

2. A rule statement should not include the definite article 'the' before a term unless either
    a. that term, as used in that rule statement, genuinely refers to all members of the set signified by the term, as in 'one of the Australian States', or
    b. that term is qualified by a qualifying clause that identifies a particular member (or members) of the set signified by that term.

---

[22]The dagger at the start of a fact type or rule statement indicates that it is in some way invalid as it stands.

R270 is an example of a rule statement that contravenes this guideline:

R270. †Each <u>flight booking confirmation</u>
must *specify* exactly one <u>escorting party</u>
  at the <u>destination city</u>
if the <u>age</u>
  of every <u>passenger</u>
  is less than <u>12 years</u>.

This rule statement does not make clear which destination city is referred to, nor which passengers, although it should be reasonably obvious to a human reader of the rule statement. Nonetheless we should qualify the terms '<u>destination city</u>' and '<u>passenger</u>', as in R271. While we're doing that, we might notice that something else in the rule statement requires qualification: the age limit refers to the age at the time of travel rather than (for example) at the time of booking.

R271. Each <u>flight booking confirmation</u>
must *specify* exactly one <u>escorting party</u>
  at the <u>destination city</u>
  specified in that <u>flight booking confirmation</u>
if the <u>age</u>
  of every <u>passenger</u>
  specified in that <u>flight booking confirmation</u>
  is less than <u>12 years</u>
  at the <u>time of travel</u>.

3. As discussed in Section 7.2.6, at least one of the terms in a conditional clause in a rule statement must (as does '<u>flight booking confirmation</u>' in R271)
  a. refer back to one of the terms in the subject of the rule statement, and
  b. be preceded by the determiner 'that'.

4. Where the same term is used more than once in the same rule statement to signify different instances of the same concept, it will be necessary to qualify which instance is referred to: for example, the third use of Party in rule statement R272 is ambiguous. While this can be clarified (in this case at least) by preceding the third use of '<u>Party</u>' by 'second', a better or more general solution is to create specific business terms for the two Parties involved and use those terms instead.

R272. †A <u>Party</u>
  who *acts on behalf of* another <u>Party</u>
must *be cited by* the <u>Party</u>
  in an <u>Authorization to Transact</u>.

5. A rule statement that includes both 'and' and 'or' in a qualifying or conditional clause may be ambiguous. For example, in R273 it is not clear whether an applicant holding an Australian passport must also hold an Australian state driving license. Note that, if this type of formulation is required, it can be made unambiguous by
  a. moving the pair of clauses to be evaluated first to the end of the qualifying or conditional clause, and
  b. inserting 'both' (if 'and') or 'either' (if 'or') before that pair of clauses, as in R274 and R275 respectively:

R273. †An <u>applicant</u>
must *hold* an <u>Australian passport</u>
or a <u>business skills visa</u>
and an <u>Australian state driving license</u>.

R274. An <u>applicant</u>
must *hold* an <u>Australian passport</u>
or both a <u>business skills visa</u> and an <u>Australian state driving license</u>.

R275. An <u>applicant</u>
must *hold* an <u>Australian state driving license</u>
and either an <u>Australian passport</u> or a <u>business skills visa</u>.

One alternative approach is to use bullets to separate clauses:

R276. Each <u>flight booking confirmation</u>
must *specify* exactly one of the following:
• a <u>mobile phone number</u>; or
• an <u>origin city daytime phone number</u> and
an <u>origin city evening phone number</u>.

6. Similarly a qualifying clause that includes both 'that' and 'and' (or 'that' and 'or') may be ambiguous. For example, 'a <u>car</u> that *belongs to* a <u>person</u> that *lives in* <u>Sydney</u> and that *is white*' does not make clear whether it is the car or the person that is white. Note that, if this type of formulation is required, it can be made unambiguous by reordering the formulation so that 'and' or 'or' precedes 'that', as in 'a <u>car</u> that *is white* and that *belongs to* a <u>person</u> that *lives in* <u>Sydney</u>'.

7. Every rule statement should include the singular rather than the plural form of the subject term: for example, R277 is correct whereas R278 is incorrect. This is because it is important to understand precisely the constraints on a single member of the set signified by the subject term.

R277. A <u>Lodgment Case</u>
contains by definition
at least one <u>Registry Instrument</u>.

R278. †<u>Lodgment Cases</u>
contain by definition
at least one <u>Registry Instrument</u>.

8. A range predicate that includes both 'at least' and '*less than*' (or '*fewer than*') may be ambiguous. Consider 'at least 2 *fewer than* the <u>number of passengers</u>': does a quantity that is three less than the number of passengers comply with that predicate or not? If this predicate is intended to mean '(at least 2) *fewer than* the <u>number of passengers</u>', that quantity does comply with the predicate, but, if it means 'at least (2 *fewer than* the <u>number of passengers</u>),' it does not. However, despite their use in use in mathematical formulae, parentheses are not used in this way in natural language.

7.4.3 **Self-contradiction**

We need to ensure that we don't use a qualifying clause in a rule statement that limits the scope of that rule statement to an ***empty set***. Consider the following examples:

1. 'An infant passenger whose age *is more than* 2 years *at* the time of travel …': here the qualifying clause contradicts the definition of the term infant passenger:

R279. An infant passenger
   is by definition
   a passenger whose age *is less than* 2 years *at* the time of travel.

2. 'A journey that *is* not a one-way journey, a return journey, or a multi-stop journey …': here the qualifying clause exhausts the categories of journey. An important point to note here is that the existence of the fact types F149, F150, and F151 is not sufficient to establish that these are the *only* categories of journey. It is therefore a good idea to add definitional rule statement R280, which makes clear that they are the only categories.

F149. return journey *is a* category *of* journey
F150. one-way journey *is a category of* journey
F151. multi-stop journey *is a category of* journey
R280. A journey
   is by definition
   a one-way journey, a return journey, or a multi-stop journey.

3. 'A flight that *has* no origin port … ', 'A flight that *has* more than one origin port …': in each case here, the qualifying clause contradicts the fact that, by definition, every flight has a single origin port (as well as a destination port: "what goes up must come down"). Again, it is important to note that the existence of fact type F152 is not sufficient to establish that *every* flight has an origin port. We therefore need the additional definitional rule statement R281 to specify that every flight has an origin port.

F152. flight *has* origin port
R281. Each flight
   has by definition
   exactly one origin port.

4. 'A flight booking request that *specifies* a passenger name …': here the qualifying clause is invalid because the fact type 'flight booking request *specifies* passenger name' does not exist. But what if we had simply created automatically (i.e., without careful thought) all the fact types that appear to support each rule statement we had created? If that were the case, we would have created the fact type 'flight booking request *specifies* passenger name' as soon as we thought we needed a rule statement with the qualifying clause 'that *specifies* a passenger name' after the term flight booking request. As a result, we would be unable to apply this type of 'sanity check' (does the necessary fact type exist?) on rule statements. Fact types are far more useful if created by way of thoughtful analysis of the organization's business through such questions as follows:
   a. What are the products and services available, what are the characteristics of those products and services, and how are they related to each other? For example:

F153. airline *serves* city
F154. flight *is operated by* airline
F155. flight *has* origin city

F156. flight *has* departure time
F157. fare class *is available on* flight
F158. port *has* minimum domestic transit time

  b. What processes and events occur and who and/or what is involved? For example:

F159. passenger *is booked on* flight
F160. passenger *checks in for* flight
F161. passenger *presents* boarding pass

  c. What information is created or used in each process? For example:

F162. flight booking request *specifies* departure date
F163. flight booking confirmation *specifies* passenger name
F164. airline *can access* postal code information *from* postal authority

5. 'A flight booking request that *specifies* no origin city …', 'A flight booking request that *specifies* more than one origin city …': in each case here the qualifying clause contradicts rule statement R282. Note that, by contrast with the example above that contradicted R281, the rule statement contradicted is an operative rule statement, which can be violated, rather than a definitional rule statement, which cannot. It is therefore possible for a flight booking request not to specify an origin city. However, it is unlikely that we would want to formulate a rule that applied only to such invalid flight booking requests. Remember that we do not include in our rule statements any statement as to how the organization or its employees or systems respond to rule violations.

R282. Each flight booking request
        must *specify* exactly one origin city.

The qualifying clauses above each contradict in some way the definition of the term being qualified. It is also possible for a qualifying clause to contradict itself as in the following examples, each of which is inappropriate in a rule statement since it would limit the scope of that statement to an empty set:

1. that *is less than* 1 year and *more than* 2 years;
2. that *is* a one-way journey and a return journey;
3. that *has* no origin port and *has* more than one origin port;
4. that *specifies* a passenger name and *does* not *specify* a passenger name.

Conditional clauses, like the following, can similarly limit rule statements to the empty set, and are therefore inappropriate:

1. the age *of* that infant passenger *is more than* 2 years *at* the time of travel;
2. that journey *is* not a one-way journey, a return journey or a multi-stop journey;
3. that flight *has* no origin port;
4. that flight *has* more than one origin port;
5. that flight booking request *specifies* a passenger name;
6. that flight booking request *specifies* no origin city;
7. that flight booking request *specifies* more than one origin city.

Similarly, a conditional clause may be self-contradictory and therefore inappropriate in a rule statement, as in the following examples:

1. the <u>age</u> *of* that <u>passenger</u> *is less than* <u>1 year</u> and *more than* <u>2 years</u>;
2. that <u>journey</u> *is* a <u>one-way journey</u> and a <u>return journey</u>;
3. that <u>flight</u> *has* no <u>origin port</u> and *has* more than one <u>origin port</u>;
4. that <u>flight booking request</u> *specifies* a <u>passenger name</u> and *does* not *specify* a <u>passenger name</u>.

While it is permissible to use both a qualifying clause and a conditional clause in the same rule state-ment, it is possible for the conditional clause to contradict the qualifying clause, as in 'A <u>flight booking request</u> that *specifies* a <u>return journey</u> must . . . if that <u>flight booking request</u> *does* not *specify* a <u>return journey</u>'. Such a combination of clauses limits the scope of the rule statement to the empty set: one of the clauses should be removed.

7.4.4 Redundant qualifying and conditional clauses

The inclusion of redundant qualifying clauses in rule statements is a common error made by overcau-tious authors. A redundant qualifying clause is one that has no effect, in that every member of the set signified by the qualified term meets the criterion expressed in the qualifying clause; thus no members of that set are excluded from the coverage of the rule statement by virtue of the qualifying clause. Here are some examples:

1. 'An <u>infant passenger</u> whose <u>age</u> *is less than* <u>2 years</u> *at* the <u>time of travel</u> . . .': since the qualifying clause repeats the definition of the term <u>infant passenger</u> provided in R283, it is true for every infant passenger.

R283. An <u>infant passenger</u>
　　　　is by definition
　　　　a <u>passenger</u> whose <u>age</u> *is less than* <u>2 years</u> *at* the <u>time of travel</u>.

2. 'A <u>journey</u> that *is* a <u>one-way journey</u>, a <u>return journey</u>, or a <u>multi-stop journey</u> . . .': since the qual-ifying clause lists all the categories of <u>journey</u> as defined in R284, it is true for every journey.

R284. A <u>journey</u>
　　　　is by definition
　　　　a <u>one-way journey</u>, a <u>return journey</u>, or a <u>multi-stop journey</u>.

3. 'A <u>flight</u> that *has* an <u>origin port</u> . . .': since the qualifying clause repeats the fact that, by definition, every flight has a single origin port, as stated in R285, and it is true for every flight.

R285. Each <u>flight</u>
　　　　has by definition
　　　　exactly one <u>origin port</u>.

4. 'A <u>flight booking request</u> that *does* not *specify* a <u>passenger name</u> . . .': this qualifying clause is irrelevant because the fact type '<u>flight booking request</u> *specifies* <u>passenger name</u>' does not exist: that is, no flight booking requests specify passenger names.

Conditional clauses that do not limit the scope of their rule statements are similarly redundant, includ-ing the following examples:

1. the <u>age</u> *of* that <u>infant passenger</u> *is less than* <u>2 years</u> *at* the <u>time of travel</u>;
2. that <u>journey</u> *is* a <u>one-way journey</u>, a <u>return journey</u>, or a <u>multi-stop journey</u>;

3. that <u>flight</u> *has* an <u>origin port</u>;
4. that <u>flight booking request</u> *does* not *specify* a <u>passenger name</u>.

It is also possible for the conditional clause to repeat the qualifying clause, as in 'A <u>flight booking request</u> that *specifies* a <u>return journey</u> must . . . if that <u>flight booking request</u> *specifies* a <u>return journey</u>'. Obviously the rule statement does not need both clauses: one should be removed.

Some qualifying clauses are inappropriate for a different reason. Consider 'A <u>flight booking request</u> that *specifies* an <u>origin city</u> . . .': this qualifying clause limits the scope of its rule statement to those flight booking requests that comply with rule statement R286. Note that, since R286 is an operative rule statement, which can be violated (rather than a definitional rule statement, which cannot) it is possible for a flight booking request to violate R286 by not specifying an origin city. Note that a principle of the Business Rules Approach is that rules are independent of each other. Thus it is unlikely that we would want to formulate a rule that applied only to those flight booking requests that comply with some other rule.

R286. Each <u>flight booking request</u>
    must *specify* exactly one <u>origin city</u>.

The corresponding conditional clause ('that <u>flight booking request</u> *specifies* an <u>origin city</u>') is similarly inappropriate.

7.4.5 Duplicate rule statements

Any two rule statements may be semantically equivalent (duplicate each other). Should this occur, one of the two rule statements should be deleted. There are many ways in which two rule statements may be equivalent. The following are just a few examples:

1. If a rule statement includes a conditional clause introduced by 'unless', it can be rephrased by changing 'unless' to 'if' and negating the first verb phrase in the conditional clause: for example, 'unless the <u>flight</u> *is domestic*' can be rephrased as 'if the <u>flight</u> *is* not *domestic*'. More insidiously, 'unless the <u>flight</u> *is domestic*' and 'if the <u>flight</u> *is international*' mean the same thing since '*is domestic*' and '*is international*' are complementary Boolean characteristics. Again, two rule statements that are identical except for such a rephrasing are equivalent.

2. Comparison operators can be expressed in alternative ways, as in the next two examples, which are equivalent.

R287. The <u>order quantity</u>
    specified in each <u>line</u>
    of an <u>order</u>
    must *be no less than* <u>1</u>.
R288. The <u>order quantity</u>
    specified in each <u>line</u>
    of an <u>order</u>
    must *be at least* <u>1</u>.

3. Comparison operators can also be expressed in an equivalent reversed form, as in the next two examples, which are equivalent.

R289. A flight booking confirmation
    must not *specify* the code
        of a special offer
    if the departure date
        specified in that flight booking confirmation
        is later than the expiry date
        of that special offer.

R290. A flight booking confirmation
    must not *specify* the code
        of a special offer
    if the expiry date
        of that special offer
        is earlier than the departure date
        specified in that flight booking confirmation.

4. A rule statement can refer to either 'an international flight' or 'a flight that *is international*', with no change of meaning. Two rule statements that are identical except for such a rephrasing are equivalent.

5. Some rules may be expressed as either an ***obligation statement*** or a ***restricted permission statement***, as in the next two examples, which are equivalent.

R291. A flight booking request
        for a one-way journey
    must not *specify* a return date.

R292. Each flight booking request
    may *specify* a return date
    only if that flight booking request *is not for* a one-way journey.

7.4.6 Overlapping rule statements

Any two rule statements may overlap, in that one implies the other. Should this occur, again one should be deleted. The following are just some of the many ways in which two rule statements may overlap:

1. Two rule statements overlap if they impose the same condition on a term and the term representing its subset. For example, R293 and R294 would overlap since an online flight booking request is a category of flight booking request; thus R293 implies R294. Again, only one should be retained; here, however, unlike with equivalent rule statements, the choice of statement to be retained has semantic implications. R293 is the correct one here, since the rule applies to all flight booking requests, whether online or not. If, however, the rule only applied to online flight booking requests, R293 should be deleted.

R293. Each flight booking request
    must *specify* exactly one origin city.

R294. Each online flight booking request
    must *specify* exactly one origin city.

2. Two rule statements overlap if they are identical except for the presence or absence of a qualifying clause. For example, R295 is implied by R296. Again, only one of these rule statements is correct: in this case, R295.

R295. Each flight booking request
    for a return journey
must *specify* exactly one return date.
R296. Each flight booking request
must *specify* exactly one return date.

3. Two rule statements overlap if they are identical except for semantically different qualifying clauses: for example,

R297. Each bag
    that *weighs more than* 20 kg
must *be labeled with* a 'heavy bag' label.
R298. Each bag
    that *weighs more than* 30 kg
must *be labeled with* a 'heavy bag' label.

4. Two rule statements overlap if they are identical except for the presence or absence of a conditional clause. For example, R299 is implied by R300. Again, only one of these rule statements is correct: in this case, R299.

R299. Each flight booking confirmation
must *specify* exactly one date of birth
    for each passenger
if that flight booking confirmation *specifies* an insurance option.
R300. Each flight booking confirmation
must *specify* exactly one date of birth
    for each passenger.

5. Two rule statements overlap if they are identical except for semantically different conditional clauses. For example, R301 is implied by R302.

R301. Each flight booking confirmation
must *specify* exactly one set of passport details
    for each passenger
if any flight
    specified in that flight booking confirmation
    is international.
R302. Each flight booking confirmation
must *specify* exactly one set of passport details
    for each passenger
if all flights
    specified in that flight booking confirmation
    are international.

7.4.7 **Contradictory rule statements**

Any two rule statements may contradict, in that they cannot both be true. Should this occur, again one should be deleted. The following are just some of the many potential ways in which two rule statements can be contradictory:

1. Two cardinality rule statements contradict each other if they are identical except for cardinality: for example,

R303. Each flight booking request
   must *specify* exactly one departure date.
R304. Each flight booking request
   must *specify* at least one departure date.

2. Two data content rules of the same type contradict each other if they are identical except for their predicates and those predicates contradict each other: for example,

R305. The travel class
      specified in each flight booking request
   must *be* first class, business class, premium economy class,
      or economy class.
R306. The travel class
      specified in each flight booking request
   must *be* first class, business class, or economy class.

7.4.8 **Using multiple complementary rule statements to state a single rule**

Consider the following rule statements:

R307. †Each flight booking request
      for a return journey
   must *specify* exactly one departure date.
R308. †Each flight booking request
      for a one-way journey
   must *specify* exactly one departure date.
R309. †Each flight booking request
      for a multi-stop journey
   must *specify* exactly one departure date.

It should be obvious that all flight booking requests, irrespective of the type of journey specified, need to specify a departure date. These three rule statements, therefore, should be replaced by

R310. Each flight booking request
   must *specify* exactly one departure date.

7.5 SUMMARY

If you follow the method outlined in this book, each operative rule statement you write will conform to one of five standard formulations. In each of these formulations, there is

1. a subject, preceded by a determiner ('Each', 'The', 'A', or 'An'), and optionally followed by a qualifying clause;
2. a predicate, preceded by a modal verb: 'must' (optionally followed by 'not') or 'may';
3. a conditional clause, preceded by a conditional conjunction (usually 'if' or 'unless', but 'after', 'during', or 'while' in certain types of rule statements); the conditional clause is optional in most cases but mandatory if the modal verb is 'may'.

Similarly, each definitional rule statement you write will conform to a standard formulation, consisting of

1. a subject, optionally preceded by a determiner ('The', 'A', or 'An'), and optionally followed by a qualifying clause;
2. a definition, preceded by a verb phrase and the phrase 'by definition'.

Which subjects and predicates are permissible in rule statements depends on the type of rule being expressed. There are also various permissible formulations for conditional and qualifying clauses. For these reasons, the next chapter includes one or more templates for each type of rule.

There are various other factors that affect the quality of a rule statement including

1. whether all terms, verb phrases and prepositions have been drawn from fact types in the fact model;
2. whether its subject signifies the object that is to be tested by the rule;
3. whether it is ambiguous and/or self-contradictory;
4. whether it includes redundant qualifying or conditional clauses;
5. whether it duplicates, overlaps (implies or is implied by), or contradicts any other rule statement;
6. whether it is one of a set of rule statements which between them express a single rule.

An end-to-end rule management methodology

This chapter describes a complete end-to-end rule writing, documentation, and management methodology, with examples drawn from some typical business scenarios.

Effective establishment and ongoing management of an organization's rule book involves the following phases:

1. discovery: finding out what rules govern the organization (discussed in Section 8.1);
2. analysis: establishing what each rule actually involves (discussed in Section 8.2);
3. developing the rule statement vocabulary as necessary (discussed in Section 8.3);
4. documentation: recording each rule statement with appropriate metadata (discussed in Section 8.4);
5. quality assurance: establishing that each rule statement is correct (discussed in Section 8.5);
6. publication: making all rule statements available to all stakeholders (discussed in Section 8.6);
7. implementation: creating new system components (or modifying existing components) to ensure that all data and automated processes comply with all relevant rules;
8. ongoing maintenance of the vocabulary and rule statements (discussed in Section 8.7).

Note that rule implementation is outside the scope of this book.

While the approach to rule discovery and analysis will vary according to the source from which you are harvesting rules, the overall methodology is much the same.

8.1 RULE DISCOVERY

The most useful sources of rules are procedural manuals and other procedural documentation for employees (and possibly customers) such as instructions for filling out forms. Additional rules can often be established by examination of paper or electronic forms, message and database schemas, and process models.

8.1.1 Sources of rules

There are many possible sources of rules, although in any one situation only some of these will be available:

1. interviews or workshops with subject matter experts or potential system users;
2. existing documented guidance, such as procedural manuals, training material, annotations on user interfaces, help screens, regulations;
3. analysis of input forms (paper or online) or input XML messages;
4. analysis of data models;

5. analysis of process models;

6. existing system specifications, program code, or DDL (data definition language).

8.1.2 Collecting rules from those sources

Each type of rule source requires different techniques for understanding what rules apply:

1. When interviewing or conducting workshops with subject matter experts or potential system users, you will generally get to hear about many different aspects of the organization and its systems, not all of which will have a bearing on the rules that govern that organization and systems. Be alert for the following:

    a. terms that are frequently used and/or have a specific meaning for the organization or its processes;

    b. descriptions of specific processes and transactions;

    c. allusions to obligations on the part of the organization or its employees, customers, or suppliers;

    d. allusions to prohibited processes or activities;

    e. allusions to processes or activities that are permitted only in certain situations;

    f. data items that are necessary for particular processes and transactions;

    g. constraints on data items.

2. When examining existing documented guidance, be alert for the same issues as you might find during interviews or workshops.

3. When analyzing an input form or message type, consider each field in turn and ask the following questions:

    a. Is this field mandatory: that is, must it be filled in on every occasion? If not, what are the occasions when it must be filled in? What are the occasions when it may be left empty?

    b. What type of field is it (in terms of permissible contents)? That is, does it require

        i. an identifier?

        ii. a value from an enumerated set?

        iii. a numeric quantity?

        iv. a date, time, or other temporal value?

        v. a person name?

        vi. an address of some kind (street address, postal delivery service address, e-mail address)?

        vii. free text?

    c. What are the constraints on the values that may be entered into the field?

        i. Must it be a value from some set?

        ii. Must it match some other value exactly?

        iii. Is there a range outside which it must not fall?

       iv. Must it be different from other values of the same field, either on the same form or in existing data?

4. When analyzing a data model

    a. analyze each attribute, in terms of whether it is mandatory and whether there are any constraints on its value (including whether it must have a different value for each instance of the entity);

    b. analyze each relationship, in terms of whether it is mandatory in each direction and whether there can be more than one instance of the entity at each end.

5. When analyzing a process model, ask for each process the following:
   a. What are the events or situations (if any) that prevent that process from occurring?
   b. What are the events or situations (if any) that require that process to occur?
   c. What are the decisions (if any) that that process is required to enact?
6. When examining existing system specifications, program code, or DDL, you are of course looking out for the same obligations, prohibitions, and restricted permissions as with any other source of rules.

8.2 ANALYZING RULES

There are three principal approaches to rule analysis:

1. one to be used when analyzing input forms or messages, or data models (the "data analysis" approach, discussed in Section 8.2.1);
2. one to be used when the source of rule intelligence is subject matter experts, potential system users, existing documented guidance, system specifications, program code, or DDL (the "raw rules" approach, discussed in Section 8.2.2);
3. one to be used when analyzing process models.

Analysis of process models is arguably the least common activity in rule discovery, and is probably the most straightforward, so I shall not dwell on it in detail. The other approaches each require some thought, so I shall now discuss each approach, with examples.

8.2.1 The "data analysis" approach

I shall illustrate this approach with two example forms:

1. a simple flight booking request form,
2. an employee leave request form,

For each data item in each form, we will be considering the questions listed in Section 8.1.2:

1. Is this data item mandatory?
2. What type of data item is it?
3. What are the constraints on the values that may be entered into the field?

8.2.1.1 Employee leave request
A typical employee leave request form is illustrated in Figure 1.
   This form includes the following data items:

1. a field for the employee number;
2. fields for the start and end dates of the leave period being requested;
3. a field in which can be selected the type of leave being requested (annual leave, sick leave, parental leave, bereavement leave, etc.);
4. a pair of radio buttons indicating 'leave with pay' and 'leave without pay' respectively;

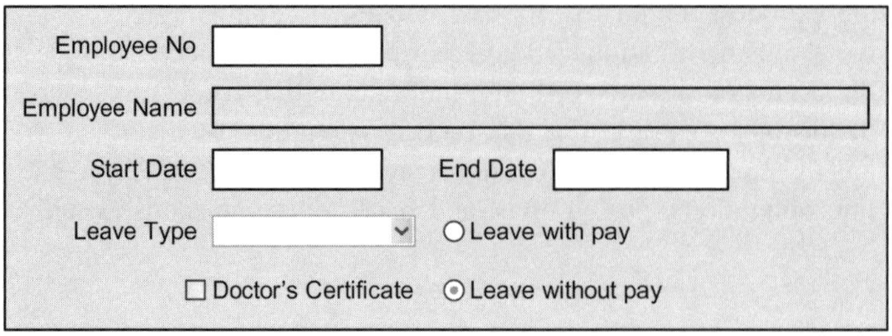

FIGURE 1

An employee leave request form.

5. a check box to indicate whether the employee has a doctor's certificate to cover a period of sick leave.

It should be clear that each individual data item is mandatory except the check box (which is either checked or is not).

The start and end date fields obviously require valid dates. The leave type field requires a value from an enumerated set. The employee number field is most likely free text.

What are the constraints on the values that may be entered into each data item?

1. The employee number must be one of the employee numbers allocated by the organization.
2. The end date must not be earlier than the start date.
3. The leave type must be one of the leave types allowed by the organization.
4. One of the pair of radio buttons must be selected.

We therefore have the following rules:

1. For the employee number field
   a. a *mandatory data item rule*,
   b. a *value set rule*;
2. For the start date field
   a. a *mandatory data item rule*,
   b. a *data item format rule*;
3. For the end date field
   a. a *mandatory data item rule*,
   b. a *data item format rule*;
4. For the start date and end date fields as a combination
   a. a *data consistency rule*;
5. For the leave type field
   a. a *mandatory data item rule*,
   b. a *value set rule*;
6. For the pair of radio buttons
   a. a *mandatory option selection rule*.

Each type of rule has its own template(s). Let's look at two different templates in turn.

8.2.1.1.1 Creating a mandatory data item rule statement

The template for this type of rule statement is T19 (described in Section 9.3.1.1.1 in Chapter 9):

Each <transaction signifier>
must {*specify*| *contain*} <cardinality> <data item term>
  {{*in*| *for*} {each|the} <subform term> {(if any)|}
  {<qualifying clause>|}|}
{{if|unless} <conditional clause>|}.

A number of steps are required to create a rule statement using this template as a basis:

1. We first need to look at the options available for the <transaction signifier> placeholder, for which there is a subtemplate (S8 in Section 9.1.2.4 in Chapter 9) as follows:

<transaction signifier>::=
{<term>|{record of a|} combination of [<term>, and]}
  {<qualifying clause>|}

2. Which option applies here? The transaction governed is an Employee Leave Request, so we can substitute the term 'employee leave request' in place of the <term> placeholder rather than refer to a combination of data items. Since each rule applies to all Employee Leave Requests, we do not need the qualifying clause, so we can omit it, meaning that all that needs to be substituted in place of the <transaction signifier> placeholder is the term 'employee leave request', yielding

Each employee leave request
must {*specify*| *contain*} <cardinality> <data item term>
  {*for* {each|the} <subform term> {(if any)|}
  {<qualifying clause>|}|}
{{if|unless} <conditional clause>|}.

3. At this point, we are in a position to establish whether the various optional elements of the rule statement are required:
a. Since there is no subform in this form, we do not need the optional element in lines 3 and 4.
b. Since each rule applies to all Employee Leave Requests, we do not need the conditional clause. Removing the unneeded elements yields

Each employee leave request
must {*specify*| *contain*} <cardinality> <data item term>.

4. We need to decide whether to use '*specify*' or '*contain*' as the verb phrase. For rule statements governing data in a transaction, '*specify*' works best, whereas '*contain*' is more appropriate for rule statements governing larger collections of data, such as messages containing multiple transactions. This rule statement governs the content of a transaction, so we will use '*specify*'.

5. We now need to substitute something for the <cardinality> placeholder. The only available options for a mandatory data item rule (as listed in Section 9.3.1.1.1) are
a. exactly <positive integer>,
b. at least <positive integer>,
c. at least <positive integer> and at most <positive integer>.

The option 'exactly one' is the appropriate one for each data item in this form, yielding

Each <u>employee leave request</u>
must *specify* exactly one <<u>data item term</u>>.

6. This formulation can now be used for each of the data items subject to a mandatory data item rule, yielding:

R311. Each <u>employee leave request</u>
must *specify* exactly one <u>employee number</u>.
R312. Each <u>employee leave request</u>
must *specify* exactly one <u>start date</u>.
R313. Each <u>employee leave request</u>
must *specify* exactly one <u>end date</u>.
R314. Each <u>employee leave request</u>
must *specify* exactly one <u>leave type</u>.

8.2.1.1.2 Creating a value set rule statement

The template for this type of rule statement is T27 (described in Section 9.3.2.1.1 in Chapter 9):

{The|Each} <<u>data item term</u>> {(if any)|}
specified {{*in*| *for*} {the|each} <<u>subform term</u>> {(if any)|}|}
in each <transaction signifier>
must *be*
{{other than|} one of the <<u>term</u>> <qualifying clause>|[<<u>literal</u>>, or]}
{{*if*|unless} <conditional clause>|}.

The following steps are required to create a rule statement using this template as a basis:

1. As with the mandatory data item rules, we can
   a. substitute the term 'employee leave request' in place of the <transaction signifier> placeholder;
   b. remove the optional element from line 2 since there is no subform;
   c. remove the conditional clause since these rules apply to all Employee Leave Requests.
   We can also remove the first '(if any)' since each of the data items for which we need a value set rule is mandatory.

   After these transforms, the embryonic rule statement now looks like this:

   The <<u>data item term</u>>
   specified
   in each <u>employee leave request</u>
   must *be*
   {{other than|} one of the <<u>term</u>> <qualifying clause>|[<<u>literal</u>>, or]}.

2. Let's deal with the employee number rule statement first. The set of Employee Numbers will change from time to time so, rather than list them in the rule (using the '[<<u>literal</u>>, or]' option), we need to refer indirectly to the set of Employee Numbers, by using the '{other than|} one of the <<u>term</u>> <qualifying clause>' option.

3. The data item governed by this rule is 'employee number' and the set of values to which it is restricted is the set of Employee Numbers allocated by the organization, so we can substitute
   a. 'employee number' in place of <data item term>, and
   b. 'employee numbers' in place of <term>, yielding

   The employee number
      specified in each employee leave request
   must *be* {other than|} one of the employee numbers <qualifying clause>.

4. Since the Employee Numbers must be the same as an existing number rather than different from any existing number, we can remove the optional preposition 'other than'.

5. We now need to substitute something for the <qualifying clause> placeholder, for which there is also a subtemplate (S14 in Section 9.1.2.10) as follows:

   <qualifying clause>::=
   {{that|who} <*verb phrase*> {<object>|}|
   <*verb part*> <object>|
   other than {<object>|[<object>, or]}|
   {<*preposition*> {which|whom}|whose} <conditional clause>|
   {that|who} <*verb phrase*> {that|if|whether} <conditional clause>|
   <and-qualifying clause>|
   <or-qualifying clause>|
   <both-and-qualifying clause>|
   <either-or-qualifying clause>}

   This subtemplate allows for a daunting nine options! We could look up the description of each of these options in Section 9.1.2.10, or take advantage of the fact that the most common option for a qualifying clause is the one that starts with a verb part (i.e., a preposition optionally preceded by a participle or adjective), so we select the '<*verb part*> <object>' option.

6. This means we need to substitute something for the <object> placeholder, for which there is also a subtemplate (S11 in Section 9.1.2.7) as follows:

   <object>::=
   {{<determiner>|the <set function> of {<determiner>|}|} <term>
      {<qualifying clause>|}|
   {<determiner>|} <literal>}

   Since the set of values that govern this rule is the set of Employee Numbers allocated by the organization, all we need to substitute in place of the various placeholders are
   a. '*allocated by*' in place of <*verb part*>, and
   b. 'the organization' in place of '<determiner> <term>' from <object>,
   yielding '*allocated by* the organization' as the qualifying clause.

7. Returning to our rule statement, we can now substitute this phrase in place of the <qualifying clause> placeholder, yielding

R315. The <u>employee number</u>
specified
in each <u>employee leave request</u>
must *be* one of the <u>employee numbers</u>
allocated by the <u>organization</u>.

8. A similar process can be used to create the leave type rule statement, yielding

R316. The <u>leave type</u>
specified
in each <u>employee leave request</u>
must *be* one of the <u>leave types</u>
allowed by the <u>organization</u>.

By now, you should have a better idea of how the templates and subtemplates set out in Chapter 9 can be used as the basis for rule statements. We shall return to this topic in Section 8.2.2.9.

8.2.1.2 Flight booking request

As a further example of rule discovery and analysis, consider the typical simple flight booking request form illustrated in Figure 2.

This form includes the following data items:

1. a pair of radio buttons to select whether the journey is one-way or return;
2. fields for the origin and destination cities;
3. fields for the departure and return dates;
4. fields for the numbers of adult, child, and infant passengers traveling;
5. a pair of radio buttons to select whether those traveling are flexible as to travel dates or must travel on the dates entered.

It should be clear that each individual field (and each pair of radio buttons) is mandatory except the return date field (which is not required if the journey is one-way). Indeed, if the journey is one-way, no return date should be entered.

The departure and return date fields obviously require valid dates, and the fields for the numbers of adult, child, and infant passengers traveling obviously require valid positive integers. Each other individual data item (and each pair of radio buttons) requires a value from an enumerated set.

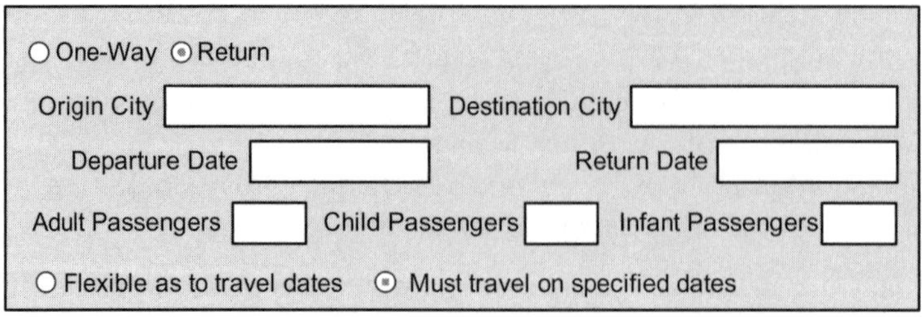

FIGURE 2

A simple flight booking request form.

What are the constraints on the values that may be entered into each field? For each pair of radio buttons, there is no constraint in addition to the requirement that for each pair one of the pair must be selected. For the other data items, it is clear that the following constraints are required:

1. The origin and destination cities must be cities that are served by the airline (there are two rules here, one for each city).
2. The origin and destination cities must be different.
3. The departure date must not be earlier than the date on which the booking is made.
4. The return date must not be earlier than the departure date.
5. There must be at least one adult traveling (a different form is required for children traveling alone, and infants cannot travel alone).
6. The number of infants must not be more than the number of adults (as each infant is required to travel on the lap of an adult).

We therefore have the following rules:

1. for the first pair of radio buttons
   a. a *mandatory option selection rule*;
2. for the origin city field
   a. a *mandatory data item rule*,
   b. a *value set rule* (one of the ports served by the airline);
3. for the destination city field
   a. a *mandatory data item rule*,
   b. a *value set rule* (again one of the cities served by the airline),
   c. an *equality rule* (different from the destination port);
4. for the departure date field
   a. a *mandatory data item rule*,
   b. a *data item format rule*,
   c. a *range rule* (no earlier than the date on which the booking is made);
5. for the return date field
   a. a *mandatory data item rule* (requiring the date if a return journey has been specified),
   b. a *prohibited data rule* (requiring no date if a one-way journey has been specified),
   c. a *data item format rule*,
   d. a *range rule* (no earlier than the departure date);
6. for the number of adult passengers field
   a. a *mandatory data item rule*,
   b. a *data item format rule*,
   c. a *range rule* (at least one);
7. for the number of child passengers field
   a. a *mandatory data item rule*,
   b. a *data item format rule*;
8. for the number of infant passengers field
   a. a *mandatory data item rule*,
   b. a *data item format rule*,
   c. a *range rule* (no more than the number of adult passengers);

9. for the second pair of radio buttons
   a. a *mandatory option selection rule*.

8.2.2 The "raw rules" approach

This approach is required when there already exist (or we have collected through consultation) various statements of the rules that apply. These statements will of course be in various syntactic forms, may use varying terminology, and some may be ambiguous when taken out of context.

To illustrate the approach, consider the following statements from a procedural manual governing the processing of real property transaction forms, under the heading 'Transfer Form':

1. *"The reference to title for the land being transferred must be stated."*
2. *"The full name of the transferor must be stated and must be identical to the name of the registered proprietor as shown on the Register."*
3. *"The consideration is optional. A consideration stated must agree with the purchase price stated in the Notice of Sale form."* [1]

Note that the process of converting these to rule statements that comply with the quality criteria set out in this book will involve a number of steps. At all intermediate stages, the rules will be rendered in italics as above, to distinguish them from compliant rule statements that will be rendered like all other rule statements in this book. At each step, the words (if any) added to each rule statement at that step are underlined.

8.2.2.1 Decomposing non-atomic rules

Each raw rule first needs to be decomposed into one or more *atomic rules*. An atomic rule is one that cannot be partially complied with, but only be completely complied with or completely contravened. Consider the three examples above:

1. The first rule is atomic. If a Transfer Form states a reference to title, that form complies with that rule, whereas if it states no reference to title, that form contravenes that rule; it cannot be partly complied with.
2. The second rule is not atomic. It can be completely complied with (by stating a transferor name that is identical to the relevant registered proprietor name) or be contravened (by not stating a transferor name), but it can also be partly complied with (by stating a transferor name that is different from the relevant registered proprietor name).
3. The third rule is atomic. It can be completely complied with (either by not stating a consideration or by stating a consideration that agrees with the relevant purchase price) or be contravened (by stating a consideration that does not agree with the relevant purchase price); it cannot be partly complied with.

Note that atomicity has nothing to do with the sentence structure of a rule statement.

---

[1] 'Consideration' is the term used to signify the money or whatever else is provided by the purchaser or receiving party to the vendor or relinquishing party in a real property transfer.

The second rule statement needs to be separated, as follows:

2A. *"The full name of the transferor must be stated."*
2B. *"The full name of the transferor must be identical to the name of the registered proprietor as shown on the Register."*

The third rule statement needs to be merged, as follows:

3. *"A consideration (if any) stated must agree with the purchase price stated in the Notice of Sale form."*

8.2.2.2 Removing context

Each rule must be independent of context. Frequently, in existing documentation of rules, section headings provide context; this is the case here. Each of these rules governs Transfer Forms: this needs to be expressed in each rule statement, as follows:

1. *"The reference to title for the land being transferred must be stated in a Transfer Form."*
2A. *"The full name of the transferor must be stated in a Transfer Form."*
2B. *"The full name of the transferor stated in a Transfer Form must be identical to the name of the registered proprietor as shown on the Register."*
3. *"A consideration (if any) stated in a Transfer Form must agree with the purchase price stated in the Notice of Sale form."*

8.2.2.3 Removing ambiguity

Each rule should be completely unambiguous by qualifying each term so that it refers only to relevant instances.

1. The first rule needs to state that only the land being transferred by way of that Transfer Form must be referenced in that Transfer Form.
2. The second rule needs to state that only the transferor taking part in the transfer documented in that Transfer Form must be referenced in that Transfer Form.
3. The third rule needs to state which registered proprietor the transferor name must match.
4. The fourth rule needs to state which Notice of Sale form is being referred to.

With the appropriate changes, the rules now look like this:

1. *"The reference to title for the land being transferred by the transfer documented in a Transfer Form must be stated in that Transfer Form."*
2A. *"The full name of the transferor taking part in the transfer documented in a Transfer Form must be stated in that Transfer Form."*
2B. *"The full name of the transferor stated in a Transfer Form must be identical to the name of the registered proprietor that is specified in the land title that*
    a. *is registered in the Register; and*
    b. *is specified in that Transfer Form."*
3. *"A consideration (if any) stated in a Transfer Form must agree with the purchase price stated in the Notice of Sale form that*
    a. *is contained in the lodgment case that contains that Transfer Form; and*
    b. *is associated with that Transfer Form."*

Note the three uses of the word '*that*' in rule 2B:

1. The first qualifies the term '*Registered Proprietor*' (enables us to establish which Registered Proprietor is being referred to).
2. The second qualifies the term '*Land Title*' (enables us to establish which Land Title is being referred to).
3. The third refers back to the reference to Transfer Form in the subject of the rule statement.

8.2.2.4 *Standardizing vocabulary*

At this point, we need to refer to the fact model, which (we hope) has the preferred terms we need to express each concept in each of these rules, as well as fact types which contain the agreed verb phrases to associate terms with each other. We may of course discover that some terms or fact types are missing. If so, we must add the required terms and/or fact types, as described in Section 6.4 in Chapter 6.

8.2.2.4.1 Standardizing the terms

Let's assume that the fact model has the following terms:

1. Land Title Reference
2. Land Title
3. Transfer
4. Transfer Instrument
5. Full Name
6. Transferor
7. Registered Proprietor
8. Land Title
9. Real Property Register
10. Consideration
11. Purchase Price
12. Notice of Sale Report
13. Lodgment Case

With the appropriate changes, the rules now look like this:

1. "The <u>Land Title Reference</u> for the <u>Land Title</u> being transferred by the <u>Transfer</u> documented in a <u>Transfer Instrument</u> must be stated in that <u>Transfer Instrument</u>."
2A. "The <u>Full Name</u> of the <u>Transferor</u> taking part in the <u>Transfer</u> documented in a <u>Transfer Instrument</u> must be stated in that <u>Transfer Instrument</u>."
2B. "The <u>Full Name</u> of the <u>Transferor</u> stated in a <u>Transfer Instrument</u> must be identical to the <u>Full Name</u> of the <u>Registered Proprietor</u> that is specified in the <u>Land Title</u> that
   a. is registered in the <u>Real Property Register</u>; and
   b. is specified in that <u>Transfer Instrument</u>."
3. "A <u>Consideration</u> (if any) stated in a <u>Transfer Instrument</u> must agree with the <u>Purchase Price</u> stated in the <u>Notice of Sale Report</u> that
   a. is contained in the <u>Lodgment Case</u> that contains that <u>Transfer Instrument</u>; and
   b. is associated with that <u>Transfer Instrument</u>."

8.2.2.4.2 Removing further ambiguity

Examination of the fact model reveals that there are two types of Consideration:

1. Monetary Consideration (i.e., money paid by a purchaser to a vendor in return for the real property being purchased), and
2. Non-Monetary Consideration (i.e., something other than money provided by a receiving party to a relinquishing party in return for the real property being transferred).

Clearly rule 3 governs only Monetary Consideration, so needs to be changed as follows:

3. *"A <u>Monetary Consideration</u> (if any) stated in a Transfer Instrument must agree with the Purchase Price stated in the Notice of Sale Report that*
   a. *is contained in the Lodgment Case that contains that Transfer Instrument; and*
   b. *is associated with that Transfer Instrument."*

8.2.2.4.3 Identifying the underlying fact types

Let's assume that the fact model has the following fact types associating the terms used in these rule statements:

F165. transfer *transfers* land title/
land title *is transferred by* transfer
F166. transfer instrument *documents* transfer/
transfer *is documented in* transfer instrument
F167. real property instrument *specifies* land title reference *for* land title
F168. transfer instrument *is a category of* real property instrument
F169. real property instrument *specifies* full name *of* transacting party/
full name *is specified for* transacting party *in* real property instrument
F170. transferor *is a category of* transacting party
F171. transferor *takes part in* transfer
F172. land title *specifies* full name *of* registered proprietor
F173. land title *is registered in* real property register
F174. transfer instrument *specifies* consideration
F175. monetary consideration *is a category of* consideration
F176. notice of sale report *specifies* purchase price
F177. lodgment case *contains* real property instrument
F178. lodgment case *contains* notice of sale report
F179. notice of sale report *is associated with* real property instrument

The principle of inheritance of fact types by **hyponyms** from their **hypernyms** allows us to infer some additional fact types that will be required to directly support the wording of our rule statements:

a. F180 from F167 and F168;
b. F181 from F168, F169, and F170;
c. F182 from F174 and F175;
d. F183 from F168 and F177;
e. F184 from F168 and F179.

F180. <u>transfer instrument</u> *specifies* <u>land title reference</u> *for* <u>land title</u>
F181. <u>transfer instrument</u> *specifies* <u>full name</u> *of* <u>transferor</u>/
      <u>full name</u> *is specified for* <u>transferor</u> *in* <u>transfer instrument</u>
F182. <u>transfer instrument</u> *specifies* <u>monetary consideration</u>
F183. <u>lodgment case</u> *contains* <u>transfer instrument</u>
F184. <u>notice of sale report</u> *is associated with* <u>transfer instrument</u>

We are now in a position to standardize the verb phrases and prepositions used in our rule statements.

8.2.2.4.4 Standardizing the verb phrases and prepositions
If we change the various verbs and prepositions to
1. match those in the relevant fact types identified in the previous section,
2. take the **simple form** (e.g., 'specify', 'specified') rather than the **progressive aspect** (e.g., 'specifying') (see Section 5.3.2.2 in Chapter 5),
the rules now look like this:

  1. *"The Land Title Reference for the Land Title <u>that is</u> transferred by the Transfer documented in a Transfer Instrument must be <u>specified</u> in that Transfer Instrument."*
2A. *"The Full Name of the Transferor <u>that</u>[2] <u>takes</u> part in the Transfer documented in a Transfer Instrument must be <u>specified</u> in that Transfer Instrument."*
2B. *"The Full Name of the Transferor <u>specified</u> in a Transfer Instrument must be identical to the Full Name of the Registered Proprietor that is specified in the Land Title that*
    a. *is registered in the Real Property Register; and*
    b. *the Land Title Reference <u>of which</u> is specified in that Transfer Instrument."*
  3. *"A Monetary Consideration (if any) <u>specified</u> in a Transfer Instrument must agree with the Purchase Price <u>specified</u> in the Notice of Sale Report that*
    a. *is contained in the Lodgment Case that contains that Transfer Instrument; and*
    b. *is associated with that Transfer Instrument."*

8.2.2.5 Exceptions and generalization
At this point, there are two questions that we need to ask:

1. Does the rule apply in all cases or only some?
2. Does the rule apply to a wider set of cases?

With respect to the first question, if there are exceptions, these can be expressed in the rule statement by way of either

1. a qualifying clause following the subject term (such as 'that *specifies* more than one <u>land title</u>' or 'that *specifies* a <u>transferor</u> that *is* an <u>organization</u>'); or
2. a conditional clause stating the conditions under which the rule applies, such as 'if the <u>land title</u> *identified by* the <u>land title reference</u> *specified in* the <u>transfer instrument</u> *specifies* more than one <u>registered proprietor</u>'.

---

[2]The relative pronoun 'that' is used rather than 'who' since a Transferor may be an organization rather than a person.

With respect to the second question, some rules do apply to a wider set of cases than might be assumed from the documentation. For example, whereas rule 3 applies only to transfer instruments (since only these involve a consideration), rules 1 and 2A apply to all instruments documenting real property transactions, the term for which is 'real property instrument'. As for rule 2B, there are likely to be analogous rules for other types of real property instruments but rule 2B applies only to transfer instruments.

Note that, in generalizing rules 1 and 2A, we may need to do more than simply generalize the subject term; verb phrases and other terms may need to be generalized too, as in the following updated versions of these two rule statements:

1. *"The Land Title Reference for the Land Title that is <u>involved in</u> the <u>Real Property Transaction</u> documented in a <u>Real Property Instrument</u> must be specified in that <u>Real Property Instrument</u>."*

2A. *"The Full Name of the <u>Transacting Party</u> that takes part in the <u>Real Property Transaction</u> documented in a <u>Real Property Instrument</u> must be specified in that <u>Real Property Instrument</u>."*

We then need check that the necessary fact types are present in the fact model:

F185. <u>real property transaction</u> *involves* <u>land title</u>/
<u>land title</u> *is involved in* <u>real property transaction</u>

F186. <u>real property instrument</u> *documents* <u>real property transaction</u>/
<u>real property transaction</u> *is documented in* <u>real property instrument</u>

F187. <u>transacting party</u> *takes part in* <u>real property transaction</u>

8.2.2.6 *Ensuring correct cardinalities*

For each concept signified by a term in a rule statement, we need to establish how many there can be of each of the concepts signified by other terms in that rule statement. This requires that we ask the following questions about each associated pair of terms x and y:

1. Can there be a y for which there is more than one x?
2. Can there be a y for which there is no x?

For example, for rule 1, the questions to ask (and the answers) are

1. Can there be a Land Title for which there is more than one Land Title Reference? No
2. Can there be a Land Title for which there is no Land Title Reference? No
3. Can there be a Real Property Instrument for which there is more than one Real Property Transaction? No
4. Can there be a Real Property Instrument for which there is no Real Property Transaction? No
5. Can there be a Real Property Instrument for which there is more than one Land Title Reference? Yes
6. Can there be a Real Property Instrument for which there is no Land Title Reference? No

The definite article ('the') can be used before a term only if there can only ever be one instance of the concept signified by that term in that context. If there can be more than one, and the rule applies to every instance, use 'each' or 'one of the'.

Taking into account the answers to the above questions requires the following change to rule statement 1:

1. *"The Land Title Reference <u>of each</u> Land Title that is involved in the Real Property Transaction documented in a Real Property Instrument must be specified in that Real Property Instrument."*

The corresponding questions and answers for rule statements 2A and 2B are as follows:

1. Can there be a Real Property Instrument (including a Transfer Instrument) for which there is more than one Transacting Party (i.e., Transferor in the case of a Transfer Instrument)? Yes
2. Can there be a Real Property Instrument for which there is no Transacting Party? No
3. Can there be a Transacting Party (including a Transferor) for which there is more than one Full Name? No[3]
4. Can there be a Transacting Party for which there is no Full Name? No
5. Can there be a Land Title for which there is more than one Registered Proprietor? Yes
6. Can there be a Land Title for which there is no Registered Proprietor? No
7. Can there be a Registered Proprietor for which there is more than one Full Name? No
8. Can there be a Registered Proprietor for which there is no Full Name? No
9. Can there be a Real Property Instrument for which there is more than one Land Title Reference? Yes
10. Can there be a Real Property Instrument for which there is no Land Title Reference? No

Taking into account the answers to these questions requires the following changes to rule statements 2A and 2B:

2A. *"The Full Name of each Transacting Party that takes part in the Real Property Transaction documented in a Real Property Instrument must be specified in that Real Property Instrument."*

2B. *"The Full Name of each Transferor specified in a Transfer Instrument must be identical to the Full Name of one of the Registered Proprietors that is specified in the Land Title that*
   a. *is registered in the Real Property Register; and*
   b. *the Land Title Reference of which is specified in that Transfer Instrument."*

The corresponding questions and answers for rule statement 3 are as follows:

1. Can there be a Transfer Instrument for which there is more than one Monetary Consideration? No
2. Can there be a Transfer Instrument for which there is no Monetary Consideration? Yes
3. Can there be a Notice of Sale Report for which there is more than one Purchase Price? No
4. Can there be a Notice of Sale Report for which there is more than one Purchase Price? No
5. Can there be a Lodgment Case for which there is more than one Notice of Sale Report associated with a particular Transfer Instrument? No
6. Can there be a Lodgment Case for which there is no Notice of Sale Report associated with a particular Transfer Instrument? Yes

Taking into account the answers to these questions requires the following changes to rule statement 3:

3. *"The Monetary Consideration (if any) specified in a Transfer Instrument must agree with the Purchase Price (if any) specified in the Notice of Sale Report (if any) that*
   a. *is contained in the Lodgment Case that contains that Transfer Instrument; and*
   b. *is associated with that Transfer Instrument."*

---

[3]People may use aliases and businesses may have trading names but only registered names may be used.

8.2.2.7 Classifying the rule appropriately

Section 4.9 in Chapter 4 sets out a complete taxonomy of rules. What types of rules do we have here?

Clearly all of these rules are **data rules**. In particular, rules 1 and 2A each require a data item to be present, so these are **mandatory data item rules**. Rule 2B requires that each Transferor Full Name match an existing Full Name, while rule 3 requires that the value entered as the Monetary Consideration be equal to another value: these rules are therefore **equality rules**.

8.2.2.8 Establishing the subject of the rule statement

The subject of a mandatory data rule statement must be the term signifying the transaction governed by the rule. In both rule 1 and rule 2A, the transaction is a Real Property Instrument.

The subject of a data content rule statement (such as one for an equality rule) must be the data item whose content is constrained. For rule 2B that data item is Transferor Full Name whereas for rule 3 it is Monetary Consideration.

8.2.2.9 Standardizing the syntax

Remember each type of rule has its own template(s). Let's look at each rule in turn, starting with rule 1, which is a mandatory data item rule.

8.2.2.9.1 Creating a mandatory data item rule statement

Section 8.2.1.1.1 describes in detail the creation of a mandatory data item rule statement based on template T19 (to be found in Section 9.3.1.1.1 in Chapter 9 and reproduced here):

Each <transaction signifier>
must {*specify*|*contain*} <cardinality> <data item term>
  {{*in*|*for*} {each|the} <subform term> {(if any)|}
  {<qualifying clause>|}|}
{{if|unless} <conditional clause>|}.

The similarities and differences between the mandatory data item rule statements described in Section 8.2.1.1.1 and the one we need now are as follows:

1. Instead of substituting 'employee leave request' in place of the <transaction signifier> placeholder, we need 'real property instrument'.
2. As with those other rule statements
   a. we do not need the qualifying clause that is an option in the transaction signifier, as this rule applies to all Real Property Instruments;
   b. this rule statement governs the data in a transaction rather than a larger collection of data, so we will use '*specify*' rather than '*contain*';
   c. since each rule applies to all Real Property Instruments, we do not need the conditional clause.
3. However, this transaction accommodates multiple Land Titles. We therefore require the subform element in lines 3 and 4 of the template, with 'land title' in place of the <subform term> placeholder.
4. The term 'land title reference' can be substituted in place of the <data item term> placeholder.

This yields

> Each <u>real property instrument</u>
> must *specify* <cardinality> <u>land title reference</u>
>   *for* {each|the} <u>land title</u> {(if any)|}
>   {<qualifying clause>|}.

Let's now look at the remaining placeholders and option sets in the rule statement.

1. The only available options for the <cardinality> placeholder in a mandatory data item rule statement (as listed in Section 9.3.1.1.1) are
   a. exactly <positive integer>,
   b. at least <positive integer>,
   c. at least <positive integer> and at most <positive integer>.
   The option 'exactly one' is the appropriate one in this case (recall there is only ever one Land Title
   Reference for a Land Title).
2. Can there be more than one Land Title specified in a Real Property Instrument? Yes, so we need
   'each' rather than 'the'.
3. Can there be a Real Property Instrument for which there is no Land Title Reference? No, so we can
   omit the '(if any)'.
4. Since this rule requires that a Registry Instrument specify a Land Title Reference not for all Land
   Titles but for all Land Titles that are being transacted by way of the Real Property Transaction documented by this Real Property Instrument, we do need the final qualifying clause.

Applying each of these transformations yields

> Each <u>real property instrument</u>
> must *specify* exactly one <u>land title reference</u>
>   *for* each <u>land title</u>
>   <qualifying clause>.

We now need to substitute something for the <qualifying clause> placeholder, for which there is a
subtemplate (S14 in Section 9.1.2.10 in Chapter 9) as follows:

> <qualifying clause>::=
> {{that|who} <*verb phrase*> {<object>|}}|
> <*verb part*> <object>|
> other than {<object>|[<object>, or]}|
> {<*preposition*> {which|whom}|whose} <conditional clause>|
> {that|who} <*verb phrase*> {that|if|whether} <conditional clause>|
> <and-qualifying clause>|
> <or-qualifying clause>|
> <both-and-qualifying clause>|
> <either-or-qualifying clause>}

As previously observed (in Section 8.2.1.1.2), this subtemplate allows for a daunting nine options! Again,
rather than look up the description of each option in Section 9.1.2.10, we can take advantage of the fact

that the most common option for a qualifying clause is the one that starts with a verb part (i.e., a preposition optionally preceded by a participle or adjective). Selecting that option, we get

> $<$ *verb part*$>$ $<$object$>$

The $<$*verb part*$>$ and $<$object$>$ placeholders each have a subtemplate (S9 and S11 in Sections 9.1.2.5 and 9.1.2.7 respectively):

> $<$*verb part*$>$::=
> {$<$*participle*$>$|$<$*adjective*$>$|} $<$*preposition*$>$
>
> $<$object$>$::=
> {{$<$determiner$>$|the $<$set function$>$ of {$<$determiner$>$|}|} $<$<u>term</u>$>$
>   {$<$qualifying clause$>$|}|
> {$<$determiner$>$|} $<$<u>literal</u>$>$}

Let's look first at the object we need, in this case a term with determiner ('the <u>real property transaction</u>') but we also need to qualify that term, so we need

> the <u>real property transaction</u>
> $<$qualifying clause$>$

Thus we have an inner qualifying clause inside a qualifying clause. Selecting again the most common qualifying clause option for the inner qualifying clause yields

> the <u>real property transaction</u>
> $<$*verb part*$>$ $<$object$>$

This time the object we need includes the term '<u>real property instrument</u>'. Since we are now referring back to the subject of the rule statement,

1. we do not need to qualify that term, and
2. we should use the determiner 'that'.

We thus now have as the object of the original (outer) qualifying clause:

> the <u>real property transaction</u>
> $<$*verb part*$>$ that <u>real property instrument</u>

Substituting that for the $<$object$>$ placeholder in the original qualifying clause yields

> $<$*verb part*$>$ the <u>real property transaction</u>
> $<$*verb part*$>$ that <u>real property instrument</u>

What verb parts do we need? We need to refer to the relevant fact types: F185 and F186 (see Section 8.2.2.5), and remember that we are creating a qualifying clause to qualify '<u>land title</u>'. Using the verb phrases in these fact types, we get

> *involved in* the <u>real property transaction</u>
>   *documented in* that <u>real property instrument</u>

Substituting this in place of the $<$qualifying clause$>$ placeholder in the rule statement (and 'exactly one' in place of $<$cardinality$>$) yields

R317. Each <u>real property instrument</u>
must *specify* exactly one <u>land title reference</u>
for each <u>land title</u>
involved in the <u>real property transaction</u>
documented in that <u>real property instrument</u>.

Much the same process is required for rule 2A, the only differences being

1. the terms '<u>full name</u>' and '<u>transacting party</u>' should be substituted in place of the placeholders <<u>data item term</u>> and <<u>subform term</u>> respectively;
2. the qualifying clause is based on fact types F187 and F186 (see Section 8.2.2.5);
3. the '{that|who} <*verb phrase*> <object>' option is better for the outer qualifying clause.

The rule statement for this rule is therefore:

R318. Each <u>real property instrument</u>
must *specify* exactly one <u>full name</u>
for each <u>transacting party</u>
that *takes part in* the <u>real property transaction</u>
documented in that <u>real property instrument</u>.

8.2.2.9.2 Creating an equality rule statement
Let's now try to standardize the syntax of rule 2B, reproduced again here for convenience.

2B. *"The Full Name of <u>each</u> Transferor specified in a Transfer Instrument must be identical to the Full Name of <u>one of</u> the Registered Proprietor<u>s</u> that is specified in the Land Title that*
 a. *is registered in the Real Property Register; and*
 b. *the Land Title Reference of which is specified in that Transfer Instrument."*

The template for this type of rule statement is T30 (described in Section 9.3.2.3 in Chapter 9):

{The|Each} <<u>data item term</u>> {(if any)|}
    specified {{*in*|*for*} {the|each} <<u>subform term</u>> {(if any)|}|}
    in each <transaction signifier>
must *be* <*equality operator*> <object>
{{*if*|*unless*} <conditional clause>|}.

The following steps are required to create a rule statement using this template as a basis:

1. Inspection of the partly processed "raw rule" reveals that we can
 a. substitute the term '<u>full name</u>' in place of the <<u>data item term</u>> placeholder;
 b. remove the first '(if any)' since Full Name is mandatory for a Transferor;
 c. since this transaction accommodates multiple Transferors, retain the subform element in line 2 of the template, with '<u>transferor</u>' in place of the <<u>subform term</u>> placeholder;
 d. use 'for' rather than 'in' since '<u>transferor</u>' signifies a real-world object rather than a collection of data;
 e. use 'each' rather than 'the' as there may be more than one Transferor in a Transfer Instrument;
 f. remove the second '(if any)' since at least one Transferor is required in a Transfer Instrument;
 g. remove the conditional clause since these rules apply to all Transfer Instruments.

After these transforms, the embryonic rule statement now looks like this:

The <u>full name</u>
   specified for each <u>transferor</u>
   in each <transaction signifier>
must *be* <*equality operator*> <object>.

2. Let's next look at the options available for each placeholder:
  a. <transaction signifier>, defined in subtemplate S8 in Section 9.1.2.4 in Chapter 9:

    <transaction signifier>::=
    {<<u>term</u>>|{record of a|} combination of [<<u>term</u>>, and]}
      {<qualifying clause>|}

  b. <*equality operator*>, defined in subtemplate S7 in Section 9.1.2.3:

    <*equality operator*>::=
    {*the same as*|*different from*|*equal to*|*unequal to*}

  c. <object>, defined in subtemplate S11 in Section 9.1.2.7:

    <object>::=
    {{<determiner>|the <set function> of {<determiner>|}|} <<u>term</u>>
      {<qualifying clause>|}|
      {<determiner>|} <<u>literal</u>>}

3. We can select the following options for these placeholders:
  a. substitute the term '<u>transfer instrument</u>' in place of <<u>term</u>> in the <transaction signifier> placeholder, and omit the optional qualifying clause (these rules apply to all Transfer Instruments);
  b. select '*the same as*' in place of <*equality operator*>;
  c. select '<determiner> <term> <qualifying clause>' in place of <object>, 'the' in place of '<determiner>' and '<u>full name</u>' in place of <<u>term</u>>, yielding

The <u>full name</u>
   specified for each <u>transferor</u>
   in each <u>transfer instrument</u>
must *be the same as* the <u>full name</u> <qualifying clause>.

4. The options available for the <qualifying clause> placeholder are defined in subtemplate S14 in Section 9.1.2.10.

<qualifying clause>::=
{{that|who} <*verb phrase*> {<object>|}|
<*verb part*> <object>|
other than {<object>|[<object>, or]}|
{<*preposition*> {which|whom}|whose} <conditional clause>|
{that|who} <*verb phrase*> {that|if|whether} <conditional clause>|
<and-qualifying clause>|
<or-qualifying clause>|
<both-and-qualifying clause>|
<either-or-qualifying clause>}

Again we're faced with nine options! We could look up the description of each of these options in Section 9.1.2.10, or again select the most common option:

> *< verb part>* <object>

Revisiting <object>, we can again select the '<determiner> <u>term</u> <qualifying clause>' option, to yield

> *< verb part>* <determiner> <u>term</u>
>   <qualifying clause>

Inspection of our "raw rule" reveals that '*of*', 'one of the', and '<u>registered proprietors</u>' are required in place of *< verb part>*, <determiner>, and <u>term</u> respectively, yielding

> *of* one of the <u>registered proprietors</u>
>   <qualifying clause>

We can repeat this process of expanding a qualifying clause by incorporating the next phrase from the "raw rule", to yield

> *of* one of the <u>registered proprietors</u>
>   *specified in* the <u>land title</u>
>   <qualifying clause>

At this point, we realize that after '*Land Title*' there are two criteria joined by '*and*' in our "raw rule", so we now select the <and-qualifying clause> option,[4] defined in subtemplate S15 in Section 9.1.2.10:

> {that|who}
> {[*< verb phrase>* {<object>|} and]|
> *is* [*< verb part>* {<object>|} and]
> *< verb phrase>* [<object> and]}

By repeating the same selection and substitution processes, we can end up with the following qualifying clause to substitute into the rule statement:

> *of* one of the <u>registered proprietors</u>
>   *specified in* the <u>land title</u>
>   that *is registered in* the <u>real property register</u>
>   and *is identified by* one of the <u>land title references</u>
>   *specified in* that <u>transfer instrument</u>

5. Substituting this qualifying clause in place of <qualifying clause> in the rule statement yields

---

[4]We could just as easily select the <both-and-qualifying clause> option since there are only two criteria.

R319. The <u>full name</u>
specified for each <u>transferor</u>
in each <u>transfer instrument</u>
must *be the same as* the <u>full name</u>
of one of the <u>registered proprietors</u>
specified in the <u>land title</u>
that *is registered in* the <u>real property register</u>
and *is identified by* one of the <u>land title references</u>
specified in that <u>transfer instrument</u>.

By a similar process we can do the same for Rule 3, reproduced again here for convenience.

3. *"<u>The Monetary Consideration (if any) specified in a Transfer Instrument must agree with the Purchase Price (if any) specified in the Notice of Sale Report (if any) that*
    a. *is contained in the Lodgment Case that contains that Transfer Instrument; and*
    b. *is associated with that Transfer Instrument."*

R320. The <u>monetary consideration</u> (if any)
specified in each <u>transfer instrument</u>
must *be the same as* the <u>purchase price</u> (if any)
specified in the <u>notice of sale report</u> (if any)
that *is contained in* the <u>lodgment case</u>
that *contains* that <u>transfer instrument</u>
and *is associated with* that <u>transfer instrument</u>.

8.3 DEVELOPING THE RULE STATEMENT VOCABULARY

As rule statements are added, additional business terms, proper names, and fact types are inevitably required.

8.3.1 Term and name metadata

As each business term or proper name is added, the following metadata should be recorded in addition to the term or name itself:

1. the definition of the term or name;
2. the status of the term or name (one of the following, for example):
    a. In Progress: being worked on by the author but not yet ready for review,
    b. Prepared: author finished, term ready to be reviewed,
    c. Approved: reviewer approves term, which may therefore be used in fact types and rule statements,
    d. Published: has been published to the wider community for implementation,
    e. Retired: previously in use, but now discontinued, inapplicable, or obsolete,
    f. Under Review: being re-examined with a view to revision, replacement, or retirement;

3. its effective date (if the term or name is only coming into use after a particular date);
4. its expiry date (if the term or name is not to be used after a particular date);
5. whether the text being recorded is a business term or a proper name;
6. the source of the term or name and/or its definition (in particular if the term, name, or definition is likely to be contentious);
7. the author and reviewer of the term or name;
8. any party other than the author with a stake in the term or name: for example, the role, position, or organization unit responsible for administering the term or name;
9. any synonyms that exist, each with
    a. whether it is an abbreviation, acronym, or label on a paper or electronic form,
    b. its source,
    c. any context in which it applies,
    d. whether or not it may be used in the description of business processes or system components[5];
10. any exclusions applicable to the term or name (i.e., if the term or name is likely to be misused or misapplied, any situations in which it is not to be used);
11. any useful notes on the use of the term or name including examples;
12. (for a business term) names of associated data items in models, schemas, or databases, including
    a. data model entities or attributes,
    b. message types, user interfaces, forms, or reports,
    c. database tables or columns,
    d. XML tags;
13. the identifiers in the Business Process Model of any associated business processes.

8.3.2 Fact type metadata

As each fact type is added, the following metadata should be recorded in addition to the fact type itself:

1. the status of the fact type (one of the following, for example):
    a. In Progress: being worked on by the author but not yet ready for review,
    b. Prepared: author finished, fact type ready to be reviewed,
    c. Approved: reviewer approves fact type, which may therefore be used in rule statements,
    d. Published: has been published to the wider community for implementation,
    e. Retired: previously in use, but now discontinued, inapplicable, or obsolete,
    f. Under Review: being re-examined with a view to revision, replacement, or retirement;
2. its effective date (if the fact type is only coming into use after a particular date);
3. its expiry date (if the fact type is not to be used after a particular date);
4. the author and reviewer of the fact type;
5. any party other than the author with a stake in the fact type: for example, the role, position, or organization unit responsible for administering the fact type;
6. any relationships in data models that represent the fact type.

---

[5]Note that the term itself will be used in all rule statements.

8.4 DOCUMENTING RULES

8.4.1 Rule metadata

As each rule statement is recorded, the following metadata should be recorded in addition to the natural language rule statement itself:

1. a unique unchanging identifier;
2. the status of the rule (one of the following, for example):
   a. In Progress: being worked on by the author but not yet ready for review,
   b. Prepared: author finished, rule ready to be reviewed,
   c. Approved: reviewer approves rule, which may therefore be published and implemented in applications, user interfaces, etc.,
   d. Published: has been published to the wider community for implementation,
   e. Retired: previously in use, but now discontinued, inapplicable, or obsolete,
   f. Under Review: being re-examined with a view to revision, replacement, or retirement;
3. its effective date (if the rule is only coming into use after a particular date);
4. its expiry date (if the rule is not to be used after a particular date);
5. the source of the rule;
6. the motivation behind the rule: that is, the reason the rule exists: for example, compliance with a particular act of legislation, integrity of the database;
7. the author and reviewer of the rule statement;
8. any party other than the author with a stake in the rule: for example, the role, position, or organization unit responsible for administering the rule;
9. the identity of the template on which the rule statement is based;
10. the fact types underlying the rule statement;
11. the enforcement level(s) that apply to the rule and (if more than one) the contexts (e.g., processes in the Business Process Model) in which those enforcement levels apply: the enforcement levels defined in (Business Rules Group, 2005) are
    a. Strict: strictly enforced, and cannot be overridden,
    b. Deferred: strictly enforced, but enforcement may be delayed,
    c. Pre-authorized: enforced, but exceptions are allowed for actors with prior approval,
    d. Post-justified: approval must be sought after violation; if approval is withheld, sanctions may be applied,
    e. Override: any violation must be accompanied by an appropriate comment,
    f. Guideline: suggested but not enforced;
12. details of each known implementation of the rule;
13. details of each document or website in which the rule statement is published;
14. membership of any groups of associated rules;
15. the rule's relationships to any other rules: for example, the rule or rules that it replaces;
16. for each quality criterion against which the rule statement has been tested, an indication whether the rule statement has passed or failed that quality criterion.

8.5 RULE BOOK QUALITY ASSURANCE

There are three aspects to rule book quality:

1. The rule book must contain rule statements for all the rules the organization requires and no rule statements for rules that it does not require.
2. Each rule statement in the rule book must accurately express the organization's requirements.
3. Each rule statement in the rule book must comply with the quality criteria listed in Section 7.4 in Chapter 7.

These are equally important. While the third aspect can largely be checked by the rule authoring team without involving business stakeholders, the other aspects cannot be checked without their involvement. However, business stakeholders can only be engaged with a few times, and if the rule authoring team has already consulted them to discover rules, I recommend the team perform an internal check of the rule book first, for compliance with quality criteria, and only then publish them to business stakeholders for review.

Inevitably, following this review there will be a need to add, delete, and modify rule statements. Ideally, the updated rule book should receive a further review. If you can obtain that further review, it will be more effective if all additions, deletions, and modifications are clearly marked as such.

8.6 RULE PUBLICATION

Once there is agreement that all required rules (and only those rules) are represented by accurate rule statements in the rule book, the latter should be published in such a manner as to provide easy access to it by all who are governed by those rules.

8.7 RULE BOOK AND FACT MODEL MAINTENANCE

Any of the following situations will require updates to the rule book and/or fact model:

1. the addition of one or more rules;
2. changes to one or more existing rules;
3. the deletion of one or more existing rules;
4. the addition of one or more
    a. databases,
    b. tables, columns, or foreign keys to a database,
    c. message types or user interfaces, or
    d. data elements to a message type or user interface;
5. the modification of an existing table or column in a database, or data element in a message type or user interface;
6. the addition of one or more software components;
7. the modification of an existing software component;
8. changes to terminology.

8.7.1 **Adding a rule**

If an additional rule is required,

1. the appropriate rule statement should be added to the rule book, with an appropriate status and effective date;
2. if the rule is a data rule,
   a. the term that is the subject of that rule statement should be identified, along with any fact types involving the terms that have been used in formulating that rule statement;
   b. the entities or attributes described by the terms identified in step a should then be identified, along with the relationships described by the fact types identified in step a;
   c. each database table, column, or foreign key implementing the entities, attributes, or relationships identified in step b should then be identified;
   d. the message types, user interfaces, and/or data elements described by the terms identified in step a should also be identified;
   e. additional logic to ensure compliance with the new rule should be added to each database table, column, foreign key, message type, user interface, and data element identified in steps c and d.
3. if the rule is an activity rule,
   a. the term that is the subject of that rule statement should be identified;
   b. the business process described by the term identified in step a should then be identified;
   c. each software component implementing the business process identified in step b should then be identified;
   d. additional logic to ensure compliance with the new rule should be added to each software component identified in step c.

8.7.2 **Changing an existing rule**

If an existing rule needs to be changed,

1. the previous version of the rule statement should be recorded with an appropriate status and expiry date;
2. the relevant rule statement should be modified in the rule book;
3. if the rule is a data rule,
   a. the term that is the subject of that rule statement should be identified, along with any fact types involving the terms that have been used in formulating that rule statement;
   b. the entities or attributes described by the terms identified in step a should then be identified, along with the relationships described by the fact types identified in step a;
   c. each database table, column, or foreign key implementing the entities, attributes, or relationships identified in step b should then be identified;
   d. the message types, user interfaces, and/or data elements described by the terms identified in step a should also be identified;
   e. the logic associated with each database table, column, foreign key, message type, user interface, and data element identified in steps c and d should be modified to ensure compliance with the new version of the rule;

4. if the rule is an activity rule,
    a. the term that is the subject of that rule statement should be identified;
    b. the business process described by the term identified in step a should then be identified;
    c. each software component implementing the business process identified in step b should then be identified;
    d. the logic within each software component identified in step c should be modified to ensure compliance with the new version of the rule.

8.7.3 Retiring an existing rule

If an existing rule needs to be retired,

1. the relevant rule statement should be marked as no longer applicable, using an appropriate status and expiry date;
2. if the rule is a data rule,
    a. the term that is the subject of that rule statement should be identified, along with any fact types involving the terms that have been used in formulating that rule statement;
    b. the entities or attributes described by the terms identified in step a should then be identified, along with the relationships described by the fact types identified in step a;
    c. each database table, column, or foreign key implementing the entities, attributes, or relationships identified in step b should then be identified;
    d. the message types, user interfaces, and/or data elements described by the terms identified in step a should also be identified;
    e. the logic associated with each database table, column, foreign key, message type, user interface, and data element identified in steps c and d should be modified to ensure that it no longer supports the deleted rule;
3. if the rule is an activity rule,
    a. the term that is the subject of that rule statement should be identified;
    b. the business process described by the term identified in step a should then be identified;
    c. each software component implementing the business process identified in step b should then be identified;
    d. the logic within each software component identified in step c should be modified to ensure that it no longer supports the deleted rule.

8.7.4 Adding an implemented data component

If a database table, column, or foreign key is to be added,

1. the entity, attribute, or relationship implemented by the table, column, or foreign key should be identified;
2. the term describing the entity or attribute (if any) identified in step 1 should then be identified;
3. the name of the new table or column should be added to the implementation metadata of the term (if any) identified in step 2;
4. the fact type describing the relationship (if any) identified in step 1 should also be identified;
5. the name of the new table or foreign key should be added to the implementation metadata of the fact type (if any) identified in step 4;

6. each rule statement involving the term or fact type identified in steps 2 and 4 should then be identified;

7. logic to ensure compliance with each rule identified in step 6 should be added to the database, table, column, or foreign key.

If a message type, user interface, or data element is to be added,

1. the term describing the message type, user interface, or data element should be identified;

2. each rule statement involving the term identified in step 1 should then be identified;

3. logic to ensure compliance with each rule identified in step 2 should be added to the message type, user interface, or data element.

8.7.5 Modifying an existing implemented data component

If a database table, column, or foreign key is to be modified,

1. each entity, attribute, or relationship implemented by the table, column, or foreign key should be identified;

2. the term describing each entity or attribute identified in step 1 should then be identified;

3. the fact type describing each relationship identified in step 1 should also be identified;

4. each rule statement involving the terms and fact types identified in steps 2 and 3 should then be identified;

5. the modified design of the table, column, or foreign key must be checked to ensure that it continues to comply with each rule identified in step 4.

If a message type, user interface, or data element is to be modified,

1. the term describing the message type, user interface, or data element should be identified;

2. each rule statement involving the term identified in step 2 should then be identified;

3. the modified design of the message type, user interface, or data element must be checked to ensure that it continues to comply with each rule identified in step 3.

8.7.6 Adding a software component

If a software component is to be added,

1. one or more process models should be prepared to model the processes to be performed by that software component;

2. the software component should be designed so as to

   a. only start an occurrence of a process if all the specified pre-conditions of that process are met;

   b. only complete an occurrence of a process if all the specified constraints on that process are met;

   c. only process an input message if the message complies with all rules governing that message type;

   d. only create instances of persistent data entities that comply with all rules governing that entity;

   e. only update instances of persistent data entities in a way that ensures that they continue to comply with all rules governing that entity.

8.7.7 Modifying an existing software component

If an existing software component is to be modified,

1. if process models already exist describing that software component, they should be modified to model the processes to be performed by the modified software component; if not, one or more process models should be prepared to model the processes to be performed by the modified software component;
2. the redesign of the software component should ensure that
   a. it only starts an occurrence of a process if all the specified pre-conditions of that process are met;
   b. it only completes an occurrence of a process if all the specified constraints on that process are met;
   c. it only processes an input message if the message complies with all rules governing that message type;
   d. it only creates instances of persistent data entities that comply with all rules governing that entity;
   e. it only updates instances of persistent data entities in a way that ensures that they continue to comply with all rules governing that entity.

8.7.8 Changing the vocabulary

If a term is to be changed, the process to be followed depends on whether the term has been published. If the term has been published, the procedure described in Section 8.7.8.1 should be followed, but if it has not been published, the procedure described in Section 8.7.8.2 should be followed.

If a synonym is to be added to a term (published or unpublished), the procedure in Section 8.7.8.3 should be followed.

If a fact type is to be changed, the procedure in Section 8.7.8.4 should be followed.

If an existing term or fact type needs to be retired, it should be marked as no longer applicable, using an appropriate status and expiry date.

A term may be retired only if

1. any rule statement using that term is itself retired, and
2. any fact type using that term is itself retired, and
3. any term using that term in its definition is itself retired.

A fact type may be retired only if any rule statement based on that fact type is itself retired.

8.7.8.1 Changing a published term
1. If the intended replacement term is already in use as a preferred term, the intended change should not occur.
2. If the replacement term is not already in use, this may be achieved by
   a. adding the replacement term as a synonym of the original term;
   b. marking the original term as non-preferred and marking the replacement term as preferred;
   c. identifying each rule statement, fact type, and term definition that uses the original term;
   d. updating each such rule statement, fact type, or term definition by replacing the original term with the replacement term (after recording the previous version with an appropriate status and expiry date);
   e. once any other terms are similarly changed, republishing all changed rule statements, fact types, and term definitions.

3. If the replacement term is already in use as a synonym (rather than a preferred term), the existing synonym must first be changed by appending a numeric discriminator (e.g., '[2]' as in 'service [2]' so as to distinguish it from the unmarked term 'service') before performing the above steps.

8.7.8.2 Changing an unpublished term

1. If the intended replacement term is already in use as a preferred term, the intended change should not occur.

2. If the replacement term is not already in use, this may be achieved by
   a. overwriting the term;
   b. identifying each rule statement, fact type, and term definition that uses the original term;
   c. updating each such rule statement, fact type, or term definition by replacing the original term with the replacement term (after recording the previous version with an appropriate status and expiry date);
   d. once any other terms are similarly changed, republishing all changed rule statements, fact types, and term definitions.

3. If the replacement term is already in use as a synonym (rather than a term as such), the existing synonym must first be changed by appending a numeric discriminator (e.g., '[2]' as in 'service [2]' so as to distinguish it from the unmarked term 'service') before performing the above steps.

8.7.8.3 Adding a non-preferred synonym to a term

1. If the synonym is not already in use, it can simply be added without any additional tasks.

2. If the synonym is already in use, it can simply be added without any additional tasks, with the proviso that the new synonym must have a numeric discriminator appended: for example, '[2]' as in 'service [2]' so as to distinguish it from the unmarked term 'service'.

8.7.8.4 Changing fact types

There are four types of fact type changes:

1. those resulting from term changes (as described in Sections 8.7.8.1 and 8.7.8.2);
2. replacing a term in the fact type by a *hypernym* (a more general term);
3. any other change to the terms used in the fact type;
4. a change to a verb phrase or preposition used in the fact type.

Any change to a fact type requires the following two tasks:

1. The previous version of the fact type should be recorded with an appropriate status and expiry date.
2. Those terms, verb phrases, and/or prepositions that need to be changed can then be changed.

Any change to the terms, verb phrases, or prepositions in a fact type other than
   a. a change resulting from term changes as described in Sections 8.7.8.1 and 8.7.8.2, or
   b. the replacement of a term by one of its hypernyms,

then requires the following tasks:

3. Each rule statement that uses the fact type should be identified.

4. Each rule statement based on the fact type must be updated as follows (after recording the previous version with an appropriate status and expiry date):

   a. updating each term that has been changed in the fact type to the replacement term;

   b. updating each verb phrase or preposition that has been changed in the fact type to the replacement verb phrase or preposition.

8.8 SUMMARY

Discovery and analysis of an organization's rules requires techniques appropriate to the source from which the rule analyst harvests those rules. Two useful techniques are documented in this chapter:

1. the "data analysis" approach, used when analyzing input forms or messages, or data models;

2. the "raw rules" approach, used when discovering rules from stakeholders or existing documentation.

Inevitably, as the rule book is developed, the rule statement vocabulary documented in the fact model also requires development. Each term and fact type in the fact models, as well as each rule in the rule book, require appropriate metadata to support effective ongoing management of these resources.

Ongoing maintenance of the rule book and fact model needs to be aligned with ongoing maintenance of data and software components.

Rule statement templates and subtemplates

This chapter lists all the ***rule statement templates*** and ***subtemplates*** that can be used as the basis for rule statements and provides guidance as to their use.

Each template in this chapter is designed as the *pro forma* for rule statements for a particular type of rule listed in Section 4.9 in Chapter 4. A template is a string of symbols, each of which is either included in the generated rule statement or used to establish the form of the generated rule statement in some way. The various types of symbols used in the templates are described in Section 9.1.1 and its subsections.

The templates and subtemplates in this book are depicted using the same sans serif font as is used for rule statements and fact types. Each template is given a unique identifier starting with the letter 'T' while each subtemplate is given a unique identifier starting with the letter 'S'.

9.1 USING THE TEMPLATES TO WRITE RULE STATEMENTS

While it is possible to formally generate a rule statement from any of these templates, this can be quite a complex process. Examples of this process are worked through in Sections 8.2.1.1 and 8.2.2.9 in Chapter 8.

In practice, rather than generate each rule statement from a template, a rule author will find examples of well-formed rule statements of each type that he or she requires and change them as necessary to meet the new requirements.

Thus these templates can be considered as simply a formal definition of the constrained natural language used for rule statements in this book, rather than as a means by which a rule author will formulate each rule statement to be written.

9.1.1 Rule statement templates

A ***rule statement template*** is a string of symbols that can be used as a *pro forma* for rule statements of a particular type. Each template consists of the following types of symbols:

1. *option sets*
2. *placeholders*
3. *list definitions*
4. *boilerplate text*

9.1.1.1 Option sets

An *option set* is delimited by braces; each option within an option set is separated from its neighbor(s) by a bar: for example, '{a|an|the}'. For each option set that appears in a template, one and only one option must be selected: in this case, exactly one of 'a', 'an', or 'the' must be included at that point in the template or subtemplate.

An option set may include a *null option*: this is indicated by the fact that there is no text between the last bar symbol and the closing brace: for example, '{a|an|the|}'. This signifies that it is permitted to select null (or nothing) as an option: in other words, at most one of 'a', 'an', or 'the' may be included at that point in the template, but nothing may be included if nothing is required at that point.

9.1.1.2 Placeholders

There are various places in a template where any term, verb phrase, etc. can be substituted. These places are denoted by enclosing a label in angle brackets, the label indicating the type of word or other symbol which may be substituted. There are five types of placeholders:

1. Any placeholder in which the designator is underlined with a single underline (e.g., <u>term</u>, <u>data item term</u>) indicates that any appropriate term from the fact model may be substituted in place of the placeholder at that point in the template. If the designator is more than just <u>term</u> (e.g., <u>data item term</u>, <u>subform term</u>), a term that signifies that type of object (a data item or a subform in these examples) should be substituted. If the designator is <u>term</u>, any term which makes sense can be substituted.

2. The placeholder <u>literal</u> indicates that any appropriate numeric value, textual value, category from a categorization scheme, date, time, or other time point may be substituted in place of the placeholder at that point in the template.

3. The placeholder <u>positive integer</u> indicates that any suitable cardinal number (e.g., 'one', 'two') may be substituted.

4. The placeholders *<verb phrase>* and *<preposition>* indicate that a verb phrase or preposition respectively from a fact type in the fact model may be substituted in place of the placeholder at that point in the template. Note that there may be restrictions in some templates on which verb phrase or preposition may be substituted: these restrictions are identified in the discussion of each template.

5. Any placeholder (other than *<verb phrase>* or *<preposition>*) in which the designator is not underlined is associated with a *subtemplate* having the same designator before the symbol '::='. The content of that subtemplate (i.e., the text after the symbol '::=') is substituted in place of the placeholder. For example one of the subtemplates is '<article>::= {a|an|the}'. Wherever the placeholder <article> appears, the option set '{a|an|the}' must be substituted (after which an option from that option set must be selected).

Numerals are used to distinguish multiple placeholders of the same type in the one template: for example, <u>term 1</u>, <u>term 2</u>. However, if it is required that the same term, verb phrase, or preposition is to be substituted in place of both of two placeholders in a template, the same numeral will be used in both placeholders. For example, if a template includes <u>term 1</u> twice, the same term is to be substituted in place of both of those placeholders.

9.1.1.3 List definitions

Where a syntactic element may be repeated indefinitely, this is denoted in a template by a ***list definition***, consisting of a pair of square brackets enclosing the repeated syntactic element and the word to be used between repetitions. For example, '[<object> and]' indicates that any of the following may appear at that point in the rule statement:

1. <object> and <object>,
2. <object> and <object> and <object>,
3. <object> and <object> and <object> and <object>,
4. and so on.

A variant form of list definition includes a punctuation mark (a comma or semicolon) before the word to be used between repetitions. For example, '[<literal>, or]' indicates that any of the following may appear at that point in the rule statement:

1. <literal> or <literal>;
2. <literal>, <literal>, or <literal>;
3. <literal>, <literal>, <literal>, or <literal>;
4. and so on.

An example of such a list is 'first class, business class, or economy class'. The same list definition may be interpreted differently by those following UK or Australian punctuation conventions, by omitting the comma before the 'and' or 'or', thus 'first class, business class or economy class'.

9.1.1.4 Boilerplate text

Any text outside the option sets, placeholders, and list definitions in a template is boilerplate, to be included in all rule statements based on that template. For example, if a template were to read '{A|An} <term 1> must <verb phrase> {a|an} <term 2>', the word 'must' is to be included in each rule statement based on that template.

9.1.2 **Subtemplates**

A ***subtemplate*** is a template for a syntactic element that may appear in more than one type of rule statement. Subtemplates also include option sets, placeholders, and boilerplate text, which are used in exactly the same way as in templates. There are subtemplates for

1. articles and other determiners (Section 9.1.2.1)
2. set functions (Section 9.1.2.2)
3. comparison operators (Section 9.1.2.3)
4. transaction signifiers (Section 9.1.2.4)
5. verb parts (Section 9.1.2.5)
6. predicates (Section 9.1.2.6)
7. objects (Section 9.1.2.7)
8. calculated data expressions (Section 9.1.2.8)
9. conditional and qualifying clauses (Sections 9.1.2.9 and 9.1.2.10)

10. format definitions (Section 9.2.7)
11. spatial operators (Section 9.3.2.7)
12. time restrictions (Section 9.4.1.1)
13. information access processes (Section 9.5.3).

As explained in Section 9.1.1.2, each subtemplate has a designator before the symbol ‘::=’. The text after the symbol ‘::=’ can be substituted in place of any placeholder (in a template or subtemplate) that has the same designator. For example, one subtemplate is

```
<determiner>::=
{<article>|each|that|those|
<cardinality>|at most <positive integer>|
the {{first|last} or only|second or any subsequent|previous|next|same}|
any {other|more}}
```

If a <determiner> placeholder is encountered in a template (or subtemplate), any of the following can be substituted in place of that placeholder:

1. any article (from those available in the <article> subtemplate);
2. ‘each’, ‘that’, or ‘those’;
3. any cardinality (from those available in the <cardinality> subtemplate);
4. ‘at most’ followed by a positive integer;
5. ‘the first or only’, ‘the last or only’, ‘the second or any subsequent’, ‘the previous’, ‘the next’;
6. ‘the same’, ‘any other’, ‘any more’.

The <determiner> subtemplate is an example of one that itself contains placeholders with associated subtemplates.

The subtemplates that follow define various syntactic elements that are used generally in rule statements.

9.1.2.1 Determiners

Determiners are defined from a grammatical point of view in Section 5.4 in Chapter 5.

S2. <article>::={a|an|the}
S3. <cardinality>::=
  {exactly|at least {<positive integer 1> and at most|}}
  <positive integer 2>

For example, ‘exactly one’, ‘at least two’, ‘at least one and at most four’.

S4. <determiner>::=
  {<article>|each|that|those|
  <cardinality>|at most <positive integer>|
  the {{first|last} or only|second or any subsequent|previous|next|same}|
  any {other|more}}

See the discussion in the previous section for a list of the alternative determiners available in rule statements.

9.1.2.2 Set functions

A set function is any scalar numeric property of a set of data items.

S5. <set function>::=
　　{number|sum|total|maximum|minimum|average|mean|median|
　　latest|earliest}

9.1.2.3 Comparison operators

There are two types of comparison operators: inequality operators and equality operators.

S6. <inequality operator>::=
　　{{no|} {more|less|later|earlier} than|
　　at {least|most} <u>literal</u>> {more|later} than|
　　{no|} {later|earlier} than <u>literal</u>> {after|before}}

Thus an inequality operator in a rule statement can be any of the following:

1. *'more than'*, *'less than'*, *'later than'*, *'earlier than'*, *'no more than'*, *'no less than'*, *'no later than'*, *'no earlier than'*;
2. *'at least* <u>literal</u>> *more than'*, *'at most* <u>literal</u>> *more than'*, *'at least* <u>literal</u>> *later than'*, *'at most* <u>literal</u>> *later than'*;
3. *'later than* <u>literal</u>> *after'*, *'earlier than* <u>literal</u>> *after'*, *'later than* <u>literal</u>> *before'*, *'earlier than* <u>literal</u>> *before'*.

S7. <equality operator>::=
　　{the same as|different from|equal to|unequal to}

9.1.2.4 Transaction signifiers

A transaction signifier is either a term or a reference to a combination of terms, possibly qualified.

S8. <transaction signifier>::=
　　{<u>term</u>>|{record of a|} combination of [<u>term</u>>, and]}
　　　{<qualifying clause>|}

Thus any of the following can be substituted in place of a <transaction signifier> placeholder:

1. a term, optionally followed by a qualifying clause;
2. a list of terms, optionally followed by a qualifying clause, and preceded by 'combination of' or 'record of a combination of'; the last two objects in the list are separated by 'and' (or a comma and 'and' if adhering to U.S. punctuation standards) and each other pair of objects in the list is separated by a comma.

9.1.2.5 Verb parts

A verb part may be used wherever *'is'* or *'be'* may be dropped from a verb phrase.

S9. <verb part>::=
　　{<participle>|<adjective>|} <preposition>

Thus any of the following can be substituted in place of a *<verb part>* placeholder:

1. a preposition preceded by a participle: for example, '*specified by*';
2. a preposition preceded by an adjective: for example, '*available in*';
3. a preposition alone: for example, '*of*'.

9.1.2.6 Predicates
Broadly speaking, a predicate is whatever may follow a subject in a clause.

S10. <predicate>::=
    {{*<verb phrase>*|*is* {<equality operator>|<inequality operator>}}
      <object>|
    <verb phrase> {[<object>, and]|[<object>, or]|}}}

Thus any of the following can be substituted in place of a <predicate> placeholder:

1. a verb phrase followed by a single object: for example, '*is specified by* that <u>transaction</u>';
2. '*is*' and an equality operator or inequality operator followed by a single object: for example, '*is equal to* the <u>fee payable</u>', '*is less than* the <u>maximum price</u>';
3. a verb phrase followed by
    a. a list of objects, the last two objects in the list separated by 'and' (or a comma and 'and' if adhering to U.S. punctuation standards), and each other pair of objects in the list separated by a comma: for example, '*specifies* a <u>discount code</u> and a <u>promotion code</u>';
    b. a list of objects, the last two objects in the list separated by 'or' (or a comma and 'or' if adhering to U.S. punctuation standards), and each other pair of objects in the list separated by a comma: for example, '*is* <u>0</u> or <u>1</u>';
4. a verb phrase alone: for example, '*is closed*'.

9.1.2.7 Objects
Broadly speaking, an object is whatever may follow a verb phrase.

S11. <object>::=
    {{<determiner>|the <set function> of {<determiner>|}|} <u>term</u>
      {<qualifying clause>|}|
    {<determiner>|} <u>literal</u>}

Thus any of the following can be substituted in place of an <object> placeholder:

1. a term optionally preceded by a determiner and optionally followed by a qualifying clause: for example, 'the <u>credit card</u> *with* which the <u>booking</u> *was paid for*', '<u>employees</u> *in receipt of* this <u>allowance</u>';
2. a term preceded by 'the <set function> of' and an optional determiner, and optionally followed by a qualifying clause: for example, 'the number of <u>employees</u> *in* the <u>team</u>', 'the sum of the <u>fares</u>';
3. a literal optionally preceded by a determiner: for example, '<u>1 January 2012</u>', 'that <u>24 h</u>'.

9.1.2.8 Calculated data expressions

An expression is a verbal statement of a calculation.

S12. <expression>::=
  {<object>|
  <set function> of {<determiner>|} <term> {<qualifying clause>|}|
  <expression> {plus|minus|multiplied by|divided by} <expression>|
  {sum|product} of [<expression>, and]|
  {square|cube} {root|} of <expression>}

Thus any of the following can be substituted in place of the <expression> placeholder:

1. an object (see subtemplate S11): for example, 'the order quantity *of* that order line';
2. a set function followed by a term with optional preceding determiner and optional following qualifying clause: for example, 'the number of order lines', 'the sum of the extensions *for* each order line';
3. any two expressions joined by 'plus', 'minus', 'multiplied by', or 'divided by': for example, '1 minus the discount *for* that customer', '1 minus the discount for that customer multiplied by the unit price *of* that product';
4. 'sum of' or 'product of', followed by a list of expressions each separated from the next by a comma and/or 'and': for example, 'the sum of the base fare, fuel levy, booking fee, and credit card charge *for* that booking';
5. 'square', 'cube', 'square root', or 'cube root', followed by an expression: for example, 'the square of the speed of light'.

9.1.2.9 Conditional clauses

Conditional clauses have been discussed in Section 7.2.6 in Chapter 7. This subtemplate defines the various forms of conditional clauses that can be used in rule statements:

S13. <conditional clause>::=
  {{<determiner> <term> {<qualifying clause>|}|<expression>|it}
  {<predicate>|[<predicate> and]|[<predicate> or]}|
  [<conditional clause> and]|[<conditional clause> or]}

Thus any of the following can be substituted in place of a <conditional clause> placeholder:

1. a single conditional clause, consisting of
   a. either
      i. a term preceded by a determiner and optionally followed by a qualifying clause: for example, 'the employee who *submitted* the application',
      ii. an expression (see subtemplate S12), or
      iii. 'it';
   b. followed by one of
      i. a single predicate (see subtemplate S10),
      ii. a list of predicates, each pair of predicates in the list separated by 'and',
      iii. a list of predicates, each pair of predicates in the list separated by 'or';
2. a list of conditional clauses, each pair of clauses in the list separated by 'and';
3. a list of conditional clauses, each pair of clauses in the list separated by 'or'.

9.1.2.10 Qualifying clauses

Qualifying clauses have been discussed in Section 7.2.7 in Chapter 7. These subtemplates define the various forms of qualifying clauses that can be used in rule statements:

S14. <qualifying clause>::=
    {{that|who} <*verb phrase*> {<object>|}|
    <*verb part*> <object>|
    other than {<object>|[<object>, or]}|
    {<*preposition*> {which|whom}|whose} <conditional clause>|
    {that|who} <*verb phrase*> {that|if|whether} <conditional clause>|
    <and-qualifying clause>|
    <or-qualifying clause>|
    <both-and-qualifying clause>|
    <either-or-qualifying clause>}

Thus any of the following can be substituted in place of a <qualifying clause> placeholder:

1. 'that' or 'who' followed by a verb phrase and an optional object (see subtemplate S11): for example, 'that *includes* an <u>international flight</u>';
2. a verb part (see subtemplate S9) followed by an object: for example, '*specified in* a <u>real property transaction</u>';
3. 'other than' followed by either
   a. an object, or
   b. a list of objects, the last two objects in the list separated by 'or' (or a comma and 'or' if adhering to U.S. punctuation standards) and each other pair of objects in the list separated by a comma: for example, 'other than a <u>cash payment</u> or a <u>direct debit payment</u>';
4. a conditional clause (see subtemplate S13) preceded by either
   a. a preposition followed by 'which' or 'whom', or
   b. 'whose':
   for example, '*for* which the <u>payment</u> *is made*', 'whose <u>name</u> *appears on* the <u>passport</u>';
5. 'that' or 'who' followed by
   a. a verb phrase,
   b. 'that', 'if', or 'whether', and
   c. a conditional clause:
   for example, 'who *checks* whether the <u>passport</u> *has expired*';
6. a qualifying clause involving multiple criteria:
   a. separated by 'and', with or without 'both', as defined in subtemplates S15 and S16,
   b. separated by 'or', with or without 'either', as defined in subtemplates S17 and S18.

Note that, given the definition of <object> in subtemplate S11, any object in a qualifying clause may itself be qualified by a qualifying clause.

S15. <and-qualifying clause>::=
    {that|who}
    {[<*verb phrase*> {<object>|}] and]|
    is [<*verb part*> {<object>|}] and]
    <*verb phrase*> [<object> and]}

Subtemplate S15 allows for any of the forms illustrated by the following examples:

1. 'who *has* a <u>passport</u> and *is booked on* an <u>international flight</u>';
2. 'that *is international* and *has* more than one <u>intermediate stop</u>';
3. 'that *is specified in* that <u>document</u> and *recorded on* the <u>register</u>';
4. 'that *is specified in* that <u>document</u> and *registered*';
5. 'that *specifies* an <u>urgency code</u> and a <u>rural delivery address</u>'.

S16. <both-and-qualifying clause>::=
    {that|who}
    {both <*verb phrase*> {<object>|} and <*verb phrase*> {<object>|}|
    {*is*|*are*} both <*verb part*> {<object>|} and <*verb part*> {<object>|}|
    <*verb phrase*> both <object> and <object>}

Subtemplate S16 allows for any of the forms illustrated by the following examples:

1. 'who both *has* a <u>passport</u> and *is booked on* an <u>international flight</u>';
2. 'that *is* both *specified in* that <u>document</u> and *recorded on* the <u>register</u>';
3. 'that *specifies* both an <u>urgency code</u> and a <u>rural delivery address</u>'.

The next two subtemplates are analogous to the previous two, using 'or' instead of 'and':

S17. <or-qualifying clause>::=
    {that|who}
    {[<*verb phrase*> {<object>|} or]|
    is [<*verb part*> {<object>|} or]
    <*verb phrase*> [<object> or]}
S18. <either-or-qualifying clause>::=
    {that|who}
    {either <*verb phrase*> {<object>|} or <*verb phrase*> {<object>|}|
    {*is*|*are*} either <*verb part*> {<object>|} or <*verb part*> {<object>|}|
    <*verb phrase*> either <object> or <object>}

9.1.2.11 *Specialized subtemplates*
Any subtemplate used only within a single template is defined in the section devoted to that template, specifically,

1. Section 9.2.7, in which a subtemplate for format definitions is defined;
2. Section 9.3.2.7, in which a subtemplate for spatial operators is defined;
3. Section 9.4.1.1, in which subtemplates are defined for phrases and clauses with which time restrictions on activities can be expressed;
4. Section 9.5.3, in which a subtemplate for access activities is defined.

9.2 DEFINITIONAL RULES

Definitional rules (introduced in Section 4.9.1 in Chapter 4) constrain how we define constructs created or used by the organization or the industry within which it operates. Each of the following subcategories of definitional rule has its own template(s):

1. *formal term definitions*, which define business terms formally:
   a. *formal intensional definitions*, for which the template is described in Section 9.2.1.1;
   b. *formal extensional definitions*, for which the template is described in Section 9.2.1.2;
   c. *symbolic literal definitions*, for which the template is described in Section 9.2.1.3;
2. *categorization scheme enumerations*, which define members of *categorization schemes*; the template for these is described in Section 9.2.2;
3. *category transition constraints*, which define constraints on the transitions between categories in a categorization scheme; the template for these is described in Section 9.2.3;
4. *complex concept structure rules*, which define constraints on the components of complex concepts:
   a. *complex concept cardinality rules*, for which the template is described in Section 9.2.4.1;
   b. *complex concept equivalence rules*, for which the template is described in Section 9.2.4.2;
   c. *complex concept set constraints*, for which the template is described in Section 9.2.4.3;
5. *valid value definitions*, which define the valid values of measures; the template for these is described in Section 9.2.5;
6. *data calculation rules*, which define algorithms or formulae for named quantities or conversion factors between units:
   a. *data calculation algorithms*, for which the template is described in Section 9.2.6.1;
   b. *conversion factor definitions*, for which the template is described in Section 9.2.6.2;
7. *standard format definitions*, which define standard formats for data items; the template for these is described in Section 9.2.7.

9.2.1 Formal term definitions

A *formal term definition* defines a particular business term in a formal manner.

9.2.1.1 Formal intensional definitions

A *formal intensional definition* defines the subject business term using an *intensional definition*: one that cites both a *hypernym* (a term that signifies a superset of the set signified by the original term) and the characteristics that distinguish members of the set signified by the original term: for example,

R321. A minor
    is by definition
    a person
        whose age *is less than* 18 years.
R322. A mother
      of a person
    is by definition
    the person
        who *is female* and *is* the parent *of* the first person.

Rule statements for this type of rule can be generated from the following template:

T7. {A|An} <term 1>
    {*of* {a|an} <term 2>|}
    is by definition
    {a|an|the} <term 3>
      <qualifying clause>.

This template has the following important options and placeholders:

1. <u>< term 1></u> is the term being defined;
2. '*of* {a|an} <u>< term 2></u>' is only required if <u>< term 1></u> is an attribute term (as defined in Section 6.2 in Chapter 6);
3. <u>< term 3></u> is the **hypernym** of <u>< term 1></u>;
4. < qualifying clause> is used to state the characteristics that distinguish members of the set signified by <u>< term 1></u> from members of the sets signified by other **hyponyms** of <u>< term 3></u>; the options for a < qualifying clause> are listed in subtemplate S14 in Section 9.1.2.10.

The following fact types should be present in the fact model (either explicitly stated, or derived as described in Section 6.3.3 in Chapter 6):

1. a categorization fact type of the form
   '<u>< term 1></u> *is a category of* <u>< term 3></u>':
   for example, F188 for R321; F191 for R322;
2. if '*of* {a|an} <u>< term 2></u>' is used, a fact type of the form
   '<u>< term 1></u> *is of* <u>< term 2></u>':
   for example, F190 for R322;
3. the fact type that links < qualifying clause> to <u>< term 3></u> (plus any fact types required for the qualifying clause itself) as described in Section 7.4.1 in Chapter 7: for example, F189 for R321; F192 and F193 for R322.

F188. <u>minor</u> *is a category of* <u>person</u>
F189. <u>age</u> *is of* <u>person</u>
F190. <u>mother</u> *is of* <u>person</u>
F191. <u>mother</u> *is a category of* <u>person</u>
F192. <u>person</u> *is female*
F193. <u>person</u> *is* <u>parent</u> *of* <u>person</u>

9.2.1.2 Formal extensional definitions

A *formal extensional definition* defines the subject business term using an **extensional definition**: one that lists a complete set of **hyponyms** (terms that signify subsets of the set signified by the original term): for example,

R323. A <u>parent</u>
   of a <u>person</u>
   is by definition
   the <u>mother</u> or <u>father</u>
   of that <u>person</u>.
R324. A <u>party</u>
   is by definition
   a <u>person</u> or an <u>organization</u>.
R325. A <u>journey</u>
   is by definition
   a <u>one-way journey</u>, a <u>return journey</u>, or a <u>multi-stop journey</u>.

Rule statements for this type of rule can be generated from the following template:

T8. {A|An} <u><term 1></u>
    {*of* {a|an} <u><term 2></u>|}
  is by definition
  [<article> <u><term 3></u>, or]
    {*of* that <u><term 2></u>|}.

This template has the following important options and placeholders:

1. <u><term 1></u> is the term being defined;
2. '*of* {a|an} <u><term 2></u>' is only required if <u><term 1></u> is an attribute term or role term (as defined in Section 6.2 in Chapter 6);
3. '[<article> <u><term 3></u>, or]' is a list of the **hyponyms** making up the definition of <u><term 1></u>, the last two articles and terms in the list separated by 'or' (or a comma and 'or' if adhering to U.S. punctuation standards), and each other pair of articles and terms in the list separated by a comma;
4. '*of* that <u><term 2></u>' is only required if <u><term 1></u> is an attribute term or role term; if it is used, the term substituted in place of <u><term 2></u> after '[<article> <u><term 3></u>, or]' should be the same as the term substituted in place of <u><term 2></u> after <u><term 1></u>.

The following fact types should be present in the fact model (either explicitly stated, or derived as described in Section 6.3.3 in Chapter 6):

1. a categorization fact type of the form
   '<u><term></u> *is a category of* <u><term 1></u>'
   for each <u><term></u> in the list of terms: for example,
   F194 and F195 for R323,
   F197 and F198 for R324,
   F199, F200, and F201 for R325;
2. if '*of* {a|an} <u><term 2></u>' is used, a fact type of the form
   '<u><term 1></u> *is of* <u><term 2></u>':
   for example, F196 for R323.

F194. <u>mother</u> *is a category of* <u>parent</u>
F195. <u>father</u> *is a category of* <u>parent</u>
F196. <u>parent</u> *is of* <u>person</u>
F197. <u>person</u> *is a category of* <u>party</u>
F198. <u>organization</u> *is a category of* <u>party</u>
F199. <u>one-way journey</u> *is a category of* <u>journey</u>
F200. <u>return journey</u> *is a category of* <u>journey</u>
F201. <u>multi-stop journey</u> *is a category of* <u>journey</u>

9.2.1.3 Symbolic literal definitions

A **symbolic literal definition** defines the subject business term using one or more **literals**: for example,

R326. <u>Freezing point</u>
  is by definition
  <u>0°C.</u>

R327. A financial <u>year</u>
     is by definition
     <u>365 days</u> or <u>366 days</u> *from* a <u>July 1</u> *to* the following <u>June 30</u>.[1]

Rule statements for this type of rule can be generated from the following template:

T9. {<<u>literal 1</u>>|{A|An} <<u>term 1</u>>
     {*of* {a|an} <<u>term 2</u>>|}}
   is by definition
   {<<u>literal 2</u>>|
   [<<u>literal 3</u>>, or] *from* a <<u>literal 4</u>> *to* the following <<u>literal 5</u>>}.

This template has the following important options and placeholders:

1. <<u>literal 1</u>> or <<u>term 1</u>> is the term being defined;
2. '*of* {a|an} <<u>term 2</u>>' is only required in conjunction with <<u>term 1</u>> if <<u>term 1</u>> is an attribute term (as defined in Section 6.2 in Chapter 6);
3. <<u>literal 2</u>> is used when a single value defines the term;
4. '[<<u>literal 3</u>>, or] *from* a <<u>literal 4</u>> *to* the following <<u>literal 5</u>>' is used for definitions of terms signifying durations that may vary depending on the year or month (as in R327).

This type of rule statement requires no fact types.

9.2.2 Categorization scheme enumerations

A *categorization scheme enumeration* defines the members of a *categorization scheme* other than by way of a formal extensional definition (already discussed in Section 9.2.1.2): for example,

R328. The <u>status</u>
     of a <u>payroll deduction</u>
   is by definition
   either <u>before-tax</u> or <u>after-tax</u>.
R329. The <u>status</u>
     of a <u>loan application</u>
   is by definition
   one of the following: <u>awaiting approval</u>, <u>approved</u>, or <u>rejected</u>.

Rule statements for this type of rule can be generated from the following template:

T10. {{A|An} <<u>category attribute term</u>>|
   The <<u>category attribute term</u>>
     of {a|an} <<u>entity class term</u>>}
   is by definition
   {either <<u>literal 1</u>> or <<u>literal 2</u>>|
   one of the following: [<<u>literal 3</u>>, or]}.

---

[1]This is the case in Australia; other dates apply in other countries.

This template has the following important options and placeholders:

1. '{A|An} <u><category attribute term></u>' is used if that term is used for category attributes (as defined in Section 6.2.3.2.2 in Chapter 6) that belong to the same categorization scheme (i.e., have the same categories) irrespective of the entity or object class in which they appear;
2. 'The <u><category attribute term></u> *of* {a|an} <u><entity class term></u>' is used if the named category attribute of the named entity class belongs to a categorization scheme that is specific to that category attribute of that entity class;
3. 'either <u><literal 1></u> or <u><literal 2></u>' is used when there are only two categories in the categorization scheme, as in R328;
4. 'one of the following: [<u><literal 3></u>, or]' is used when there are more than two categories in the categorization scheme, as in R329: the categories are listed separated by commas (with the last two categories in the list separated by 'or' or, if adhering to U.S. punctuation conventions, a comma and 'or').

The following fact type should be present in the fact model (either explicitly stated, or derived as described in Section 6.3.3 in Chapter 6):

1. if 'The <u><category attribute term></u> *of* {a|an} <u><entity class term></u>' is used, an attribute fact type of the form
   '<u><category attribute term></u> *is of* <u><entity class term></u>':
   for example, F202 for R328; F203 for R329.

F202. <u>status</u> *is of* <u>payroll deduction</u>
F203. <u>status</u> *is of* <u>loan application</u>

9.2.3 Category transition constraints

A ***category transition constraint*** defines a constraint on the transitions between categories in a categorization scheme: for example,

R330. A transition
　　　　of the <u>marital status</u> *of* a <u>person</u>
　　　　from <u>married</u>, <u>widowed</u>, <u>separated</u>, or <u>divorced</u>
　　　　to <u>never married</u>
　　is by definition
　　impossible.
R331. A transition
　　　　of the <u>marital status</u> *of* a <u>person</u>
　　　　from <u>divorced</u>
　　　　to <u>widowed</u> or <u>separated</u>
　　is by definition
　　impossible.

Rule statements for this type of rule can be generated from the following template:

T11. A transition
     of the <u><category attribute term></u> *of* {a|an} <u><entity class term></u>
     from {<<u>literal 1</u>>|[<<u>literal 2</u>>, or]}
     to {<<u>literal 3</u>>|[<<u>literal 4</u>>, or]}
   is by definition
   impossible.

This template has the following important options and placeholders:

1. <<u>category attribute term</u>> is the term used for the category attribute (as defined in Section 6.2.3.2.2 in Chapter 6) which is subject to the transition constraint;
2. <<u>entity class term</u>> is the term used for the entity or object class in which the category attribute appears;
3. if there is only one category from which the quoted transition is impossible, use <<u>literal 1</u>>, otherwise list the categories separated by commas (with the last two categories in the list separated by 'or' or, if adhering to U.S. punctuation conventions, a comma and 'or');
4. if there is only one category to which the quoted transition is impossible, use <<u>literal 3</u>>, otherwise list the categories.

The following fact type should be present in the fact model (either explicitly stated, or derived as described in Section 6.3.3 in Chapter 6):

1. an attribute fact type of the form
   '<<u>category attribute term</u>> *is of* <<u>entity class term</u>>':
   for example, F204 for both R330 and R331;

F204. <u>marital status</u> *is of* <u>person</u>

9.2.4 Complex concept structure rules

A *complex concept structure rule* defines a constraint on one or more components of a complex concept.

9.2.4.1 Complex concept cardinality rules

A *complex concept cardinality rule* defines the number of (or minimum and/or maximum number of) components of a particular type within a particular concept: for example,

R332. A <u>flight</u>
     has by definition
     exactly one <u>departure time</u>.

Rule statements for this type of rule can be generated from the following template:

T12. {A|An} <u><term 1></u>
     <u><verb phrase></u> by definition
     {<cardinality>|at most <positive integer>} <u><term 2></u>
       {{*for*|*in*} {each|the} <u><term 3></u>|}.

This template has the following important options and placeholders:

1. <u>\<term 1></u> is the term used for the complex concept;
2. *\<verb phrase>* is the verb phrase used for the relationship between <u>\<term 1></u> and <u>\<term 2></u>;
3. \<cardinality> defines the number of (or the minimum number of) components; \<cardinality> options are listed in subtemplate S3 in Section 9.1.2.1;
4. <u>\<term 2></u> is the term used for the components;
5. '{*for*|*in*} {each|the} <u>\<term 3></u>' is optional:
   a. it can be used with 'each' where there is a restriction on the number of components of one type for each component of some other type: for example, a return journey (consisting of two flights) has only one departure port for each flight: in this case, <u>\<term 3></u> is the term used for the component of the other type (<u>flight</u> in this example);
   b. it can be used with 'the' where there is a restriction on the number of components of one type for a single component of some other type: for example, a one-way journey (consisting of one flight) has only one departure port for that flight: in this case, <u>\<term 3></u> is the term used for the component of the other type (<u>flight</u> in this example).

The following fact types should be present in the fact model (either explicitly stated, or derived as described in Section 6.3.3 in Chapter 6):

1. if '{*for*|*in*} {each|the} <u>\<term 3></u>' is not used, a fact type of the form
   '<u>\<term 1></u> *\<verb phrase>* <u>\<term 2></u>':
   for example, F205;
2. if '{*for*|*in*} {each|the} <u>\<term 3></u>' is used, a fact type of the form
   '<u>\<term 1></u> *\<verb phrase>* <u>\<term 2></u> \<preposition> <u>\<term 3></u>'.

F205. <u>flight</u> *has* <u>departure time</u>

9.2.4.2 Complex concept equivalence rules
A ***complex concept equivalence rule*** defines a pair of components within a particular concept that are of necessity the same: for example,

R333. The <u>departure date</u>
  of a <u>journey</u>
 is by definition
 the same as the <u>departure date</u>
  of the <u>outgoing flight</u> *of* that <u>journey</u>.

Rule statements for this type of rule can be generated from the following template:

T13. The <u>\<term 1></u>
  \<qualifying clause 1>
 is by definition
 the same as the <u>\<term 2></u>
  \<qualifying clause 2>.

This template has the following placeholders:

1. <u>\<term 1></u> is the term used for the component that must match;

2. <qualifying clause 1> defines the relationship of that component to the complex concept; the options for a <qualifying clause> are listed in subtemplate S14 in Section 9.1.2.10;
3. <term 2> is the term used for the component that the <term 1> component must match;
4. <qualifying clause 2> defines the relationship of the <term 2> component either to the complex concept or to the <term 1> component.

Each qualifying clause should be supported by at least one fact type in the fact model as described in Section 7.4.1 in Chapter 7 (either explicitly stated, or derived as described in Section 6.3.3 in Chapter 6). For example

1. F206 supports the first qualifying clause in R333;
2. a fact type can be derived from F207 and F208 to support the second qualifying clause in R333.

F206. departure date *is of* journey
F207. departure date *is of* flight *of* journey
F208. outgoing flight *is a category of* flight

9.2.4.3 Complex concept set constraints

A *complex concept set constraint* defines two sets of components within a particular concept that must be identical: for example,

R334. The set of flights
      booked for each passenger *in* a flight booking confirmation
  is by definition
  the same as the set of flights
      booked for each other passenger *in* that flight booking confirmation.

Rule statements for this type of rule can be generated from the following template:

T14. The set of <term 1>
      <qualifying clause 1>
  is by definition
  the same as the set of <term 1>
      <qualifying clause 2>.

This template has the following placeholders:

1. <term 1> is the term used for the components in the set that must match;
2. <qualifying clause 1> defines the relationship of that set of components to the complex concept; the options for a <qualifying clause> are listed in subtemplate S14 in Section 9.1.2.10;
3. <qualifying clause 2> defines the relationship of the second set of components to the complex concept.

Each qualifying clause should be supported by at least one fact type in the fact model as described in Section 7.4.1 in Chapter 7 (either explicitly stated, or derived as described in Section 6.3.3 in Chapter 6). For example, F209 supports both qualifying clauses in R334.

F209. flight *is booked for* passenger *in* flight booking confirmation

9.2.5 Valid value definitions

A *valid value definition* defines the valid values of a particular measure, as a range or (occasionally) as a list of discrete values: for example,

R335. Discount rate
    is by definition
    at least 0% and *at most* 100%.

Rule statements for this type of rule can be generated from the following template:

T15. {The|} <attribute term>
    {*of* {a|an} <entity class term>|}
    is by definition
    {<inequality operator> <literal 1>
      {*and* <inequality operator> <literal 2>|}|
      [<literal 3>, or]}.

This template has the following important options and placeholders:

1. <attribute term> is the term used for the quantitative attribute (as defined in Section 6.2.3.2.3 in Chapter 6) used to record the measure;
2. '*of* {a|an} <entity class term>' is optional and can be used if the values of the quantitative attribute are specific to the use of that attribute by that entity class;
3. use one or both '<inequality operator> <literal>' elements to define the minimum and/or maximum values of the attribute, or (if there is a set of discrete valid values) list them, separated by commas (with the last two values in the list separated by 'or' or, if adhering to U.S. punctuation conventions, a comma and 'or'); the options for an <inequality operator> are listed in subtemplate S6 in Section 9.1.2.3.

The following fact type should be present in the fact model (either explicitly stated, or derived as described in Section 6.3.3 in Chapter 6):

1. if '*of* {a|an} <entity class term>' is used, an attribute fact type of the form '<attribute term> *is of* <entity class term>'.

9.2.6 Data calculation rules

A *data calculation rule* defines the algorithm or formula for a particular quantity or a conversion factor between two units.

9.2.6.1 Data calculation algorithms

A *data calculation algorithm* defines how a particular quantity or amount is calculated: for example,

R336. The extension
    for an order line
    is by definition *calculated as*
    the product of the order quantity and the unit price
    for that order line.

R337. The <u>total order value</u>
        of an <u>order</u>
    is by definition *calculated as*
    the sum of the <u>extensions</u>
        for each <u>order line</u>.

Rule statements for this type of rule can be generated from the following template:

T16. {The|} <<u>attribute term</u>>
        {*of*|*for*} {a|an} <<u>entity class term</u>>
        {<qualifying clause>|}
    is by definition *calculated as*
    <expression>.

This template has the following important options and placeholders:

1. <<u>attribute term</u>> is the term used for the quantitative attribute (as defined in Section 6.2.3.2.3 in Chapter 6) for which the calculation is being defined;
2. <<u>entity class term</u>> is the term used for the entity class to which the attribute belongs;
3. <qualifying clause> is optional, to be used if the calculation does not apply to all instances of the nominated entity class; the options for <qualifying clause> are listed in subtemplate S14 in Section 9.1.2.10;
4. the options for <expression> are listed in subtemplate S12 in Section 9.1.2.8.

The following fact types should be present in the fact model (either explicitly stated, or derived as described in Section 6.3.3 in Chapter 6):

1. an attribute fact type of the form
   '<<u>attribute term</u>> *is* {*of* | *for*} <<u>entity class term</u>>':
   for example, F210 for R336; F213 for R337;
2. at least one fact type for any qualifying clause in the expression, as described in Section 7.4.1 in Chapter 7: for example, F211 and F212 for R336; F210 for R337.

F210. <u>extension</u> *is for* <u>order line</u>
F211. <u>order quantity</u> *is of* <u>order line</u>
F212. <u>unit price</u> *is of* <u>order line</u>
F213. <u>total order value</u> *is of* <u>order</u>

9.2.6.2 Conversion factor definitions

A ***conversion factor definition*** defines a conversion factor between two units of measurement: for example,

R338. <u>1 mile</u>
    is by definition *approximately equal to*
    <u>1.6 km</u>.

Rule statements for this type of rule can be generated from the following template:

T17. <u><literal 1></u>
is by definition {*approximately*|} *equal to*
<<u>literal 2</u>>.

This template has the following options and placeholders:

1. <<u>literal 1</u>> is a standard quantity (usually 1) together with one of the units of measurement;
2. '*approximately*' is used if and only if the conversion is approximate;
3. <<u>literal 2</u>> is the corresponding quantity for the other unit of measurement, together with that unit of measurement.

This type of rule statement requires no fact types.

9.2.7 **Standard format definitions**

A *standard format definition* defines the standard format for data items of a particular type in terms of individual characters and/or component data items: for example,

R339. A valid <u>airline code</u>
is by definition *composed of*
exactly two <u>letters</u>.

Rule statements for this type of rule can be generated from the following template:

T18. A valid <<u>term</u>>
is by definition *composed of*
<format definition>.

This template has the following placeholders:

1. <<u>term</u>> is the term used for the type of data item;
2. the <format definition> placeholder can be replaced by anything defined in the following subtemplate:

S19. <format definition>::=
{{exactly|at least|up to} <positive integer 1>|
from <positive integer 2> to <positive integer 3>} <<u>term</u>>
{followed by <format definition>|}

Thus any of the following can be substituted in place of the <format definition> placeholder:

1. 'exactly', 'at least', or 'up to', followed by a positive integer and a term: for example, 'exactly two <u>digits</u>', 'at least three <u>letters</u>', 'up to nine <u>digits</u>';
2. 'from', a positive integer, 'to', and another positive integer followed by a term: for example, 'from two to seven <u>digits</u>';
3. any number of any of the above, each separated from the next by 'followed by'.

This type of rule statement requires no fact types.

9.3 DATA RULES

Data rules (introduced in Section 4.9.2 in Chapter 4) constrain the data included in a transaction (a form or message) or a persistent data set (e.g., a database record). Each of the following subcategories of data rule has its own template(s):

1. *data cardinality rules*, which place restrictions on the maximum or minimum number of occurrences of data items:
   a. *mandatory data rules*, which mandate the presence of data; the templates for these are described in Section 9.3.1.1;
   b. *prohibited data rules*, which mandate the absence of some data item in a particular situation; the template for these is described in Section 9.3.1.2;
   c. *maximum cardinality rules*, which place an upper limit (usually but not necessarily one) on how many instances of a particular data item there may be; the template for these is described in Section 9.3.1.3;
   d. *multiple data rules*, which mandate the presence of two or more instances of a particular data item in a particular situation; the template for these is described in Section 9.3.1.4;
   e. *dependent cardinality rules*, which mandate how many of a particular data item must be present based on other data item(s); the template for these is described in Section 9.3.1.5;
2. *data content rules*, which place restrictions on the values contained in data items:
   a. *value set rules*, which require
      i. that the content of a data item be (or not be) one of a particular set of values (either a fixed set or a set that may change over time),
      ii. that the content of a combination of data items match or not match a corresponding combination in a set of records, or
      iii. that the values contained in two or more data items form a valid combination;
      the templates for these are described in Section 9.3.2.1;
   b. *range rules*, which require that the content of a data item be a value within a particular inclusive or exclusive single-bounded or double-bounded range; the template for these is described in Section 9.3.2.2;
   c. *equality rules*, which require that the content of a data item be the same as or not the same as that of some other data item; the template for these is described in Section 9.3.2.3;
   d. *uniqueness constraints*, which require that the content of a data item (or combination of data items) be different from that of the corresponding data item(s) in the same or other records or transactions; the templates for these are described in Section 9.3.2.4;
   e. *data consistency rules*, which require the content of multiple data items to be consistent with each other, other than as provided for by a value set rule, range rule, or equality rule; the template for these is described in Section 9.3.2.5;
   f. *temporal data constraints*, which constrain one or more *temporal data* items (data items that represent time points or time periods); the templates for these are described in Section 9.3.2.6;
   g. *spatial data constraints*, which prescribe or prohibit relationships between spatial properties (points, line segments or polygons) specified in a record or set of records; the template for these is described in Section 9.3.2.7;

  h. *data item format rules*, which specify the required format of a data item; the template for these is described in Section 9.3.2.8;

3. *data update rules*, which either prohibit update of a data item or place restrictions on the new value of a data item in terms of the existing value:

  a. *data update prohibition rules*, which prohibit update of a particular data item or set of data items; the template for these is described in Section 9.3.3.1;

  b. *state transition constraints*, which limit the changes in a data item to a set of valid transitions; the template for these is described in Section 9.3.3.2;

  c. *monotonic transition constraints*, which require that a numeric value can either only increase or only decrease; the template for these is described in Section 9.3.3.3.

9.3.1 Data cardinality rules

A *data cardinality rule* places a restriction on the maximum or minimum number of occurrences of a data item in a transaction (i.e., a paper or online form) or a persistent data set.

9.3.1.1 Mandatory data rules

A *mandatory data rule* mandates the presence of data: that is, requires that a data item be entered in a transaction form or be present in a message, or that a persistent data record include a value for a data item.

  There are three subcategories of mandatory data rule, each with its own template(s):

1. *mandatory data item rules*, which require that a particular data item be present; the template for these is described in Section 9.3.1.1.1;

2. *mandatory option selection rules*, which require that one of a set of pre-defined options be specified; the template for these is described in Section 9.3.1.1.2;

3. *mandatory group rules*, which require that at least one of a group of data items be present; the template for these is described in Section 9.3.1.1.3.

9.3.1.1.1 Mandatory data item rules

A *mandatory data item rule* requires that a particular data item be present: for example,

R340. Each <u>flight booking request</u>
    that *is for* a <u>multi-stop journey</u>
   must *specify* exactly one <u>travel date</u>
    for each <u>flight</u> *in* that <u>journey</u>
   unless that <u>flight booking request</u> *is for* an <u>open-dated journey</u>.

Rule statements for this type of rule can be generated from the following template:

T19. Each <transaction signifier>
   must {*specify*| *contain*} <cardinality> <u><data item term></u>
    {{*in*| *for*} {each|the} <u><subform term></u> {(if any)|}
    {<qualifying clause>|}|}
   {{if|unless} <conditional clause>|}.

This template has the following important options and placeholders:

1. <transaction signifier> is the term used for the transaction (paper or electronic form or message) or persistent data record in which a data item is required; the options for <transaction signifier> are listed in subtemplate S8 in Section 9.1.2.4 and discussed below;
2. <cardinality> must be one of
   a. exactly <positive integer>,
   b. at least <positive integer>,
   c. at least <positive integer> and at most <positive integer>;
3. <data item term> is the name of the required data item;
4. '{*in*|*for*} {each|the} <subform term> {(if any)|} {<qualifying clause>|}':
   a. this phrase is required if the data item signified by <data item term> is (if present) contained in a complex data item or subform (as discussed in Section 7.2.3.2.2 in Chapter 7);
   b. 'each' is required if the complex data item or subform can appear more than once in an instance of the transaction, whereas 'the' is required if the complex data item or subform can appear only once in an instance of the transaction (see examples in Section 7.2.4.1);
   c. <subform term> is the name of the complex data item or subform;
   d. '(if any)' is required if and only if the complex data item or subform may be omitted from an instance of the transaction (again see examples in Section 7.2.4.1);
   e. <qualifying clause> is required if and only if it is necessary to relate <subform term> back to a term in <transaction signifier>; the options for <qualifying clause> are listed in subtemplate S14 in Section 9.1.2.10;
5. '{if|unless} <conditional clause>' (or a qualifying clause in <transaction signifier>) is only required if not all instances of the transaction are subject to the rule; the options for <conditional clause> are listed in subtemplate S13 in Section 9.1.2.9.

In rule statement R340, a simple term ('flight booking request') can be used to signify the transaction being recorded. Sometimes what is being recorded is an association between two or more real-world objects for which it is impractical to use a single term. For example, the term 'flight' (e.g., QF1) refers to something which may occur each day (or at least the same days every week). There is no obvious term by which we can refer to a particular flight on a particular day. Furthermore, a particular flight may cover more than one leg: for example, QF1 flies from Sydney to London Heathrow via Bangkok. If we want to refer to seat allocations, these may be different on a particular day between Sydney and Bangkok and between Bangkok and Heathrow, but there is even less likely to be an obvious term by which we can refer to a particular leg of a particular flight on a particular day.

Rule statement R341 gets around this by referring to 'combination of departure date, flight number, and departure city' rather than to some artificial term that may be misinterpreted.

R341. Each combination of departure date, flight number, and departure city
must *be allocated*
exactly one flight crew.

Another example of a data cardinality rule statement governing a combination of objects is

R342. Each record of a combination of student and course
must *specify* exactly one year of initial study.

Each of these options is allowed for in the <transaction signifier> subtemplate.

The following fact types should be present in the fact model (either explicitly stated, or derived as described in Section 6.3.3 in Chapter 6):

1. if <transaction signifier> includes a term (as in R340), rather than a list of terms (as in R341 or R342)[2]:

    a. if <subform term> is included, a fact type of the form

    '<transaction term> *specifies* <data item term>
        {*in*|*for*} <subform term>', or
    '<transaction term> *specifies* <data type> *as* <data item term>
        {*in*|*for*} <subform term>',

    where <transaction term> signifies the transaction: for example, for R340, F215;

    b. if <subform term> is not included, a fact type of the form

    '<transaction signifier> *specifies* <data item term>', or
    '<transaction term> *specifies* <data type> *as* <data item term>',

    where <transaction term> signifies the transaction;

2. at least one fact type for each qualifying clause (if any), including any within the transaction signifier, as described in Section 7.4.1 in Chapter 7: for example, for R340:

    a. F214 supports the qualifying clause within the transaction signifier ('that *is for* a multi-stop journey');

    b. F216 supports the qualifying clause following the data item term ('*in* that journey');

3. at least one fact type for the conditional clause (if any), as also described in Section 7.4.1: for example, for R340, F217.

F214. flight booking request *is for* multi-stop journey
F215. flight booking request *specifies* travel date *for* flight
F216. flight *is part of* journey
F217. flight booking request *is for* open-dated journey

9.3.1.1.2 Mandatory option selection rules

A ***mandatory option selection rule*** requires that one of a set of pre-defined options be specified: for example,

R343. Each flight booking request
    must *specify* whether it
    is for a return journey, a one-way journey, or a multi-stop journey.
R344. Each flight booking confirmation
    must *specify* whether the payment
        specified in that flight booking confirmation
    is a credit card payment or an electronic funds transfer payment.

---

[2]As at the time of writing, the literature on fact models does not provide fact types that document associations between combinations of objects and data items. This gap will no doubt be filled in due course.

R345. Each <u>flight booking confirmation</u>
must *specify* whether or not the <u>paying party</u>
specified in the <u>flight booking confirmation</u>
wishes to include a CO2 offset payment.

R346. Each record of a combination of <u>supplier</u> and <u>product</u>
must *specify* whether or not that <u>supplier</u>
is a <u>preferred supplier</u> *for* that <u>product</u>.

R347. Each <u>flight booking confirmation</u>
that *specifies* a <u>destination city</u> that *is in* a <u>country</u> other than <u>Australia</u>
must *specify* whether each <u>passenger</u>
specified in that <u>flight booking confirmation</u>
has a <u>passport</u> *issued by* that <u>country</u> or a <u>visa</u> *issued by* that <u>country</u>.

Note that alternative formulations are available in rule statements for this type of rule:

1. There may be two or more options (as in R343, R344, and R347) or a single option which may or may not be the case (as in R345 and R346), in which case 'whether' is followed by 'or not'.
2. The subject of what is being specified by the transaction may be a term ('<u>payment</u>', '<u>paying party</u>', '<u>supplier</u>', '<u>passenger</u>' in the above examples) or the transaction itself (as in R343), in which case (provided the transaction signifier contains no intervening qualifying clause) 'it' can be used.

Rule statements for rules with two or more options can be generated from the following template:

T20. Each <transaction signifier>
must
{({if|unless} <conditional clause>)|}
specify whether {it|{the|each} <u><term></u>
{<qualifying clause>|}}
<*verb phrase*> [<object>, or].

Rule statements for rules with a single option which may or may not be the case can be generated from the following template:

T21. Each <transaction signifier>
must
{({if|unless} <conditional clause>)|}
specify whether {or not|} {it|{the|each} <u><term></u>
{<qualifying clause>|}}
<*verb phrase*> {<object>|}.

Both these templates have the following options and placeholders:

1. <transaction signifier> is the term used for the transaction (paper or electronic form or message) or persistent data record in which a data item is required; options for <transaction signifier> are listed in subtemplate S8 in Section 9.1.2.4 and discussed in Section 9.3.1.1.1;
2. '({if|unless} <conditional clause>)' (or a qualifying clause in <transaction signifier>) is only required if not all instances of the transaction are subject to the rule; options for <conditional clause> are listed in subtemplate S13 in Section 9.1.2.9;
3. 'it' is used if and only if the subject of what is being specified by the transaction is the transaction itself and the transaction signifier contains no intervening qualifying clause (as in R343); otherwise

a term is used, preceded by 'the' or 'each' as appropriate, and optionally followed by a qualifying clause; options for <qualifying clause> are listed in subtemplate S14 in Section 9.1.2.10;

4. <verb phrase> is followed either by
   a. a single <object> (in T21), or
   b. a list of as many alternative <objects> as are required (in T20), the last two separated by 'or' (or a comma and 'or' if adhering to U.S. punctuation standards) and each other pair of alternatives separated by a comma;
   options for <object> are listed in subtemplate S11 in Section 9.1.2.7.

The following fact types should be present in the fact model (either explicitly stated, or derived as described in Section 6.3.3 in Chapter 6):

1. if <transaction signifier> includes a term (as in R343, R344, R345, and R347), rather than a list of terms (as in R346):
   a. a fact type of the form
      '<transaction term> *specifies* proposition',
      where <transaction term> signifies the transaction: for example,
      F218 for R343;
      F222 for R344, R345, and R347;
   b. if the rule statement is based on template T20 and includes a term rather than 'it' after 'whether', one of the following for each <object> in the list of alternatives:
      i. a fact type of the form
         '<term> <verb phrase> <object>': for example,
         F231 and F233 for R347, or
      ii. (if <verb phrase> is 'is') one of the form
         '<object> *is a category of* <term>': for example,
         F224 and F225 for R344;
   c. if the rule statement is based on template T20 and includes 'it' rather than a term after 'whether', a fact type of the form
      '<transaction term> <verb phrase> <object>'
      for each <object> in the list of objects, where <transaction term> signifies the transaction: for example, F219, F220, and F221 for R343;
   d. if the rule statement is based on template T21 and includes a term rather than 'it' after 'whether', either
      i. (if <verb phrase> is followed by an <object>) a fact type of the form
         '<term> <verb phrase> <object term>',
         where <object term> is the first term in <object>, or
      ii. (if <verb phrase> is not followed by an <object>) a fact type of the form
         '<term> <verb phrase>':
         for example, F227 for R345;
   e. if the rule statement is based on template T21 and includes 'it' rather than a term after 'whether', either:
      i. (if <verb phrase> is followed by an <object>) a fact type of the form
         '<transaction term> <verb phrase> <object term>',
         where <transaction term> signifies the transaction and <object term> is the first term in <object>, or

    ii. (if *<verb phrase>* is not followed by an *<object>*) a fact type of the form
       '<u>\<transaction term></u> *\<verb phrase>*',
   where *<transaction term>* signifies the transaction;

2. at least one fact type for each qualifying clause (if any), including any within the transaction signifier or any object, as described in Section 7.4.1 in Chapter 7: for example,
   a. F223 for R344;
   b. F226 for R345;
   c. in R347:
     i. F228 and F229 support the qualifying clause within the transaction signifier ('that *specifies* a <u>destination city</u> that *is in* a <u>country</u> other than <u>Australia</u>'),
     ii. F230 supports the qualifying clause following the data item term ('*specified in* that <u>flight booking confirmation</u>'),
    iii. F232 and F234 support the qualifying clauses within the objects in the object list ('*issued by* that <u>country</u>');

3. at least one fact type for the conditional clause (if any), as also described in Section 7.4.1.

F218. <u>flight booking request</u> *specifies* <u>proposition</u>
F219. <u>flight booking request</u> *is for* <u>return journey</u>
F220. <u>flight booking request</u> *is for* <u>one-way journey</u>
F221. <u>flight booking request</u> *is for* <u>multi-stop journey</u>
F222. <u>flight booking confirmation</u> *specifies* <u>proposition</u>
F223. <u>payment</u> *is specified in* <u>flight booking confirmation</u>
F224. <u>credit card payment</u> *is a category of* <u>payment</u>
F225. <u>electronic transfer payment</u> *is a category of* <u>payment</u>
F226. <u>paying party</u> *is specified in* <u>flight booking confirmation</u>
F227. <u>paying party</u> *wishes to include a CO2 offset payment*
F228. <u>flight booking confirmation</u> *specifies* <u>city</u> *as* <u>destination city</u>
F229. <u>city</u> *is in* <u>country</u>
F230. <u>passenger</u> *is specified in* <u>flight booking confirmation</u>
F231. <u>passenger</u> *has* <u>passport</u>
F232. <u>passport</u> *is issued by* <u>country</u>
F233. <u>passenger</u> *has* <u>visa</u>
F234. <u>visa</u> *is issued by* <u>country</u>

9.3.1.1.3 Mandatory group rules

A ***mandatory group rule*** requires that at least one of a group of data items be present: for example,

R348. Each <u>customer complaint</u>
    must *specify* a <u>mobile phone number</u>, an <u>e-mail address</u>,
      or both.
R349. Each <u>flight booking confirmation</u>
     for an <u>international journey</u>
    must *specify for* each <u>passenger</u>
     specified in that <u>flight booking request</u>
     a <u>passport number</u> or a <u>visa number</u>
     but not both.

R350. Each <u>concert ticket purchase</u>
must *specify* exactly one of the following:
a <u>postal address</u>, an <u>e-mail address</u>, or a <u>fax number</u>.

Note that alternative formulations are available in rule statements for this type of rule depending on the number of data items in the group.

If there are only two data items in the group, use the following template:

T22. Each <transaction signifier>
must {*specify*|*contain*}
{{*in*|*for*} {each|the} <u><subform term></u> {(if any)|}
{<qualifying clause>|}|}
{a|an} <u><data item term 1></u>, {a|an} <u><data item term 2></u>
{, or|but not} both
{{if|unless} <conditional clause>|}.

If there are more than two data items in the group, use the following template:

T23. Each <transaction signifier>
must
{(({if|unless} <conditional clause>)|}
{*specify*|*contain*}
{{*in*|*for*} {each|the} <u><subform term></u> {(if any)|}
{<qualifying clause>|}|}
<cardinality> of the following:
[<u><data item term></u>, or].

Both these templates have the following options and placeholders:

1. <transaction signifier> is the term used for the transaction (paper or electronic form or message) or persistent data record which contains the group of data; options for <transaction signifier> are listed in subtemplate S8 in Section 9.1.2.4 and discussed in Section 9.3.1.1.1;
2. '{*in*|*for*} {each|the} <u><subform term></u> {(if any)|} {<qualifying clause>|}':
    a. this phrase is required if the group of data items (signified by <u><data item term 1></u> and <u><data item term 2></u>, or by <u><data item term></u>) is contained in a complex data item or subform (as discussed in Section 7.2.3.2.2 in Chapter 7);
    b. 'each' is required if the complex data item or subform can appear more than once in an instance of the transaction, whereas 'the' is required if the complex data item or subform can appear only once in an instance of the transaction (see examples in Section 7.2.4.1);
    c. <u><subform term></u> is the name of the complex data item or subform;
    d. '(if any)' is required if and only if the complex data item or subform may be omitted from an instance of the transaction (again see examples in Section 7.2.4.1);
    e. <qualifying clause> is required if and only if it is necessary to relate <u><subform term></u> back to a term in <transaction signifier>; options for <qualifying clause> are listed in subtemplate S14 in Section 9.1.2.10;

3. The data items in the group are specified using either
   a. <data item term 1> and <data item term 2> (in T22), or
   b. '[<data item term>, or]' (in T23), in which as many terms as required are listed, separated by commas except for the last two, which are separated by 'or' (or a comma and 'or' if U.S. punctuation standards are followed); in this case <cardinality> (options for which are listed in subtemplate S3 in Section 9.1.2.1) is used to indicate how many data items are required;
4. '({if|unless} <conditional clause>)' (or a qualifying clause in <transaction signifier>) is only required if not all instances of the transaction are subject to the rule; options for <conditional clause> are listed in subtemplate S13 in Section 9.1.2.9.

The following fact types should be present in the fact model (either explicitly stated, or derived as described in Section 6.3.3 in Chapter 6):

1. if <transaction signifier> includes a term rather than a list of terms, then
   a. if the rule statement is based on template T22 and <subform term> is not included, fact types of the form
      '<transaction term> *specifies* <data item term 1>' and
      '<transaction term> *specifies* <data item term 2>', or
      '<transaction term> *specifies* <data type> *as* <data item term 1>' and
      '<transaction term> *specifies* <data type> *as* <data item term 2>',
      where <transaction term> signifies the transaction: for example, F235 and F236 for R348;
   b. if the rule statement is based on template T22 and <subform term> is included, fact types of the form
      '<transaction term> *specifies* <data item term 1>
         {*in*|*for*} <subform term>' and
      '<transaction term> *specifies* <data item term 2>
         {*in*|*for*} <subform term>', or
      '<transaction term> *specifies* <data type> *as* <data item term 1>
         {*in*|*for*} <subform term>' and
      '<transaction term> *specifies* <data type> *as* <data item term 2>
         {*in*|*for*} <subform term>',
      where <transaction term> signifies the transaction: for example, F238 and F239 for R349;
   c. if the rule statement is based on template T23 and <subform term> is not included, a fact type of the form
      '<transaction term> *specifies* <data item term>', or
      '<transaction term> *specifies* <data type> *as* <data item term>'
      for each data item term in the list of data item terms, where <transaction term> signifies the transaction: for example, F241, F242, and F243 for R350;
   d. if the rule statement is based on template T23 and <subform term> is included, a fact type of the form
      '<transaction term> *specifies* <data item term>
         {*in*|*for*} <subform term>' or
      '<transaction term> *specifies* <data type> *as* <data item term>
         {*in*|*for*} <subform term>',
      for each data item term in the list of data item terms, where <transaction term> signifies the transaction;

    2. at least one fact type for each qualifying clause (if any), including any within the transaction signifier, as described in Section 7.4.1 in Chapter 7: for example, F237 and F240 for R349;

    3. at least one fact type for the conditional clause (if any), as also described in Section 7.4.1.

F235. customer complaint *specifies* mobile phone number
F236. customer complaint *specifies* e-mail address
F237. flight booking confirmation *is for* international journey
F238. flight booking confirmation *specifies* passport number *for* passenger
F239. flight booking confirmation *specifies* visa number *for* passenger
F240. passenger *is specified in* flight booking request
F241. concert ticket purchase *specifies* postal address
F242. concert ticket purchase *specifies* e-mail address
F243. concert ticket purchase *specifies* fax number

9.3.1.2 Prohibited data rules

A ***prohibited data rule*** mandates the absence of some data item in a particular situation: for example,

R351. A flight booking confirmation
        that *specifies* an insurance option
    must not *specify* an electronic funds transfer payment receipt.

Rule statements for this type of rule can be generated from the following template:

T24. {A|An} <transaction signifier>
      must not {*specify*|*contain*} a <data item term>
        {{*in*|*for*} {any|the} <subform term> {(if any)|}
        {<qualifying clause>|}|}
      {{*if*|*unless*} <conditional clause>|}.

This template has the following important options and placeholders:

    1. <transaction signifier> is the term used for the transaction (paper or electronic form or message) or persistent data record in which a data item is required; options for <transaction signifier> are listed in subtemplate S8 in Section 9.1.2.4 and discussed in Section 9.3.1.1.1;

    2. <data item term> is the name of the data item that must be absent;

    3. '{*in*|*for*} {any|the} <subform term> {(if any)|} {<qualifying clause>|}':

        a. this phrase is required if the data item signified by <data item term> would (if present) be contained in a complex data item or subform (as discussed in Section 7.2.3.2.2 in Chapter 7);

        b. 'any' is required if the complex data item or subform can appear more than once in an instance of the transaction, whereas 'the' is required if the complex data item or subform can appear only once in an instance of the transaction (see examples in Section 7.2.4.1);

        c. <subform term> is the name of the complex data item or subform;

        d. '(if any)' is required if and only if the complex data item or subform may

           i. appear only once in an instance of the transaction, and

          ii. be omitted from an instance of the transaction (again see examples in Section 7.2.4.1);

e. <u>qualifying clause</u> is required if and only if it is necessary to relate <u>subform term</u> back to a term in <u>transaction signifier</u>; options for <u>qualifying clause</u> are listed in subtemplate S14 in Section 9.1.2.10;

4. '{if|unless} <conditional clause>' (or a qualifying clause in <transaction signifier>) is always required since a prohibited data rule only makes sense when applied to a subset of the governed transactions; options for <conditional clause> are listed in subtemplate S13 in Section 9.1.2.9.

The following fact types should be present in the fact model (either explicitly stated, or derived as described in Section 6.3.3 in Chapter 6):

1. if <u>transaction signifier</u> includes a term rather than a list of terms, then
   a. if <u>subform term</u> is included, a fact type of the form
   '<u>transaction term</u> *specifies* <u>data item term</u>
       {*in*|*for*} <u>subform term</u>', or
   '<u>transaction term</u> *specifies* <u>data type</u> *as* <u>data item term</u>
       {*in*|*for*} <u>subform term</u>',
   where <u>transaction term</u> signifies the transaction;
   b. if <u>subform term</u> is not included, a fact type of the form
   '<u>transaction term</u> *specifies* <u>data item term</u>', or
   '<u>transaction term</u> *specifies* <u>data type</u> *as* <u>data item term</u>',
   where <u>transaction term</u> signifies the transaction: for example, F245;
2. at least one fact type for each qualifying clause (if any), including any within the transaction signifier, as described in Section 7.4.1 in Chapter 7: for example, F244;
3. at least one fact type for the conditional clause (if any), as also described in Section 7.4.1.

F244. <u>flight booking confirmation</u> *specifies* <u>insurance option</u>
F245. <u>flight booking confirmation</u> *specifies* <u>electronic funds transfer payment receipt</u>

9.3.1.3 Maximum cardinality rules

A *maximum cardinality rule* places an upper limit (usually but not necessarily one) on how many instances of a particular data item there may be: for example,

R352. A <u>change of name registration</u>
       must not *specify* more than one <u>party</u>.
R353. A <u>purchase order</u>
       must not *specify* more than one <u>discount code</u> *for* any one <u>product</u>.

Rule statements for this type of rule can be generated from the following template:

T25. {A|An} <transaction signifier>
       must not {*specify*|*contain*} more than <positive integer>
          <data item term>
       {{*in*|*for*} {any one|the} <subform term> {(if any)|}
       {<qualifying clause>|}|}
       {{if|unless} <conditional clause>|}.

This template has the following important options and placeholders:

1. <u>\<transaction signifier></u> is the term used for the transaction (paper or electronic form or message) or persistent data record in which a data item is required; options for \<transaction signifier> are listed in subtemplate S8 in Section 9.1.2.4 and discussed in Section 9.3.1.1.1;
2. <u>\<data item term></u> is the name of the restricted data item;
3. '{*in*|*for*} {any one|the} <u>\<subform term></u> {(if any)|} {\<qualifying clause>|}':
   a. this phrase is required if the data item signified by <u>\<data item term></u> is (if present) contained in a complex data item or subform (as discussed in Section 7.2.3.2.2 in Chapter 7);
   b. 'any one' is required if the complex data item or subform can appear more than once in an instance of the transaction, whereas 'the' is required if the complex data item or subform can appear only once in an instance of the transaction (see examples in Section 7.2.4.1);
   c. <u>\<subform term></u> is the name of the complex data item or subform;
   d. '(if any)' is required if and only if the complex data item or subform may
      i. appear only once in an instance of the transaction, and
      ii. be omitted from an instance of the transaction (again see examples in Section 7.2.4.1);
   e. <u>\<qualifying clause></u> is required if and only if it is necessary to relate <u>\<subform term></u> back to a term in \<transaction signifier>; options for \<qualifying clause> are listed in subtemplate S14 in Section 9.1.2.10;
4. '{*if*|*unless*} \<conditional clause>' (or a qualifying clause in \<transaction signifier>) is only required if not all instances of the transaction are subject to the rule; options for \<conditional clause> are listed in subtemplate S13 in Section 9.1.2.9.

The following fact types should be present in the fact model (either explicitly stated, or derived as described in Section 6.3.3 in Chapter 6):

1. if <u>\<transaction signifier></u> includes a term rather than a list of terms, then
   a. if <u>\<subform term></u> is not included, a fact type of the form
      '<u>\<transaction term></u> *specifies* <u>\<data item term></u>', or
      '<u>\<transaction term></u> *specifies* <u>\<data type></u> *as* <u>\<data item term></u>',
      where <u>\<transaction term></u> signifies the transaction: for example, F246 for R352;
   b. if <u>\<subform term></u> is included, a fact type of the form
      '<u>\<transaction term></u> *specifies* <u>\<data item term></u>
         {*in*|*for*} <u>\<subform term></u>', or
      '<u>\<transaction term></u> *specifies* <u>\<data type></u> *as* <u>\<data item term></u>
         {*in*|*for*} <u>\<subform term></u>',
      where <u>\<transaction term></u> signifies the transaction: for example, F247 for R353;
2. at least one fact type for each qualifying clause (if any), including any within the transaction signifier, as described in Section 7.4.1 in Chapter 7;
3. at least one fact type for the conditional clause (if any), as also described in Section 7.4.1.

F246. <u>change of name registration</u> *specifies* <u>party</u>
F247. <u>purchase order</u> *specifies* <u>discount code</u> *for* <u>product</u>

9.3.1.4 Multiple data rules

A *multiple data rule* mandates the presence of two or more instances of a particular data item in a particular situation.

Rule statements for this type of rule can also be generated from template T19, but in these rule statements <cardinality> may only take one of the following forms:

1. exactly <positive integer>, where <positive integer> is at least two;
2. at least <positive integer>, where <positive integer> is at least two;
3. at least <positive integer 1> and at most <positive integer 2>, where <positive integer 1> is at least two.

For example, a parcel of real property may be held by way of a sole tenancy, a joint tenancy (in which on the death of one of the proprietors the proprietorship passes automatically to the remaining proprietors), or a tenancy in common (in which the proprietors each own shares of the whole): a joint tenancy or tenancy in common must involve at least two proprietors.

9.3.1.5 Dependent cardinality rules

A *dependent cardinality rule* mandates how many of a particular data item must be present based on the value of another data item: for example,

R354. The number of <u>flights</u>
    specified in each <u>round-trip special booking</u>
  must *be* no *less than* the <u>minimum number of flights</u>
    defined for the <u>special offer code</u>
    specified in that <u>round-trip special booking</u>.

Rule statements for this type of rule can be generated from the following template:

T26. The number of <<u>data item term 1</u>>
    {*specified*| *contained*}
    {{*in*| *for*} {the | each} <<u>subform term</u>> {(if any)|}|}
    in each <transaction signifier>
  must *be* {{no|} {*more*| *less*} *than*| *equal to*} the <<u>data item term 2</u>>
    {<qualifying clause>|}
    {{*if*| unless} <conditional clause>|}.

This template has the following important options and placeholders:

1. <<u>data item term 1</u>> is the name of the data item for which the cardinality is constrained;
2. '{*in*| *for*} {the | each} <<u>subform term</u>> {(if any)|}|}':
   a. this phrase is required if the data item signified by <<u>data item term 1</u>> is contained in a complex data item or subform (as discussed in Section 7.2.3.2.2 in Chapter 7);
   b. 'each' is required if the complex data item or subform can appear more than once in an instance of the transaction, whereas 'the' is required if the complex data item or subform can appear only once in an instance of the transaction (see examples in Section 7.2.4.1);
   c. <<u>subform term</u>> is the name of the complex data item or subform;
   d. '(if any)' is required if and only if the complex data item or subform may be omitted from an instance of the transaction (again see examples in Section 7.2.4.1);

3. <transaction signifier> is the term used for the transaction (paper or electronic form or message) or persistent data record in which a data item is required; options for <transaction signifier> are listed in subtemplate S8 in Section 9.1.2.4 and discussed in Section 9.3.1.1.1;

4. <u>data item term 2</u> is the name of the data item whose value constrains the cardinality of the data item signified by <u>data item term 1</u>;

5. <qualifying clause> is required if and only if it is necessary to relate <u>data item term 2</u> back to a term in <transaction signifier>; options for <qualifying clause> are listed in subtemplate S14 in Section 9.1.2.10;

6. '{if|unless} <conditional clause>' (or a qualifying clause in <transaction signifier>) is only required if not all instances of the transaction are subject to the rule; options for <conditional clause> are listed in subtemplate S13 in Section 9.1.2.9.

The following fact types should be present in the fact model (either explicitly stated, or derived as described in Section 6.3.3 in Chapter 6):

1. if <transaction signifier> includes a term rather than a list of terms, then:
   a. if <u>subform term</u> is not included, a fact type of the form
   '<u>transaction term</u> *specifies* <u>data item term 1</u>', or
   '<u>transaction term</u> *specifies* <u>data type</u> *as* <u>data item term 1</u>'
   where <u>transaction term</u> signifies the transaction: for example, F248;
   b. if <u>subform term</u> is included, a fact type of the form
   '<u>transaction term</u> *specifies* <u>data item term 1</u>
      {*in*|*for*} <u>subform term</u>', or
   '<u>transaction term</u> *specifies* <u>data type</u> *as* <u>data item term 1</u>
      {*in*|*for*} <u>subform term</u>',
   where <u>transaction term</u> signifies the transaction;

2. at least one fact type for each qualifying clause (if any), including any within the transaction signifier, as described in Section 7.4.1 in Chapter 7: for example, F249 and F250;

3. at least one fact type for the conditional clause (if any), as also described in Section 7.4.1.

F248. <u>flight</u> *is specified in* <u>round-trip special booking</u>
F249. <u>minimum number of flights</u> *is defined for* <u>special offer code</u>
F250. <u>special offer code</u> *is specified in* <u>round-trip special booking</u>

9.3.2 Data content rules

A ***data content rule*** places a restriction on the values contained in a data item or set of data items (rather than whether or not they must be present and how many there may or must be).

9.3.2.1 Value set rules

A ***value set rule*** requires that the content of a data item (or combination of data items) be or not be a member of a particular set of values (or combinations of values). There are two subcategories of value set rule, each with its own template:

1. those constraining a single data item, discussed in Section 9.3.2.1.1;
2. those constraining a combination of data items, discussed in Section 9.3.2.1.2.

9.3.2.1.1 Value set rules constraining single data items

Examples of value set rules constraining a single data item are as follows:

R355. The <u>frequent flier membership number</u>
      specified for each <u>passenger</u>
      in each <u>flight booking confirmation</u>
   must *be* one of the <u>frequent flier membership numbers</u>
      recognized by the <u>airline</u>
      with which that <u>flight booking confirmation</u> *is made.*

R356. The <u>departure date</u>
      specified in each <u>award flight booking request</u>
   must *be* other than one of the <u>award flight unavailability dates</u>
      nominated by the <u>airline</u>
      to which that <u>award flight booking request</u> *is made.*

Rule statements for this type of rule can be generated from the following template:

T27. {The|Each} <<u>data item term</u>> {(if any)|}
      specified {{*in*|*for*} {the|each} <<u>subform term</u>> {(if any)|}|}
      in each <transaction signifier>
   must *be*
      {{other than|} one of the <<u>term</u>> <qualifying clause>|[<<u>literal</u>>, or]}
      {{if|unless} <conditional clause>|}.

This template has the following important options and placeholders:

1. <<u>data item term</u>> is the name of the data item whose values are constrained;
2. 'Each' is required if that data item can appear more than once in an instance of the transaction or subform, whereas 'The' is required if that data item can appear only once in an instance of the transaction or subform;
3. '(if any)' is required if and only if the data item is optional;
4. '{*in*|*for*} {the|each} <<u>subform term</u>> {(if any)|}':
  a. this phrase is required if the data item signified by <<u>data item term</u>> is contained in a complex data item or subform (as discussed in Section 7.2.3.2.2 in Chapter 7);
  b. 'each' is required if the complex data item or subform can appear more than once in an instance of the transaction, whereas 'the' is required if the complex data item or subform can appear only once in an instance of the transaction (see examples in Section 7.2.4.1);
  c. <<u>subform term</u>> is the name of the complex data item or subform;
  d. '(if any)' is required if and only if the complex data item or subform may be omitted from an instance of the transaction (again see examples in Section 7.2.4.1);
5. <transaction signifier> is the term used for the transaction (paper or electronic form or message) or persistent data record in which a data item is required; options for <transaction signifier> are listed in subtemplate S8 in Section 9.1.2.4 and discussed in Section 9.3.1.1.1;
6. if used, <<u>term</u>> must be the name of the data item with which values of the constrained data item are to be compared, in which case <qualifying clause> is required to relate <<u>term</u>> back to a term in <transaction signifier>; options for <qualifying clause> are listed in subtemplate S14 in Section 9.1.2.10;

7. as an alternative to <u>\<term\></u>, '[\<<u>literal</u>\>, or]' is a list of the literal values with which the constrained data item is to be compared, in which the last two are separated with 'or' (or a comma and 'or' if adhering to U.S. punctuation standards) and each other pair of values is separated with a comma;

8. '{if|unless} \<conditional clause\>' (or a qualifying clause in \<transaction signifier\>) is only required if not all instances of the transaction are subject to the rule; options for \<conditional clause\> are listed in subtemplate S13 in Section 9.1.2.9.

The following fact types should be present in the fact model (either explicitly stated, or derived as described in Section 6.3.3 in Chapter 6):

1. if \<transaction signifier\> includes a term rather than a list of terms, then
   a. if \<<u>subform term</u>\> is included, a fact type of the form
      '\<<u>transaction term</u>\> *specifies* \<<u>data item term</u>\>
         {*in*|*for*} \<<u>subform term</u>\>', or
      '\<<u>transaction term</u>\> *specifies* \<<u>data type</u>\> *as* \<<u>data item term</u>\>
         {*in*|*for*} \<<u>subform term</u>\>',
      where \<<u>transaction term</u>\> signifies the transaction: for example, F251 for R355;
   b. if \<<u>subform term</u>\> is not included, a fact type of the form
      '\<<u>transaction term</u>\> *specifies* \<<u>data item term</u>\>', or
      '\<<u>transaction term</u>\> *specifies* \<<u>data type</u>\> *as* \<<u>data item term</u>\>',
      where \<<u>transaction term</u>\> signifies the transaction: for example, F254 for R356;

2. at least one fact type for each qualifying clause (if any), including any within the transaction signifier, as described in Section 7.4.1 in Chapter 7: for example, F252, F253 for R355; F255, F256 for R356;

3. at least one fact type for the conditional clause (if any), as also described in Section 7.4.1.

F251. <u>flight booking confirmation</u> *specifies* <u>frequent flier membership number</u> *for* <u>passenger</u>
F252. <u>frequent flier membership number</u> *is recognized by* <u>airline</u>
F253. <u>flight booking confirmation</u> *is made with* <u>airline</u>
F254. <u>award flight booking request</u> *specifies* <u>departure date</u>
F255. <u>award flight unavailability date</u> *is nominated by* <u>airline</u>
F256. <u>award flight booking request</u> *is made to* <u>airline</u>

9.3.2.1.2 Value set rules constraining combinations of data items
An example of a value set rule constraining a combination of data items is as follows:

R357. The combination of <u>reward program</u> and <u>reward membership number</u>
         specified in each <u>online order</u>
      must *be* one of the combinations of
         <u>reward program</u> and <u>reward membership number</u>
         recognized by the <u>vendor</u>
         with which that <u>online order</u> *is placed*.

Rule statements for this type of rule can be generated from the following template:

T28. {The|Each} combination of [<u>data item term 1</u>>, and] {(if any)|}
     specified {{*in*| *for*} {the|each} <<u>subform term</u>> {(if any)|}|}
     in each <transaction signifier>
    must *be* one of the combinations of [<<u>data item term 2</u>>, and]
     {<qualifying clause>|}
    {{if|unless} <conditional clause>|}.

This template has the following important options and placeholders:

1. '[<<u>data item term 1</u>>, and]' is a list of the data items whose values are constrained, in which the last two are separated with 'or' (or a comma and 'or' if adhering to U.S. punctuation standards) and each other pair of data item names is separated with a comma;
2. 'Each' is required if the combination of data items can appear more than once in an instance of the transaction or subform, whereas 'The' is required if the combination of data items can appear only once in an instance of the transaction or subform;
3. '(if any)' is required if and only if the data items are optional;
4. '{*in*|*for*} {the|each} <<u>subform term</u>> {(if any)|}':
   a. this phrase is required if the data item signified by <<u>data item term</u>> is contained in a complex data item or subform (as discussed in Section 7.2.3.2.2 in Chapter 7);
   b. 'each' is required if the complex data item or subform can appear more than once in an instance of the transaction, whereas 'the' is required if the complex data item or subform can appear only once in an instance of the transaction (see examples in Section 7.2.4.1);
   c. <<u>subform term</u>> is the name of the complex data item or subform;
   d. '(if any)' is required if and only if the complex data item or subform may be omitted from an instance of the transaction (again see examples in Section 7.2.4.1);
5. <transaction signifier> is the term used for the transaction (paper or electronic form or message) or persistent data record in which a data item is required; options for <transaction signifier> are listed in subtemplate S8 in Section 9.1.2.4 and discussed in Section 9.3.1.1.1;
6. '[<<u>data item term 2</u>>, and]' is a list of the data items with which values of the constrained combination of data items are to be compared, in which the last two are separated with 'or' (or a comma and 'or' if adhering to U.S. punctuation standards) and each other pair of data item names is separated with a comma;
7. <qualifying clause> is required to relate the listed terms back to a term in <transaction signifier>; options for <qualifying clause> are listed in subtemplate S14 in Section 9.1.2.10;
8. '{if|unless} <conditional clause>' (or a qualifying clause in <transaction signifier>) is only required if not all instances of the transaction are subject to the rule; options for <conditional clause> are listed in subtemplate S13 in Section 9.1.2.9.

The following fact types should be present in the fact model (either explicitly stated, or derived as described in Section 6.3.3 in Chapter 6):

1. if <transaction signifier> includes a term rather than a list of terms, then
   a. if <<u>subform term</u>> is not included, a fact type of the form
   '<<u>transaction term</u>> *specifies* <<u>data item term</u>>', or
   '<<u>transaction term</u>> *specifies* <<u>data type</u>> *as* <<u>data item term</u>>',
   for each data item term in the list of data item terms, where <<u>transaction term</u>> signifies the transaction: for example, F257 and F258;

b. if <subform term> is included, a fact type of the form
'<transaction term> *specifies* <data item term>
{*in*|*for*} <subform term>', or
'<transaction term> *specifies* <data type> *as* <data item term>
{*in*|*for*} <subform term>',
for each data item term in the list of data item terms, where <transaction term> signifies the transaction;
2. at least one fact type for each qualifying clause (if any), including any within the transaction signifier, as described in Section 7.4.1 in Chapter 7: for example, F259, F260, and F261;
3. at least one fact type for the conditional clause (if any), as also described in Section 7.4.1.

F257. online order *specifies* reward program
F258. online order *specifies* reward membership number
F259. reward program *is recognized by* vendor
F260. reward membership number *is recognized by* vendor
F261. online order *is placed with* vendor

9.3.2.2 Range rules

A *range rule* requires that the content of a data item be a value within a particular inclusive or exclusive single- or double-bounded range: for example,

R358. The order quantity
specified for each product
in each online order
must *be at least* 1.
R359. The return date (if any)
specified in each flight booking request
must *be no earlier than* the departure date
specified in that flight booking request.
R360. The departure time
of the return flight (if any)
specified in each flight booking confirmation
must *be no earlier than* 1 h
after the arrival time
of the outgoing flight
specified in that flight booking confirmation.

Rule statements for this type of rule can be generated from the following template:

T29. {The|Each} <data item term> {(if any)|}
specified {{*in*| *for*} {the|each} <subform term> {(if any)|}|}
in each <transaction signifier>
must *be* <inequality operator> <object> {and <inequality operator> <object>|}
{{if|unless} <conditional clause>|}.

There are various inequality operators, some appropriate to temporal comparisons and others to non-temporal comparisons. Options for <inequality operator> are listed in subtemplate S6 in Section 9.1.2.3, reproduced here. Options for <object> are listed in subtemplate S11 in Section 9.1.2.7.

<inequality operator>::=
{{*no*|} {*more*| *less*| *later*| *earlier*} *than*|
at {*least*| *most*} <u>literal</u> {*more*| *later*} *than*|
{*no*|} {*later*| *earlier*} *than* <u>literal</u> {*after*| *before*}}

The same conditions apply to the use of each other option or placeholder as in template T27 described in Section 9.3.2.1.1.

The same conditions also apply as in template T27 regarding the fact types that should be present in the fact model. In addition, the comparison should be supported by a fact type. Thus the following fact types are required to support the example rule statements at the start of this section:

F262. <u>online order</u> *specifies* <u>quantity</u> *as* <u>order quantity</u> *for* <u>product</u>
F263. <u>quantity</u> *is at least* <u>quantity</u>
F264. <u>flight booking request</u> *specifies* <u>date</u> *as* <u>return date</u>
F265. <u>flight booking request</u> *specifies* <u>date</u> *as* <u>departure date</u>
F266. <u>date</u> *is no earlier than* <u>date</u>
F267. <u>flight booking confirmation</u> *specifies* <u>time</u> *as* <u>departure time</u> *of* <u>return flight</u>
F268. <u>flight booking confirmation</u> *specifies* <u>time</u> *as* <u>arrival time</u> *of* <u>outgoing flight</u>
F269. <u>time</u> *is no earlier than* <u>time</u>

9.3.2.3 Equality rules

A *equality rule* requires that the content of a data item be the same as or not the same as that of some other data item: for example,

R361. The <u>origin city</u>
　　　　of the <u>outgoing flight</u>
　　　　specified in a <u>flight booking confirmation</u>
　　　must *be the same as* the <u>origin city</u>
　　　　specified in the <u>flight booking request</u>
　　　　that *gives rise to* that <u>flight booking confirmation</u>.
R362. The <u>new full name</u>
　　　　specified in each <u>change of name request</u>
　　　must *be different from* the <u>previous full name</u>
　　　　specified in that <u>change of name request</u>.
R363. The <u>payment amount</u>
　　　　specified in a <u>flight booking payment confirmation</u>
　　　must *be equal to* the <u>total amount payable</u>
　　　　specified in the <u>flight booking confirmation response</u>
　　　　that *gives rise to* that <u>flight booking payment confirmation</u>.
R364. The <u>registry instrument count</u>
　　　　specified in each <u>lodgment information report</u>
　　　must *be equal to* the number of <u>registry instruments</u>
　　　　contained in the <u>lodgment case</u>
　　　　that *contains* that <u>lodgment information report</u>.

Rule statements for this type of rule can be generated from the following template:

T30. {The|Each} <u><data item term></u> {(if any)|}
      specified {{*in*|*for*} {the|each} <u><subform term></u> {(if any)|}|}
      in each <transaction signifier>
      must *be* <*equality operator*> <object>
      {{*if*|*unless*} <conditional clause>|}.

There are various equality operators, some appropriate to non-quantitative comparisons and others to quantitative comparisons. Options for <*equality operator*> are listed in subtemplate S7 in Section 9.1.2.3, reproduced here. Options for <object> are listed in subtemplate S11 in Section 9.1.2.7.

    <*equality operator*>::=
    {*the same as*|*different from*|*equal to*|*unequal to*}

The same conditions apply to the use of each other option or placeholder as in template T27 described in Section 9.3.2.1.1.

    The same conditions also apply as in template T27 regarding the fact types that should be present in the fact model. In addition, the comparison should be supported by a fact type. Thus the following fact types are required to support the first three example rule statements at the start of this section:

F270. flight booking confirmation *specifies* city *as* origin city *of* outgoing flight
F271. flight booking request *specifies* city *as* origin city
F272. city *is the same as* city
F273. flight booking request *gives rise to* flight booking confirmation
F274. change of name request *specifies* full name *as* new full name
F275. change of name request *specifies* full name *as* previous full name
F276. full name *is different from* full name
F277. flight booking payment confirmation *specifies* amount *as* payment amount
F278. flight booking confirmation response *specifies* amount *as* total amount payable
F279. amount *is equal to* amount
F280. flight booking confirmation response *gives rise to* flight booking payment confirmation

9.3.2.4 Uniqueness constraints

A **uniqueness constraint** requires that the content of a data item (or combination or set[3] of data items) be different from that of other data items (or combinations or sets of data items) of the same kind in the same or other records or transactions. There are three subcategories of uniqueness constraint, each with its own template:

1. those constraining a single data item, described in Section 9.3.2.4.1;
2. those constraining a combination of data items, described in Section 9.3.2.4.2;
3. those constraining a set of data items, described in Section 9.3.2.4.3.

---

[3]The difference between a combination and a set of data items is discussed in Section 7.2.3.2.2 in Chapter 7.

9.3.2.4.1 Uniqueness constraints constraining single data items

Examples of uniqueness constraints constraining single data items are as follows:

R365. The <u>customer number</u>
      allocated to each <u>customer</u>
  must *be different from* the <u>customer number</u>
      allocated to any other <u>customer</u>.

R366. Each <u>allowance code</u>
      specified in each <u>employee payroll record</u>
  must *be different from* any other <u>allowance code</u>
      specified in that <u>employee payroll record</u>.

R367. The <u>seat number</u>
      specified for each <u>passenger</u>
      in each <u>advance seat allocation</u>
  must *be different from* the <u>seat number</u>
      specified for any other <u>passenger</u>
      in that <u>advance seat allocation</u>

Rule statements for this type of rule can be generated from the following template:

T31. {The|Each} <<u>data item term 1</u>> {(if any)|}
    <*verb part*> {the <<u>subform term 1</u>> {(if any)|}
    in|} each <transaction signifier 1>
    {<qualifying clause 1>|}
  must *be different from* the <<u>data item term 1</u>>
    <*verb part*> {{the|any other} <<u>subform term 1</u>> {(if any)|}
    in|} {that|any other} <transaction signifier 1>
    {<qualifying clause 2>|}
  {{if|unless} <conditional clause>|}.

Much the same conditions apply to the use of each option or placeholder as in template T27 described in Section 9.3.2.1.1. In addition

1. the same term must be substituted in place of each <<u>data item term 1</u>>;
2. 'the <<u>subform term 1</u>> {(if any)|} *in*' and
  '{the|any other} <<u>subform term 1</u>> {(if any)|}*in*'
  are the phrases required if the data item signified by <<u>data item term</u>> is contained in a complex data item or subform (as discussed in Section 7.2.3.2.2 in Chapter 7);
3. the same term must be substituted in place of each <<u>subform term 1</u>> (if used);
4. the same term(s) and qualifying clause(s) (if any) must be substituted in place of each <transaction signifier 1>;
5. if <qualifying clause 1> is used, <qualifying clause 2> should also be used and will generally be the same as <qualifying clause 1>;
6. the words 'any other' must appear either before the second appearance of <<u>subform term 1</u>> or the second appearance of <transaction signifier 1>.

The same conditions also apply as in template T27 regarding the fact types that should be present in the fact model. In addition, the difference between instances of the subject data item should be supported by a fact type. Thus the following fact types are required to support the example rule statements at the start of this section:

F281. customer number *is allocated to* customer
F282. customer number *is different from* customer number
F283. allowance code *is specified in* employee payroll record
F284. allowance code *is different from* allowance code
F285. seat number *is specified for* passenger *in* advance seat allocation
F286. seat number *is different from* seat number

9.3.2.4.2 Uniqueness constraints constraining combinations of data items

An example of a uniqueness constraint constraining a combination of data items is as follows:

R368. The combination of employee ID and project code
    specified in each employee assignment
    must *be different from* the combination of employee ID and project code
    specified in any other employee assignment.

Rule statements for this type of rule can be generated from the following template:

T32. {The|Each} combination of [<data item term 1>, and] {(if any)|}
    <verb part> {the <subform term 1> {(if any)|}
    in|} each <transaction signifier 1>
    {<qualifying clause 1>|}
    must *be different from* the combination of [<data item term 1>, and]
    <verb part> {{the|any other} <subform term 1> {(if any)|}
    in|} {that|any other} <transaction signifier 1>
    {<qualifying clause 2>|}
    {{if|unless} <conditional clause>|}.

Much the same conditions apply to the use of each option or placeholder as in template T31 described in Section 9.3.2.4.1. In addition, both lists of terms ('[<data item term 1>, and]') should in general be the same.

The same conditions apply as in template T28 (described in Section 9.3.2.1.2) regarding the fact types that should be present in the fact model. Thus the following fact types are required to support the example rule statement at the start of this section:

F287. employee assignment *specifies* employee ID
F288. employee assignment *specifies* project code

9.3.2.4.3 Uniqueness constraints constraining sets of data items

An example of a uniqueness constraint constraining a set of data items is as follows:

R369. The set of full names
    specified for each share received
    in each real property transfer instrument
    must *be different from* the set of full names
    specified for any other share received
    in that real property transfer instrument.

Rule statements for this type of rule can be generated from the following template:

T33. {The|Each} set of <u><data item term 1></u> {(if any)|}
       <verb part> {the <u><subform term 1></u> {(if any)|}
       in|} each <transaction signifier 1>
       {<qualifying clause 1>|}
     must *be different from* the set of <u><data item term 1></u>
       <verb part> {{the|any other} <u><subform term 1></u> {(if any)|}
       in|} {that|any other} <transaction signifier 1>
       {<qualifying clause 2>|}
     {{if|unless} <conditional clause>|}.

The same conditions apply to the use of each option or placeholder as in template T31 described in Section 9.3.2.4.1.

    The same conditions apply as in template T27 (described in Section 9.3.2.1.1) regarding the fact types that should be present in the fact model. Thus the following fact type is required to support the example rule statement at the start of this section:

F289. <u>real property transfer instrument</u> *specifies* <u>full name</u> *for* <u>share received</u>

9.3.2.5 Data consistency rules

A *data consistency rule* requires the content of multiple data items to be consistent with each other, other than as provided for by a value set rule, range rule, or equality rule. There are three subcategories of data consistency rule, each with its own template:

1. those constraining a combination of data items, described in Section 9.3.2.5.1;
2. those constraining a set function on a data item, described in Section 9.3.2.5.2;
3. those constraining a set of data items, described in Section 9.3.2.5.3.

9.3.2.5.1 Data consistency rules constraining a combination of data items

An example of a data consistency rule constraining a combination of data items is as follows:

R370. The combination of <u>start date</u> and <u>end date</u>
      specified in each <u>project assignment</u>
     must *be* such that the <u>end date</u> *is no earlier than* the <u>start date</u>.

Rule statements for this type of rule can be generated from the following template:

T34. {The|Each} combination of [<u><data item term></u>, and] {(if any)|}
      specified {{*in*|*for*} {the|each} <u><subform term></u> {(if any)|}|}
      in each <transaction signifier>
      {<qualifying clause>|}
     must *be such that* <conditional clause 1>
     {{if|unless} <conditional clause 2>|}.

Much the same conditions apply to the use of each option or placeholder as in template T28 described in Section 9.3.2.1.2.

The same conditions also apply as in template T28 regarding the fact types that should be present in the fact model. Thus the following fact types are required to support the example rule statements at the start of this section:

F290. project assignment *specifies* date *as* start date
F291. project assignment *specifies* date *as* end date
F292. date *is no earlier than* date

9.3.2.5.2 Data consistency rules constraining a set function

An example of a data consistency rule constraining a set function on a data item is as follows:

R371. The sum of the shares transferred
specified in each real property transfer instrument
must *be no more than* 100%.

Rule statements for this type of rule can be generated from the following template:

T35. The <set function> of {the|} <data item term> {(if any)|}
specified {{in| for} {the|each} <subform term> {(if any)|}|}
in each <transaction signifier>
{<qualifying clause>|}
must *be* {<inequality operator>|<equality operator>} <object>
{{if|unless} <conditional clause>|}.

There are various set functions. Options for <set function> (defined in subtemplate S5 in Section 9.1.2.2) are the following:

{number|sum|total|maximum|minimum|average|mean|median|
latest|earliest}

There are also various comparison operators, both inequality operators and equality operators. Options for <inequality operator> (defined in subtemplate S6 in Section 9.1.2.3) are

{{no|} {more|less|later|earlier} than|
at {least|most} <literal> {more|later} than|
{no|} {later|earlier} than <literal> {after|before}}

There are also various equality operators, some appropriate to non-quantitative comparisons and others to quantitative comparisons: only quantitative comparisons are relevant for this type of rule statement. Options for <equality operator> are defined in subtemplate S7 in Section 9.1.2.3, of which the quantitative options are the following:

{equal to| unequal to}

Options for <object> are listed in subtemplate S11 in Section 9.1.2.7.

The same conditions apply to the use of each other option and placeholder as in template T27 described in Section 9.3.2.1.1.

The same conditions also apply as in template T27 regarding the fact types that should be present in the fact model. In addition, the comparison should be supported by a fact type. Thus the following fact types are required to support the example rule statements at the start of this section:

F293. <u>real property transfer instrument</u> *specifies* <u>share transferred</u>
F294. <u>quantity</u> *is no more than* <u>quantity</u>

9.3.2.5.3 Data consistency rules constraining a set

An example of a data consistency rule constraining a set of data items is as follows:

R372. The set of <u>passengers</u>
      specified for each <u>flight</u>
      in each <u>flight booking confirmation</u>
    must *be the same as* the set of <u>passengers</u>
      specified for each other <u>flight</u>
      in that <u>flight booking confirmation</u>.

Rule statements for this type of rule can be generated from the following template:

T36. {The|Each} set of <<u>data item term</u>> {(if any)|}
    specified {{*in*|*for*} {the|each} <<u>subform term</u>> {(if any)|}|}
    in each <transaction signifier>
    {<qualifying clause 1>|}
    must {*be* {*the same as*|*different from*}|*include*} the set of <<u>term</u>>
    {<qualifying clause 2>|}
    {{*if*|*unless*} <conditional clause>|}.

Much the same conditions apply to the use of each option and placeholder as in template T35 described in Section 9.3.2.5.2.

The following fact types should be present in the fact model (either explicitly stated, or derived as described in Section 6.3.3 in Chapter 6):

1. if <<u>subform term</u>> is not included, a fact type of the form
   '<transaction signifier> *specifies* <<u>data item term</u>>', or
   '<transaction signifier> *specifies* <<u>data type</u>> *as* <<u>data item term</u>>';
2. if <<u>subform term</u>> is included, a fact type of the form
   '<transaction signifier>*specifies* <<u>data item term</u>>
       {*in*|*for*} <<u>subform term</u>>', or
   '<transaction signifier> *specifies* <<u>data type</u>> *as* <<u>data item term</u>>
       {*in*|*for*} <<u>subform term</u>>': for example, F295;
3. at least one fact type for each qualifying clause (if any), including any within the transaction signifier, as described in Section 7.4.1 in Chapter 7;
4. at least one fact type for the conditional clause (if any), as also described in Section 7.4.1.

F295. <u>flight booking confirmation</u> *specifies* <u>passenger</u> *for* <u>flight</u>

9.3.2.6 Temporal data constraints

A **temporal data constraint** constrains one or more **temporal data** items (data items that represent time points or time periods).

There are six subcategories of temporal data rule, each with its own template(s):

1. **simple temporal data constraints**, which require that particular dates or times fall within a certain temporal range: these are simply range rules, as described in Section 9.3.2.6.1;
2. **temporal data non-overlap constraints**, which require that the time periods specified in sets of records do not overlap each other, described in Section 9.3.2.6.2;
3. **temporal data completeness constraints**, which require that the time periods specified in a set of records are contiguous and between them completely span some other time period, described in Section 9.3.2.6.3;
4. **temporal data inclusion constraints**, which require that the time periods specified in a set of records do not fall outside some other time period, described in Section 9.3.2.6.4;
5. **temporal single record constraints**, which require that a temporal state of affairs be recorded using a single record rather than multiple records: these are simply uniqueness constraints, as described in Section 9.3.2.6.5;
6. **day type constraints**, which restrict a date to one or more days of the week or a particular type of day such as a working day (typically but not necessarily any day other than a Saturday, Sunday, or public holiday), described in Section 9.3.2.6.6.

9.3.2.6.1 Simple temporal data constraints

A **simple temporal data constraint** requires that a particular date or time fall within a certain temporal range: for example,

R373. The <u>departure time</u> *of* the <u>outgoing flight</u>
　　　　　specified in each <u>flight booking confirmation</u>
　　　　　that *is made online*
　　　　must *be no earlier than* <u>3 h</u>
　　　　　after the <u>booking confirmation time</u>
　　　　　of that <u>flight booking confirmation</u>.

Such a rule statement is simply a range rule using a temporal inequality operator, as described in Section 9.3.2.2.

9.3.2.6.2 Temporal data non-overlap constraints

A **temporal data non-overlap constraint** requires that the time periods specified in a set of records do not overlap each other: for example,

R374. The <u>time period</u>
　　　　　specified in each <u>employee grade record</u>
　　　　must not *overlap* the <u>time period</u>
　　　　　specified in any other <u>employee grade record</u>
　　　　　for the same <u>employee</u>.

Rule statements for this type of rule can be generated from the following template:

T37. {The|Each} <u><time</u> period <u>term 1</u>> {(if any)|}
    specified {{*in*|*for*} {the|each} <<u>subform term 1</u>> {(if any)|}|}
    in each <transaction signifier 1>
    {<qualifying clause 1>|}
    must not *overlap* the <<u>time period term 1</u>>
    specified {{*in*|*for*} {the|each} <<u>subform term 1</u>> {(if any)|}|}
    in any other <transaction signifier 1>
    {<qualifying clause 2>|}
    {{*if*|*unless*} <conditional clause>|}.

Much the same conditions apply to the use of each option or placeholder as in template T27 described in Section 9.3.2.1.1. In addition

1. the same term must be substituted in place of each <time period term 1>;
2. the same term(s) and qualifying clause(s) (if any) must be substituted in place of each <transaction signifier 1>;
3. if <qualifying clause 1> is used, <qualifying clause 2> should also be used and will generally be the same as <qualifying clause 1>.

The following fact types should be present in the fact model (either explicitly stated, or derived as described in Section 6.3.3 in Chapter 6):

1. if <subform term> is not included, a fact type of the form
   '<transaction signifier> *specifies* <time period term 1>': for example, F296;
2. if <subform term> is included, a fact type of the form
   '<transaction signifier> *specifies* <time period term 1>
        {*in*|*for*} <subform term>';
3. at least one fact type for each qualifying clause (if any), including any within either transaction signifier, as described in Section 7.4.1 in Chapter 7;
4. at least one fact type for the conditional clause (if any), as also described in Section 7.4.1.

F296. <u>employee grade record</u> *specifies* <u>time period</u>

9.3.2.6.3 Temporal data completeness constraints
A ***temporal data completeness constraint*** requires that the time periods specified in a set of records be contiguous and between them completely span some other time period: for example,

R375. Each <u>day</u>
        within the <u>employment period</u>
        specified in each <u>employee record</u>
    must *be within* the <u>time period</u>
        specified in exactly one <u>employee grade record</u>
        for the same <u>employee</u>.

Rule statements for this type of rule can be generated from the following template:

T38. Each <time period term 1>
       within the <time period term 2> {(if any)|}
       specified {{*in*| *for*} {the|each} <subform term 1> {(if any)|}|}
       in each <transaction signifier 1>
       {<qualifying clause 1>|}
    must *be within* the <time period term 3>
       specified {{*in*| *for*} {the|each} <subform term 2> {(if any)|}|}
       in <cardinality> <transaction signifier 2>
       {<qualifying clause 2>|}
    {{*if*|*unless*} <conditional clause>|}.

Much the same conditions apply to the use of each option or placeholder as in template T27 described in Section 9.3.2.1.1. In addition note that <u>day</u> is the most common term to be substituted in place of <time period term 1> although any term signifying a time period may be used as required.

    The following fact types should be present in the fact model (either explicitly stated, or derived as described in Section 6.3.3 in Chapter 6):

1. fact types of the form
   '<time period term 1> *is within* <time period term 2>', and
   '<time period term 1> *is within* <time period term 3>': for example, F297 and F299;
2. if <subform term 1> is not included, a fact type of the form
   '<transaction signifier 1> *specifies* <time period term 2>': for example, F298;
3. if <subform term 1> is included, a fact type of the form
   '<transaction signifier 1> *specifies* <time period term 2>
         {*in*|*for*} <subform term 1>';
4. if <subform term 2> is not included, a fact type of the form
   '<transaction signifier 2> *specifies* <time period term 3>': for example, F300;
5. if <subform term 2> is included, a fact type of the form
   '<transaction signifier 2> *specifies* <time period term 3>
         {*in*|*for*} <subform term 2>';
6. at least one fact type for each qualifying clause (if any), including any within either transaction signifier, as described in Section 7.4.1 in Chapter 7: for example, F301;
7. at least one fact type for the conditional clause (if any), as also described in Section 7.4.1.

F297. day *is within* employment period
F298. employee record *specifies* employment period
F299. day *is within* time period
F300. employee grade record *specifies* time period
F301. employee grade record *is for* employee

9.3.2.6.4 Temporal data inclusion constraints

A *temporal data inclusion constraint* requires that the time periods specified in a set of records do not fall outside some other time period: for example,

R376. Each <u>date</u>
        within the <u>time period</u>
        specified in each <u>employee grade record</u>
     must *be within* the <u>time period</u>
        specified in the <u>employment record</u>
        for the same <u>employee</u>.

Rule statements for this type of rule can be generated from template T38 described in the previous section.

9.3.2.6.5 Temporal single record constraints

A *temporal single record constraint* requires that a temporal state of affairs be recorded using a single record rather than multiple records: for example,

R377. Each <u>leave type</u>
        specified in an <u>employee leave record</u>
     must *be different from* the <u>leave type</u>
        specified in the latest of the earlier <u>employee leave records</u>
        for the same <u>employee</u>.

Rule statements for this type of rule can be generated from the following templates (T39 where a single data item is involved, T40 where a combination of data items is involved):

T39. {The|Each} <<u>data item term 1</u>> {(if any)|}
        specified {{*in*| *for*} {the|each} <<u>subform term 1</u>> {(if any)|}|}
        in each <transaction signifier 1>
     must *be different from* the <<u>data item term 1</u>>
        specified {{*in*| *for*} {the|each} <<u>subform term 1</u>> {(if any)|}|}
        in the latest of the earlier <transaction signifier 1>
     {{*if*|*unless*} <conditional clause>|}.
T40. {The|Each} combination of [<<u>data item term 1</u>>, and] {(if any)|}
        specified {{*in*| *for*} {the|each} <<u>subform term 1</u>> {(if any)|}|}
        in each <transaction signifier 1>
     must *be different from* the combination of [<<u>data item term 1</u>>, and]
        specified {{*in*| *for*} {the|each} <<u>subform term 1</u>> {(if any)|}|}
        in the latest of the earlier <transaction signifier 1>
     {{*if*|*unless*} <conditional clause>|}.

If using template T39, much the same conditions apply to the use of each option or placeholder as in template T27 described in Section 9.3.2.1.1. If using template T40, much the same conditions apply to the use of each option or placeholder as in template T28 described in Section 9.3.2.1.2.

The same conditions also apply as in those templates regarding the fact types that should be present in the fact model. Thus the following fact types are required to support the example rule statement at the start of this section:

F302. leave type *is specified in* employee leave record
F303. employee leave record *is for* employee

9.3.2.6.6 Day type constraints

A ***day type constraint*** restricts a date to one or more days of the week or a particular type of day such as a working day (typically but not necessarily any day other than a Saturday, Sunday, or public holiday): for example,

R378. Each instalment due date
       specified in each property tax notice[4]
    must *be* a working day.

Rule statements for this type of rule can be generated from the following template:

T41. {The|Each} <data item term> {(if any)|}
      specified {{*in*|*for*} {the|each} <subform term> {(if any)|}|}
      in each <transaction signifier>
    must *be* a {<term>|<literal 1>|[<literal 2>, or]}
    {{if|unless} <conditional clause>|}.

Much the same conditions apply to the use of each option or placeholder as in template T27 described in Section 9.3.2.1.1. Note that, if only one day of the week is permitted, use <literal 1>, otherwise list the days of the week separated by commas (with the last two day names in the list separated by 'or' or, if adhering to U.S. punctuation conventions, a comma and 'or');

The same conditions also apply as in template T27 regarding the fact types that should be present in the fact model. Thus the following fact type is required to support the example rule statement at the start of this section:

F304. instalment due date *is specified in* property tax notice

9.3.2.7 Spatial data constraints

A ***spatial data constraint*** prescribes or prohibits relationships between spatial properties (points, line segments or polygons) specified in a record or set of records: for example,

R379. The polygon
      that *constitutes* each individual parcel
      in a real estate subdivision
    must *be within* the polygon
      that *constitutes* the real estate subdivision.

---

[4]Council Tax in the United Kingdom, "Rates" in Australia.

Rule statements for this type of rule can be generated from the following template:

T42. {The|Each|A|An} <u><spatial term 1></u> {(if any)|}
     <qualifying clause 1>
    must {not|} <*spatial operator*> the <u><spatial term 2></u>
     <qualifying clause 2>
    {{if|unless} <conditional clause>|}.

This template has the following important options and placeholders:

1. <u><spatial term 1></u> is the name of the spatial data item whose values are constrained;
2. if 'must' is not followed by 'not', 'Each' is required if that data item can appear more than once in an instance of the transaction or subform, whereas 'The' is required if that data item can appear only once in an instance of the transaction or subform;
3. if 'must' is followed by 'not', 'A' or 'An' is required;
4. '(if any)' is required if and only if the data item is optional;
5. the <*spatial operator*> placeholder can be replaced by anything defined in the following subtemplate:

S20. <*spatial operator*>::=
    {*overlap*| *be within*| *enclose*| *span*| *intersect*| *meet*| *be on*}

Each qualifying clause and the conditional clause (if any) should be supported by at least one fact type in the fact model as described in Section 7.4.1 in Chapter 7. In addition, the spatial operator should be supported by a fact type. Thus the following fact types are required to support the example rule statement at the start of this section:

F305. <u>polygon</u> *constitutes* <u>individual parcel</u>
F306. <u>individual parcel</u> *is in* <u>real estate subdivision</u>
F307. <u>polygon</u> *is within* <u>polygon</u>
F308. <u>polygon</u> *constitutes* <u>real estate subdivision</u>

9.3.2.8 Data item format rules

A *data item format rule* specifies the required format of a data item: for example,

R380. The <u>contact phone number</u>
    specified in each <u>online order</u>
  must *be* a valid <u>phone number</u>.

Rule statements for this type of rule can be generated from the following template:

T43. The <u><data item term></u> {(if any)|}
    specified {{*in*| *for*} {the|each} <u><subform term></u> {(if any)|}|}
    in each <transaction signifier>
  must *be* {*represented using*|} a valid <u><term></u>
  {{if|unless} <conditional clause>|}.

Much the same conditions apply to the use of each option or placeholder as in template T27 described in Section 9.3.2.1.1. In addition

1. *'represented using'* should be included in the rule statement if the data type is one that admits different representations: for example, the same date can be represented as '25/12/2011', '12/25/2011', or '25 December 2011';
2. <u>term</u> must be defined in a **standard format definition** (see Section 9.2.7).

The same conditions also apply as in template T27 regarding the fact types that should be present in the fact model. Thus the following fact type is required to support the example rule statement at the start of this section:

F309. <u>contact phone number</u> *is specified in* <u>online order</u>

9.3.3 Data update rules

A *data update rule* either prohibits update of a data item or places restrictions on the new value of a data item in terms of its existing value.

There are three subcategories of data update rule, each with its own template(s):

1. *data update prohibition rules*, which prohibit update of a particular data item or set of data items, described in Section 9.3.3.1;
2. *state transition constraints*, which limit the changes in a data item to a set of valid transitions, described in Section 9.3.3.2;
3. *monotonic transition constraints*, which require that a numeric value can either only increase or only decrease, described in Section 9.3.3.3.

9.3.3.1 Data update prohibition rules

A *data update prohibition rule* prohibits update of a particular data item or set of data items: for example,

R381. A <u>data item</u>
     in a <u>financial transaction</u>
  must not *be updated.*

In particular, a data update prohibition rule can be used to specify that a recorded relationship is *non-transferable*: for example,

R382. An <u>order</u>
  must not *be transferred*
    from one <u>customer</u> *to* another <u>customer</u>.

Rule statements for rules governing non-transferable relationships can be generated from the following template:

T44. {A|An} <transaction signifier 1>
  must not *be transferred*
    from one <transaction signifier 2> *to* another <transaction signifier 2>
  {{if|unless} <conditional clause>|}.

<transaction signifier 1> is the term used for the transaction (paper or electronic form or message) or persistent data record which is not allowed to be updated while <transaction signifier 2> is the term used for those objects to which <transaction signifier 1> refers; options for <transaction signifier> are listed in subtemplate S8 in Section 9.1.2.4 and discussed in Section 9.3.1.1.1;

There should be a fact type connecting the principal term in each transaction signifier, although the verb phrase in that fact type does not appear in this type of rule statement. Thus the following fact type supports rule statement R382:

F310. order *is raised by* customer

Rule statements for other data update prohibition rules can be generated from the following template:

T45. {The|A|An} <data item term> {(if any)|}
    {{*in*| *for*} {any|the} <subform term> {(if any)|}|}
    {*in*| *of*} a <transaction signifier>
    must not *be updated*
    {{if|unless} <conditional clause>|}.

Much the same conditions apply to the use of each option or placeholder in this template as in template T27 described in Section 9.3.2.1.1. In addition, the term 'data item' can be used in place of the <data item term> placeholder.

The same conditions that apply in template T27 regarding the fact types that should be present in the fact model also apply to this template, except when 'data item' is used in place of the <data item term> placeholder.

9.3.3.2 State transition constraints

A *state transition constraint* limits the changes in a data item to a set of valid transitions: for example,

R383. The status
    of a loan application
    may *be updated to* approved
    only if the status
    of that loan application
    is review complete.

Rule statements for this type of rule can be generated from the following template:

T46. The <data item term> {(if any)|}
    {{*in*| *for*} {any|the} <subform term> {(if any)|}|}
    {*in*| *of*} a <transaction signifier>
    may *be updated to* {<literal 1>|[<literal 2>, or]}
    only if <conditional clause>.

Much the same conditions apply to the use of each option or placeholder as in template T27 described in Section 9.3.2.1.1. In addition, if the rule covers only transitions to a single category, use <literal 1>, otherwise list the categories separated by commas (with the last two categories in the list separated by 'or' or, if adhering to U.S. punctuation conventions, a comma and 'or').

The same conditions also apply as in template T27 regarding the fact types that should be present in the fact model. Thus the following fact type is required to support the example rule statement at the start of this section:

F311. <u>status</u> *is of* <u>loan application</u>

9.3.3.3 Monotonic transition constraints

A ***monotonic transition constraint*** requires that a numeric value either only increase or only decrease: for example,

R384. The <u>hourly pay rate</u>
   of an <u>employee</u>
  must not *be decreased.*

Rule statements for this type of rule can be generated from the following template:

T47. The <<u>data item term</u>> {(if any)|}
  {{*in*| *for*} {any|the} <<u>subform term</u>> {(if any)|}|}
  {*in*|*of*} a <transaction signifier>
  must not *be* {*increased*|*decreased*}
  {{*if*|unless} <conditional clause>|}.

Much the same conditions apply to the use of each option or placeholder as in template T27 described in Section 9.3.2.1.1.

 The same conditions also apply as in template T27 regarding the fact types that should be present in the fact model. Thus the following fact type is required to support the example rule statement at the start of this section:

F312. <u>hourly pay rate</u> *is of* <u>employee</u>

9.4 ACTIVITY RULES

Activity rules (introduced in Section 4.9.3 in Chapter 4) constrain the operation of one or more business processes or other activities. Each of the following subcategories of activity rule has its own template(s):

1. *activity restriction rules*, which restrict business processes or other activities in various ways:
   a. *activity time limit rules*, which restrict business processes or other activities to within particular time periods; the templates for these are described in Section 9.4.1.1;
   b. *activity exclusion period rules*, which prohibit business processes or other activities during particular time periods; the templates for these are also described in Section 9.4.1.1;
   c. *activity pre-condition rules*, which prohibit business processes or other activities unless some other activity or event has previously occurred or some prerequisite condition exists; the templates for these are described in Section 9.4.1.2;

    d. ***activity prohibition rules***, which prohibit business processes or other activities if some event or other process has previously occurred or some dangerous or illegal condition exists; the templates for these are described in Section 9.4.1.3;

    e. ***activity conflict rules***, which restrict the simultaneous occurrence of multiple processes or other activities; the templates for these are described in Section 9.4.1.1;

    f. ***information retention rules***, which define the minimum period for which a particular type of information is retained; the templates for these are described in Section 9.4.1.4;

2. ***activity obligation rules***, which require business processes or other activities to occur either within a maximum time after a particular event (such as the completion of some other process) or as soon as practical after a particular event; the templates for these are described in Section 9.4.1.1;

3. ***process decision rules***, which determine what action a business process or device is to take in specific situations; the templates for these are described in Section 9.4.2.

9.4.1 Activity restriction rules

An ***activity restriction rule*** restricts a business process or other activity in some way.

9.4.1.1 *Rules restricting when an activity can occur*

Many activity restriction rules place time restrictions on activities. Such restrictions may be expressed in various ways:

1. as a requirement that the subject activity be before, after, during, or not during some other activity or event expressed using a complete clause (with a subject and verb phrase): for example,
    a. after that <u>passenger</u> *undergoes* <u>security screening</u>;
    b. after that <u>passenger</u> *checks in for* that <u>flight</u>;
    c. until a <u>cabin crew member</u> *advises* that
        <u>electronic devices</u> *may be operated safely*;
    d. while the <u>seat belt signs</u> *are illuminated*;

2. as a requirement that the subject activity be before, after, during, or not during some other activity, event, or time period expressed using a qualified term: for example,
    a. *within* the <u>time period</u>
        specified in the <u>employment record</u>
        for the same <u>employee</u>;
    b. *after* the <u>day</u>
        on which the <u>ticket</u> *is validated*;

3. as a requirement that the subject activity be before, after, during, or not during some time period before or after some other activity, event, or time period: for example,
    a. *during* the <u>24 h</u>
        before the <u>departure time</u> *of* that <u>flight</u>;
    b. *earlier than* <u>24 h</u>
        before the <u>departure time</u> *of* that <u>flight</u>;
    c. *during* the <u>7 years</u>
        after the <u>end</u> *of* that <u>financial year</u>;

4. as a requirement that the subject activity be before or after some time point during some other activity, event, or time period: for example,

   a. *before* <u>5 pm</u>
      on the <u>day</u> *on* which that <u>request</u> *is made*;

5. as a combination of two such requirements: for example,

   a. *at* any <u>time</u> *after* <u>pushback</u>
      until a <u>cabin crew member</u> *advises* that
         <u>electronic devices</u> *may be operated safely*;

Note that the word 'after' may be used as a conjunction (in which case it is shown as 'after') or a preposition (in which case it is shown as '*after*'). This is also true of 'before' and 'until'. Other words and phrases operate only as one or the other: for example, 'while' operates only as a conjunction, while '*during*', '*within*', '*earlier than*', and '*later than*' operate only as prepositions.

    All of the above are accommodated by the following subtemplate:

S21. <time restriction>::=
    {*at* any <u>time</u>|}
    {{*before*|*after*|*during*|*until*|*within*|{*no*|} {*earlier*|*later*} *than*} <object>|}
    {{*before*|*after*|*during*|*until*|*within*|*on*} <object>|
    {before|after|while|until} <conditional clause>}

An ***activity time limit rule*** restricts a process or other activity to within a particular time period: for example,

R385. <u>Bag drop</u> *for* a <u>flight</u>
    may *occur*
    only *during* the <u>4 h</u> *before* the <u>departure time</u> *of* that <u>flight</u>.

R386. <u>Acknowledgment</u> *of* a <u>service request</u>
      that *is made before* <u>2 pm</u>
    must *occur*
    before <u>5 pm</u> *on* the <u>day</u> *on* which that <u>service request</u> *is made*.

R387. A <u>daily ticket</u>
    may *be used*
    only *until* <u>2 am</u> *on* the <u>day</u>
      after the <u>day</u> *on* which the <u>ticket</u> *is validated*.

An ***activity exclusion period rule*** achieves a similar effect by prohibiting a process or other activity during a particular time period: for example,

R388. <u>Construction machinery</u>
    must not *be operated*
      in a <u>residential area</u>
         before <u>7:30 am</u> or *after* <u>7:30 pm</u> *on* a <u>weekday</u>.

An ***activity conflict rule*** restricts the simultaneous occurrence of multiple processes or other activities: for example,

R389. <u>Online banking</u>
must not *occur*
during <u>system maintenance</u>.

An ***activity obligation rule*** requires a business process or other activity to occur either within a maximum time after a particular event (such as the completion of some other process) or as soon as practical after a particular event: for example,

R390. A <u>replenishment order</u>
must *be raised for* a <u>part</u>
no later than <u>24 h</u>
after the <u>quantity on hand</u> *of* that <u>part</u> *falls below*
the <u>reorder point</u> *for* that <u>part</u>.

Rule statements for all these types of rules can be generated from the following templates:

1. T48 for those rule statements in which the subject is the term signifying the process or other activity, such as R385, R386, and R389;
2. T49 for those rule statements in which the subject is either:
   a. the term signifying the object of the process or other activity, such as R387, R388, or R390, or
   b. the term signifying the party or device performing the process or other activity.

T48. {The|} <<u>process</u> term> {*of*| *for*} {a|an} <<u>object term</u>>
    {<qualifying clause>|}
    {must {not|} *occur*|may *occur* only}
    <time restriction 1> {{and|or} <time restriction 2>|}
    {{if|unless} <conditional clause>|}.
T49. {Each|A|An} <<u>term</u>>
    {<qualifying clause 1>|}
    {must {not|} <*verb phrase 1*> {<object 1>|}
    {<qualifying clause 2>|}|
    may <*verb phrase 2*> {<object 2>|}
    {<qualifying clause 3>|} only}
    <time restriction 1> {{and|or} <time restriction 2>|}
    {{if|unless} <conditional clause>|}.

These templates have the following important options and placeholders:

1. <<u>process term</u>> is the term used for the activity that is subject to the restriction;
2. <<u>object term</u>> is the term used for the object of the activity;
3. <<u>term</u>> is the term used for either the object of the activity or the party or device performing the activity;
4. each <qualifying clause> is used only if not all instances of the object, party, or device are subject to the rule; the options for <qualifying clause> are listed in subtemplate S14 in Section 9.1.2.10;
5. 'must' should be used if the activity must occur during the period defined by the <time restrictions>, whereas 'must not' should be used if the activity must not occur during that period, and 'may' with 'only' should be used if the activity may only occur during that period;

6. *<verb phrase>* after 'must', 'must not', or 'may' is followed by an *<object>* if transitive (e.g., '*be used by*', '*be operated by*') but not if intransitive (e.g., '*be used*', '*be operated*');
7. up to two *<time restriction>*(s) may be used to define the period during which the activity must occur, must not occur, or may only occur; the options for *<time restriction>* are listed in subtemplate S21 at the start of this section;
8. '{if|unless} *<conditional clause>*' is required if and only if no *<time restriction>* is used; the options for *<conditional clause>* are listed in subtemplate S13 in Section 9.1.2.9.

The following fact types should be present in the fact model (either explicitly stated, or derived as described in Section 6.3.3 in Chapter 6):

1. if template T48 is used, a fact type of the form
    '<u>process term</u> *is of* <u>object term</u>', or
    '<u>process term</u> *is for* <u>object term</u>':
    for example, F313 and F316;
2. if template T49 is used, a fact type of the form
    '<u>term</u> *<verb phrase>* *<object>*'
    (if *<verb phrase>* is followed by an *<object>*): for example, F323, F327, or
    '<u>term</u> *<verb phrase>*'
    (if not): for example, F320;
3. if either of the *<time restriction>*(s) uses a preposition rather than a conjunction, a fact type of the form
    '<u>activity</u> *occurs* *<preposition>* <u>term</u>'
    (if *<object>* within *<time restriction>* includes <u>term</u>): for example, F326, or
    '<u>activity</u> *occurs* *<preposition>* <u>temporal term</u>'
    (if not, where *<temporal term>* is '<u>time</u>' or '<u>time period</u>', depending on the preposition): for example, F314, F318, F321, F324, and F328;
4. at least one fact type for each qualifying clause (if any), including any within any *<object>*, as described in Section 7.4.1 in Chapter 7: for example, F315, F317, F319, and F322;
5. at least one fact type for each conditional clause (if any), including any within either *<time restriction>*, as also described in Section 7.4.1: for example, F329, F330, and F331.

F313. <u>bag drop</u> *is for* <u>flight</u>
F314. <u>activity</u> *occurs during* <u>time period</u>
F315. <u>departure time</u> *is of* <u>flight</u>
F316. <u>acknowledgment</u> *is of* <u>service request</u>
F317. <u>service request</u> *is made before* <u>time</u>
F318. <u>activity</u> *occurs before* <u>time</u>
F319. <u>service request</u> *is made on* <u>day</u>
F320. <u>daily ticket</u> *is used*
F321. <u>activity</u> *occurs until* <u>time</u>
F322. <u>ticket</u> *is validated on* <u>day</u>
F323. <u>construction machinery</u> *is operated in* <u>residential area</u>
F324. <u>activity</u> *occurs after* <u>time</u>
F325. <u>online banking</u> *occurs*
F326. <u>activity</u> *occurs during* <u>system maintenance</u>

F327. <u>replenishment order</u> *is raised for* <u>part</u>
F328. <u>activity</u> *occurs no later than* <u>time</u>
F329. <u>quantity on hand</u> *is of* <u>part</u>
F330. <u>quantity on hand</u> *falls below* <u>reorder point</u>
F331. <u>reorder point</u> *is of* <u>part</u>

9.4.1.2 Activity pre-condition rules

An ***activity pre-condition rule*** prohibits a business process or other activity unless some other activity or event has previously occurred or some prerequisite condition exists: for example,

R391. A <u>passenger</u>
 may *board* an <u>international flight</u>
 only after that <u>passenger</u> *undergoes* <u>departure control</u>.
R392. A <u>laptop computer</u>
 may *undergo* <u>security screening</u>
 only if that <u>laptop computer</u> *has been removed from* any <u>bag</u>.

Rule statements for this type of rule can be generated from the following template:

T50. {A|An} <u><subject term></u>
  {<qualifying clause>|}
  may *<verb phrase>* {<object>|}
  only {<time restriction>|if <conditional clause>}.

These templates have the following important options and placeholders:

1. <u><subject term></u> is the term used for the parties or things that are the focus of the activity;
2. <qualifying clause> is used if not every instance of <u><subject term></u> is subject to the rule; the options for <qualifying clause> are listed in subtemplate S14 in Section 9.1.2.10;
3. *<verb phrase>* is followed by <object> if transitive (e.g., '*board*', '*undergo*') but not if intransitive (e.g., '*be deleted*');
4. <time restriction> is used if the activity is prohibited unless some other activity or event has previously occurred, whereas 'if <conditional clause>' is used if the activity is prohibited unless some prerequisite condition exists; the options for <time restriction> are listed in subtemplate S21 in Section 9.4.1.1, while the options for <conditional clause> are listed in subtemplate S13 in Section 9.1.2.9.

The following fact types should be present in the fact model (either explicitly stated, or derived as described in Section 6.3.3 in Chapter 6):

1. a fact type of the form
 '<u><subject term></u> *<verb phrase>* <object>'
 (if *<verb phrase>* is followed by an <object>), e.g., F332 and F334, or
 '<u><subject term></u> *<verb phrase>*'
 (if not);
2. at least one fact type for the qualifying clause (if any), including any within the time restriction, as described in Section 7.4.1 in Chapter 7

3. at least one fact type for the conditional clause (if any), including any within the time restriction, as also described in Section 7.4.1: for example, F333 and F335.

F332. passenger *boards* international flight
F333. passenger *undergoes* departure control
F334. laptop computer *undergoes* security screening
F335. laptop computer *is removed from* bag

9.4.1.3 Activity prohibition rules

An *activity prohibition rule* prohibits a business process or other activity if some event or other process has previously occurred or some dangerous or illegal condition exists: for example,

R393. A driver
  must not *operate* any vehicle
  if that driver *is intoxicated.*

Rule statements for this type of rule can be generated from the following template:

T51. {A|An} <subject term>
  {<qualifying clause>|}
  must not <*verb phrase*> {<object>|}
  if <conditional clause>.

These templates have the following important options and placeholders:

1. <subject term> is the term used for the parties or things that are the focus of the activity;
2. <qualifying clause> is used if not every instance of <subject term> is subject to the rule; the options for <qualifying clause> are listed in subtemplate S14 in Section 9.1.2.10;
3. <*verb phrase*> is followed by <object> if transitive (e.g., '*board*', '*undergo*') but not if intransitive (e.g., '*be deleted*');
4. the options for <conditional clause> are listed in subtemplate S13 in Section 9.1.2.9.

The following fact types should be present in the fact model (either explicitly stated, or derived as described in Section 6.3.3 in Chapter 6):

1. a fact type of the form
 '<subject term> <*verb phrase*> <object>'
 (if <*verb phrase*> is followed by an <object>), e.g., F336, or
 '<subject term> <*verb phrase*>'
 (if not);
2. at least one fact type for the qualifying clause (if any), as described in Section 7.4.1 in Chapter 7;
3. at least one fact type for the conditional clause, as also described in Section 7.4.1: for example, F337.

F336. driver *operates* vehicle
F337. driver *is intoxicated*

9.4.1.4 Information retention rules

An ***information retention rule*** defines the minimum period for which a particular type of information is retained: for example,

R394. An <u>order</u>
>   must not *be deleted*
>   *until* <u>6 months</u> *after* the <u>payment</u> *for* that <u>order</u>.

Rule statements for this type of rule can be generated from template T49 described in Section 9.4.1.1.

The same conditions also apply as in template T49 regarding the fact types that should be present in the fact model. Thus the following fact types are required to support rule statement R394:

F338. <u>order</u> *is deleted*
F339. <u>activity</u> *occurs until* <u>time</u>
F340. <u>payment</u> *is for* <u>order</u>

9.4.2 Process decision rules

A ***process decision rule*** determines what action a business process or device is to take in specific situations: for example,

R395. Each <u>ticket barrier</u>
>   must *retain* each <u>ticket</u>
>   that *is* not *valid for* any more <u>journeys</u>.
R396. Each <u>ticket barrier</u>
>   must *retain* each <u>ticket</u>
>   that *is expired.*

Rule statements for this type of rule can be generated from the following template:

T52. Each <<u>actor term</u>>
>   must <*verb phrase*> {<object>|}
>   {<qualifying clause>|}
>   {{if|unless} <conditional clause>|}.

These templates have the following important options and placeholders:

1. <<u>actor term</u>> is the term signifying the business process or device;
2. <*verb phrase*> (and <object>, if present) defines the action to be taken in the situation defined by <qualifying clause> or <conditional clause>.

The following fact types should be present in the fact model (either explicitly stated, or derived as described in Section 6.3.3 in Chapter 6):

1. a fact type of the form
   '<<u>actor term</u>> <*verb phrase*> <object>':
   for example, F341;

2. at least one fact type for the qualifying clause (if any), as described in Section 7.4.1 in Chapter 7: for example, F342 or F343;
3. at least one fact type for the conditional clause (if any), as also described in Section 7.4.1.

F341. ticket *retains* ticket
F342. ticket *is valid for* journey
F343. ticket *is expired*

9.5 PARTY RULES

Party rules (introduced in Section 4.9.4 in Chapter 4) restrict the parties who can perform processes or activities or play roles. Each of the following subcategories of party rule has its own template(s):

1. *party restriction rules* place restrictions on who can perform some processes or activities or play some roles; the template for these is described in Section 9.5.1;
2. *role separation rules* prohibit the same party from performing two activities, while *role binding rules* require that the party performing the second of two activities must be the same as the party who performed the first of those activities; the template for both of these is described in Section 9.5.2;
3. *information access rules* define who can view, create, or update particular information; the template for these is described in Section 9.5.3;
4. *responsibility rules* define who is responsible for performing particular processes or liable for particular fees, duties, or taxes; the template for these is described in Section 9.5.4.

9.5.1 Party restriction rules

A *party restriction rule* places restrictions on who can perform some processes or activities or play some roles, based on age, some other physical characteristic or capability, or training, testing, and certification in the appropriate skills: for example,

R397. A person
　　　may *be rostered as* the pilot in command
　　　　　on a flight crew
　　　only if that person *holds* a command endorsement
　　　　　that *is current*.
R398. A person
　　　may *be rostered as* a flight crew member
　　　only if the current medical status *of* that person *is* A1.

Rule statements for this type of rule can be generated from the following template:

T53. A <party signifier 1>
　　　{<qualifying clause>|}
　　　may <predicate 1>
　　　only if {the <attribute signifier> of|} that <party signifier 1>
　　　　　<predicate 2>.

These templates have the following important options and placeholders:

1. <party signifier 1> is a generic term signifying all parties covered by the rule, such as 'person', 'employee', or 'organization';
2. the same term must be substituted in place of each<party signifier 1>;
3. <qualifying clause> is used if the rule governs some proper subset of the parties signified by <party signifier 1>; the options for a <qualifying clause> are listed in subtemplate S14 in Section 9.1.2.10;
4. <predicate 1> signifies the restricted activity or role;
5. 'the <attribute signifier> of' is used if some attribute of a party qualifies that party to perform the activity or play the role;
6. <predicate 2> signifies the value of <attribute signifier>, if used, or some relationship in which a party must participate in order to qualify for the activity or role.

The following fact types should be present in the fact model (either explicitly stated, or derived as described in Section 6.3.3 in Chapter 6):

1. a fact type based on <party signifier 1> and <predicate 1>: for example, F344 and F347;
2. if <attribute signifier> is not used, a fact type based on <party signifier 1> and <predicate 2>: for example, F345;
3. if <attribute signifier> is used, a fact type of the form
   '<attribute signifier> *is of* <party signifier 2>':
   for example, F348;
4. at least one fact type for the qualifying clause (if any), including any within either predicate, as described in Section 7.4.1 in Chapter 7: for example, F346.

F344. person *is rostered as* pilot in command *on* flight crew
F345. person *holds* command endorsement
F346. command endorsement *is current*
F347. person *is rostered as* flight crew member
F348. current medical status *is of* person

9.5.2 Role separation and binding rules

A *role separation rule* prohibits the same party from performing two activities: for example,

R399. The consultant
      who *performs* the quality review
      of a project deliverable
   must not *be* one of the consultants
      who *updated* that project deliverable.

A *role binding rule* requires that the party performing the second of two activities be the same as the party who performed the first of those activities: for example,

R400. The consultant
   who *signs* the quality review report
  must *be* the same consultant
   who *performed* the quality review
   documented in that quality review report.

Rule statements for both these types of rules can be generated from the following template:

T54. The <party signifier 1>
   <qualifying clause 1>
  must {not|} *be* {the same|one of the} <party signifier 1>
   <qualifying clause 2>
  {{if|unless} <conditional clause>|}.

These templates have the following important options and placeholders:

1. <party signifier 1> is a generic term signifying all parties covered by the rule, such as 'person', 'employee', or 'organization';
2. the same term must be substituted in place of each <party signifier 1>;
3. <qualifying clause 1> defines one of the activities while <qualifying clause 2> defines the other; the options for a <qualifying clause> are listed in subtemplate S14 in Section 9.1.2.10.

The following fact types should be present in the fact model (either explicitly stated, or derived as described in Section 6.3.3 in Chapter 6):

1. at least one fact type for each qualifying clause, as described in Section 7.4.1 in Chapter 7: for example,
 a. F349 and F350 for R399;
 b. F351, F352, and F353 for R400;
2. at least one fact type for the conditional clause (if any), as also described in Section 7.4.1.

F349. consultant *performs* quality review *of* project deliverable
F350. consultant *updates* project deliverable
F351. consultant *signs* quality review report
F352. consultant *performs* quality review
F353. quality review *is documented in* quality review report

9.5.3 Information access rules

An ***information access rule*** defines who can view, create, or update particular information: for example,

R401. A payroll record
   of an employee
  may *be viewed by*
  only that employee, the supervisor *of* that employee, or a payroll officer.

Rule statements for this type of rule can be generated from the following template:

T55. {The|A|An} <u><information signifier></u>
      <qualifying clause>
    may *be* <*information access process*> *by*
    only {<object 1>|[<object 2>, or]}
    {{if|unless} <conditional clause>|}.

These templates have the following important options and placeholders:

1. <u><information signifier></u> is the term signifying the information item to which access is restricted;
2. <qualifying clause> is used to specify precisely which instances of that information item are subject to restricted access;
3. <*information access process*> defines the form of access that is restricted; the <*information access process*> placeholder can be replaced by anything defined in the following subtemplate:

S22. <*information access process*>::=
    {*viewed*|*created*|*updated*|*deleted*}

4. the verb phrase defining the form of access is followed by
    a. a single <object> if only one role or position is allowed access, or
    b. a list of the roles or positions allowed access, the last two separated by 'or' (or a comma and 'or' if adhering to U.S. punctuation standards) and each other pair separated by a comma.
    Options for <object> are listed in subtemplate S11 in Section 9.1.2.7.

The following fact types should be present in the fact model (either explicitly stated, or derived as described in Section 6.3.3 in Chapter 6):

1. a fact type of the form
    '<u><information signifier></u> *is* <*information access process*> *by* <object>'
    for each role or position listed: for example, F355;
2. at least one fact type for the qualifying clause, as described in Section 7.4.1 in Chapter 7: for example, F354;
3. at least one fact type for the conditional clause (if any), as also described in Section 7.4.1.

F354. <u>payroll record</u> *is of* <u>employee</u>
F355. <u>payroll record</u> *is viewed by* <u>person</u>

9.5.4 Responsibility rules

A ***responsibility rule*** defines who is responsible for performing a particular process or liable for a particular fee, duty, or tax: for example,

R402. The <u>final quality review</u>
      of each <u>project deliverable</u>
    must *be performed by* the <u>quality assurance officer</u>.

Rule statements for this type of rule can be generated from the following template:

T56. {The|A|An|} <u><responsibility signifier></u>
   {<qualifying clause 1>|}
   must <*verb phrase*> {the|a|an} <u><party signifier></u>
   {<qualifying clause 2>|}
   {{if|unless} <conditional clause>|}.

These templates have the following important options and placeholders:

1. <u><responsibility signifier></u> is the term signifying the process, fee, duty, or tax;
2. <qualifying clause 1> is used if necessary to specify precisely which instances of that process, fee, duty, or tax are subject to the responsibility rule;
3. <u><party signifier></u> is the term signifying the party responsible for performing the process or liable for the fee, duty, or tax;
4. <qualifying clause 2> is used if necessary to specify precisely which instance or instances of that party are responsible.

The following fact types should be present in the fact model (either explicitly stated, or derived as described in Section 6.3.3 in Chapter 6):

1. a fact type of the form
   '<u><responsibility signifier></u> <*verb phrase*> <u><party signifier></u>':
   for example, F357;
2. at least one fact type for each qualifying clause (if any), as described in Section 7.4.1 in Chapter 7:
   for example, F356;
3. at least one fact type for the conditional clause (if any), as also described in Section 7.4.1.

F356. <u>final quality review</u> *is of* <u>project deliverable</u>
F357. <u>final quality review</u> *is performed by* <u>person</u>

9.6 SUMMARY

The templates and subtemplates in this chapter constitute a formal definition of the constrained natural language used for rule statements in this book. One or more templates is provided for each type of rule statement listed in Chapter 4. Associated with each template is information about

1. what may be substituted in place of each placeholder in the template;
2. when to use particular options;
3. the fact types that should be present in the fact model to support a rule statement based on that template.

Bibliography

Barker, R., 1990. Case Method: Tasks and Deliverables. Addison-Wesley, Wokingham, UK.

BusinessDictionary.com, n.d. Plain language law. Retrieved from: www.businessdictionary.com/definition/plain-language-law.html.

Business Rules Group, 2000, July. Defining Business Rules ~ What Are They Really? Retrieved from: http://www.businessrulesgroup.org/first_paper/br01c0.htm.

Business Rules Group, 2003. The Business Rules Manifesto. Retrieved from: http://www.businessrulesgroup.org/brmanifesto.htm.

Business Rules Group, 2005, September. The Business Motivation Model ~ Business Governance in a Volatile World. Retrieved from: http://www.BusinessRulesGroup.org.

Business Rules Group, n.d. The Business Rules Approach. Retrieved from: http://www.businessrulesgroup.org/bra.shtml.

Chen, P.P., 1976. The entity relationship model—toward a unified view of data. ACM Trans. Database Syst 1(1), pp. 9–36.

Crystal, D., 2006. How Language Works. Penguin, Melbourne, Victoria, Australia.

Date, C.J., 2005. Database in Depth—Relational Theory for Practitioners. O'Reilly, Sebastopol, CA, USA.

Date, C.J., Darwen, H., Lorentzos, N.A., 2003. Temporal Data and the Relational Model. Morgan Kaufman, San Francisco, CA, USA.

Finch, G., 2005. Key Concepts in Language and Linguistics, second ed. Palgrave Macmillan, Basingstoke, UK.

Halliday, M.A., 1985. An Introduction to Functional Grammar. Arnold, London, UK.

Halliday, M.A., Matthiessen, C.M., 2004. An Introduction to Functional Grammar, third ed. Arnold, London, UK.

Halpin, T.A., 2001. Information Modeling and Relational Databases, Morgan Kaufman, San Francisco, CA, USA.

Halpin, T.A., 2003, April. Verbalizing business rules: Part 1. Retrieved from Business Rules Journal: http://www.BRCommunity.com/a2003/b138.html.

Halpin, T.A., n.d. Object Role Modeling. Retrieved from: http://www.orm.net/.

Halpin, T.A., Harding, J., 1993. Automated support for verbalization of conceptual schemas. In: Proceedings of the 4th Workshop on Next Generation CASE Tools. Twente Memoranda Informatica, Paris, France.

Morgan, T., 2002. Business Rules and Information Systems. Addison-Wesley, Indianapolis, IN, USA.

Nijssen, G.M., Halpin, T.A., 1989. Conceptual Schema and Relational Database Design. Prentice Hall, New York, NY, USA.

Object Management Group, 2008, January. Semantics of Business Vocabulary and Business Rules. Retrieved from: www.omg.org/spec/SBVR/1.0/PDF/.

Object Management Group, n.d. Business Process Management Initiative. Retrieved from BPMN: http://www.bpmn.org/.

Object Management Group, n.d. UML Resource Page. Retrieved from UML Resource Site: www.uml.org.

Ross, R.G., 1997. The Business Rule Book—Classifying, Defining, and Modeling Rules, second ed. Business Rule Solutions, Inc., Houston, TX, USA.

Ross, R.G., 1998. Business Rule Concepts—Getting to the Point of Knowledge, first ed. Business Rule Solutions, Inc., Houston, TX, USA.

Ross, R.G., 2003. Principles of the Business Rule Approach, Addison-Wesley, Longman, Reading, MA, USA.

Ross, R.G., 2009. RuleSpeak Sentence Forms—Specifying Natural-Language Business Rules in English. Retrieved from Business Rules Journal: http://www.BRCommunity.com/b472.php.

Ross, R.G., 2009, February. In: Seiner, R.S., (Ed.) Are Integrity Constraints Business Rules? Not! Retrieved from The Data Administration Newsletter: http://www.tdan.com/view-featured-columns/9611.

Ross, R.G., Lam, G.S., 2001. RuleSpeak Sentence Templates—Developing Rule Statements Using Sentence Patterns. Retrieved from http://www.brsolutions.com/rulespeak_download.shtml.

Silver, B., 2009. BPMN Method and Style, Cody-Cassidy, Aptos.

Simsion, G.C., Witt, G.C., 2004. Data Modeling Essentials, third ed. Morgan Kaufmann, San Francisco, CA, USA.

Stonebraker, M., Moore, D., 1996. Object-Relational DBMSs: The Next Great Wave. Morgan Kaufmann, San Francisco, CA, USA.

von Halle, B., 2001. Business Rules Applied, John Wiley & Sons, Inc., New York, NY, USA.

Witt, G.C., 1999. Modelling Business Rules for School Student Administration: a Case Study, *ER99*. Paris, France.

Witt, G.C., 2009, February. A Practical Method of Developing Natural Language Rule Statements: Part 1. Retrieved from Business Rules Journal: http://www.BRCommunity.com/a2009/b461.html.

Glossary

This glossary includes a definition for each technical term used in this book. Where appropriate, source(s) of the term and/or the definition are indicated in brackets. Any definition not attributed is by the author.

action assertion A *rule statement* that defines allowable actions, in particular, allowable changes to data. (Term: Business Rules Group Final Report, 2000)

active verb phrase A *verb phrase* in the *active voice*.

active voice The use of a *verb phrase* such that the subject of that verb phrase is the person or thing performing the action signified by that verb phrase (i.e., the *actor* or *agent*), as in "the passenger presents a boarding pass". By contrast, the subject of a verb phrase in *passive voice* (as in "a boarding pass is presented by the passenger") is the person or thing on which the action is performed (the *patient* or *target*).

activity conflict rule An *activity restriction rule* that restricts the simultaneous occurrence of multiple processes or other activities. (Term: Author)

activity exclusion period rule An *activity restriction rule* that prohibits a business process or other activity during a particular time period. (Term: Author)

activity obligation rule An *activity rule* that requires a business process or other activity to occur either within a maximum time after a particular event (such as the completion of some other process) or as soon as practical after a particular event. (Term: Author)

activity pre-condition rule An *activity restriction rule* that prohibits a business process or other activity unless some other activity or event has previously occurred or some prerequisite condition exists. (Term: Author)

activity prohibition rule An *activity restriction rule* that prohibits a business process or other activity if some event or other process has previously occurred or some dangerous or illegal condition exists. (Term: Author)

activity restriction rule An *activity rule* that restricts a business process or other activity in some way. (Term: Author)

activity rule An *operative rule* that constrains the operation of one or more *business processes* or other activities. (Term: Author)

activity rule statement A *rule statement* that expresses an *activity rule*. (Term: Author)

activity time limit rule An *activity restriction rule* that restricts a business process or other activity to within a particular time period. (Term: Author)

actor The person or thing performing the action signified by a *verb phrase*.

adjectival An *adjective* or a *simple noun* acting as an adjective. (Term: Finch, 2005)

adjective A word (e.g., 'international') that specifies an attribute or property of an entity signified by a *noun*, such as its color, shape, size, or appearance, and that can appear as either

  1. a *pre-modifier* of that noun (an *attributive adjective*), as in "the international flight" or
  2. part of a *predicate* following that noun and the word 'is' (in which case it is a *predicative adjective*), as in "this flight is international". (Definition: after Finch, 2005)

adverb A word that qualifies a *verb*, "by giving circumstantial information about the time, place, or manner in which an action, event, or process takes place". (Definition: after Finch, 2005)

advice statement A statement advising of the absence of a rule. (Term: SBVR)

agent See *actor*

alethic modality The interpretation of a *modal auxiliary* as stating a logical conclusion, as in "he must be out" (since he is not home), or possibility, as in "he may come home" (meaning "it is possible that he will come home") as distinct from *deontic modality* or *epistemic modality*.

arithmetic attribute See *quantitative attribute*.

article An *indefinite article* ('a' or 'an' in English) or a *definite article* ('the' in English).

aspect The ability of a *verb phrase* to express
1. continuous activity, using the *progressive aspect* (e.g., 'am specifying', 'was specifying', 'will be specifying'),
2. activity at an indeterminate time, using the *perfect aspect* (e.g., 'have specified', 'had specified', 'will have specified'), or
3. both (e.g., 'have been specifying', 'had been specifying', 'will have been specifying').

assertion A statement about a particular artifact in a data model. (Term: Author)

association A *relationship* between *object classes*. (Term: object-oriented programming)

association class An *association* represented using an *object class*. (Term: object-oriented programming)

associative fact A fact that associates phenomena with each other: for example, a person with the city in which he or she resides, a flight with the ports that it flies between. (Term: Author)

associative fact type A *fact type* that is a *pro forma* for one or more *associative facts*. (Term: SBVR)

assortment fact type A *fact type* that defines the set to which the individual concept signified by a *proper name* belongs. (Term: SBVR)

atomic rule A *rule* that cannot be partially complied with, but only be completely complied with or completely contravened.

attribute A property (of interest to an organization) of each instance of an *entity class* (or *object class*).

attribute fact type A *fact type* that associates an *attribute term* used to signify a non-Boolean property of an *entity class* (or *object class*) with the term that signifies that class. (Term: Author)

attribute term A *term* that signifies a non-Boolean property of an *entity class* (or *object class*). (Term: Author)

attributive adjective An *adjective* used as a *pre-modifier* of a *noun* (as in "the international flight") as distinct from a *predicative adjective*, which follows a noun and the verb 'is' (as in "this flight is international").

auxiliary verb A verb that can be used in front of a simple verb to generate different forms of that verb: for example, 'is'/'are', 'has'/'have', 'does'/'do', 'will', 'must', 'may', 'might', 'can', 'could', 'shall', 'should', 'would'.

basic constraint A *rule pattern* that establishes a constraint on a subject that exhibits no more than one particular characteristic. (Term: Morgan; definition: Author, after Morgan)

binary fact type A *fact type* involving two terms. (Term: ORM)

boilerplate text All text in a *template* other than the *option sets*, *placeholders*, and *list definitions*: that is, all text that is included in all rule statements based on that template.

Boolean A property or attribute of a class of objects that each individual object either exhibits or does not exhibit: for example, a person is either deceased or not deceased, a loan is either approved or not approved.

Boolean attribute An *attribute* in which only values representing 'True' and 'False' can be recorded and which can thus be used to record a *Boolean* property. (Term: Author)

BPMN Business Process Modeling Notation.

business glossary A collection of the *business terms* used by an organization, each with a definition.

business process An activity (or set of activities) that is managed by an organization to produce some result of value to that organization, its customers, its suppliers, and/or its partners.

business process model A model of some subset of the *business processes* performed by an organization, depicting participants in those processes, events giving rise to those processes, information inputs to those processes, sequential relationships between those processes, decisions taken by those processes, and information outputs from those processes.

business rule "A statement that defines or constrains some aspect of the business. It is intended to assert business structure or to control or influence the behavior of the business." (Definition: Business Rules Group, 2000) "A condition that govern[s] . . . business event[s] so that [they] occur in such a way that is acceptable to the business." (Definition: von Halle, 2001)

business term See *term*.

cardinal number The numbers 'one', 'two', 'three', etc.

CASE tool A software product that, in its simplest form, enables a data model to be developed and an empty database reflecting that model to be generated (the acronym CASE stands for "computer aided system engineering").

categorization fact type A *fact type* that defines a term's *hypernym* (the term signifying the superset of the set signified by the original term). (Term: SBVR)

categorization scheme A set of *categories* used to classify a particular set of people, places, or things.

categorization scheme enumeration A *definitional rule* that defines the members of a *mutually exclusive* and *jointly exhaustive categorization scheme*. (Term: Author)

category One of the classifications in a *categorization scheme*: for example, 'male' and 'female' are categories in the 'gender' categorization scheme.

category attribute An *attribute* that can only take one of a defined set of values, each representing a *category* in the relevant *categorization scheme*. (Term: Author)

category transition constraint A *definitional rule* that specifies allowed or disallowed transitions between categories or statuses. (Term: Author)

chained qualifying clause A *qualifying clause* that includes a term that is itself qualified by a qualifying clause: for example, "*specified in* the flight booking request that *gives rise to* that flight booking confirmation", in which 'flight booking request' is itself qualified. (Term: Author)

characteristic See *unary fact type*.

circumstantial An attribute of the verb 'be' whereby it has not only a *subject* but a circumstance of the subject: for example, "Manuel is in the garden".

classification A *rule pattern* that establishes a definition for a *term* in the *fact model*. (Term and definition: Morgan)

column A structure in a *table* in a *relational database* that holds one value of the same type for each *row* in that table.

common noun A *noun* that can be used to refer to either a set of similar persons, organizations, places, or things, or any member of that set. For example, 'city' can be used to refer to a set of places, as in "most cities have historic buildings", or to assert that an individual place belongs to that set, as in "Sydney is a city". By contrast, a *proper name* is the name of a single entity instance: for example, 'Sydney'.

complement A reference to another facet, quality, characteristic, or attribute of the subject of the verb 'be': for example, 'old' as in "that man is old".

complex concept cardinality rule A *complex concept structure rule* that defines the number of (or minimum and/or maximum number of) components of a particular type within a particular concept. (Term: Author)

complex concept equivalence rule A *complex concept structure rule* that defines a pair of components within a particular concept that are of necessity the same. (Term: Author)

complex concept set constraint A *complex concept structure rule* that defines two sets of components within a particular concept that must be identical. (Term: Author)

complex concept structure rule A *definitional rule* that defines a particular constraint on one or more components of a complex concept. (Term: Author)

complex data item A data item that consists of other data items: for example, a street address. (Term: Author)

compound noun A *noun* consisting of more than one word, as distinct from a *simple noun*. This may be a simple noun either preceded by one or more *pre-modifiers* (*adjectives*, simple nouns, or *cardinal numbers* or *ordinal numbers*) or followed by a *post-modifier* (either an adjective or a preposition and another simple noun). Alternatively, it may be two simple nouns joined by a *conjunction*.

compound verb A *verb phrase* consisting of more than one word, as distinct from a *simple verb*.

computation A *rule pattern* that establishes a relationship between *terms* in the *fact model* sufficient to allow the computation or establishment of a value. (Term and definition: Morgan)

conditional clause A clause in a *rule statement* following 'if' or 'unless' and consisting of either a single *subject* and *predicate* or two or more subject-predicate pairs separated by 'and' or 'or'.

conditional start event An event in a process model which causes the following business process to be initiated when a particular condition becomes true. (Term: BPMN)

conjunction A word, such as 'and', 'or', 'if', or 'unless', that can be used to join two or more *nouns*, clauses, (less commonly) *verbs*, *determiners*, or *prepositions*.

connector (in a **fact type**) A *verb phrase* or *preposition* used in one or more *fact types*. (Term: Ross, 2009)

constrained natural language A subset of a *natural language* (e.g., English), in which both vocabulary and syntax are constrained: that is,
1. only certain words of each type are used and
2. only certain sentence forms are used.

constraint See *action assertion*.

containment The concept wherein objects of a particular class act as containers for other objects: for example, a form contains fields for data entry and may also contain *subforms* which in turn contain fields and/or other subforms.

controlled natural language See *constrained natural language*.

conversion factor definition A *data calculation rule* that defines a conversion factor between two units of measurement. (Term: Author)

count noun See *countable noun*.

countable noun A noun that can be meaningfully used after the word 'each' and that has both *singular* and *plural* forms (e.g., 'customer', 'order', 'business day'), as distinct from a *non-countable noun* (e.g., 'information', 'governance').

data calculation algorithm A *data calculation rule* that defines how a particular quantity or amount (whether for operational purposes, such as a fee, or for business intelligence purposes, such as a performance measure) is calculated. (Term: Author)

data calculation rule A *definitional rule* that defines the algorithm or formula for a particular quantity or a conversion factor between two units. (Term: Author)

data cardinality rule A *data rule* that requires the presence or absence of a data item and/or places a restriction on the maximum or minimum number of occurrences of a data item. (Term: Author)

data cardinality rule statement A *rule statement* that expresses a *data cardinality rule*. (Term: Author)

data consistency rule A *data content rule* that requires the content of multiple data items to be consistent with each other, other than as provided for by a *value set rule*, *range rule*, or *equality rule*. (Term: Author)

data content rule A *data rule* that places a restriction on the values contained in a data item or set of data items (rather than whether or not they must be present and how many there may or must be). (Term: Author)

data content rule statement A *rule statement* that expresses a *data content rule*. (Term: Author)

data dictionary A repository of *metadata* specifying the meaning of, and rules governing the content of, individual data items in an organization's data resources or intersystem messages.

data item format rule A *data content rule* that specifies the required format of a data item. (Term: Author)

data item format rule statement A *rule statement* that expresses a *data item format rule*. (Term: Author)

data model A model of the structure (and to some extent the content) of a database and at least some of the rules governing the data therein.

data rule An *operative rule* that constrains the data included in a transaction (a form or message) or a persistent data set (e.g., a database record). (Term: Author)

data rule statement A *rule statement* that expresses a *data rule*. (Term: Author)

data update prohibition rule A *data update rule* that prohibits update of a particular data item or set of data items. (Term: Author)

data update prohibition rule statement A *rule statement* that expresses a *data update prohibition rule*. (Term: Author)

data update rule A *data rule* that either prohibits update of a data item or places restrictions on the new value of a data item in terms of its existing value. (Term: Author)

data update rule statement A *rule statement* that expresses a *data update rule*. (Term: Author)

day type constraint A *temporal data constraint* that restricts a date to one or more days of the week or a particular type of day such as a working day (typically but not necessarily any day other than a Saturday, Sunday, or public holiday). (Term: Author)

DDL Data Definition Language: a language, forming part of *SQL*, in which the properties of the tables and columns of a database can be defined.

decision point A point in a process model from which flow two or more sequences of processes depending on some logical condition.

decision table A table documenting the different decisions or actions to be taken in different sets of conditions.

declarative mood One of the two forms of the *indicative mood*, used to state a fact (as in "the form specifies the departure date"), as distinct from the other form of the indicative mood, the *interrogative mood*, which is used to question the truth of a proposition (as in "does the form specify the departure date?").

declarative programming language A programming language that can be used to specify the desired result, as distinct from a *procedural programming language*, which can only be used to specify the actions to be taken to achieve that result.

declarative rule statement A *rule statement* that states the condition or set of conditions that some information, process, person, or thing is to comply with and leaves unstated the action to be taken if that condition or set of conditions is not complied with (as distinct from a *procedural rule statement*).

default value A value assigned to each instance of a particular data item for which no value has been provided.

definite article An *article* (taking the form 'the' in English) that indicates that the following noun refers on that occasion to a specific instance or instances of the signified concept, as distinct from an *indefinite article*, which indicates that the following noun refers on that occasion to a single unspecified instance of that concept.

definitional rule A *rule* that constrains how an organization (or the industry within which it operates) defines a construct created or used by that organization or industry, as distinct from an *operative rule*. (Term: SBVR)

definitional rule statement A *rule statement* that expresses a *definitional rule*. (Term: Author)

demonstrative determiner One of the *determiners* 'that', 'those', 'this', or 'these'.

deontic modality The interpretation of a *modal auxiliary* as stating an obligation, as in "he must be out before the doors are locked", or a permission, as in "he may come home" (meaning "he is allowed to come home") as distinct from *alethic modality* or *epistemic modality*.

dependent cardinality rule A *data cardinality rule* that mandates how many of a particular data item must be present based on the value of another data item. (Term: Author)

dependent cardinality rule statement A *rule statement* that expresses a *dependent cardinality rule*. (Term: Author)

derivation A *rule statement* that "define[s] how knowledge in one form may be transformed into other knowledge, possibly in a different form". (Term and definition: Business Rules Group, 2000)

derivation rule A rule that can be modeled in *ORM*, which specifies how values of a particular type can be derived or calculated. (Term: ORM)

descriptive rule See *definitional rule*.

determiner A word or phrase used before a noun to provide some information as to which instance (or instances) of the noun's concept are being referred to, such as 'the', 'my', 'this'.

difference (of two sets) The set that contains all members that are in one of those sets but not the other.

digital signature Data that assures the authenticity of a digital message or document, namely that the message was created by a known sender and not altered in transit.

dynamic data constraint A constraint which defines valid changes to a set of persistent data, as distinct from a *static data constraint*, which defines valid states of that set.

empty set A set with no members.

entity See *entity class*.

entity class An artifact in a *data model* that represents a class of people, places, things, or other concepts of interest to an organization.

Entity-Relationship Model A type of *data model*, using *entity classes*, *attributes*, and *relationships* to represent objects of interest to an organization, their properties and relationships.

Entity-Relationship Modeling The use of *Entity-Relationship Models* to represent objects of interest to an organization, their properties and relationships.

enumerated set A set of values that may be assigned to a particular *attribute*.

enumeration A *rule pattern* that establishes the range of values that can legitimately be taken by a *term* in the *fact model*. (Definition: Morgan)

epistemic modality The interpretation of a *modal auxiliary* as asserting a belief, as in "surely he must be out", as distinct from *alethic modality* or *deontic modality*.

equality rule A *data content rule* that requires that the content of a data item be the same as or not the same as that of some other data item. (Term: Author)

ER Model See *Entity-Relationship Model*.

exclusion constraint A constraint that can be modeled in *ORM*, in which no instance of a particular *object type* may participate in more than one of a set of particular *fact types*. (Term: ORM)

exclusive gateway A *decision point* in a process model which allows only one of a set of following processes to proceed based on some condition established in the preceding process. (Term: BPMN)

exclusive-or constraint A constraint that can be modeled in *ORM*, in which each instance of a particular *object type* must participate in exactly one of two particular *fact types*. (Term: ORM)

extensional definition A definition that (unlike an *intensional definition*) lists the members of the set signified by the term being defined: for example, "Immediate family member: a spouse, child, or parent".

fact Either
1. something which is the case or which has occurred, or
2. a true statement.

Fact-Based Modeling See *Natural Language Information Analysis Method*.

fact model A set of *fact types* describing one or more aspects of an enterprise or the environment in which it operates.

fact symbol The *connectors* (*verb phrase* and optional *prepositions*) used in a *fact type* as distinct from the *terms*.

fact type An artifact originally used in *ORM* to model a set of associations between instances of two or more object types and now also used to describe such associations in *fact models*. (Term: ORM)

first person A form of a verb phrase indicating an action or relationship involving the speaker or writer rather than the audience (*second person*) or any other party (*third person*); in modern English, only the verb 'to be' has a distinct first person form (in the *indicative present tense* and *singular number*), namely, 'am'.

first person pronoun A *pronoun* that refers to the speaker or writer of an utterance: that is, (in English) 'I', 'me', 'we', 'us'.

flag attribute See *Boolean attribute*.

foreign key A *column* or set of columns in one *table* referring to a specific *row* in another table or another row in the same table.

formal extensional definition A *formal term definition* that defines the subject business term by using an *extensional definition*. (Term: Author)

formal intensional definition A *formal term definition* that defines the subject business term by using an *intensional definition*. (Term: Author)

formal term definition A *definitional rule* that defines a particular business term in a formal manner, using a *formal intensional definition*, a *formal extensional definition*, or a *symbolic literal definition*. (Term: Author)

frequency constraint A constraint that can be modeled in *ORM*, which constrains the number of instances of a particular *fact type* that an instance of a particular *object type* (or set of instances of different object types) may participate in. (Term: ORM)

functional grammar See *systemic functional grammar*.

fundamental term A *term* that is not a *relationship term*, *role term*, or *attribute term*: that is, a term that corresponds to an *entity class* (but not an *intersection entity class*) in a *entity-relationship model* or an *object class* (but not an *association class*) in a UML object class model. (Term: Author)

future tense A form of a ***verb phrase*** that indicates that the action or relationship signified by that verb phrase occurs in the future (e.g., 'will write', 'will have written'), as distinct from the ***past tense*** ('wrote', 'used to write', 'was writing', 'have written', 'had written') and ***present tense*** ('write', 'be writing') forms.

general determiner A ***determiner*** that limits the number of instances referred to by a noun without being specific as to which instance or instances are referenced, as distinct from a ***specific determiner***, which is used to limit the noun to referring only to a specific instance or instances.

genitive case A form of a noun that indicates that the following noun signifies a quality, characteristic, property, circumstance, or asset of the object signified by the first noun. For example, in "this man's house", the house is an asset belonging to the man: the noun 'man' is therefore marked in the genitive case by the suffixed apostrophe and 's'.

hash key A scalar value returned by a function applied to a large data set such as a message.

head noun The most significant ***simple noun***(s) in a ***compound noun***
1. the last or only simple noun in a compound noun without ***prepositions*** or ***conjunctions*** (e.g., 'unit' in 'business unit');
2. the first or only simple noun in a compound noun using ***prepositions*** (e.g., 'date' in 'date of birth');
3. all nouns in a compound noun using one or more ***conjunctions*** (e.g., 'terms' and 'conditions' in 'terms and conditions').

homonym One of the meanings of a ***noun*** that has more than one meaning: for example, 'range' has meanings of "collection of mountains", "continuous set of numerical values", "item of kitchen equipment".

hypernym A ***noun*** that signifies a ***superset*** of the set signified by another noun: for example, 'adult' is a hypernym of 'woman'. (Term: Finch, 2005)

hyponym A ***noun*** that signifies a ***subset*** of the set signified by another noun: for example, 'woman' is a hyponym of 'adult'. (Term: Finch, 2005)

identification fact type An ***attribute fact type*** that uses the verb phrase '*is identified using*' to associate an ***entity class*** (or ***object class***) with one of its ***identifier attributes***. (Term: Author)

identifier A ***column*** or combination of columns in a ***table*** in a ***database*** that uniquely identify each row of that table.

identifier attribute An ***attribute*** that exists purely to identify entity instances and does not imply any properties of those instances. (Term: Author)

if-statement A statement that can be used in a ***procedural programming language*** to specify that an action is only to occur if some condition holds.

imperative mood A form of a ***verb phrase*** that directs a person or person(s) (or an intelligent device) to do something (as in "go away", "insert record"), as distinct from the ***indicative mood***, which states a fact (as in "the form specifies the departure date") or questions the truth of a proposition (as in "does the form specify the departure date?") or the ***subjunctive mood***, which expresses a wish or non-factual condition (e.g., 'be' and 'were' in "I insist he be there" and "if this were true" respectively). (Definition: after Finch, 2005)

impersonal pronoun The pronoun 'it' when used to refer not to a previous noun but to the world in general, as in "it is raining".

impossibility statement A ***rule statement*** that expresses an impossibility: that is, states that something is impossible (see Section 3.3.8.4 for a more detailed definition). (Term: SBVR)

inclusive-or constraint A constraint that can be modeled in ***ORM***, in which each instance of a particular ***object type*** must participate in at least one of a set of particular ***fact types***. (Term: ORM)

indefinite article An ***article*** (taking the form 'a' or 'an' in English) that indicates that the following noun refers on that occasion to a single unspecified instance of the signified concept, as distinct from a ***definite article***, which indicates that the following noun refers on that occasion to a specific instance or instances of that concept.

indicative mood A form of a ***verb phrase*** that states a fact (as in "the form specifies the departure date") or questions the truth of a proposition (as in "does the form specify the departure date?"), as distinct from the ***imperative mood***, which directs a person or person(s) (or an intelligent device) to do something (as in "go away", "insert record"), or the *subjunctive mood*, which expresses a wish or non-factual condition (e.g., 'be' and 'were' in "I insist he be there" and "if this were true" respectively). (Definition: after Finch, 2005)

indicator attribute See *Boolean attribute*.

infinitive The form of a verb that may be used after 'must' or 'may'.

inflection A change that can occur to a word in certain contexts: for example, 'man' to 'men'; 'girl' to 'girls'; 'speak' to 'speaks', 'spoke', 'spoken', or 'speaking'; 'talk' to 'talks', 'talked', or 'talking'.

information access rule A *party rule* that defines who can view, create, or update particular information. (Term: Author)

information retention rule An *activity restriction rule* that defines the minimum period for which a particular type of information is retained. (Term: Author)

inheritance The phenomenon whereby members of a *entity class* can be assumed to exhibit the properties of members of a *superclass* of that entity class.

intensional definition A definition that (unlike an *extensional definition*) cites both a *hypernym* (a term that signifies a superset of the set signified by the original term) and the characteristics that distinguish members of the set signified by the term being defined: for example, "Woman: an adult who is female".

intensive An attribute of the verb 'be' whereby it has not only a *subject* but a *complement* of the subject (i.e., another facet of the subject or one of its qualities, characteristics, or attributes): for example, "Ahmed is a man", "Indira is happy".

interrogative mood One of the two forms of the *indicative mood*, used to question the truth of a proposition (as in "does the form specify the departure date?"), as distinct from the other form of the indicative mood, the *declarative mood*, which is used to state a fact (as in "the form specifies the departure date").

interrupting event An event which causes the process to which it is attached to be aborted. (Term: BPMN)

intersection (of two or more sets) The set that contains all members that are in all of those sets.

intersection entity class A *relationship* represented using an *entity class*.

intransitive (of a *verb phrase*) Having a *subject* but no *object*.

irregular verb A *verb* for which the *past participle* is different from the *simple past tense*: for example, 'give', for which the past participle is 'given' and the simple past tense is 'gave'.

is-property-of fact type See *attribute fact type*. (Term: SBVR)

jointly exhaustive (with respect to a *categorization scheme*) Classifies that categorization scheme as consisting of a set of categories such that each member of the set of objects classified using that categorization scheme must belong to at least one of those categories.

list constraint A *rule pattern* that establishes a constraint on a subject that exhibits one or more characteristics, taken from a list. (Term: Morgan)

list definition An indication in a template that a syntactic element can be repeated indefinitely. (Term: Author)

literal A reference to a numeric value, textual value, category in a categorization scheme, date, time, or other time point in a programming language statement or rule statement.

mandatory column constraint An integrity constraint by which a DBMS ensures that a particular *column* has a value in every *row*. (Term: Author)

mandatory data item rule A *mandatory data rule* that requires that a particular data item be present. (Term: Author)

mandatory data rule A *data cardinality rule* that mandates the presence of data: that is, requires that a data item be entered in a transaction form or present in a message, or that a persistent data record include a value for a data item. (Term: Author)

mandatory dependent row constraint A requirement that, where a *row* in one *table* can be associated with multiple rows in a second table, there be at least one row in the second table for each row in the first table. (Term: Author)

mandatory group rule   A *mandatory data rule* that requires that at least one of a group of data items be present. (Term: Author)

mandatory group rule statement   A *rule statement* that expresses an *mandatory group rule*. (Term: Author)

mandatory option selection rule   A *mandatory data rule* that requires that one of a set of pre-defined options be specified. (Term: Author)

mandatory option selection rule statement   A *rule statement* that expresses an *mandatory option selection rule*. (Term: Author)

mandatory role constraint   A *constraint* that specifies the mandatory participation of each instance of a particular object type in at least one instance of a particular fact type: for example, each order must have at least one order line. (Term: ORM)

many-to-many relationship   A type of *relationship* between *entity classes* in which a member of either entity class can be associated with more than one member of the other entity class.

mass noun   See *non-countable noun*.

maximum cardinality rule   A *data cardinality rule* that places an upper limit (usually but not necessarily one) on how many instances of a particular data item there may be. (Term: Author)

metadata   Data about an artifact used in the design or implementation of a system: for example, data about an *entity class*, *attribute*, or *relationship* in a *data model*, a process in a process model, a *term* or *fact type* in a *fact model*, a *rule* or *rule statement*, a database *table* or *column*, or a *reusable service*.

modal auxiliary   An *auxiliary verb* that expresses obligation, prohibition, permission, necessity, possibility, intention, etc. The modal auxiliaries in English are 'may'/'might', 'must', 'can'/'could', 'shall'/'should', 'will'/'would'.

modality   One of the possible interpretations of a *modal auxiliary*, namely, *alethic modality*, *deontic modality*, or *epistemic modality*.

monotonic transition constraint   A *data update rule* that requires that a numeric value either only increase or only decrease. (Term: Author)

mood   A feature displayed by verb phrases which indicates whether the signified action, relationship, or state of being is actual, hypothetical, anticipated, or commanded.

motivation   The organizational reason for a rule, such as minimization of exposure to risk, cost reduction, revenue protection, maintenance of market share, or system simplicity.

multiple data rule   A *data cardinality rule* that mandates the presence of two or more instances of a particular data item in a particular situation. (Term: Author)

mutually exclusive (with respect to a *categorization scheme*)   Classifies that categorization scheme as consisting of a set of categories such that no member of the set of objects classified using that categorization scheme can belong to more than one of those categories.

n-ary association   An *association* involving more than two *object classes*.

name   See *proper name*.

named relationship fact type   An *associative fact type* other than a *partitive fact type* or *attribute fact type*.

Natural Language Information Analysis Method   The original name given to *Object-Role Modeling*.

necessity statement   A *rule statement* that expresses a necessity: that is, something that is necessarily the case (see Section 3.3.8.4 for a more detailed definition). (Term: SBVR)

negated (of a *verb phrase*)   The form of that verb phrase (using the word 'not') that indicates that the action, relationship, or state of being does not exist or is not to exist.

nested table   A datatype that allows a *column* in a database *table* to hold multiple values in any *row* in the form of subtables containing more than one row or more than one column.

NIAM   See *Natural Language Information Analysis Method*.

Nijssen's Information Analysis Method   An alternative interpretation of the acronym *NIAM*.

non-countable noun A noun that cannot be meaningfully used after the word 'each', and that does not have *singular* or *plural* forms (e.g., 'information', 'governance'), as distinct from a *countable noun* (e.g., 'customer', 'order', 'business day').

non-necessity statement A *statement of advice of possibility* advising that a situation is not necessarily the case. (Term: SBVR)

non-null A constraint on a *column* in a database *table* requiring there to be a value in every *row*.

non-obligation statement A *statement of advice of permission* advising that an action or situation is not obligatory. (Term: SBVR)

non-transferable relationship A *relationship* that is constrained so that instances of that relationship cannot be changed to involve different entity instances from those involved initially. For example, an Order Line cannot be transferred from one Order to another. (Term: Barker, 1990)

normative rule See *operative rule*.

noun A label which we can apply to one or more instances of a concept: that is, a person, organization, place, or concrete or abstract thing.

null option The option (if allowed) of including none of the options in an *option set* in a *template*.

number (of a *verb phrase*) The marking of that verb phrase to indicate whether the *subject* is *singular* or *plural*.

object (of a *transitive verb phrase*) The noun phrase following that verb phrase.

object class An artifact in an *object class model* that corresponds (more or less) to an *entity class* in an *entity-relationship model*.

object class model A type of *data model* used in *UML*, using *object classes*, *attributes*, and *associations* to represent objects of interest to an organization, their properties and relationships.

Object-Role Modeling A data modeling notation using *object types*, *fact types*, and *roles* to represent objects of interest to an organization (with their properties and relationships).

object type An artifact used in *Object-Role Modeling* to model an *entity class* or an *attribute*. (Term: ORM)

obligation statement A *rule statement* that expresses an obligation (see Section 3.3.8.3 for a more detailed definition). (Term and definition: SBVR)

on-screen form A form displayed on a computer monitor.

on-statement A statement specifying a condition and an associated action at the beginning of a block of code, such that that condition is then automatically tested each time there is a relevant change to any of the data item(s) covered by the condition, without that test having to be explicitly coded each time. (Term: PL/1)

operative rule A *rule* that states what must or must not happen in particular circumstances and which can therefore be contravened, as distinct from a *definitional rule* (or *structural rule*). (Term: SBVR)

operative rule statement A *rule statement* that expresses an *operative rule*. (Term: Author)

option set A set of options, available in a *template*, from which one may be chosen each time the template is used as the basis for a *rule statement*.

ordinal number One of the *determiners* 'first', 'second', 'third', etc.

ORM See *Object-Role Modeling*.

partitive fact type A *fact type* that expresses an association between a complex object and a part thereof: for example, between a form and a field therein. (Term: SBVR)

party restriction rule A *party rule* that places restrictions on who can perform some processes or activities or play some roles, based on age, some other physical characteristic or capability, or training, testing, and certification in the appropriate skills. (Term: Author)

party rule An *operative rule* that makes a distinction between different parties or the roles they play. (Term: Author)

party rule statement A *rule statement* that expresses a *party rule*. (Term: Author)

passive voice The use of a *verb phrase* such that the subject of that verb phrase is the person or thing on which the action is performed (the *patient* or *target*), as in "a boarding pass is presented by the passenger". By contrast, the subject of a verb phrase in ***active voice*** (as in "the passenger presents a boarding pass") is the person or thing performing the action signified by that verb phrase (i.e., the ***actor*** or ***agent***).

past participle The form of a ***verb phrase*** that can be used after 'be' to indicate the ***passive voice*** or after 'have' to indicate the ***perfect aspect***: for example, "It is written", "I have written".

past tense A form of a ***verb phrase*** that indicates that the action or relationship signified by that verb phrase occurs in the past (e.g., 'wrote', 'used to write', 'was writing', 'have written', 'had written'), as distinct from the ***present tense*** ('write', 'be writing') and ***future tense*** ('will write', 'will have written') forms.

patient See ***target***.

perfect aspect A form of a ***verb phrase*** that indicates that the time of the activity is indeterminate: for example, 'have specified', 'had specified', 'will have specified'.

perfective aspect An aspect of a verb used in some languages to indicate a completed activity.

permission statement A ***statement of advice of permission*** advising that an action or situation is permitted rather than prohibited. (Term: SBVR)

person One of the ways in which a verb phrase can vary, in this case to distinguish the speaker or writer (***first person***), the audience (***second person***), and other parties (***third person***): for example, the verb 'to be' has (in the indicative present tense) the forms 'am' (first person singular), 'is' (third person singular), and 'are' (second person singular and all persons plural). All other English verbs differ only in the third person singular: for example, 'pays', 'pay'.

personal pronoun A ***pronoun*** such as 'he', 'him', 'she', 'her', 'it', 'they', and 'them' (of which only 'it' should be used in rule statements, and that with care).

phrasal verb A ***transitive verb phrase***, such as 'check out' or 'look up', that involves a ***preposition*** (acting as an ***adverb***) that can either precede or follow the object of the verb phrase: for example, one can check out something or check something out, look up something or look something up.

placeholder A position in a ***template*** in place of which a ***term***, ***verb phrase***, ***literal***, or ***subtemplate*** is to be substituted when the template is used as the basis for a ***rule statement***. (Term: Author)

plural (of a ***noun***) The form of a noun that signifies that more than one instance of the concept signified by the noun is meant (e.g., 'persons') as distinct from the ***singular*** form (in this case, 'person') which signifies that only one instance of the concept is meant.

positive (of a ***verb phrase***) A form of a verb phrase that is not ***negated***.

possibility statement A ***statement of advice of possibility*** advising that a situation is possible. (Term: SBVR)

post-modifier (with respect to a ***noun***) An ***adjective*** following that noun and thus qualifying the meaning of that noun.

predicate A phrase expressing a state or condition that may or may not be true of each associated ***subject***: for example, 'is a citizen of the United States' is true of 'Ron Ross' but not true of 'Graham Witt'. A predicate can be used after a ***subject term*** in a ***conditional clause***, as in "if the passenger is a citizen of the United States".

predicative adjective An ***adjective*** that is part of a ***predicate*** following a ***noun*** and the word 'is' (as in "this bag is checked") as distinct from an ***attributive adjective***, which is used as a ***pre-modifier*** of a noun (as in "the international flight").

pre-modifier (with respect to a ***noun***) An ***adjective***, ***noun***, or (occasionally) a ***cardinal number*** or ***ordinal number*** preceding that noun and thus qualifying the meaning of that noun.

preposition One or more words that can be used in either or both of the following ways

1. after the ***verb*** 'be' and before a ***noun*** to express a relationship between the object signified by the noun before 'be' and the object signified by the noun after the preposition, as with 'on' in "the message is on the screen";

2. after the verb 'go' and before a noun to express movement by the object signified by the noun before the verb with respect to the object signified by the noun after the preposition, as with 'into' in "the flight crew goes into the aircraft";

3. after other verbs, as with 'into' in "enter into an agreement" and 'through' in "read through the document";

4. after nouns, as with 'on' in "the fields on this form".

prepositional verb A *transitive verb phrase* formed from a *simple verb* followed immediately by a *preposition* which cannot be moved to after the *object* of the verb phrase (e.g., 'apply for', 'buy into', 'act as'), as distinct from a *phrasal verb* (e.g., 'check out' or 'look up'), that involves a preposition that can either precede or follow the object of the verb phrase.

prescriptive rule See *operative rule*.

present tense A form of a *verb phrase* that indicates that the action or relationship signified by that verb phrase occurs now (e.g., 'write', 'be writing'), as distinct from the *past tense* ('wrote', 'used to write', 'was writing', 'have written', 'had written') and *future tense* ('will write', 'will have written') forms.

primary key The *column* (or combination of columns) in a *table* in a *relational database* that, holding a unique value (or combination of values) in each *row* of that table, enables other tables to hold unambiguous references (*foreign keys*) to individual rows.

procedural programming language A programming language that can only be used to specify the actions to be taken to achieve a desired result, as distinct from a *declarative programming language*, which can be used to specify that result.

procedural rule statement A rule statement that states what is to be done if a certain condition or set of conditions occurs (as distinct from a *declarative rule statement*).

process decision rule An *activity rule* that determines what action a business process or device is to take in specific situations. (Term: Author)

process sequence A set of processes in which each process other than the first must not start until the preceding process is completed.

progressive aspect A form of a verb phrase that expresses continuous activity, (e.g., 'am specifying', 'was specifying', 'will be specifying') as distinct from the *simple form* of the verb (e.g., 'specify', 'specified', 'will specify').

prohibited data rule A *data cardinality rule* that mandates the absence of some data item in a particular situation. (Term: Author)

prohibition statement A rule statement that expresses a prohibition (see Section 3.3.8.3 for a more detailed definition). (Term and definition: SBVR)

pronoun A word that may stand in place of a *noun* (or other pronoun) previously referred to: for example, 'him' as in "when Paul arrived, we recognized him".

proper name The name of a single entity instance, such as a person, business or other organization, place, time period, musical or other artistic work, or brand or product.

proper noun See *proper name*.

pseudo-code A description of the computational logic to be used in a system that uses one or more conventions of a programming language but is intended for comprehension by a human being rather than a system.

qualifying clause A clause used after a *term* in two ways

1. following the *subject term* of a rule statement, to restrict the scope of that rule statement to a subset of the set of objects signified by that term, rather than the set of all objects signified by that term (e.g., '*for* a return journey' in "Each flight booking request *for* a return journey must *specify* exactly one return date.")

2. following any other term in a rule statement, to make a constraint more specific than if the qualifying clause were absent (e.g., 'that *is current*' in "Each passenger must *present* a passport that *is current*.") (Term: Author)

quantifier A *general determiner* that gives some indication as to the number of instances meant, such as 'all', 'both', 'every', 'each', 'any', 'no'.

quantitative attribute An *attribute* on which some arithmetic can be performed (e.g., addition, subtraction) and on which comparisons other than '=' and '≠'[1] can be performed. (Term: Author)

---

[1]Note that the comparisons '=' and '≠' can be performed on any type of attribute.

quaternary fact type A *named relationship fact type* with four *terms* and three *connectors*, of which one is a *verb phrase* and the others are *prepositions*. (Term: inferred from SBVR)

range rule A *data content rule* that requires that the content of a data item be a value within a particular inclusive or exclusive single- or double-bounded range, or that the values contained in two data items in a transaction or record have a particular relationship to each other. (Term: Author)

recurrent (of a *business process*, activity, or event) occurring repeatedly, at regular or irregular intervals.

recursive foreign key A *foreign key* that refers to another *row* in the same *table* rather than a row in a different table.

recursive relationship A *relationship* between two instances of the same *entity class* or *object class*.

reference scheme One or more numbers, names, or codes that together uniquely identify each instance of a concept of interest. (Term: SBVR)

referential integrity constraint An integrity constraint by which a *DBMS* ensures that, in every *row* of a *table* in a *database*, a particular *column* (or combination of columns) has a value or values that match the value(s) in a specific column or columns in either
1. one of the rows of another database table or
2. another row of the same database table.

regular verb A *verb* for which the *past participle* is the same as the *simple past tense*: for example, 'specify', for which both past participle and simple past tense are 'specified'.

relational database A database that organizes data into *tables* and uses common values to associate *rows* in different tables (or different rows in the same table).

relationship A set of associations between instances of *entity classes* (e.g., 'Customer places Order' is a relationship that signifies each instance of a customer placing an order).

relationship term A *term* that signifies a *relationship* between entity classes signified by other terms (e.g., employment is a relationship term signifying the relationship between an organization in the role of employer and a person employed as an employee by that organization. (Term: Author)

relative clause A clause that is introduced by a *relative pronoun* (such as 'that', 'who', 'which', and 'whose' in "that Jack built", "who stole my heart", "which is very tasty", or "whose life is covered by the policy" respectively) or a relative pronoun such as 'which' or 'whom' preceded by a *preposition* (as in "at which those flights connect" or "for whom the bell tolls").

relative pronoun A *pronoun* that acts as the subject or object of the first or only verb in a *relative clause*.

responsibility rule A *party rule* that defines who is responsible for performing a particular process or liable for a particular fee, duty, or tax. (Term: Author)

restricted permission statement A *rule statement* that allows a situation to exist only if a particular condition applies (see Section 3.3.8.3 for a more detailed definition). (Term: SBVR)

restricted possibility statement A *rule statement* that expresses a situation that is possible only if a particular condition applies (see Section 3.3.8.4 for a more detailed definition). (Term: SBVR)

restrictive relative clause See *qualifying clause*.

reusable service A system component with defined request and response messages that can be used generally across an enterprise.

ring constraint A constraint that can be modeled in *ORM*, which governs a *recursive relationship*. (Term: ORM)

role An artifact used in *ORM* to model the part played by an *object type* in a *fact type*. (Term: ORM)

role binding rule A *party rule* that requires that the party performing the second of two activities be the same as the party who performed the first of those activities. (Term: Author)

role separation rule A *party rule* that prohibits the same party from performing two activities. (Term: Author)

role term A *term* that signifies the role played by one of the participating parties or objects in a relationship: for example, employer and employee are role terms (with respect to the relationship whereby an organization employs a person), whereas organization and person are not role terms. (Term: Author)

row A single record in a *table* in a *relational database*.

rule "One of a set of explicit or understood regulations or principles governing conduct or procedure within a particular area of activity ... a law or principle that operates within a particular sphere of knowledge, describing, or prescribing what is possible or allowable." (Definition: SBVR)

rule book A collection of rule statements expressing the rules governing an organization. (Term: SBVR)

rule pattern A template for a *rule statement* proposed in Morgan (2002). (Term: Morgan)

rule statement A guidance statement that expresses an operative or definitional rule. (Term: SBVR)

rule statement template A string of symbols that can be used as a *pro forma* for *rule statements* of a particular type. (Term: Author)

second person A form of a verb phrase indicating an action or relationship involving the audience rather than the speaker or writer (*first person*) or any other party (*third person*); in modern English, the second person form of all verb phrases is indistinguishable from the third person plural form: for example, 'speak', 'are', as in "you speak" ("they speak") and "you are" ("they are").

second person pronoun A *pronoun* that refers to the audience of an utterance: that is, (in English) 'you'.

set equality constraint A constraint that can be modeled in *ORM*, in which the set of instances of a particular *object type* that participate in one particular *fact type* must be identical to the set of instances of that object type that participate in another particular fact type. (Term: ORM)

set function A function that returns a single scalar value from a set: for example, sum, maximum, minimum, average.

signify Used throughout this book in to express the relationship between a *term* and the concept that the term is used for: that is, the term signifies the concept.

simple form (with respect to a *verb phrase*) A form of a verb phrase (such as 'specify', 'specified', 'will specify') that does not express either
   1. continuous activity (the *progressive aspect*, e.g., 'am specifying', 'was specifying', 'will be specifying') or
   2. activity at an indeterminate time (the *perfect aspect*, e.g., 'have specified', 'had specified', 'will have specified').
   (Term: Author)

simple noun A *noun* consisting of only one word, as distinct from a *compound noun*. (Term: Author)

simple past tense The *past tense* form of a *verb phrase* that does not use 'have', 'has', 'were', 'was', 'used to', or 'had': for example, 'gave', 'loved'.

simple qualifying clause A *qualifying clause* that does not include a *term* or *literal* that is itself qualified by a further qualifying clause (Term: Author)

simple temporal data constraint A *temporal data constraint* that requires that a particular date or time fall within a certain temporal range. (Term: Author)

simple verb A *verb* consisting of only one word, as distinct from a *compound verb*. (Term: Author)

singular (of a *noun*) The form of a noun that signifies that only one instance of the concept signified by the noun is meant (e.g., 'person') as distinct from the *plural* form (in this case, 'persons') which signifies that more than one instance of the concept is meant.

spatial data constraint A *data content rule* that prescribes or prohibits relationships between spatial properties (points, line segments, or polygons) specified in a record or set of records. (Term: Author)

specific determiner A *determiner* that limits the noun to referring only to a specific instance or instances, as distinct from a *general determiner*, which is used to limit the number of instances referred to by a noun without being specific as to which instance or instances are referenced.

SQL Structured Query Language: a standard language, in which the properties of the tables and columns of a database can be defined (using *DDL*—the Data Definition Language), and the data to be written to or read from a database can be defined (using DML—the Data Manipulation Language).

standard format definition A *definitional rule* that defines the standard format for data items of a particular type in terms of individual characters and/or component data items. (Term: Author)

state transition constraint A *data update rule* that limits the changes in a data item to a set of valid transitions. (Term: Author)

statement of advice See *advice statement*.

statement of advice of permission An *advice statement* advising of the absence of an *operative rule*. (Term: SBVR)

statement of advice of possibility An *advice statement* advising of the absence of a *definitional rule*. (Term: SBVR)

static data constraint A constraint which defines valid states of a set of persistent data, as distinct from a *dynamic data constraint*, which defines valid changes to that set.

structural assertion A *fact type* or a definition of a *term*. (Term and definition: Business Rules Group, 2000)

structural rule See *definitional rule*. (Term: SBVR)

structured business vocabulary See *fact model*.

subclass (of a *superclass*) An *object class* that contains some (but not all) of the members of the superclass but no object instances that are not members of the superclass: for example, the class of wide-body aircraft is a subclass of the class of aircraft (all wide-body aircraft are aircraft but not all aircraft are wide-body aircraft).

subclass name See *hyponym*.

subform A feature of a form that can be used to support the recording of
1. multiple records, each containing similar sets of data,
2. an optional set of data,
3. a set of data grouped to make data entry easier.

(Term: Author)

subject (of a *rule statement* or *conditional clause*) The *term* (possibly preceded by a *determiner* and possibly followed by a *qualifying clause*) that precedes the first *verb phrase* that is not part of a qualifying clause: for example,
1. 'Each passenger' in "Each passenger must present a boarding pass."
2. 'Each flight booking request that is for a return journey' in "Each flight booking request that is for a return journey must specify a return date."
3. 'That flight booking request' in "That flight booking request is for a return journey."

subject term (of a *rule statement*) The first or only *term* in the *subject* of that rule statement.

subjunctive mood A form of a *verb phrase* that expresses a wish or non-factual condition (e.g., 'be' and 'were' in "I insist he be there" and "if this were true" respectively), as distinct from the *indicative mood*, which states a fact (as in "the form specifies the departure date") or questions the truth of a proposition (as in "does the form specify the departure date?"), or the *imperative mood*, which directs a person or person(s) (or an intelligent device) to do something (as in "go away", "insert record"). (Definition: after Finch, 2005).

subset (of a *superset*) A set that contains some of the members of the superset but has no members that are not members of the superset: for example, the set of wide-body aircraft is a subset of the set of aircraft (all wide-body aircraft are aircraft but not all aircraft are wide-body aircraft).

subset constraint A constraint that can be modeled in *ORM*, in which all instances of a particular *object type* that participate in one particular *fact type* must participate in another particular fact type. (Term: ORM)

subset term See *hyponym*.

subtemplate A template for a syntactic element that may appear in more than one type of rule statement. (Term: Author)

subtype See *subclass*.

subtype constraint A constraint in an *ORM* model that specifies that each instance of a particular *object type* is an instance of another object type.

subtype name See *hyponym*.

suffix One or more letters added to the end of word to mark some aspect of that word: for example, 's' to denote the plural form of a noun as in 'cats', 'ed' to denote the simple past form of a verb as in 'warmed'.

superclass (of a *subclass*) An *object class* that contains all of the members of the subclass as well as object instances that are not members of the subclass: for example, the class of aircraft is a superclass of the class of wide-body aircraft (all wide-body aircraft are aircraft but not all aircraft are wide-body aircraft).

superclass name See *hypernym*.

superset (of a *subset*) A set that contains all of the members of the subset but may have members that are not members of the subset: for example, the set of aircraft is a superset of the set of wide-body aircraft (all wide-body aircraft are aircraft but not all aircraft are wide-body aircraft).

superset term See *hypernym*.

supertype See *superclass*.

supertype name See *hypernym*.

symbolic literal definition A *formal term definition* that defines the subject business term using one or more *literals*. (Term: Author)

synchronizing gateway A gateway in a process model which allows the following process to proceed only after all preceding processes are completed. (Term: BPMN)

synonym A noun that has the same meaning as another noun: for example, 'client' is often a synonym of 'customer'.

system rule A rule enforced by technology (hardware or software) as distinct from a business rule, which governs the behavior of the organization, its employees, and/or customers. (Term: Ross, Are Integrity Constraints Business Rules? Not!, 2009)

systemic functional grammar A theory of language, focused (as its name suggests) both on language as a set of systems and the function of language, first described in Halliday (1985) and developed in Halliday and Matthiessen (2004).

table A structure in a *relational database* in which each real-world object instance is represented by (usually) one *row* and in which each *attribute* that is recorded for each object instance is recorded in a separate *column*.

target The person or thing on which the action signified by a *verb phrase* in the *passive voice* is performed: for example, 'door' in 'the door is closed by the flight attendant'.

taxonomic fact type A *categorization fact type* or *assortment fact type*. (Term: Author)

taxonomic relationship A relationship between
1. a specialized concept and a more general concept that includes that specialized concept,
2. a *term* signifying a specialized concept and a term signifying a more general concept that includes that specialized concept (i.e., a *hyponym* and one of its *hypernyms*), or
3. a *proper name* and a *term* that signifies the concept that includes the object having that proper name.

taxonomy A collection of concepts and the terms that signify those concepts, each with definitions, in which each concept (except for a small set of top-level concepts) is recorded as being a specialized variety of some more general concept: for example, businesses, government bodies, and not-for-profit organizations are each particular types of organizations.

template See *rule statement template*.

temporal data Data that represent time points or time periods.

temporal data completeness constraint A *temporal data constraint* that requires that the time periods specified in a set of records (e.g., an employee's pay records) be contiguous and between them completely span some other time period (in this case, that employee's employment period). (Term: Author)

temporal data constraint A *data content rule* that constrains one or more *temporal data* items.

temporal data inclusion constraint A *temporal data constraint* that requires that the time periods specified in a set of records (e.g., an employee's leave and pay records) do not fall outside some other time period (such as that employee's employment period). (Term: Author)

temporal data non-overlap constraint A *temporal data constraint* that requires that the time periods specified in a set of records (e.g., an employee's leave records) do not overlap each other. (Term: Author)

temporal single record constraint A *temporal data constraint* that prohibits two records with two contiguous time periods and all other content identical. (Term: Author)

tense A feature displayed by verb phrases which indicates whether the signified action, relationship, or state of being is in the present, the past, or the future.

term A *noun* used to refer to a person, organization, place, or thing that is of interest to the organization for which the *fact model* is being developed. (Term: SBVR)

ternary fact type A *named relationship fact type* with three *terms* and two *connectors*, of which one is a *verb phrase* and the other a *preposition*. (Term: SBVR)

text attribute An *attribute* that can hold any string of characters that the user may choose to enter. (Term: Author)

third person A form of a verb phrase indicating an action or relationship involving a party other than the speaker or writer (*first person*) or the audience (*second person*); in modern standard English, all verbs (except the *modal auxiliaries*) have a distinct third person form in the *indicative present tense* and *singular number*: for example, 'writes' (as in "she writes"), compared with 'write' for the third person plural ("they write"), first person ("I write"), and second person ("you write").

third person plural personal pronoun In English, 'they'.

third person singular personal pronoun: In English, 'he', 'she', or 'it'.

third person singular present indicative (of a *verb phrase*) The distinct form of a verb phrase after a *third person singular personal pronoun* in the *present tense* and *indicative mood*: for example, 'writes'.

timer event An event which causes the following process in a process model to be initiated after a particular duration of time has elapsed. (Term: BPMN)

transitive (of a *verb phrase*) Having a *subject* and an *object*.

UML See *Unified Modeling Language*.

unary fact type A fact type with one *term* and one *connector*. (Term: SBVR)

Unified Modeling Language A synthesized object-oriented modeling approach, which includes a variety of model types, including *object class models*, which are used in many organizations as an alternative to *Entity-Relationship models*.

union (of two or more sets) The set that contains all members that are in at least one of those sets.

unique (with respect to a *column*) Classifies that column as having a different value in every *row* (i.e., being subject to a *uniqueness constraint*).

uniqueness constraint
1. An integrity constraint by which a DBMS ensures that a particular *column* (or combination of columns) in a *table* has different values in every *row*.
2. In ORM, a constraint in which each instance of a particular *object type* may participate in no more than one instance of a particular *fact type*.
3. A *data content rule* that requires that the content of a data item (or combination of data items) be different from that of the corresponding data item(s) in the same or other records or transactions.

valid value definition A *definitional rule* that defines the valid values of a particular measure, as a range or (occasionally) as a list of discrete values. (Term: Author)

value constraint A constraint that can be modeled in *ORM*, which constrains the values that a particular *object type* may take. (Term ORM)

value set rule A *data content rule* that requires that the content of a data item be (or not be) one of a particular set of values (either a fixed set or a set that may change over time), that the content of a combination of data items match or not match a corresponding combination in a set of records, or that the values contained in two or more data items form a valid combination. (Term: Author)

verb A word that signifies a process or relationship, such as
1. an action performed in the physical world, such as 'open', as in "open the bag", "open the door";
2. a mental process, such as 'like', 'know', 'think', 'understand';

3. a behavioral process, such as 'laugh', 'sneeze', 'walk', 'sleep';

4. a verbal process, such as 'say', 'tell', 'inform', 'explain', 'specify', 'ask';

5. a relationship, such as those expressed using 'be' or 'have'.

Every English verb other than a ***modal auxiliary*** exhibits the following two behavioral characteristics, which are only exhibited by verbs:

1. It inflects, in that the form after 'he', 'she', 'it', or a ***singular noun*** (e.g., 'is' and 'specifies') is different from the form after 'they' or a ***plural noun*** ('are' and 'specify' respectively).

2. It has a form (the ***infinitive***) that can follow the ***modal auxiliaries*** (including 'must' and 'may'). Except for 'is'/'are' (for which the infinitive form is 'be'), the infinitive form of all verbs is the same as the form after 'they' or a ***plural noun***.

verb phrase A ***simple verb*** or ***compound verb***.[2]

word class A set of words with similar characteristics: for example, ***noun, verb, determiner, adjective, preposition, conjunction, pronoun***.

---

[2]Note that the term ***verb phrase*** is used throughout this book with this meaning rather than the alternative meaning ascribed to this term by linguists, which more closely corresponds to that of ***predicate***.

Index

Note: Page numbers followed by *f* indicate figures and *ge* indicate glossary terms.

A

Access control, 15–16
Action assertion, 58, 305*ge*
Active verb phrase, 145, 305*ge*
Active voice, 108–109, 305*ge*
Activity conflict rule, 96, 97, 291, 292, 305*ge*
    fact types, 294–295
    options and placeholders, 293–294
    rule statement examples, 97, 293
    templates, 293
Activity exclusion period rule, 96, 290, 292, 305*ge*
    fact types, 294–295
    options and placeholders, 293–294
    rule statement examples, 96, 292
    templates, 293
Activity, human, 21–22, 84
Activity obligation rule, 82, 96, 97, 291, 293, 305*ge*
    fact types, 294–295
    options and placeholders, 293–294
    rule statement examples, 97, 293
    templates, 293
Activity pre-condition rule, 96–97, 290, 295–296, 305*ge*
    fact types, 295–296
    options and placeholders, 295
    rule statement examples, 97, 295
    template, 295
Activity prohibition rule, 96, 97, 291, 296, 305*ge*
    fact types, 296
    options and placeholders, 296
    rule statement examples, 97, 296
    template, 296
Activity restriction rule, 81, 96–97, 291–297, 305*ge*
    activity conflict rule, 97, 292, 305*ge*
    activity exclusion period rule, 96, 292, 305*ge*
    activity pre-condition rule, 96–97, 295, 305*ge*
    activity prohibition rule, 97, 296, 305*ge*
    activity time limit rule, 96, 292, 305*ge*
    categories, 96, 290
    information retention rule, 97, 297, 312*ge*
Activity rule, 84, 96–97, 231, 232, 290–298, 305*ge*
    activity obligation rule, 82, 97, 305*ge*
    activity restriction rule, 81, 96–97, 291–297, 305*ge*
    categories, 96, 290
    process decision rule, 96, 97, 297–298, 316*ge*
Activity rule statement, 172, 180–181, 305*ge*
    predicates, 180–181
    subjects, 172

Activity time limit rule, 96, 290, 292, 305*ge*
    fact types, 294–295
    options and placeholders, 293–294
    rule statement examples, 96, 292
    templates, 293
Actor, 108–109, 305*ge*
Adjectival, 103, 305*ge*
Adjective, 101, 102, 112, 115, 130, 134, 136, 138, 211, 223, 242, 305*ge*
    attributive, 109, 112, 113, 115, 306*ge*
    predicative, 109, 115, 315*ge*
    pre-modifier, 103, 115, 315*ge*
    use in compound nouns, 103, 115, 122, 131, 135
    use in standard format definition, 115
Adverb, 101, 110, 138, 181, 189, 305*ge*
Advice statement, 57, 61, 62, 305*ge*
    non-necessity statement, 62, 314*ge*
    non-obligation statement, 61, 314*ge*
    permission statement, 61, 315*ge*
    possibility statement, 62, 315*ge*
    SBVR formulation, 61, 62
    statement of advice of permission, 61–62, 319*ge*
    statement of advice of possibility, 62, 319*ge*
Agent. *See* Actor
Airline industry, 6, 9, 17, 22, 28, 68, 69, 128–129, 130–132, 137
Alethic modality, 111, 305*ge*
Algorithm, 14, 48, 85, 88, 246, 254–255
Ambiguity, 194–196
Analysis of rules
    "data analysis" approach, 207–214
    principal approaches, 207
    "raw rules" approach, 214–227
Arithmetic attribute. *See* Quantitative attribute
Article, 101–103, 112–113, 176–178, 240, 248, 306*ge*
    definite, 112–113, 137, 194, 219, 309*ge*
    indefinite, 103, 112, 114, 137, 311*ge*
Aspect, 106, 107, 306*ge*
    perfect, 107, 315*ge*
    perfective, 107, 315*ge*
    progressive, 107, 218, 316*ge*
Assertion, 42, 49–52, 49, 306*ge*
    action, 58, 305*ge*
    attribute, 50–51
    constraint, 52
    entity class, 49
    for intersection entity class, 51–52
    relationship, 49–50
    structural, 58, 319*ge*

Association, 34, 37, 39, 146, 151, 156, 157, 259, 306*ge*
  n-ary, 40, 43, 44, 313*ge*
Association class, 133, 306*ge*
Associative fact, 128, 306*ge*
Associative fact type, 128, 144–151, 306*ge*
Assortment fact type, 105, 144, 151–152, 153, 306*ge*
ATM. *See* Automated Teller Machine
Atomic rule, 214–215, 306*ge*
Attribute, 11, 34–37, 39, 45, 46, 58, 59, 61, 65–67, 72, 80–81,
    118, 124, 125, 127, 129, 130, 133, 140–143, 147,
    150, 151, 157, 166, 191, 206, 228, 231–233, 247,
    249, 299, 306*ge*
  arithmetic. *See* Attribute, quantitative
  Boolean, 141, 157, 306*ge*
  category, 86, 140, 141, 165, 250, 251, 307*ge*
  flag. *See* Attribute, Boolean
  identifier, 140, 141, 148, 311*ge*
  indicator. *See* Attribute, Boolean
  multi-valued, 50, 51
  of relationship, 50–51
  quantitative, 130, 140, 141–143, 149–150, 254, 255, 316*ge*
  text, 140, 321*ge*
Attribute assertion, 50–51
Attribute fact type, 129–130, 144, 147, 148–149, 157, 250, 251,
    254, 255, 306*ge*
  identification fact type, 147, 148–149, 311*ge*
  unary fact type, 143, 147–148, 157, 192, 321*ge*
Attribute term, 130, 133, 157, 191, 247, 248, 254, 255, 306*ge*
Attributive adjective, 109, 112, 113, 115, 306*ge*
Automated Teller Machine (ATM), 15, 17
Auxiliary verb, 109, 111, 306*ge*
  modal, 106, 108, 111, 313*ge*

B

Bachman, C., 34
Barker, R., 34, 37, 314
Basel II, 3
Basic constraint, 48, 306*ge*
Best practice, 5–6
Binary fact type, 143, 144, 157, 306*ge*
Boilerplate text, 239, 306*ge*
Boolean, 147, 148, 200, 306*ge*
Boolean attribute, 141, 157, 306*ge*
BPMN. *See* Business process modeling notation
Business glossary, 123–125, 136, 154, 306*ge*
Business jurisdiction, 1, 56
Business process, 15–18, 81–84, 306*ge*
  characteristics
    environmental knowledge, 16
    recurrent, 16
    subprocesses, 17
    trigger event, 17
  rules
    calculations, 18
    constraints on individuals or roles, 18
    decisions, 18
    'go/no-go' rule, 16
    pre-conditions, 17
Business process model, 40–41, 124, 125, 158, 228, 229, 306*ge*
  conditional start event, 41
  decision point, 40, 309*ge*
  interrupting event, 41, 312*ge*
  process sequence, 40, 41, 316*ge*
  synchronizing gateway, 40, 320*ge*
  timer event, 41, 321*ge*
Business process modeling notation (BPMN), 40
Business rule, 1–4, 56, 67, 68, 306*ge*
  importance, 4–5
Business Rules Approach, 2, 53, 56, 200
Business Rules Community, 2, 42, 68
Business Rules Group, 1–4, 53, 58, 229, 305
Business Rules Manifesto, 2, 3, 53–56
Business term. *See* Term

C

Calculation, 18, 48, 69, 88, 246, 254–256
Calendar gadget, 19
Cardinal number, 103, 114, 119, 159, 163, 238, 307*ge*
  use in compound nouns, 114
Case, genitive, 102, 311*ge*
CASE tool, 37, 307*ge*
Categorization fact type, 122, 144, 151, 153, 157, 247, 248, 307*ge*
Categorization scheme, 29, 68, 85, 86, 118, 130–132, 138, 140,
    155, 163, 165, 238, 246, 249–251, 307*ge*
  jointly exhaustive, 86, 130, 312*ge*
  mutually exclusive, 14, 44, 86, 130, 138, 313*ge*
Categorization scheme enumeration, 85, 86, 165, 246,
    249–250, 307*ge*
  fact types, 250
  options and placeholders, 250
  rule statement examples, 86, 249
  template, 249
Category, 14, 29, 68, 74, 76, 85, 87, 118, 130–132, 140, 141,
    163, 197, 199, 238, 246, 250–251, 289, 307*ge*
Category attribute, 86, 140, 141, 165, 250, 251, 307*ge*
Category transition constraint, 85, 87, 165, 250–251, 307*ge*
  fact types, 251
  options and placeholders, 251
  rule statement examples, 87, 250
  template, 251
Chained qualifying clause, 173, 187, 307*ge*
Characteristic. *See* Unary fact type
Chen, P.P., 34
Circumstantial (of the verb 'be'), 106, 307*ge*

Classification, 48, 307*ge*
Clause
  conditional, 116, 162, 180, 182, 183–185, 187–188,
    190–192, 195, 198–200, 202, 209, 210, 218, 221, 222,
    224, 243, 244, 258–261, 263–274, 276–281, 283–290,
    292–298, 300–302, 308*ge*
  qualifying, 112, 113, 116–118, 120, 162–164, 167, 168,
    172–174, 176–178, 181, 182, 184, 185–188, 190–194,
    196–200, 202, 209–211, 218, 221–226, 241–243,
    244–245, 246, 247, 252, 253, 255, 258–274, 277–281,
    283, 284, 287, 293–302, 316*ge*
  relative, 117, 317*ge*
  restrictive relative. *See* Clause, qualifying
Cobol, 25–26
Column, 11, 19, 21, 29, 140, 228, 230–233, 307*ge*
  non-null, 30, 314*ge*
  unique, 30, 321*ge*
Combo box, 19, 79
Common noun, 104, 307*ge*
Comparison operator, 200, 241, 280
Complement, 106, 307*ge*
Complex concept cardinality rule, 85, 87, 165, 246, 251–252,
    307*ge*
  fact types, 252
  options and placeholders, 252
  rule statement examples, 87, 251
  template, 251
Complex concept equivalence rule, 85, 87, 165, 246, 252–253,
    307*ge*
  fact types, 253
  options and placeholders, 252–253
  rule statement examples, 87, 252
  template, 252
Complex concept set constraint, 85, 87, 165, 246, 253, 307*ge*
  fact types, 253
  options and placeholders, 253
  rule statement examples, 87, 253
  template, 253
Complex concept structure rule, 87, 251–253, 307*ge*
  categories, 85, 246
  complex concept cardinality rule, 85, 87, 165, 246, 251–252,
    307*ge*
  complex concept equivalence rule, 85, 87, 165, 246,
    252–253, 307*ge*
  complex concept set constraint, 85, 87, 165, 246, 253,
    307*ge*
Complex data item, 167, 168–169, 171–174, 259, 264, 266, 268,
    269, 271, 273, 277, 307*ge*
Compound noun, 103–104, 113–117, 122, 131, 132, 134–135,
    157, 307*ge*
Compound verb, 109–110, 115, 116, 131, 307*ge*
Computation, 48, 307*ge*

Conditional clause, 116, 162, 180, 182, 183–185, 187–188,
    190–192, 195, 198–200, 202, 209, 210, 218, 221, 222,
    224, 243, 244, 258–261, 263–274, 276–281, 283–290,
    292–298, 300–302, 308*ge*
Conditional conjunction, 162, 182–183
  use in restricted permission statement, 182–183
Conditional start event, 41, 308*ge*
Conjunction, 116–117, 308*ge*
  conditional, 162, 182–183
  use in compound nouns, 104, 116, 117
  use in qualifying clauses, 116
  use in rule statements, 116
Connector, 11, 128, 150, 308*ge*
Constrained natural language, 8–10, 42, 102, 111, 237,
    308*ge*
  standardized syntax, 10
  standardized vocabulary, 8–10
Constraint
  action assertion, 58, 305*ge*
  basic, 48, 306*ge*
  category transition, 85, 87, 165, 246, 250–251, 307*ge*
  complex concept set, 85, 87, 165, 246, 253, 307
  data
    dynamic, 37, 71–72, 309*ge*
    static, 71, 319*ge*
    temporal, 92–94, 257, 282–286, 320*ge*
  database integrity, 20–21, 30–31
    temporal equivalents, 21
  day type, 94, 282, 286, 309*ge*
  dynamic data, 37, 71–72, 309*ge*
  exclusion, 38, 44, 310*ge*
  exclusive-or, 38, 44, 310*ge*
  frequency, 38, 40, 44, 310*ge*
  inclusive-or, 38, 44, 311*ge*
  list, 48, 312*ge*
  mandatory column, 21, 312*ge*
  mandatory dependent row, 21, 312*ge*
  mandatory role, 38, 42, 313*ge*
  monotonic transition, 89, 95, 258, 288, 290, 313*ge*
  referential integrity, 21, 317*ge*
  ring, 39, 45, 317*ge*
  set equality, 39, 44, 318*ge*
  spatial data, 89, 94, 257, 286–287, 318*ge*
  state transition, 89, 95, 258, 288, 289–290, 319*ge*
  static data, 71, 319*ge*
  subset, 39, 44, 319*ge*
  subtype, 39, 44, 319*ge*
  temporal data, 92–94, 257, 282–286, 320*ge*
  uniqueness, 21, 38, 43, 89, 92, 174, 176, 257, 276–279,
    321*ge*
  value, 39, 44, 321*ge*
Constraint assertion, 52

Construct, organizational, 68–69, 78
Containment, 147, 308*ge*
Contradiction, 203
Controlled natural language. *See* Constrained natural language
Conversion factor definition, 85, 88, 165, 246, 255–256, 308*ge*
    options and placeholders, 256
    rule statement examples, 88, 256
    template, 256
Countable noun, 102–103, 104, 114, 132, 308*ge*
Count noun. *See* Countable noun
Crystal, D., 101, 102, 154

D

Darwen, H., 93
"Data analysis" approach to rule analysis, 207–214
Database, 7, 8, 11, 19, 20–21, 29, 30–31, 34, 37, 70, 78, 84, 125, 137, 139–141, 228–230. *See also* Relational database
Database constraint, 30–31
    mandatory column, 21, 312*ge*
    mandatory dependent row, 21, 312*ge*
    referential integrity, 21, 317*ge*
    temporal equivalents, 21
    uniqueness, 21, 321*ge*
Database integrity constraint. *See* Database constraint
Database management system (DBMS), 30, 31, 157
    object-relational, 169
    relational, 169
Data calculation algorithm, 85, 88, 165, 246, 254–255, 308*ge*
    fact types, 255
    options and placeholders, 255
    rule statement examples, 88, 254–255
    template, 255
Data calculation rule, 88, 254–256, 308*ge*
    categories, 85, 246
    conversion factor definition, 85, 88, 165, 246, 255–256, 308*ge*
    data calculation algorithm, 85, 88, 165, 246, 254–255, 308*ge*
Data cardinality rule, 70, 89–91, 257, 258–270, 308*ge*
    categories, 88
    dependent cardinality rule, 88, 91, 166, 257, 269–270, 309*ge*
    mandatory data item rule, 88, 89, 221–224, 258–260, 312*ge*
    mandatory data rule, 70, 89–90, 257, 258–266, 312*ge*
    mandatory group rule, 88, 90, 258, 263–266, 313*ge*
    mandatory option selection rule, 88, 90, 258, 260–263, 313*ge*
    maximum cardinality rule, 88, 90, 257, 267–268, 313*ge*
    multiple data rule, 88, 90, 257, 269, 313*ge*
    prohibited data rule, 88, 90, 257, 266–267, 316*ge*
Data cardinality rule statement, 166–167, 172–174, 308*ge*
    predicates, 172–174
    subjects, 166–167
Data collection and recording, 69–72
    data cardinality rules, 70
    data content rules, 70–71

    dynamic data constraints, 71–72
    environments, 70
Data consistency rule, 89, 92, 257, 279–281, 308*ge*
    fact types, 280, 281
    options and placeholders, 279, 280, 281
    rule statement examples, 92, 279, 280, 281
    templates, 279, 280, 281
Data content rule, 70–71, 75, 91–95, 270–288, 308*ge*
    categories, 89, 257
    data consistency rule, 89, 92, 257, 279–281, 308*ge*
    data item format rule, 89, 95, 258, 287–288, 308*ge*
    equality rule, 89, 92, 174, 176, 221, 257, 275–276, 310*ge*
    range rule, 89, 91, 174, 176, 257, 274–275, 317*ge*
    spatial data constraint, 89, 94, 257, 286–287, 318*ge*
    temporal data constraint, 92–94, 257, 282–286, 320*ge*
    uniqueness constraint, 89, 92, 174, 176, 257, 276–279, 321*ge*
    value set rule, 89, 91, 174, 176, 210–212, 257, 270–274, 321*ge*
Data content rule statement, 166, 167–172, 174, 308*ge*
    predicates, 174–180
    subjects, 167–172
Data Definition Language (DDL), 6, 30, 33, 206, 207, 309*ge*
Data dictionary, 123, 125, 308*ge*
Data item format rule, 89, 95, 258, 287–288, 308*ge*
    fact types, 288
    options and placeholders, 288
    rule statement examples, 95, 171, 287
    template, 288
Data item format rule statement, 171, 308*ge*
Data, missing, 74–75
Data model, 7, 11, 34–40, 156–157, 205, 308*ge*
Data rule, 69–81, 84, 85, 88–95, 221, 231, 232, 257–290, 308*ge*
    categories, 88–89, 257–258
    data cardinality rule, 70, 89–91, 257, 258–270, 308*ge*
    data consistency rule, 89, 92, 257, 279–281, 308*ge*
    data content rule, 70–71, 75, 91–95, 270–288, 308*ge*
    data item format rule, 89, 95, 258, 287–288, 308*ge*
    data update rule, 95, 288–290, 308*ge*
    dependent cardinality rule, 88, 91, 166, 257, 269–270, 309*ge*
    equality rule, 89, 92, 174, 176, 221, 257, 275–276, 310*ge*
    mandatory data item rule, 88, 89, 221–224, 258–260, 312*ge*
    mandatory data rule, 70, 89–90, 257, 258–266, 312*ge*
    mandatory group rule, 88, 90, 258, 263–266, 313*ge*
    mandatory option selection rule, 88, 90, 258, 260–263, 313*ge*
    maximum cardinality rule, 88, 90, 257, 267–268, 313*ge*
    multiple data rule, 88, 90, 257, 269, 313*ge*
    prohibited data rule, 88, 90, 257, 266–267, 316*ge*
    range rule, 89, 91, 174, 176, 257, 274–275, 317*ge*
    spatial data constraint, 89, 94, 257, 286–287, 318*ge*
    temporal data constraint, 92–94, 257, 282–286, 320*ge*
    uniqueness constraint, 89, 92, 174, 176, 257, 276–279, 321*ge*
    value set rule, 89, 91, 174, 176, 210–212, 257, 270–274, 321*ge*

Data rule statement, 166–172, 308*ge*

Data update prohibition rule, 89, 95, 258, 288–289, 308*ge*
  fact types, 289
  options and placeholders, 289
  rule statement examples, 95, 288
  templates, 288, 289

Data update prohibition rule statement, 166, 308*ge*

Data update rule, 95, 288–290, 308*ge*
  categories, 89, 258, 288
  data update prohibition rule, 89, 95, 258, 288–289, 308*ge*
  monotonic transition constraint, 89, 95, 258, 288, 290, 313*ge*
  state transition constraint, 89, 95, 258, 288, 289–290, 319*ge*

Data update rule statement, 166, 180, 309*ge*
  predicates, 180

Date, C.J., 20, 74–75, 93

Day type constraint, 94, 282, 286, 309*ge*
  fact types, 286
  options and placeholders, 286
  rule statement examples, 94, 286
  template, 286

DBMS. *See* Database Management System

DDL. *See* Data Definition Language

Decision point, 40, 309*ge*

Decision table, 27–28, 309*ge*

Declarative mood, 107, 309*ge*

Declarative programming language, 25, 40, 309*ge*

Declarative rule statement, 58, 309*ge*

Default value, 19, 309*ge*

Definite article, 112–113, 137, 194, 219, 309*ge*

Definition, 136–137
  extensional, 86, 247, 310*ge*
  intensional, 85, 246, 312*ge*

Definitional rule, 14–15, 15, 58, 75, 76, 78–79, 84, 85–88, 164, 166, 177, 245–256, 309*ge*
  categories, 85, 245
  categorization scheme enumeration, 85, 86, 165, 246, 249–250, 307*ge*
  category transition constraint, 85, 87, 165, 246, 250–251, 307*ge*
  complex concept cardinality rule, 85, 87, 165, 246, 251–252, 307*ge*
  complex concept equivalence rule, 85, 87, 165, 246, 252–253, 307*ge*
  complex concept set constraint, 85, 87, 165, 246, 253, 307*ge*
  complex concept structure rule, 85, 87, 246, 251–253, 307*ge*
  conversion factor definition, 85, 88, 165, 246, 255–256, 308*ge*
  data calculation algorithm, 85, 88, 165, 246, 254–255, 308*ge*
  data calculation rule, 88, 254–256, 308*ge*
  formal extensional definition, 85, 86, 246, 247–248, 249, 310*ge*
  formal intensional definition, 85, 246–247, 310*ge*
  formal term definition, 85–86, 165, 246–249, 310*ge*
  standard format definition, 85, 88, 165, 246, 256, 318*ge*
  symbolic literal definition, 85, 86, 246, 248–249, 320*ge*
  valid value definition, 85, 87, 165, 246, 254, 321*ge*

Definitional rule statement, 60, 61, 164, 165, 179, 197, 198, 200, 309*ge*
  formulations, 60–61, 164
  subjects, 165
  templates, 164, 246–256

Demonstrative determiner, 113, 309*ge*

Deontic modality, 111, 309*ge*

Dependent cardinality rule, 88, 91, 166, 257, 269–270, 309*ge*
  fact types, 270
  options and placeholders, 269–270
  rule statement examples, 91, 167, 269
  template, 269

Dependent cardinality rule statement, 167, 309*ge*

Derivation, 58, 309*ge*

Derivation rule, 39, 45, 309*ge*

Derived fact type, 39, 153

Descriptive rule. *See* Definitional rule

Determiner, 47, 93, 103, 112–114, 186, 240, 309*ge*
  article, 101–103, 112–113, 176–178, 240, 248, 306*ge*
    definite, 112–113, 137, 194, 219, 309*ge*
    indefinite, 103, 112, 114, 137, 311*ge*
  demonstrative, 113, 309*ge*
  general, 114, 311*ge*
    cardinal number, 114
      use in compound nouns, 114
  specific, 113, 114, 318*ge*
    ordinal number, 113
      use in compound nouns, 113

Diagramming notation, 41, 45

Difference (of two sets), 178–179, 309*ge*

Documenting rules, 33–52, 229
  business process models, 40–41, 125
  business stakeholders, 7, 8, 33, 41, 230
  data models, 7, 34–40, 125
    Entity-Relationship (ER) Modeling, 34–37
    object class models, 34, 39–40
    Object-Role Modeling (ORM), 34, 37–39
    Unified Modeling Language (UML), 34, 39–40

Dynamic data constraint, 37, 71–72, 309*ge*

E

Electronic message, 20, 70

Empty set, 196–199, 309*ge*

Entity, 11, 125, 127, 129, 157, 206, 228, 231–234.
    See also Entity class

Entity class, 34–37, 39, 46, 49, 52, 124, 129, 130, 133, 147–149, 250, 251, 254, 255, 309*ge*

Entity class (*continued*)
    intersection, 51, 52, 132–133, 312*ge*
    subtype, 34, 35, 37–39, 44, 45, 49, 151, 157, 319*ge*
    supertype, 151, 320*ge*
Entity class assertion, 49
Entity-Relationship (ER) Model, 34–37, 39, 124, 125, 133, 157, 310*ge*
    attributes, 34–37
    data constraints, 34–37
    entities, 34–37
    example, 35–36, 35*f*
    relationships, 34–37
    subtypes, 34
    supertypes, 151
Entity-Relationship Modeling, 34, 37, 38, 40, 43, 310*ge*
Enumerated set, 33, 206, 208, 212, 310*ge*
Enumeration, 14, 49, 310*ge*
Environmental knowledge, 16
Epistemic modality, 111, 310*ge*
Equality rule, 89, 92, 174, 176, 221, 257, 275–276, 310*ge*
    fact types, 276
    options and placeholders, 276
    rule statement examples, 92, 275
    template, 276
Equality rule statement, 224–227
ER Model. *See* Entity-Relationship Model
Error message, 19, 25, 26
Event
    conditional start, 41, 308*ge*
    interrupting, 41, 312*ge*
    timer, 41, 321*ge*
    trigger, 17
Exclusion constraint, 38, 44, 310*ge*
Exclusive gateway, 40, 310*ge*
Exclusive, mutually (with respect to a categorization scheme), 14, 44, 86, 130, 138, 313*ge*
Exclusive-or constraint, 38, 44, 310*ge*
Execution, conditional, 25–26
Exhaustive, jointly (with respect to a categorization scheme), 86, 130, 312*ge*
Expression, 174, 176, 179, 243, 255
Extensible Markup Language (XML), 11, 20, 31–33, 124, 125, 169, 205, 228
Extensional definition, 86, 247, 310*ge*

F

Fact, 48, 55, 58, 128, 129, 132, 143, 310*ge*
    associative, 128
    vs. fact type, 55–56, 128, 143
Fact-Based Modeling. *See* Object-Role Modeling (ORM)
Fact model, 48, 58, 104, 121–158, 159, 163, 189, 190, 216, 217, 219, 238, 310*ge*
    attribute types, 140–143
    categories, 130–132, 140
    categorization schemes, 130–132, 140
    components, 126
    concepts, 126–127
    data item types, 140–143
    development process
        "bottom up" approach, 154–155
        deriving from data model, 156–157
        fact type discovery, 156
        maintenance, 227–228, 234–236
        publication, 156
        "top down" approach, 155
        workshops, 155–156
    fact types, 11, 37–39, 122, 123, 126, 128, 129–130, 131, 143–154, 157, 163, 190–194, 197, 216–219, 223, 224, 228, 229, 231–236, 247, 248, 250–255, 260, 262–263, 265–268, 270, 272, 273–281, 283, 284, 286–290, 294–297, 299–302, 310*ge*
    identification, 128–129
    maintenance, 227–228, 234–236
    object/identifier equivalence, 153–154
    proper names, 126, 133, 151, 227
    term definitions, 127, 136–137, 227
    terms
        attribute term, 130, 133, 157, 191, 247, 248, 254, 255, 306*ge*
        business term, 122, 125, 126, 132, 136, 137, 143, 151, 156, 227
        compound noun, 103–104, 113–117, 122, 131, 132, 134–135, 157, 307*ge*
        decisions, 133
        definitions, 127, 136–137, 227
        fundamental term, 133, 144, 146, 157, 191, 310*ge*
        homonyms, 133–134, 311*ge*
        hypernyms, 126, 138, 151, 153, 217, 311*ge*
        hyponyms, 126, 135, 138, 151, 153, 154–155, 217, 311*ge*
        relationship term, 132–133, 317*ge*
        role term, 133, 146–147, 248, 317*ge*
        synonyms, 123, 124, 126, 127, 133, 134, 189, 228, 234, 235, 320*ge*
        taxonomies, 124, 133, 138–143, 156, 320*ge*
        word choices, 133–136
    typographical conventions, 121–122
    uses, 122–124
Fact symbol, 128, 310*ge*
Fact type, 11, 37–39, 122, 123, 126, 128, 129–130, 131, 143–154, 157, 163, 190–194, 197, 216–219, 223, 224, 228, 229, 231–236, 247, 248, 250–255, 260, 262–263, 265, 268, 270, 272, 273–281, 283, 284, 286–290, 294–297, 299–302, 310*ge*
    associative, 128, 144–151, 306*ge*
    assortment, 105, 144, 151–152, 153, 306*ge*

Fact type (*continued*)
    attribute, 129–130, 144, 147–149, 157, 250, 251, 254,
        255, 306*ge*
    binary, 143, 144, 157, 306*ge*
    categorization, 122, 144, 151–153, 157, 247, 248, 307*ge*
    for comparison of quantitative attributes, 149–150
    derived, 39, 153
    higher-order, 143, 144, 145–146, 157
    identification, 147, 148–149, 311*ge*
    is-property-of. *See* Fact type, attribute
    named relationship, 144–147, 157, 313*ge*
    partitive, 144, 147, 157, 314*ge*
    quaternary, 143, 145, 317*ge*
    taxonomic, 144, 151–153, 320*ge*
    ternary, 143, 144, 145–146, 157, 192, 321*ge*
    unary, 143, 147–148, 157, 192, 321*ge*
    using role terms, 146–147
Finch, G., 102–103, 305, 311, 312
First person, 108, 310*ge*
First person pronoun, 108, 310*ge*
Flag attribute. *See* Boolean attribute
Flight booking, 15, 17, 20, 22, 28, 38, 39, 40, 60, 70, 75, 77, 83,
        109, 112, 114, 117, 122, 137, 144, 146, 165, 168, 170*f*,
        170–171, 172, 185, 189, 193–195, 197–201, 203,
        212–214, 259
Foreign key, 21, 30, 230–233, 310*ge*
    recursive, 30, 317*ge*
Formal extensional definition, 85, 86, 246, 247–248, 249, 310*ge*
    fact types, 248
    options and placeholders, 248
    rule statement examples, 86, 247
    template, 248
Formal intensional definition, 85, 246–247, 310*ge*
    fact types, 247
    options and placeholders, 247
    rule statement examples, 85, 246
    template, 246
Formal term definition, 85–86, 165, 246–249, 310*ge*
    categories, 85, 246
    formal extensional definition, 85, 86, 246, 247–248, 249, 310*ge*
    formal intensional definition, 85, 246–247, 310*ge*
    symbolic literal definition, 85, 86, 246, 248–249, 320*ge*
Frequency constraint, 38, 40, 44, 310*ge*
Functional grammar. *See* Systemic functional grammar
Fundamental term, 133, 144, 146, 157, 191, 310*ge*
Future tense, 107, 111, 311*ge*

G

Gateway, exclusive, 40, 310*ge*
General determiner, 114, 311*ge*
Genitive case, 102, 311*ge*
Global Financial Crisis, 3

Glossary. *See* Business glossary
Grammar, 101, 105
    functional. *See* Grammar, systemic functional
    systemic functional, 105–106, 320*ge*
GUIDE Business Rules Project, 1, 3, 4, 306

H

Halliday, M.A., 105, 106, 320
Halpin, T.A., 34, 37, 42, 45, 47
Hammurabi, 25
Harding, J., 42
Head noun, 103, 104, 134, 311*ge*
Higher-order fact type, 143, 144, 145–146, 157
Human activity, 21–22, 84
Hypernym, 85, 126, 138, 151, 153, 217, 235, 246, 311*ge*
Hyponym, 86, 126, 135, 138, 151, 153, 154, 155, 217,
        247, 311*ge*

I

Identification fact type, 147, 148–149, 311*ge*
Identifier, 21, 34, 141, 148, 153–154, 206, 311*ge*
Identifier attribute, 140, 141, 148, 311*ge*
If-statement, 26, 311*ge*
Imperative mood, 108, 311*ge*
Impersonal pronoun, 118, 311*ge*
Implementation of rules, 25–33
    in data, 28–29
    database constraints, 30–31
        data definition language (DDL) statements, 30
    graphical user interface building tools, 31
    program code, 25–27
        Cobol, 26
        if-statements, 26
        Java, 27
        .NET, 26–27
        on-statements, 27
        PL/1, 26, 27
        problems, 25
        Visual Basic, 26
    rules engines, 33
    XML schemas, 31–33
Impossibility statement, 60, 311*ge*
Impossible situation, 2, 75–78
    impossible placement, 76–77
    impossible sequence, 78
    impossible structure, 78
    impossible transition, 76
    impossible value, 75–76
Inclusive-or constraint, 38, 44, 311*ge*
Indefinite article, 103, 112, 114, 137, 311*ge*
Indicative mood, 107, 108, 311*ge*
Indicator attribute. *See* Boolean attribute

Industry
    airline, 6, 9, 17, 22, 28, 68, 69, 128–129, 130–132, 137
    insurance, 18, 27, 33, 41, 73–74, 82, 83, 127, 129
    passenger rail transport, 16, 22, 83, 127
    public transport, 16, 22, 57, 77, 79
Inequality operator, 254
Infinitive, 106–110, 143, 312*ge*
Inflection, 101, 102, 312*ge*
Information access rule, 98, 99, 172, 181, 298,
        300–301, 312*ge*
    fact types, 301
    options and placeholders, 301
    rule statement examples 99, 182, 300
    template, 301
Information retention rule, 97, 297, 312*ge*
    fact types, 297
    rule statement examples, 97, 297
    template, 297
Inheritance, 123, 153, 217, 312*ge*
"In-practice" model, 56, 73–74
Insurance industry, 18, 27, 33, 41, 73–74, 82, 83, 127, 129
Integrity constraint, database, 19
    mandatory column, 21, 312*ge*
    mandatory dependent row, 21, 312*ge*
    referential integrity, 21, 317*ge*
    temporal equivalents, 21
    uniqueness, 21, 321*ge*
Intensional definition, 85, 246, 312*ge*
Intensive, 106, 109, 312*ge*
Interface, user, 19–20, 31, 70, 79, 131, 205, 228, 230–233
Interrogative mood, 107, 312*ge*
Interrupting event, 41, 312*ge*
Intersection (of two or more sets), 178–179, 312*ge*
Intersection entity class, 51, 52, 133, 312*ge*
Inter-system message, 125, 139
Intransitive (of a verb phrase), 106, 110, 143, 148, 186, 294–296,
        312*ge*
Irregular verb, 109, 312*ge*
Is-property-of fact type. *See* Attribute fact type

J
Jacobson, I., 34
Java, 25, 26, 27
Jointly exhaustive (with respect to a categorization scheme), 86,
        130, 312*ge*
Jurisdiction, business, 1, 56

K
Key
    foreign, 21, 30, 230–233, 310*ge*
    primary, 30, 35, 316*ge*
    recursive foreign, 30, 317*ge*

L
Lam, G.S., 42, 46
Language, natural, 5, 7, 33, 56, 101, 137, 196
    constrained, 8–10, 42, 102, 111, 237, 308*ge*
    controlled. *See* Language, natural, constrained
    rule expression, 19, 42–52, 55, 57
        assertions, 49–52
        Morgan's rule patterns, 47–49
        ORM verbalization, 42–45
        RuleSpeak®, 46–47
Legislation, 1, 2–3, 4, 6, 33, 57, 65, 67–68, 127, 136, 139, 155,
        229
List constraint, 48, 312*ge*
List definition, 239, 312*ge*
Literal, 86, 118–120, 149, 150, 163, 165, 176, 183, 186, 187,
        242, 248, 249, 250, 251, 254, 272, 312*ge*
    typographical conventions, xvii, 122, 159
Lorentzos, N.A., 93

M
Magritte, R., 72
Maintenance
    fact model, 227–228, 234–236
    rule book, 230–236
Mandatory column constraint, 21, 312*ge*
Mandatory data item rule, 88, 89, 221–224, 258–260, 312*ge*
    fact types, 260
    options and placeholders, 259
    rule statement examples, 89, 258, 259
    template, 258
Mandatory data rule, 70, 89–90, 257, 258–266, 312*ge*
    categories, 88, 258
    mandatory data item rule, 88, 89, 221–224, 258–266, 312*ge*
    mandatory group rule, 88, 90, 258, 263–266, 313*ge*
    mandatory option selection rule, 88, 90, 258, 260–263,
        313*ge*
Mandatory dependent row constraint, 21, 312*ge*
Mandatory group rule, 88, 90, 258, 263–266, 313*ge*
    fact types, 265–266
    options and placeholders, 264–265
    rule statement examples 90, 174, 263–264
    templates, 264
Mandatory group rule statement, 174, 313*ge*
Mandatory option selection rule, 88, 90, 258, 260–263, 313*ge*
    fact types, 262–263
    options and placeholders, 261–262
    rule statement examples, 90, 173–174, 260–261
    templates, 261
Mandatory option selection rule statement, 173–174, 313*ge*
Mandatory role constraint, 38, 42, 313*ge*
Many-to-many relationship, 43, 313*ge*
Martin, J., 34

Mass noun. *See* Non-countable noun

Matthiessen, C.M., 105, 320

Maximum cardinality rule, 88, 90, 257, 267–268, 313*ge*
    fact types, 268
    options and placeholders, 268
    rule statement examples, 90, 267
    template, 267

Measurement, 14, 69, 75, 88, 255, 256

Message
    electronic, 20, 70
    error, 19, 25, 26
    inter-system, 125, 139
    XML, 169, 205

Message schema, 11

Metadata, 10–11, 137, 205, 227–229, 232, 313*ge*

Methodology, rule management, 205–236
    analysis, 207–227
        "data analysis" approach, 207–214
        "raw rules" approach, 214–227
    documentation, 229
    implementation, 231–232
    maintenance, 230–236
    metadata, 227–229
        fact type, 228
        name, 227–228
        rule, 229
        term, 227–228
    publication, 230
    quality assurance, 230
    rule sources, 205–207

Missing data, 74–75

Modal auxiliary, 106, 108, 111, 313*ge*

Modality, 111, 313*ge*
    alethic, 111, 305*ge*
    deontic, 111, 309*ge*
    epistemic, 111, 310*ge*

Model
    data, 7, 11, 34–40, 125, 156–158, 205, 308*ge*
    fact, 48, 58, 104, 121–158, 159, 163, 189, 190, 216, 217, 219, 238, 310*ge*
    "in-practice", 56, 73–74
    object class, 34, 39–40, 124, 125, 133, 146, 147, 151, 157, 314*ge*
    process, 40–41, 124, 125, 158, 228, 229, 306*ge*
    "reality", 56, 73

Monotonic transition constraint, 89, 95, 258, 288, 290, 313*ge*
    fact types, 290
    options and placeholders, 290
    rule statement examples, 95, 290
    template, 290

Mood, 107–108, 313*ge*
    declarative, 107, 309*ge*

imperative, 108, 311*ge*
    indicative, 107, 108, 311*ge*
    interrogative, 107, 312*ge*
    subjunctive, 108, 319*ge*

Moore, D., 169

Morgan, T., 42, 47–49, 306, 307, 310, 312
    basic constraint, 48
    classification, 48
    components, 47–48
    computation, 48
    enumeration, 49
    list constraint, 48
    rule pattern, 47–49

Motivation, 4, 67, 229, 313*ge*

Multiple data rule, 88, 90, 257, 269, 313*ge*
    rule statement examples, 90
    template, 269

Multi-valued attribute, 50, 51

Mutually exclusive (with respect to a categorization scheme), 14, 44, 86, 130, 138, 313*ge*

N

Name. *See* Name, proper

Named relationship fact type, 144–147, 157, 313*ge*
    binary, 143, 144, 157, 306*ge*
    higher-order, 145–146
    using role terms, 146–147

Name, proper, 102, 104–105, 121, 126, 133, 134, 138, 151, 227, 228, 316*ge*
    typographical conventions, xvii, 122, 159
    n-ary association, 40, 43, 44, 313*ge*

Natural language, 5, 7, 33, 56, 101, 137, 196
    constrained, 8–10, 42, 102, 111, 237, 308*ge*
    controlled. *See* Natural language, constrained
    rule expression, 19, 42–52, 55, 57
        assertions, 49–52
        Morgan's rule patterns, 47–49
        ORM verbalization, 42–45
        RuleSpeak®, 46–47

Natural Language Information Analysis Method (NIAM). *See* Object-Role Modeling (ORM)

Natural language rule statement, 5, 6, 10, 45, 55, 101, 159, 229
    adjectives, 101, 102, 112, 115, 130, 134, 136, 138, 211, 223, 242, 305*ge*
    adverbs, 101, 110, 138, 181, 189, 305*ge*
    articles, 101–103, 112–113, 176–178, 240, 248, 306*ge*
    conditional clauses, 116, 162, 180, 182, 183–185, 187–188, 190–192, 195, 198–200, 202, 209, 210, 218, 221, 222, 224, 243, 244, 258–261, 263–274, 276–281, 283–290, 292–298, 300–302, 308*ge*
    conditional conjunctions, 162, 182–183

Natural language rule statement (*continued*)
  definitional, 60–61, 164, 165, 179, 197, 198, 200, 309*ge*
  determiners, 47, 93, 103, 112–114, 186, 240, 309*ge*
    general, 114, 311*ge*
    specific, 113, 114, 318*ge*
  literals, 86, 118–120, 149, 150, 163, 165, 176, 183, 186, 187, 242, 248, 249, 250, 251, 254, 272, 312*ge*
  nouns, 101, 102–104, 314*ge*
    countable and non-countable, 102–103
    simple and compound, 103–104
  operative, 58–60, 62, 78, 161–163, 164, 166, 172–182, 198, 200, 314*ge*
  predicates, 172–182, 242, 315*ge*
  prepositions, 11, 103, 109, 110, 115–116, 118, 122, 128, 135, 143–145, 163, 186, 192, 211, 223, 235, 236, 238, 252, 292, 294, 315*ge*
  pronouns, 108, 117–118, 120, 160, 183, 186, 189, 194, 316*ge*
  proper names, 102, 104–105, 121, 126, 133, 134, 138, 151, 227, 228, 316*ge*
  punctuation conventions, 160
  qualifying clauses, 112, 113, 116–118, 120, 162–164, 167, 168, 172–174, 176–178, 181, 182, 184, 185–188, 190–194, 196–200, 202, 209–211, 218, 221–226, 241–243, 244–245, 246, 247, 252, 253, 255, 258–274, 277–281, 283, 284, 287, 293–302, 316*ge*
  quality
    ambiguity, 194–196
    contradiction, 203
    criteria, 189–190
    duplication, 200–201
    fact type support, 190–194
    multiple complementary rule statements, 203
    overlap, 201–202
    redundant clauses, 199–200
    self-contradiction, 196–199
  subjects, 164–172
  templates, 42, 164, 172, 188–189, 237–302
    multiple formulations, 189
    sentence forms, 42–45, 46–47, 161–163, 188
  'that', uses of
    conjunction, 120
    determiner, 120
    relative pronoun, 120
  typographical conventions
    literal values, 159
    prepositions, 160
    proper names, 159
    terms, 159
    verb phrases, 160
  verbs, 105–112

Necessity statement, 60, 313*ge*
Negated (of a verb phrase), 107, 109, 186, 313*ge*
Nested table, 169, 313*ge*
.NET, 25–27
NIAM. *See* Object-Role Modeling (ORM)
Nijssen, G.M., 34, 37
  Information Analysis Method. *See* Object-Role Modeling (ORM)
Non-countable noun, 102–103, 104, 114, 314*ge*
Non-necessity statement, 62, 314*ge*
Non-null, 30, 314*ge*
Non-obligation statement, 61, 314*ge*
Non-transferable relationship, 37, 95, 166, 288, 314*ge*
Normative rule. *See* Operative rule
Notation, diagramming, 41, 45
Noun, 101, 102–104, 314*ge*
  common, 104, 307*ge*
  compound, 103–104, 113–117, 122, 131, 132, 134–136, 157, 307*ge*
  count. *See* Noun, countable
  countable, 102–103, 104, 114, 132, 308*ge*
  head, 103, 104, 134, 311*ge*
  mass. *See* Noun, non-countable
  non-countable, 102–103, 104, 114, 314*ge*
  simple, 103, 104, 116, 122, 132, 318*ge*
  use in fact types, 104
  use in rule statements, 104
Null option, 162, 238, 314*ge*
Number
  cardinal, 103, 114, 119, 159, 163, 238, 307*ge*
  ordinal, 103, 113, 114, 314*ge*
Number (of a verb phrase), 108, 314*ge*
  plural, 108
  singular, 108

O

Object (of a transitive verb phrase), 106, 110, 117, 148, 174, 242, 244, 314*ge*
Object class, 11, 39, 40, 124, 125, 127, 129, 130, 133, 147–149, 157, 250, 251, 314*ge*
Object class model, 34, 39–40, 124, 125, 133, 146, 147, 151, 157, 314*ge*
Object Constraint Language (OCL), 25, 40
Object Management Group (OMG), xvii, 1, 3, 34, 40, 56, 108, 122, 143, 146
Object-Role Modeling (ORM), 34, 37–39, 40, 42–45, 124, 125, 133, 314*ge*
  comparison with ER modeling and UML, 37–39
  data constraints, 38–39
    derivation rule, 39, 45, 309*ge*
    exclusion constraint, 38, 44, 310*ge*
    exclusive-or constraint, 38, 44, 310*ge*

Object-Role Modeling (ORM) (*continued*)
  frequency constraint, 38, 40, 44, 310*ge*
  inclusive-or constraint, 38, 44, 311*ge*
  mandatory role constraint, 38, 42, 313*ge*
  ring constraints, 39, 45, 317*ge*
  set equality constraint, 39, 44, 318*ge*
  subset constraint, 39, 44, 319*ge*
  subtype constraint, 39, 44, 319*ge*
  uniqueness constraint, 38, 43, 321*ge*
  value constraint, 39, 44, 321*ge*
  fact types, 37–39
  object types, 37–39, 314*ge*
  roles, 37–39
  verbalization
    combined mandatory and uniqueness constraint, 43
    derivation rule, 45
    exclusion constraint, 44
    exclusive-or constraint, 44
    frequency constraint, 44
    inclusive-or constraint, 44
    mandatory role constraint, 42
    many-to-many relationship, 43
    n-ary association, 43
    ring constraints, 45
    set equality constraint, 44
    subset constraint, 44
    subtype constraint, 44
    uniqueness constraint, 43
    value constraint, 44
Object type, 37–39, 314*ge*
Obligation statement, 58–59, 201, 314*ge*
OCL. *See* Object Constraint Language
OMG. *See* Object Management Group
OMT. *See* Object Modeling Technique
On-screen form, 15, 16, 19, 31, 314*ge*
On-statement, 27, 314*ge*
Operative rule, 13, 15, 56, 58–60, 61, 67, 68, 75, 76, 78, 79, 84, 161–163, 314*ge*
  activity rule, 84, 96–97, 231, 232, 290–298, 305*ge*
  categories, 84
  data rule, 69–81, 84, 85, 88–95, 221, 231, 232, 257–290, 308*ge*
  party rule, 84, 98–99, 172, 181, 182, 298–302, 314*ge*
Operative rule statement, 58–60, 62, 78, 161–163, 164, 166, 172–182, 198, 200, 314*ge*
  formulations, 58–60, 161–163
  obligation statement, 58–59, 201, 314*ge*
  predicates, 172–182
  prohibition statement, 59, 60, 173, 316*ge*
  restricted permission statement, 59, 60, 182, 201, 317*ge*
  subjects, 166–172
  templates, 161–163, 257–302

Operator, comparison, 200, 241, 280
Option set, 222, 238, 239, 314*ge*
Order entry, 21, 30–31, 34–37
Ordinal number, 103, 113, 114, 314*ge*
Organizational construct, 68–69, 78
ORM. *See* Object-Role Modeling

P

Participle, past, 109, 110, 315*ge*
Partitive fact type, 144, 147, 157, 314*ge*
Party restriction rule, 98, 298–299, 314*ge*
  fact types, 299
  options and placeholders, 299
  rule statement examples, 98, 298
  template, 299
Party rule, 84, 98–99, 172, 181, 182, 298–302, 314*ge*
  categories, 98, 298
  information access rule, 98, 99, 172, 181, 298, 300–301, 312*ge*
  party restriction rule, 98, 298–299, 314*ge*
  responsibility rule, 98, 99, 172, 182, 298, 301–302, 317*ge*
  role binding rule, 98, 182, 298, 299–300, 317*ge*
  role separation rule, 98, 182, 298, 299–300, 317*ge*
Party rule statement, 172, 181, 314*ge*
  predicates, 181–182
  subjects, 172
Passenger rail transport, 16, 22, 83, 127
Passive voice, 109, 145, 167, 181, 314*ge*
Past participle, 109, 110, 315*ge*
Past tense, 107, 143, 315*ge*
  simple, 109, 318*ge*
Patient. *See* Target
Perfect aspect, 107, 315*ge*
Perfective aspect, 107, 315*ge*
Permission statement, 61, 315*ge*
Person, 107, 108, 315*ge*
  first, 108, 310*ge*
  second, 108, 318*ge*
  third, 108, 321*ge*
Personal pronoun, 108, 117, 189, 194, 315*ge*
  third person plural, 108, 321*ge*
  third person singular, 108, 321*ge*
Phrasal verb, 104, 110, 315*ge*
Physical world, impact of on rule expression
  invariant attributes and relationships, 81
  mandatory attributes and relationships, 80
  multi-valued attributes and relationships, 80
  optional attributes and relationships, 80
  single-valued attributes and relationships, 80
  variant attributes and relationships, 81
Physical world, rules governing
  constraints between attributes, 66

Physical world, rules governing (*continued*)
    definitional rules, 14–15
    illegal/unsafe situations, 79–80
    impossible situations
      impossible placement, 76–77
      impossible sequence, 78
      impossible structure, 78
      impossible transition, 76
      impossible value, 75–76
    invariant attributes and relationships, 66
    mandatory attributes and relationships, 65–66, 80
    multi-valued attributes and relationships, 66, 80
    optional attributes and relationships, 65–66, 80
    single-valued attributes and relationships, 66, 80
    variant attributes and relationships, 66
Physical world, taking account of, 72–81
Physics, laws of, 1, 2, 3, 6, 57, 76
Pick list, 19, 79
PL/1, 25, 26
Placeholder, 128, 162, 163, 209, 210, 211, 221–225, 238–244,
    315*ge*
Plural (of a noun), 11, 102, 104, 106, 108, 112, 132, 196,
    315*ge*
Positive (of a verb phrase), 107, 315*ge*
Possibility statement, 62, 315*ge*
Postgres, 169
Post-modifier, 103, 315*ge*
Predicate, 172–182, 242, 315*ge*
    in activity rule statements, 180–181
    in data cardinality rule statements, 172–174
    in data content rule statements
      constraining combinations of data items, 177–178
      constraining format of data items, 177
      constraining sets of data items, 178–180
      constraining values of single data items, 174–177
    in data update rule statements, 180
    in operative rule statements, 172–182
    in party rule statements, 181–182
Predicative adjective, 109, 115, 315*ge*
Pre-modifier, 103, 115, 315*ge*
Preposition, 11, 103, 109, 110, 115–116, 118, 122, 128, 135,
    143–145, 163, 186, 192, 211, 223, 235, 236, 238, 252,
    292, 294, 316*ge*
    standardization, 122, 218
    typographical conventions, 160
Prepositional verb, 110, 117, 316*ge*
Prescriptive rule. *See* Operative rule
Present tense, 107, 108, 316*ge*
Primary key, 30, 35, 316*ge*
Procedural programming language, 25, 31,
    316*ge*
Procedural rule statement, 58, 316*ge*

Process decision rule, 96, 97, 297–298, 316*ge*
    fact types, 297–298
    options and placeholders, 297
    rule statement examples, 297
    template, 297
Process model. *See* Business process model
Process sequence, 40, 41, 316*ge*
Program code, 6, 7, 25–27, 28–29, 33, 55, 206, 207
Programming language
    declarative, 25, 40, 309*ge*
    procedural, 25, 31, 316*ge*
Program module, 11
Progressive aspect, 107, 218, 316*ge*
Prohibited data rule, 88, 90, 257, 266–267, 316*ge*
    fact types, 267
    options and placeholders, 266–267
    rule statement examples, 90, 266
    template, 266–267
Prohibition statement, 59, 60, 173, 316*ge*
Prolog, 25
Pronoun, 108, 117–118, 120, 160, 183, 186, 189, 194,
    316*ge*
    first person, 108, 310*ge*
    impersonal, 118, 311*ge*
    personal, 108, 117, 189, 194, 315*ge*
    relative, 117, 120, 160, 186, 317*ge*
    second person, 108, 318*ge*
    third person plural, 108, 321*ge*
    third person singular, 108, 321*ge*
    use in rule statements, 118, 189, 194
Proper name, 102, 104–105, 121, 126, 133, 134, 138, 151, 227,
    228, 316*ge*
    typographical conventions, xvii, 122, 159
Proper noun. *See* Proper name
Pseudo-code, 6, 7, 8, 316*ge*
Public transport, 16, 22, 57, 77, 79

Q

Qualifying clause, 112, 113, 116–118, 120, 162–164,
    167, 168, 172–174, 176–178, 181, 182, 184,
    185–188, 190–194, 196–200, 202, 209–211, 218,
    221–226, 241–243, 244–245, 246, 247, 252, 253,
    255, 258–274, 277–281, 283, 284, 287, 293–302,
    316*ge*
    chained, 173, 187, 307*ge*
    simple, 171, 187, 318*ge*
Quality criteria, 189–190
Quantifier, 114, 316*ge*
Quantitative attribute, 130, 140, 141–143, 149–150, 254, 255,
    316*ge*
Quaternary fact type, 143, 145, 317*ge*

R

Range rule, 89, 91, 174, 176, 257, 274–275, 317*ge*
  fact types, 275
  options and placeholders, 274–275
  rule statement examples, 91, 274
  template, 275
"Raw rules" approach to rule analysis, 214–227
  ambiguity removal, 215–216, 217
  cardinalities, 219–220
  context removal, 215
  exceptions and generalization, 218–219
  fact type identification, 217–218
  non-atomic rule, decomposition, 214–215
  rule classification, 221
  subject, rule statement, 221
  syntax standardization, 221–227
  vocabulary standardization
    terms, 216
    verb phrases and prepositions, 218
"Reality" model, 56, 73
Real property, 41, 67, 71, 78–79, 214–227, 269
Recurrent, 16, 119, 142, 317*ge*
Recursive foreign key, 30, 317*ge*
Recursive relationship, 39, 45, 49, 317*ge*
Redundant clauses, 199–200
Reference scheme, 128–129, 149, 317*ge*
Referential integrity constraint, 21, 317*ge*
Regular verb, 109, 317*ge*
Regulation, 1, 2–3, 3, 4, 5, 6, 33, 57, 65, 67–68, 80, 127, 139, 205
Relational database, 135, 317*ge*
  column, 11, 19, 21, 29, 140, 228, 230–233, 307*ge*
    non-null, 30, 314*ge*
    unique, 30, 321*ge*
  foreign key, 21, 30, 230–233, 310*ge*
    recursive, 30, 317*ge*
  nested table, 169, 313*ge*
  primary key, 30, 35, 316*ge*
  row, 19, 21, 29, 30, 317*ge*
  table, 8, 11, 19, 21, 29, 30, 228, 230–233, 320*ge*
Relationship, 21, 34–37, 39, 46, 49, 50, 51, 52, 65–67, 72, 80–81, 124, 127, 140, 157, 206, 228, 231, 232, 233, 317*ge*
  many-to-many, 43, 313*ge*
  non-transferable, 37, 95, 166, 288, 314*ge*
  recursive, 39, 45, 49, 317*ge*
  taxonomic, 125–126, 320*ge*
Relationship assertion, 49–50
Relationship term, 132–133, 317*ge*
Relative clause, 117, 317*ge*
Relative pronoun, 117, 120, 160, 186, 317*ge*
Repository, rule, 10, 11, 145, 160
Responsibility rule, 98, 99, 172, 182, 298, 301–302, 317*ge*
  fact types, 302
  options and placeholders, 302
  rule statement examples, 99, 182, 301
  template, 302
Restricted permission statement, 59, 60, 182, 201, 317*ge*
Restricted possibility statement, 60, 317*ge*
Restrictive relative clause. *See* Qualifying clause
Reusable service, 8, 11, 317*ge*
Ring constraint, 39, 45, 317*ge*
Role, 37–39, 317*ge*
Role binding rule, 98, 182, 298, 299–300, 317*ge*
  fact types, 300
  options and placeholders, 300
  rule statement examples, 98, 300
  template, 300
Role separation rule, 98, 182, 298, 299–300, 317*ge*
  fact types, 300
  options and placeholders, 300
  rule statement examples, 98, 182, 299
  templates, 300
Role term, 133, 146–147, 248, 317*ge*
Ross, R.G., 1, 4, 41, 42, 46, 47, 53, 56, 59, 123, 151
  diagramming notation, 41, 45
  rule taxonomy, 41
Row, 19, 21, 29, 30, 317*ge*
Rule, 318*ge*
  activity, 84, 96–97, 231, 232, 290–298, 305*ge*
  atomic, 214–215, 306*ge*
  business, 1–4, 56, 67, 68, 306*ge*
  data, 69–81, 84, 85, 88–95, 221, 231, 232, 257–290, 308*ge*
  definitional, 14–15, 15, 58, 75, 76, 78–79, 84, 85–88, 164, 166, 177, 245–256, 309*ge*
  derivation, 39, 45, 309*ge*
  descriptive. *See* Rule, definitional
  motivation, 4, 67, 229, 313*ge*
  normative. *See* Rule, operative
  operative, 13, 15, 56, 58–60, 61, 67, 68, 75, 76, 78, 79, 84, 161–163, 314*ge*
  party, 84, 98–99, 172, 181, 182, 298–302, 314*ge*
  prescriptive. *See* Rule, operative
  vs. rule statement, 56–57
  system, 3–4, 320*ge*
Rule analysis
  "data analysis" approach, 207–214
  principal approaches, 207
  "raw rules" approach, 214–227
Rule book, 9–10, 125, 318*ge*
  maintenance, 230–236
    implemented data component addition/modification, 233–233
    rule addition, 231
    rule change, 231–232

Rule book (*continued*)
  rule retirement, 232
  software component addition/modification, 233–234
  vocabulary change, 234–236
    quality assurance, 230
Rule discovery
  collection, 206–207
  sources, 205–206
Rule documentation. *See* Documenting rules
Rule engine. *See* Rules engine
Rule implementation. *See* Implementation of rules
Rule management, 205–236
  analysis, 207–227
    "data analysis" approach, 207–214
    "raw rules" approach, 214–227
  documentation, 229
  implementation, 231–232
  maintenance, 230–236
  metadata, 227–229
    fact type, 228
    name, 227–228
    rule, 229
    term, 227–228
  publication, 230
  quality assurance, 230
  rule sources, 205–207
Rule pattern, 47–49, 318*ge*
  basic constraint, 48
  classification, 48
  components, 47–48
  computation, 48
  enumeration, 49
  list constraint, 48
Rule repository, 10, 11, 145, 160
Rules engine, 6, 7, 10, 33
RuleSpeak®, 46–47, 59, 60–61, 61, 62, 111
  business rule statements, 46
  statements of advice, 47
Rule statement, 318*ge*
  quality
    ambiguity, 194–196
    contradiction, 203
    criteria, 189–190
    duplication, 200–201
    fact type support, 190–194
    multiple complementary rule statements, 203
    overlap, 201–202
    self-contradiction, 196–199
  vs. rule, 56–57
  types
    action assertion, 58, 305*ge*
    activity rule statement, 172, 180–181, 305*ge*

data cardinality rule statement, 166–167, 172–174, 308*ge*
data content rule statement, 166, 167–172, 174, 308*ge*
data item format rule statement, 171, 308*ge*
data rule statement, 166–172, 308*ge*
data update prohibition rule statement, 166, 308*ge*
data update rule statement, 166, 180, 309*ge*
declarative, 58, 309*ge*
dependent cardinality rule statement, 167, 309*ge*
impossibility statement, 60, 311*ge*
mandatory group rule statement, 174, 313*ge*
mandatory option selection rule statement, 173–174, 313*ge*
necessity statement, 60, 313*ge*
non-obligation statement, 61, 314*ge*
obligation statement, 58–59, 59, 201, 314*ge*
party rule statement, 172, 181, 314*ge*
procedural, 58, 316*ge*
prohibition statement, 59, 60, 173, 316*ge*
restricted permission statement, 59, 60, 182, 201, 317*ge*
restricted possibility statement, 60, 317*ge*
structural assertion, 58, 319*ge*
vocabulary, 5, 8, 55, 122–123, 188, 216, 227–228, 234
  names, 104–105, 227–228
  prepositions, 122, 143, 218
  terms, 122, 132–143, 227–228
  verbs, 122, 143, 218
Rule statement template, 190, 237–302, 318*ge*
  boilerplate text, 239
  list definitions, 239
  multiple formulations, 189
  option sets, 238
    null option, 162, 238
  placeholders, 238
  subtemplates, 163, 209, 211, 222, 223, 225, 226, 238, 239–245, 319*ge*
    comparison operators, 241
    conditional clauses, 243
    determiners, 240
    expressions, 243
    objects, 242
    predicates, 242
    qualifying clauses, 244–245
    set functions, 241
    transaction signifiers, 241
    verb parts, 241–242
  use, 189
Rule taxonomy, 41, 46–47, 84–99
Rumbaugh, J., 34

S

Sarbanes-Oxley, 3
SBVR. *See* Semantics of Business Vocabulary and Business Rules

Schema, message, 11
Screen control, 19–20
Second person, 108, 318*ge*
Second person pronoun, 108, 318*ge*
Self-contradiction, 196–199
Semantics of Business Vocabulary and Business
    Rules (SBVR), 2, 3, 14, 55–62, 67, 73–74, 105, 118,
    122, 132, 143, 144, 159
  definitions
    business rule, 1
    rule statement, 56
  models
    "in-practice model", 56, 73–74
    "reality model", 56, 73
Service, reusable, 8, 11, 317*ge*
Set
  difference, 178–179, 309*ge*
  empty set, 196–199, 309*ge*
  intersection, 178–179, 312*ge*
  set function, 71, 168, 241–243, 279, 280, 318*ge*
  subset, 179–180, 319*ge*
  superset, 179–180, 320*ge*
  union, 178–179, 321*ge*
Set equality constraint, 39, 44, 318*ge*
Set function, 71, 168, 241–243, 279, 280, 318*ge*
Signify, 101, 318*ge*
Silver, B., 40
Simple form (with respect to a verb phrase), 107, 218, 318*ge*
Simple noun, 103, 104, 116, 122, 132, 318*ge*
Simple past tense, 109, 318*ge*
Simple qualifying clause, 171, 187, 318*ge*
Simple temporal data constraint, 89, 92, 282, 318*ge*
  rule statement examples, 93, 282
Simple verb, 109–111, 318*ge*
Simsion, G.C., 42, 49, 51, 52
Singular (of a noun), 102–104, 106, 108, 112, 132, 196, 318*ge*
Spatial data constraint, 89, 94, 257, 286–287, 318*ge*
  fact types, 287
  options and placeholders, 287
  rule statement examples, 94, 286
  template, 287
Specific determiner, 113, 114, 318*ge*
SQL. *See* Structured Query Language
Stakeholder, 7, 8, 10, 22, 25, 33, 40, 41, 45, 46, 79, 135, 155,
    156, 157, 205, 230,
Standard format definition, 85, 88, 165, 246, 256, 318*ge*
  options and placeholders, 256
  rule statement examples, 88, 95, 256
  template, 256
Statement of advice. *See* Advice statement
Statement of advice of permission, 61–62, 319*ge*
Statement of advice of possibility, 62, 319*ge*

State transition constraint, 89, 95, 258, 288, 289–290, 319*ge*
  fact types, 290
  options and placeholders, 289
  rule statement examples, 95, 289
  template, 289
Static data constraint, 71, 319*ge*
Stonebraker, M., 169
Structural assertion, 58, 319*ge*
Structural rule. *See* Definitional rule
Structured business vocabulary. *See* Fact model
Structured Query Language (SQL), 25, 318*ge*
Subclass (of a superclass), 39, 151, 157, 319*ge*
Subclass name. *See* Hyponym
Subform, 168–169, 209, 210, 221, 224, 238, 259, 264, 266, 268,
    269, 271, 273, 277, 287, 319*ge*
Subject, 60, 62, 106, 107, 108, 117, 135, 148, 164–172,
    319*ge*
  in activity rule statements, 172
  in data cardinality rule statements, 166–167
  in data content rule statements, 167–172
  in definitional rule statements, 165
  in party rule statements, 172
Subject term (of a qualifying clause), 183, 184, 186
Subject term (of a rule statement), 152, 164, 176, 185, 188, 196,
    218, 219, 319*ge*
Subjunctive mood, 108, 319*ge*
Subset (of a superset), 86, 126, 135, 179–180, 185, 201, 247,
    319*ge*
Subset constraint, 39, 44, 319*ge*
Subset term. *See* Hyponym
Subtemplate, 163, 209, 211, 222, 223, 225, 226, 238, 239–245,
    319*ge*
  comparison operators, 241
  conditional clauses, 243
  determiners, 240
  expressions, 243
  objects, 242
  predicates, 242
  qualifying clauses, 244–245
  set functions, 241
  transaction signifiers, 241
  verb parts, 241–242
Subtype, 34, 35, 37–39, 44, 45, 49, 151, 157, 319*ge*
Subtype constraint, 39, 44, 319*ge*
Subtype name. *See* Hyponym
Suffix, 102, 319*ge*
Superclass (of a subclass), 39, 151, 157, 319*ge*
Superclass name, 37, 38, 39, 44, 45, 151, 157, 320*ge*
Superset (of a subset), 85, 151, 179–180, 246, 320*ge*
Superset term. *See* Hypernym
Supertype, 37–39, 44, 45, 151, 157, 320*ge*
Supertype name, 37–39, 44, 45

Symbolic literal definition, 85, 86, 246, 248–249, 320*ge*
  options and placeholders, 249
  rule statement examples, 86, 249
  template, 249
Synchronizing gateway, 40, 320*ge*
Synonym, 9, 11, 116, 123, 124, 126, 127, 133, 134, 189, 228,
    234, 235, 320*ge*
Syntax, 5, 8, 10, 55, 137, 173, 221–227
Systemic functional grammar, 105–106, 320*ge*
System rule, 3–4, 320*ge*

T

Table, 8, 11, 19, 21, 29, 30, 228, 230–233, 320*ge*
  nested, 169, 313*ge*
Target, 109, 320*ge*
Taxonomic fact type, 144, 151–153, 320*ge*
  assortment, 105, 144, 151–152, 153, 306*ge*
  categorization, 122, 144, 151, 153, 157, 247, 248, 307*ge*
  features, 152–153
Taxonomic relationship, 125–126, 320*ge*
Taxonomy, 320*ge*
  of rules, 41, 46–47, 84–99, 221
  of terms, 138–143, 151–153, 153, 154, 155–156
Template. *See* Rule statement template
Temporal data, 92, 257, 282, 320*ge*
Temporal data completeness constraint, 89, 93, 282, 283–284,
    320*ge*
  fact types, 284
  options and placeholders, 284
  rule statement examples, 283
  template, 284
Temporal data constraint, 92–94, 257, 282–286, 320*ge*
  categories, 89, 282
  day type constraint, 94, 282, 286, 309*ge*
  simple temporal data constraint, 89, 92, 282, 318*ge*
  temporal data completeness constraint, 89, 93, 282,
    283–284, 320*ge*
  temporal data inclusion constraint, 89, 93, 282, 285, 320*ge*
  temporal data non-overlap constraint, 89, 93, 94, 177,
    282–283, 320*ge*
  temporal single record constraint, 89, 94, 282, 285–286,
    321*ge*
Temporal data inclusion constraint, 89, 93, 282, 285, 320*ge*
  rule statement examples, 93, 285
  template, 285
Temporal data non-overlap constraint, 89, 93, 94, 177, 282–283,
    320*ge*
  fact types, 283
  options and placeholders, 283
  rule statement examples, 93, 283
  template, 283
Temporal single record constraint, 89, 94, 282, 285–286, 321*ge*
  fact types, 286

options and placeholders, 285
rule statement examples, 94, 285
templates, 285
Tense, 106, 107, 321*ge*
  future, 107, 111, 311*ge*
  past, 107, 143, 315*ge*
  present, 107, 108, 316*ge*
  simple past, 109, 318*ge*
Term, 132–143, 320*ge*
  attribute term, 130, 133, 157, 191, 247, 248, 254, 255,
    306*ge*
  business term, 122, 125, 126, 132, 136, 137, 143, 151, 156, 227
  compound noun, 103–104, 113–117, 122, 131, 132,
    134–135, 157, 307*ge*
  decisions, 133
  definitions, 127, 136–137, 227
  fundamental term, 133, 144, 146, 157, 191, 310*ge*
  homonyms, 133–134, 311*ge*
  hypernyms, 126, 138, 151, 153, 217, 311*ge*
  hyponyms, 126, 135, 138, 151, 153, 154–155, 217, 311*ge*
  relationship term, 132–133, 317*ge*
  role term, 133, 146–147, 248, 317*ge*
  standardization, 256
  synonyms, 9, 11, 116, 123, 124, 126, 127, 133, 134, 189,
    228, 234, 235, 320*ge*
  taxonomies, 124, 133, 138–143, 156, 320*ge*
  typographical conventions, 121–122, 159
  word choices, 133–136
Ternary fact type, 143, 144, 145–146, 157, 192, 321*ge*
Text attribute, 140, 321*ge*
'that', uses of, 120
Third person, 108, 321*ge*
Third person plural personal pronoun, 108, 321*ge*
Third person singular personal pronoun, 108, 321*ge*
Third person singular present indicative (of a verb phrase), 59,
    143, 321*ge*
Timer event, 41, 321*ge*
Timesheet, employee, 20
Train station, 16, 17, 18, 22, 57
Transaction signifier, 209, 210, 221, 224–227, 241, 258, 260,
    263, 266–270, 274, 276–281, 283–285
Transitive (of a verb phrase), 106, 109, 110, 181–183, 294, 295,
    296, 321*ge*
Trigger event, 17
Typographical conventions, xvi–xvii, 121–122, 159–160

U

UML. *See* Unified Modeling Language
Unary fact type, 143, 147–148, 157, 192, 321*ge*
Unified Modeling Language (UML), 11, 25, 34, 37, 38, 39–40,
    43, 124, 125, 133, 146, 147, 151, 157, 321*ge*
  associations, 39
  attributes, 39

Unified Modeling Language (UML) (*continued*)
    data constraints, 40
    object classes, 39
    object constraint language (OCL), 40
Union (of two or more sets), 178–179, 321*ge*
Unique (with respect to a column), 30, 321*ge*
Uniqueness constraint, 21, 38, 43, 89, 92, 174, 176, 257,
       276–279, 321*ge*
    fact types, 277, 278, 279
    options and placeholders, 277, 278, 279
    rule statement examples, 92, 277, 278
    templates, 277, 278, 279
User interface, 19–20, 31, 70, 79, 131, 205, 228, 230–233

V

Valid value definition, 85, 87, 165, 246, 254, 321*ge*
    fact types, 254
    options and placeholders, 254
    rule statement examples, 254
    template, 254
Value constraint, 39, 44, 321*ge*
Value set rule, 89, 91, 174, 176, 210–212, 257, 270–274, 321*ge*
    fact types, 272, 273–274
    options and placeholders, 271–272, 273
    rule statement examples, 91, 271, 272
    templates, 271, 273
Verb, 105–112, 321*ge*
    aspect, 106, 107, 306*ge*
    auxiliary, 109, 111, 306*ge*
    circumstantial, 106, 307*ge*
    complement, 106, 307*ge*
    compound, 109–110, 115, 116, 131, 307*ge*
    declarative, 107, 309*ge*
    first person, 108, 310*ge*
    future, 107, 111, 311*ge*
    imperative, 108, 311*ge*
    indicative, 107, 108, 311*ge*
    infinitive, 106–110, 143, 312*ge*
    intensive, 106, 109, 312*ge*
    interrogative, 107, 312*ge*
    intransitive, 110
    involving 'if', 111–112
    involving 'that', 111–112
    involving 'to', 110
    involving 'whether', 111–112
    irregular, 109, 312*ge*
    modal auxiliary, 106, 108, 111, 313*ge*
    mood, 107–108, 313*ge*
    negated, 109
    passive, 109, 145, 167, 181, 314*ge*
    past, 107, 143, 315*ge*
    past participle, 109, 110, 315*ge*

    perfect, 107, 315*ge*
    perfective, 107, 315*ge*
    person, 107, 108, 315*ge*
    phrasal, 104, 110, 315*ge*
    plural, 106, 108
    positive, 107, 315*ge*
    prepositional, 110, 117, 316*ge*
    present, 107, 108, 316*ge*
    progressive, 107, 218, 316*ge*
    regular, 109, 317*ge*
    second person, 108, 318*ge*
    simple, 109–111, 318*ge*
    simple form, 107, 218, 318*ge*
    simple past, 109, 318*ge*
    singular, 108
    subjunctive, 59, 108, 319*ge*
    tense, 106, 107, 321*ge*
    third person, 108, 321*ge*
    third person singular present indicative, 59, 143, 321*ge*
    transitive, 106, 109, 110, 181–183, 294, 295, 296,
       321*ge*
    typographical conventions, 160
Verbalization, 42–45
Verb part, 211, 223, 226, 241–242, 244
Verb phrase, 56, 128, 143–145, 147, 148, 150–151, 159–164,
       167, 174, 176–178, 181–183, 186, 188–192, 200, 209,
       211, 216, 218, 219, 222–226, 235, 236, 238, 239, 241,
       242, 244, 245, 251, 252, 261–263, 289, 291, 293–297,
       301, 302, 322*ge*
    active, 145, 305*ge*
    intransitive, 106, 110, 143, 148, 186, 294–296, 312*ge*
    negated, 107, 109, 186, 313*ge*
    number, 108, 314*ge*
    object of, 106, 110, 117, 148, 174, 242, 244, 314*ge*
    positive, 107, 315*ge*
    simple form, 107, 218, 318*ge*
    standardization, 218
    third person singular present indicative, 59, 143, 321*ge*
    transitive, 106, 109, 110, 181–183, 294–296, 321*ge*
    typographical conventions, 160
Visual Basic, 25, 26
Vocabulary, 5, 8, 55, 122, 188, 216, 227–228, 234
Voice, 107, 108
    active, 108–109, 305*ge*
    passive, 109, 145, 167, 181, 314*ge*
von Halle, B., 1, 306

W

Witt, G.C., 42, 51, 52
Word class, 101, 322*ge*
    adjective, 101, 102, 112, 115, 130, 134, 136, 138, 211, 223,
       242, 305*ge*

Word class (*continued*)
    adverb, 101, 110, 138, 181, 189, 305*ge*
    article, 101–103, 112–113, 176–178, 240, 248,
        306*ge*
    conjunction, 116–117, 308*ge*
    determiner, 47, 93, 103, 112–114, 186, 240, 309*ge*
    literal, 86, 118–120, 149, 150, 163, 165, 176, 183,
        186, 187, 242, 248, 249, 250, 251, 254, 272,
        312*ge*
    noun, 101, 102–104, 314*ge*

preposition, 11, 103, 109, 110, 115–116, 118, 122, 128, 135,
    143–145, 163, 186, 192, 211, 223, 235, 236, 238, 252,
    292, 294, 316*ge*
pronoun, 117–118, 183, 316*ge*
proper name, 102, 104–105, 121, 126, 133, 134, 138, 151,
    227, 228, 316*ge*
verb, 105–112, 321*ge*

X

XML. *See* Extensible Markup Language